SCIENTIFIC PERSPECTIVES ON PSEUDOSCIENCE AND THE PARANORMAL:

Readings for General Psychology

Edited by

TIMOTHY J. LAWSON

College of Mount St. Joseph

PEARSON

Prentice
Hall

Library of Congress Cataloging-in-Publication Data
Scientific perspectives on pseudoscience and the paranormal / Timothy J. Lawson.
 p. cm.
 ISBN 0-13-194101-1
 1. Pseudoscience. 2. Parapsychology. I. Lawson, Timothy J., 1963-
Q172.5.P77S35 2006
500--dc22   2006032311

VP/Editorial Director: Leah Jewell
Executive Editor: Jessica Mosher
**AVP/Director of Production and
Manufacturing:** Barbara Kittle
Assistant Managing Editor: Maureen
Richardson
Production Liaison: Nicole
Girrbach-Ramirez
Production Editor: Vijay Kataria
Manufacturing Manager: Nick Sklitsis
Manufacturing Buyer: Sherry Lewis
Cover Director: Jayne Conte
Cover Design: Bruce Kenselaar
Cover Illustration/Photo: Simon
Borns/Getty Images Inc. – Illustration
Works, Inc.

**Director, Image Resource
Center:** Melinda Patelli
Manager, Rights & Permissions: Zina
Arabia
Manager, Visual Research: Beth Brenzel
**Manager, Cover Visual Research &
Permissions:** Karen Sanatar
Image Permission Coordinator:
Angelique Sharps
**Composition/Full-Service Project
Management:** *Techbooks*
Printer/Binder: RR Donnelley/
Harrisonburg
Director of Marketing: Brandy Dawson
Sr. Marketing Manager: Jeanette Moyer

This book was set Garamond by *Techbooks*. It was printed and bound by RR Donnelley.
The cover was printed by RR Donnelley.

Photo Credits: p. 224: Yoav Levy/Phototake NYC.

Pearson Education Ltd.
Pearson Education Singapore Pte. Ltd.
Pearson Education Canada, Ltd.
Pearson Education—Japan

Pearson Education Australia Pty. Limited
Pearson Education North Asia Ltd.
Pearson Educación de Mexico, S.A. de C.V.
Pearson Education Malaysia Pte. Ltd.

10 9 8 7 6 5 4 3 2 1
ISBN: 0-13-194101-1

DEDICATION

To Anna, Alexandra, and Ryan

CONTENTS

Preface / ix

CHAPTER 1 **What Is Pseudoscience? / 1**

Science Versus Pseudoscience, TIMOTHY J. LAWSON / 1

CHAPTER 2 **Methodological and Statistical Reasoning / 13**

2.1 *Why bogus therapies seem to work,* BARRY BEYERSTEIN / 13

2.2 *The suggestibility of young children,* MAGGIE BRUCK AND STEPHEN CECI / 24

2.3 *On the belief that arthritis pain is related to the weather,* DONALD REDELMEIER AND AMOS TVERSKY / 33

2.4 *The "Mozart Effect": An example of the scientific method in operation,* KENNETH STEELE /39

CHAPTER 3 **Neuroscience and Consciousness / 47**

3.1 *Whence cometh the myth that we only use 10% of our brains?* BARRY BEYERSTEIN / 47

3.2 *Can minds leave bodies? A cognitive science perspective,* D. ALAN BENSLEY / 62

3.3 *Dream interpretation and false beliefs,* GIULIANA MAZZONI, PASQUALE LOMBARDO, STEFANO MALVAGIA, AND ELIZABETH LOFTUS / 73

CHAPTER 4 **Child Development / 87**

4.1 *Common myths of children's behavior,* CATHERINE FIORELLO / 87

4.2 *Separating fact from fiction in the etiology and treatment of autism: A scientific review of the evidence,* JAMES HERBERT, IAN SHARP, AND BRANDON GAUDIANO / 93

4.3 *Project DARE: No effects at 10-year follow-up,* DONALD LYNAM, RICHARD MILICH, RICK ZIMMERMAN, SCOTT NOVAK, T. K. LOGAN, CATHERINE MARTIN, CARL LEUKEFELD, AND RICHARD CLAYTON / 104

CHAPTER 5 Sensation and Perception / 115

5.1 *What's that I smell? The claims of aromatherapy,*
Lynn McCutcheon / 115

5.2 *What you expect is what you believe (but not necessarily what you get):
A test of the effectiveness of subliminal self-help audiotapes,* Anthony
Pratkanis, Jay Eskenazi, and Anthony Greenwald / 121

5.3 *Psychic crime detectives: A new test for measuring their successes
and failures,* Richard Wiseman, Donald West, and
Roy Stemman / 140

CHAPTER 6 Learning and Memory / 149

6.1 *Different strokes for different folks? A critique of learning styles,*
Steven Stahl / 149

6.2 *Past-life identities, UFO abductions, and satanic ritual abuse: The
social reconstruction of memories,* Nicholas Spanos, Cheryl Burgess,
and Melissa Faith Burgess / 160

6.3 *Memory recovery techniques in psychotherapy: Problems and pitfalls,*
Steven Jay Lynn, Elizabeth Loftus, Scott Lilienfeld, and
Timothy Lock / 173

CHAPTER 7 Cognition / 189

7.1 *Nostradamus's clever 'clairvoyance': The power of ambiguous
specificity,* Maziar Yafeh and Chip Heath / 189

7.2 *Like goes with like: The role of representativeness in erroneous and
pseudoscientific beliefs,* Thomas Gilovich and
Kenneth Savitsky / 198

7.3 *Some systematic biases of everyday judgment,* Thomas Gilovich / 211

CHAPTER 8 Personality and Psychological Testing / 221

8.1 *What's wrong with this picture?* Scott Lilienfeld, James Wood,
and Howard Garb / 221

8.2 *Polygraph testing and sexual abuse: The lure of the magic Lasso,*
Theodore Cross and Leonard Saxe / 232

8.3 *A position statement by the International Graphonomics Society on
the use of graphology in personnel selection testing,* Marvin Simner
and Richard Goffin / 251

CHAPTER 9 Psychological Disorders and Therapies / 263

9.1 *Multiple personality disorder: Witchcraft survives in the twentieth century,* AUGUST PIPER JR. / 263

9.2 *Can we really tap our problems away? A critical analysis of thought field therapy,* BRANDON GAUDIANO AND JAMES HERBERT / 278

9.3 *Perception of conventional sensory cues as an alternative to the postulated "human energy field" of therapeutic touch,* REBECCA LONG, PAUL BERNHARDT, AND WILLIAM EVANS / 289

CHAPTER 10 Social Psychology / 301

10.1 *Mass delusions and hysterias: Highlights from the past millennium,* ROBERT BARTHOLOMEW AND ERICH GOODE / 301

10.2 *How to sell a pseudoscience,* ANTHONY PRATKANIS / 315

10.3 *The social psychology of false confessions: Compliance, internalization, and confabulation,* SAUL KASSIN AND KATHERINE KIECHEL / 328

"In a world in which the media, self-help industry, and Internet are disseminating psychological pseudoscience at an ever-increasing pace, the critical thinking skills needed to distinguish science from pseudoscience should be considered mandatory for all psychology students." Scott Lilienfeld (2005)

Unless you have avoided all popular media in the past few years, you've probably seen a number of extraordinary claims about therapies, products, and people's abilities that seem to defy what we know about physics, biology, and psychology. You may have seen people who claim they can communicate with the dead, psychic detectives who can apparently solve crimes by "seeing" a crime scene that is miles away, nurses who claim to heal people simply by waving their hands above their patients' bodies, and people who claim they were abducted by aliens who conducted horrific experiments on them. Recent Gallup polls (e.g., Moore, 2005) suggest that many people believe in paranormal phenomena. For example, 41% of Americans believe in extrasensory perception (ESP), 21% believe that people can communicate mentally with someone who has died, and 25% believe in astrology. Scientists have actually studied these phenomena and a wide variety of other paranormal and pseudoscientific phenomena. In this book you will read what they have discovered and how they think about such claims.

The fact that some college students hold beliefs in pseudoscientific and paranormal phenomena became apparent to me early in my career. Several years after I became a psychology professor, I took several of my brightest students to a professional psychology conference in Chicago. One night, while walking to a restaurant, they spotted a psychic's office. When they told me that they had a strong belief in psychic abilities, I wondered how they could hold such a belief after I had taught them about psychology, critical thinking, and the scientific method. It was at that point that I realized that even though I had taught them what science *is,* I had not specifically addressed what science is *not* (i.e., pseudoscience). Since then I have been teaching students what scientists know about pseudoscience and the paranormal, and we've all found it to be a fascinating lesson in scientific reasoning as well as the cognitive and social forces that conspire to create pseudoscientific and paranormal beliefs.

PURPOSE OF THE BOOK

As Lilienfeld, Lohr, and Morier (2001) noted, psychologists are becoming increasingly aware of and concerned about the problem of pseudoscience in psychology. Psychology students and the general public are constantly exposed to pseudoscientific and paranormal claims through the media, the Internet, and pop psychology books. Psychology professors are becoming more concerned about teaching students to think critically about these claims. I hope that instructors will find this book of readings to be a useful tool for educating psychology students about such claims.

This book was designed to give beginning psychology students the opportunity to read original sources from psychologists and other scientists who have investigated pseudoscientific and paranormal phenomena related to psychology. These original sources allow students to get a close-up look at how scientists think about these phenomena, how they design research studies to investigate such phenomena, and why they are critical of pseudoscientific and paranormal claims. Students will also learn about scientific perspectives on a wide variety of specific pseudoscientific and paranormal phenomena. Along the way, they will encounter interesting examples that bring to life important psychological concepts (e.g., representativeness heuristic, confirmation bias) and scientific principles (e.g., correlation does not mean causation; the importance of replication of research findings).

I carefully selected the readings in each chapter to ensure that (a) the articles were fairly brief, (b) they were written by scientists knowledgeable about the scientific research related to each topic, and (c) introductory psychology students would find them interesting and understandable. For articles that were somewhat longer or more complex, I edited their length and excluded sections that seemed too complex for introductory psychology students.

ORGANIZATION OF THE BOOK

The chapters in this book are organized around typical introductory psychology topics (e.g., sensation and perception, learning and memory, social psychology), making it easy for instructors to relate this material to topics that students are learning in an introductory psychology course. Although Chapter 1 is an introduction to the topic of pseudoscience and the paranormal that students should read before the other sections of the book, the other chapters and articles are designed to stand on their own. Thus, instructors have the flexibility to assign articles in the order that best fits with the content and organization of their courses.

SUGGESTIONS FOR INSTRUCTORS

At the end of each article, I've included several review questions that might be used for in-class exercises, homework assignments, or quizzes. I've also written several multiple-choice questions related to each article that instructors may obtain from the Prentice Hall Web site. The multiple-choice questions were designed in such a way that students who have correctly answered the review questions for an article should perform well on the multiple-choice questions.

Thus, instructors who choose to use only the multiple-choice questions to assess students' understanding of the articles might encourage students to use the review questions as a tool for studying.

There are a variety of ways that this book could be used in a psychology course. Students could be asked to read an article or two from each chapter as the relevant topics are covered in their course. Some of the review questions could be assigned as homework to assess how well students learned the material in the article. Instructors who would like to add in-class activities related to each article might assign students to small groups and have each student answer a different review question; they could then discuss their answers with each other in class. Another idea is to assign brief projects or presentations related to some of the articles. For example, for a few articles, I ask students to find a Web-based article that advocates the claim critiqued in the article; then students are asked to compare and contrast the quality of the Web-based source with that of the article (i.e., they evaluate the credibility of the author, whether the information is supported with research evidence, etc.).

ACKNOWLEDGMENTS

This book was inspired, in part, by psychologists such as Scott Lilienfeld, Elizabeth Loftus, and Ray Hyman, who have worked tirelessly to investigate pseudoscientific practices and to teach students to distinguish between science and pseudoscience. I thank Hank Cetola for prompting me to discuss the idea for this book with publishers much earlier than I had anticipated. I also greatly appreciate the guidance and suggestions from Jennifer Gilliland as well as the production efforts of Vijay Kataria, Nicole Girrbach, and Andrea Howe. Finally, thanks to the following reviewers who took time out of their busy schedules to provide advice and guidance: David N. Bader, Endicott College; Kevin J. Filter, Minnesota State University; Andrew Peck, Penn State University; Dean G. Purcell, Oakland University; Adriane Seiffert, Vanderbilt University; and Chris Ward, Stonehill College.

Enjoy the book!
Timothy J. Lawson

References

Lilienfeld, S. O. (2005, September). The 10 commandments of helping students distinguish science from pseudoscience in psychology. *APS Observer, 18*, 39–40, 49–51.

Lilienfeld, S. O., Lohr, J. M., & Morier, D. (2001). The teaching of courses in the science and pseudoscience of psychology: Useful resources. *Teaching of Psychology, 28*, 182–191.

Moore, D. W. (2005, June 16). *Three in four Americans believe in paranormal.* Gallup News Service.

CHAPTER 1
What Is Pseudoscience?

Science Versus Pseudoscience/
TIMOTHY J. LAWSON

Several years ago I came across an interesting advertisement for an amazing bracelet—the Q-Ray ionized bracelet—that was designed to provide pain relief and other health benefits. The manufacturer claimed that the Q-Ray could relieve pain from a variety of sources (e.g., arthritis, cancer), improve sports performance, restore energy, and improve muscle flexibility (see Barrett, 2004). Here are some of the testimonials that were offered by the manufacturer as evidence for the bracelet's effectiveness:

> My hands became so stiff I couldn't make a fist with either hand and I couldn't snap my fingers. Within minutes after putting on the Q-Ray, the stiffness began to lessen. I'd say that has been a pretty good investment. Thank you Q-Ray! [Resident of Columbia, MD]
>
> Q-Ray is the talk among my colleagues. They love its comfortable fit and its beautiful design. My game is significantly improved since wearing Q-Ray. [LPGA Tour Professional]
>
> The feedback is generally positive from those who are wearing the bracelets and the consensus among the players is that the Q-Ray is stylish. Others have reported a decrease in headaches and better sleep since wearing the bracelets. [Head Athletic Trainer, professional soccer team]
>
> I was introduced to the Bracelet after the 1997-98 season, over the summer I noticed a decrease in soreness and stiffness I normally experienced in my back and knees from summer activities. I felt that if during an entire NHL season, I could decrease any soreness in any of my athletes, that they would be able to compete at a higher level, hopefully contributing to greater success. Although the season is still young, the players are still wearing them with some results. Thanks again for your support and I'll keep you posted on the results that we experience. [Head Athletic Trainer, professional hockey club]

Who developed this amazing bracelet, and how does it work? According to the manufacturer, the Q-Ray ionized bracelet was developed in 1973 by Dr. Manuel L. Polo, a chiropractor. The Web site for the bracelet stated that it was based on ancient oriental principles that are more than

2,000 years old, and that the Q-Ray provided "natural holistic pain relief" and regulated "the imbalance of both positive and negative ions in your body the Natural Way." The Web site went on to explain (see Barrett, 2004, for more detail):

> The Q-RAY bracelet is designed to achieve many of the same goals as traditional Chinese acupuncture. Acupuncture was developed to balance the body's Yin (negative ions) and Yang (positive ions), the two inseparable, complementary energies that permanently circulate in the human body. When these energies become unbalanced, the body's functioning is thought to be altered—which can be at least very annoying and at worst debilitating, depending on the size and nature of the energy imbalance. Oriental medicine, through acupuncture, is believed to regulate these two energies, discharging from the body excess positive ions and providing access to blocked negative ions, by stimulating meridian acupuncture points.
>
> In the human body, which is electromagnetic by nature, biomagnetic alpha and beta waves circulate throughout the vital centers. When the flow is cut off and these alpha and beta waves become stagnant in one particular area of the body, bioelectrical alterations and ionic imbalances can result. Designed by Dr. Polo with polarized multimetallic metals, the Q-RAY bracelet's circular form and spherical terminals offer low resistance to the bioelectrical conductibility of the alpha and beta waves, facilitating the discharge of excess positive ions or static electricity. Excess of positive ions is associated with poor nutrition, incorrect breathing, sedentary life style, and the use of electrical instruments or exposure to EMF (Electronic Magnetic Field). Loss of negative ions is associated with symptoms such as anxiety, stress, fear, hatred, and physical exhaustion.

If you were experiencing pain as a result of a sports-related injury, would you purchase this bracelet? You just read some glowing testimonials for this bracelet and a very scientific-sounding explanation for how it works; perhaps you would view this as fairly convincing evidence that the bracelet is an effective pain reliever. Does any aspect of the information you have seen so far suggest to you that this bracelet might *not* be the miracle pain reliever it was claimed to be by the manufacturer?

We will come back to the Q-Ray bracelet in a moment, but first let's discuss the main topic of this chapter: some important differences between science and pseudoscience. As you may have learned by now, the field of psychology is a science. But what is it about psychology that makes it a science? Stanovich (2004) described three important features:

■ **Systematic Empiricism:** Psychologists gain knowledge about behavior and mental processes by collecting data and making observations to test their theories and hypotheses. Unlike our everyday observations, psychologists make their observations in a carefully planned, systematic manner in order to help them rule out alternative explanations for the phenomena they are trying to understand.

- **Publicly Verifiable Knowledge:** After psychologists conduct their research, they communicate their findings to the broader scientific community. Other scientists can then critique the research, attempt to replicate the findings, and conduct related studies to further examine the phenomenon being investigated. These other scientists play a crucial role in judging and criticizing the research (this is called "peer review") before it is deemed worthy of being published in a scientific journal. Research that is judged to be too flawed or unimportant never reaches the pages of such a journal. Other researchers also play a crucial role in scientific progress by attempting to replicate the original research findings. If others cannot obtain the same findings as the original researcher, the original findings may have been a fluke.
- **Empirically Solvable Problems:** Scientists examine research questions that can be answered with current research techniques. If a question or theory is not testable, it is not within the realm of science. Thus, a scientist might not examine the question of whether people have souls (this would be very difficult to test), but he or she could examine whether an unconventional treatment for depression actually works.

To illustrate these features of science, consider how a scientist might examine whether a new drug effectively treats depression. The scientist might recruit a number of patients who have been diagnosed with depression and are willing to participate in the study. After informing the patients about the purpose and design of the study, those who consented to participate could be randomly assigned either to an experimental group that receives the new drug or to a control group that receives a sugar pill (i.e., a placebo). The scientist would measure the level of depression in both groups of patients to determine if those who received the new drug experienced more improvement in their depression than did the control group. Let's assume the scientist found that this new drug significantly improved the patients' level of depression compared to the control group. The scientist would then write a report about this study and would send it to a scientific journal for publication. Peer reviewers would evaluate the quality of this study and determine whether it merits publication in the journal. After it is published, other scientists would critique the study and try to replicate the results. If other scientists conducted studies that also found positive results for this new drug, they would become more confident that it is a beneficial treatment for depression.

WHAT IS PSEUDOSCIENCE?

Contrast the aforementioned scientific approach with a pseudoscientific approach to testing a treatment for depression. A pseudoscientist might sell an herbal remedy for depression to a number of people, and some of them might report an improvement in their symptoms after taking the herbal remedy. The pseudoscientist might then create an advertisement for this new herbal remedy and include the testimonials of these satisfied customers as evidence of the effectiveness of the treatment. Notice that the pseudoscientific approach did not involve systematic empiricism; in other words, the pseudoscientist did not conduct a study that was carefully planned to rule out alternative explanations for the improvement in patients' symptoms. We do not know for sure whether the people who tried the herbal remedy were clinically depressed before taking the remedy (i.e., they might have been temporarily dispirited), we do not know how many of those who tried the remedy did not improve, and we cannot determine whether the improvements experienced by some of those who tried the remedy were caused by factors other than the herbal remedy. Their symptoms might have improved even without the herbal remedy, perhaps because of improvements in their social relationships, a decrease in stressful conditions at work, or simply the passage of time. Control groups used in scientific studies on treatments for depression help us rule out these alternative explanations.

Unlike science, pseudoscience (literally, "false" or "sham" science) is not characterized by carefully controlled studies that result in publicly verifiable knowledge. Instead, pseudoscientists often gain knowledge through "ancient wisdom," claims of a supposed "authority," illogical thinking, personal experience, or testimonials. Although the line between science and pseudoscience can be fuzzy at times, below I describe six of the important characteristics of pseudoscience (based on Bunge, 1984; Coker, 2001; Lilienfeld, 1998; Ruscio, 2006; see these sources for additional characteristics).

- **Imprecise, Scientific-Sounding Language:** Although the language used by pseudoscientists sometimes sounds scientific, they use terms in an imprecise, illogical, or incorrect manner. Scientists, on the other hand, define their terms in a precise, measurable way. As Ruscio (2006) pointed out, "energy" and "holistic" are terms that pseudoscientists often use in imprecise ways that have little or no connection to reality. For example, practitioners of a procedure called Therapeutic Touch claim that by moving their hands slightly above a person's body, they can realign that person's "human energy field" and heal that person, but these practitioners cannot even demonstrate to scientists that they are able to detect such "energy" (Rosa, Rosa, Sarner, & Barrett, 1998). Imprecise terms such as these are often red flags that one is dealing with a pseudoscientist.

- **Lack of Progress:** Science progresses and changes over time. For example, what we know today about how the brain works is vastly different from what we knew 10 years ago. Pseudoscience, on the other hand, tends not to progress. Because pseudoscientific claims and theories do not undergo rigorous testing and critical peer review, they are rarely modified. Although pseudoscientists sometimes point out that their claims are based on "ancient wisdom" to give the impression that they have stood the test of time, this is often a good sign that such claims are based on stagnant, inaccurate ideas.

■ **Overreliance on Testimonials and Personal Experience:** Rather than conducting carefully controlled studies, pseudoscientists often rely on personal experience or testimonials. For example, while in his twenties, Peter Halvorson drilled a hole in his head to cure his depression (a procedure called "trepanation" or "trephining"). Today, more than 30 years later, he claims that the procedure not only cured his depression, but improved his energy and vitality. Halvorson is a strong advocate for the use of the procedure to cure depression; in fact, he's the senior director of the International Trepanation Advocacy Group (visit http://www.trepan.com for more information). Why shouldn't we be convinced by stories like this one? If a person's depression lifts after trying some treatment, can't we conclude that the treatment worked? The problem with relying on testimonials and personal experience as evidence for treatments or claims is they do not allow us to rule out alternative explanations. For example, maybe Peter Halvorson's depression would have disappeared without any treatment (i.e., spontaneous remission), or perhaps his positive expectation that the "treatment" would work is what produced the improvement (i.e., a placebo effect). Controlled scientific studies employ control groups of participants who receive no treatment or fake treatments (i.e., placebos) to rule out these alternative explanations.

■ **Appeals to False Authority:** Pseudoscientists urge us to believe their claims based on the word of an "authority" on the subject, even though the person claimed to be an authority may be untrustworthy or have little expertise in the subject. For example, it is not uncommon to hear supposed experts on talk shows give advice about child rearing or romantic relationships when they have no scientific training in psychology or related sciences. Although these "experts" use "Dr." in front of their name to give the impression that they have a doctorate in psychology, their doctoral degrees are often in a completely unrelated field. Scientists, on the other hand, do not rely on authority to answer important questions, even if the authority has the appropriate scientific training from a respected institution. As I mentioned earlier, it is convincing, empirical data that drive scientists' understanding of the world, not the word of an authority.

■ **Extraordinary Claims Without Convincing Evidence:** Pseudoscientists often make extraordinary claims that are unconstrained by reality, physical laws, or human limitations. However, they back up these claims with little or no compelling, publicly verifiable evidence. For example, pseudoscientists may claim that we can transfer the "positive" or "negative" energy within us to a bottle of water simply by touching it, and that others who drink that water will be influenced by the energy within it. Before believing such an extraordinary claim that appears to contradict well-researched physical laws, a scientist would want to see some very convincing evidence.

In some cases, pseudoscientists have managed to publish a large number of articles supporting their claims, and advocates can point to the "growing literature" supporting the pseudoscience as evidence for their claims. One question to ask yourself is whether this literature consists of well-controlled, scientific research that has been published in peer-reviewed, scientific journals. If you find some articles that meet this criterion, ask yourself whether the results of this research have been replicated by other researchers. Although the evidence collected by pseudoscientists is generally not worthy of publication in peer-reviewed journals, sometimes they are able to get articles published in such outlets. For example, advocates of Therapeutic Touch have published a number of articles in peer-reviewed journals, and they point to these studies as evidence for their claims. However, in general, these journals are not reputable medical journals, and the studies published in these journals are not designed well enough to rule out alternative explanations (e.g., placebo effects or effects of relaxation).

■ **Emphasis on Confirmation Rather Than Refutation:** Pseudoscientists tend to focus only on information that is consistent with their claims, failing to seek out information that contradicts their claims. A person who claims to predict the future, for example, might make numerous, vague predictions (e.g., "A popular leader will die in the near future"; "scientists will soon make an amazing discovery in outer space."). Later, when assessing his or her accuracy, this "psychic" might point out the predictions that were apparently correct and overlook predictions that were inaccurate. In contrast, scientists deliberately attempt to falsify their own and other scientists' predictions and theories to make sure that their ideas hold up under very rigorous tests.

Now that you have a sense of the meaning of the term *pseudoscience,* I'd like to point out the difference between pseudoscience and paranormal phenomena. Paranormal phenomena (e.g., a psychic's ability to "see" the future) are those that are beyond our normal experience, and they fall outside of a scientific understanding of the world. The topics of pseudoscience and the paranormal often overlap; for example, some people claim to use paranormal abilities—such as the ability to detect a human energy field—to heal others, and they use testimonials as evidence for the effectiveness of their therapy. However, the topics of pseudoscience and the paranormal can also be distinct, as illustrated by pseudoscientific therapies that do not necessarily involve paranormal phenomena. For instance, the use of bee pollen to treat allergies may be pseudoscientific but does not involve the paranormal.

Q-RAY REVISITED

Now that we have discussed some major characteristics of pseudoscience, can you apply any of them to the example of the amazing Q-Ray bracelet? Which of these characteristics seem most relevant for assessing the claims made about the Q-Ray? I'll point out a couple of relevant characteristics, and I'll leave the rest for you to identify when you answer the questions at the end of this chapter.

When you first read the Q-Ray example, did you recognize the use of imprecise, scientific-sounding language? What exactly is "natural holistic pain relief," and how can a man-made bracelet be "natural"? Also, can our bodies actually have an "imbalance of positive and negative ions," and can such an imbalance cause pain? As Barrett (2004) pointed out, "there is no such thing as an ionic imbalance of the body, and no scientifically recognized connection between allegedly 'ionized' objects and pain relief. . . . even if 'ionic imbalance' could exist, the claim that the Q-Ray could influence the body's 'electrical energy' supply is preposterous."

After reading the section on pseudoscience, you probably quickly recognized the relevance of one of the characteristics of pseudoscience: the overuse of testimonials as evidence for the effectiveness of the Q-Ray. The numerous positive testimonials, some from seemingly credible people, might be enough to convince many people that this bracelet works. However, there are alternative explanations for people's pain relief after wearing the Q-Ray. As mentioned earlier, a placebo effect and spontaneous remission are just a couple of possibilities. We'll explore other possible explanations for the apparent effectiveness of bogus treatments in Chapter 2. Another problem with testimonials is that we do not know what percentage of the people who tried the product liked it. It might be the case that the vast majority of those who tried the Q-Ray did not experience any benefits, and the manufacturer chose the few positive testimonials to feature on the Q-Ray Web site. My quick search of the Web turned up a number of very negative reviews of the Q-Ray by those who purchased it; of course, these reviews are not mentioned on the Q-Ray Web site. Below is an example of one of the negative reviews:

> I purchased this bracelet for my mother, who has consistent back pain. I felt a little foolish calling in for it, but the customers on the infomercial seemed to be very excited about it and seemed sincere. I would have tried anything to help my mom's quality of life to be better. To make a long story short, it did nothing for my mother, and I felt kind of ridiculous for believing in such a thing. Not only did it not work, but my mom seemed to have substantially more pain and less sleep at night.

You might be wondering at this point whether I really have any grounds for implying that the Q-Ray bracelet is a worthless, pseudoscientific treatment for pain. Although I have pointed out a number of problems with the claims made by the Q-Ray manufacturer, I have not presented much evidence that the Q-Ray does *not* work. In response, my first point would be that the burden of proof is not mine; it's the job of the person making the claims for the effectiveness of the Q-Ray to prove that the bracelet *does* work. Although pseudoscientists often try to shift the burden of proof on to critics rather than themselves, scientists assume the burden of proof when they make a claim. For instance, a true scientist would not claim that a new drug alleviates depression better than other drugs on the market without scientific evidence to support that claim, and a scientist without such evidence would not tell critics that they should believe the claim unless they can disprove it. In fact, the Food and Drug Administration (FDA) would never approve a new drug if the manufacturer took such an approach. Likewise, we should not be expected to believe extraordinary claims made by pseudoscientists—for example, claims that beings from outer space abduct people and perform experiments on them—without convincing, scientific evidence to support such claims.

My second point would be that, in this particular case, there is some evidence that suggests the Q-Ray does not live up to the extraordinary claims made by the manufacturer. In 2003, the Federal Trade Commission (FTC) issued a temporary restraining order against the manufacturer of the Q-Ray for making false and unsubstantiated claims. The restraining order "prohibits defendants from making any misleading or deceptive claims about the Q-Ray Bracelet and freezes defendants' assets" (see Federal Trade Commission, 2003). The FTC also explained that "a recent study conducted by the Mayo Clinic in Jacksonville, Florida, shows that the Q-Ray Bracelet is no more effective than a placebo bracelet at relieving muscular and joint pain."

You might think that this is the end of the road for the Q-Ray bracelet, but stay tuned. The manufacturer is still selling the bracelet, and their Web site still exists (http://www.qray.com). On the current version of their Web site, you will not find any of the exaggerated claims mentioned earlier. But you will still find some familiar-looking testimonials, although they have been edited to soften the unsubstantiated claims.

CONCLUSION

I hope that you have found our discussion of the Q-Ray bracelet and the differences between science and pseudoscience to be interesting, informative, and relevant to your everyday life. This chapter is just the beginning of our examination of the fascinating realm of pseudoscience and the paranormal. In the following chapters, you will read psychologists' and other scientists' critiques of a variety of pseudoscientific and paranormal phenomena—such as psychic abilities, lie detector tests, and memories of past lives—that are related to many of the major topics in an introductory psychology course. As implied by the features of psychological science described earlier, the conclusions reached by the scientists featured in this book are based on carefully planned and controlled research studies (i.e., systematic empiricism) that have been published in scientific journals (i.e., publicly verifiable knowledge). My hope is that this book will not only help you understand the science of psychology, but also help you think critically about the many pseudoscientific and paranormal claims you are likely to encounter through the media, the Internet, and the pop psychology books in your local bookstore.

THEMES IN THIS BOOK

Although the articles in this book are independent readings that can be read in any order, there are some important themes that can be found throughout the book. Below are a couple of important themes to watch for as you read the articles.

1. **Science Versus Pseudoscience:** As implied by the topic of this chapter, one of the themes that you will encounter throughout this book is the distinction between science and pseudoscience. The articles in this book will give you a variety of examples of the differences between scientific and pseudoscientific approaches to gaining knowledge. While reading the articles, watch for the characteristics of pseudoscience discussed in this chapter (e.g., lack of progress, extraordinary claims without convincing evidence). You will also see examples of scientific research, which will illustrate how psychologists and other scientists design studies to investigate pseudoscientific and paranormal claims.

2. **Normal Cognitive and Social Processes Contribute to Pseudoscientific and Paranormal Beliefs:** Another important theme that you will encounter throughout the book is that beliefs in pseudoscientific and paranormal phenomena can result from normal cognitive and social processes. Although some of the phenemona discussed in this book may seem so bizarre or unbelievable to you that you will be tempted to conclude that only people with low intelligence could believe in them, you should resist that temptation. You will learn about a variety of cognitive and social processes that may lead even the most intelligent among us to develop beliefs in phenomena that are not real. Here are a couple of cognitive processes to watch for:

   ■ **Heuristics:** These are quick strategies we use to make decisions and judgments in our daily lives. For example, one heuristic we commonly use can lead us to believe that the cure for a disease should resemble the symptoms of the disease. Thus, a pseudoscientific health practitioner might advise a person with a liver ailment to consume an herbal remedy made from a plant that contains parts shaped like a liver.

   ■ **Difficulties in Statistical and Methodological Reasoning:** One difficulty people have with statistical reasoning is the tendency to sometimes perceive associations between events where none exist. For example, based on a couple of past experiences of winning games while wearing the same socks, a baseball player might believe that wearing his lucky socks will help his team win the next game.

TYPES OF ARTICLES IN THIS BOOK

You will find several types of readings in this book, including scientific journal articles and magazine articles. Below, I describe some differences between these two sources of articles and give some tips on reading the journal articles.

- **Journal Articles:** Articles published in peer-reviewed, scientific journals (e.g., *Journal of the American Medical Association, Professional Psychology: Research and Practice, The Scientific Review of Mental Health Practice*) typically undergo a rigorous evaluation process before they are published. After the author submits a manuscript for publication in such a journal, it is reviewed by experts in the field (i.e., a process called "peer review") to determine whether the research described in the article is of high quality and is important enough to warrant publication in a scientific journal. Thus, articles published in prestigious scientific journals are usually among the best sources of information because they reflect important, high-quality research conducted by reputable scientists.

  When reading a typical journal article about a scientific study, you will find the following sections:
  - **Introduction:** reviews the previous research relevant to the topic of the article.
  - **Method:** describes how the researcher conducted the study.
  - **Results:** states the findings and statistical analyses. If you find some of the statistical presentations in journal articles difficult to understand, focus on the author's description of the findings.
  - **Discussion:** contains the author's interpretation of the results and describes the implications of the findings.
- **Magazine Articles:** Magazine articles can vary widely in the quality of information they contain. For example, an article published in *Teen Magazine* is not as likely to contain high-quality, scientific information as is an article published in a peer-reviewed, scientific journal. Some magazines are designed more for entertainment than for education, and magazine articles typically do not go through a rigorous peer-review process before being published. Nevertheless, some scientifically oriented magazines, such as *Scientific American* and *Skeptical Inquirer,* contain high-quality articles written by respected scientists. For this book, I've selected a number of high-quality magazine articles written by scientists who are knowledgeable about the scientific research related to the topic they discuss.
- **Other Resources:** In the table that follows, I list a number of other resources that you might find useful for finding information about scientific perspectives on pseudoscience and the paranormal.

SELECTED RESOURCES FOR SCIENTIFIC PERSPECTIVES ON PSEUDOSCIENCE AND THE PARANORMAL

Below is a sample of specific journals, Web sites, and searchable databases that can be used to find scientific perspectives on the ever-expanding variety of pseudoscientific and paranormal phenomena.

Scientific Journals Devoted to Evaluating Suspected Pseudoscience

1. *The Scientific Review of Mental Health Practice* (www.srmhp.org): "the only peer-reviewed journal devoted exclusively to distinguishing scientifically-supported claims from scientifically-unsupported claims in clinical psychology, psychiatry, social work, and allied disciplines."

2. *The Scientific Review of Alternative Medicine* (www.sram.org): "the only peer-reviewed journal devoted exclusively to objectively analyzing the claims of 'alternative medicine.'"

Searchable Databases of Journal Articles and Books (consult your librarian for access)

1. *PsycINFO:* Indexes journal articles, books, and dissertations in psychology and related disciplines.

2. *MEDLINE:* Indexes journal articles related to the health sciences, including medicine, nursing, dentistry, veterinary medicine, and the health-care system.

Organizations and Web Sites

1. *National Council Against Health Fraud* (www.ncahf.org): "a private nonprofit, voluntary health agency that focuses upon health misinformation, fraud, and quackery as public health problems."

2. *Committee for the Scientific Investigation of Claims of the Paranormal* (www.csicop.org): "CSICOP encourages the critical investigation of paranormal and fringe-science claims from a responsible, scientific point of view and disseminates factual information about the results of such inquiries to the scientific community and the public."

3. *The Skeptics Society* (www.skeptic.com): "a scientific and educational organization of scholars, scientists, historians, magicians, professors and teachers, and anyone curious about controversial ideas, extraordinary claims, revolutionary ideas, and the promotion of science. Our mission is to serve as an educational tool for those seeking clarification and viewpoints on those controversial ideas and claims."

4. *James Randi Educational Foundation* (www.randi.org): "The James Randi Educational Foundation is a not-for-profit organization founded in 1996. Its aim is to promote critical thinking by reaching out to the public and media with reliable

information about paranormal and supernatural ideas so widespread in our society today."

5. *Quackwatch* (www.quackwatch.org): "a nonprofit corporation whose purpose is to combat health-related frauds, myths, fads, fallacies, and misconduct. Its primary focus is on quackery-related information that is difficult or impossible to get elsewhere."

Review and Contemplate

1. Name and describe three important features of psychology that make it a science.
2. Name and describe six important characteristics of pseudoscience.
3. This chapter described two characteristics of pseudoscience that are relevant to the example of the Q-Ray bracelet. What other pseudoscience characteristics seem relevant (name at least two and explain why you chose them)?
4. Can you think of other examples of products or practices that seem to be pseudoscientific? Which characteristics of pseudoscience are related to these examples?

References

Barrett, S. (2004, May 19). *Q-Ray bracelet marketed with preposterous claims.* Retrieved from http://www.quackwatch.org/01QuackeryRelatedTopics/PhonyAds/qray.html.

Bunge, M. (1984, Fall). What is pseudoscience? *Skeptical Inquirer, 9,* 36–46.

Coker, R. (2001, May 30). *Distinguishing science and pseudoscience.* Retrieved from http://www.quackwatch.org/01QuackeryRelatedTopics/pseudo.html.

Federal Trade Commission. (2003, June 2). *Marketers of Q-Ray ionized bracelet charged by FTC.* Retrieved from http://www.ftc.gov/opa/2003/06/qtinc.htm.

Lilienfeld, S. O. (1998, Fall). Pseudoscience in contemporary clinical psychology: What it is and what we can do about it. *The Clinical Psychologist, 51*(4), 3–9.

Rosa, L., Rosa, E., Sarner, L., & Barrett, S. (1998). A close look at therapeutic touch. *JAMA, 279,* 1005–1010.

Ruscio, J. (2006). *Critical thinking in psychology: Separating sense from nonsense* (2nd ed.). Pacific Grove, CA: Wadsworth.

Stanovich, K. E. (2004). *How to think straight about psychology* (7th ed.). Needham Heights, MA: Allyn & Bacon.

CHAPTER 2
Methodological and Statistical Reasoning

2.1   *Why Bogus Therapies Seem to Work/*
BARRY BEYERSTEIN

Chapter 1 briefly discussed the story of Peter Halvorson, who believes that trepanation (i.e., drilling a hole in his head) cured his depression. People's tendency to believe in the effectiveness of implausible—and sometimes bizarre—treatments never ceases to fascinate me. Some people believe that the Q-Ray bracelet cures pain, that bee pollen treats allergies, and that homeopathic medicines that contain few to no active ingredients are effective drugs for treating a wide variety of ailments. People whose symptoms improve after using these treatments may conclude that the treatments caused the improvement. However, it's important to keep in mind that although effective treatments should produce improved symptoms, improved symptoms do not necessarily mean the treatment was effective.

In this article, Barry Beyerstein discusses reasons bogus therapies may seem to work when, in fact, they are ineffective. Although this article is also relevant to Chapter 9, I chose to put it here because it illustrates some important methodological principles. Chapter 1 explained that the difficulties people have in statistical and methodological reasoning may lead them to develop beliefs in pseudoscientific or paranormal phenomena. This article discusses some important methodological principles to keep in mind when assessing the effectiveness of a therapy. First, it's important to keep in mind that correlation does not mean causation. In other words, just because you feel better after a therapy doesn't necessarily mean the therapy produced the improvement. Second, in order to infer that a therapy caused an improvement in one's health, one needs to be able to rule out alternative explanations for the improvement. Beyerstein discusses a number of alternative explanations to consider.

APA Reference

Beyerstein, B. L. (1997, September/October). Why bogus therapies seem to work. *Skeptical Inquirer, 21,* 29–34.

At least ten kinds of errors and biases can convince intelligent, honest people that cures have been achieved when they have not.

Nothing is more dangerous than active ignorance—Goethe

Those who sell therapies of any kind have an obligation to prove, first, that their treatments are safe and, second, that they are effective. The latter is often the more difficult task because there are many subtle ways that honest and intelligent people (both patients and therapists) can be led to think that a treatment has cured someone when it has not. This is true whether we are assessing new treatments in scientific medicine, old nostrums in folk medicine, fringe treatments in "alternative medicine," or the frankly magical panaceas of faith healers.

To distinguish causal from fortuitous improvements that might follow any intervention, a set of objective procedures has evolved for testing putative remedies. Unless a technique, ritual, drug, or surgical procedure can meet these requirements, it is ethically questionable to offer it to the public, especially if money is to change hands. Since most "alternative" therapies (i.e., ones not accepted by scientific biomedicine) fall into this category, one must ask why so many customers who would not purchase a toaster without consulting Consumer Reports shell out, with trusting naïveté, large sums for unproven, possibly dangerous, health remedies.

For many years, critics have been raising telling doubts about fringe medical practices, but the popularity of such nostrums seems undiminished. We must wonder why entrepreneurs' claims in this area should remain so refractory to contrary data. If an "alternative" or "complementary" therapy:

a.   is implausible on a priori grounds (because its implied mechanisms or putative effects contradict well-established laws, principles, or empirical findings in physics, chemistry, or biology),

b.   lacks a scientifically acceptable rationale of its own,

c.   has insufficient supporting evidence derived from adequately controlled outcome research (i.e., double-blind, randomized, placebo-controlled clinical trials),

d.   has failed in well-controlled clinical studies done by impartial evaluators and has been unable to rule out competing explanations for why it might seem to work in uncontrolled settings, and,

e.   should seem improbable, even to the lay person, on "commonsense" grounds,

why would so many well-educated people continue to sell and purchase such a treatment?

The answer, I believe, lies in a combination of vigorous marketing of unsubstantiated claims by "alternative" healers (Beyerstein and Sampson 1996), the poor level of scientific knowledge in the public at large (Kiernan 1995), and the "will to believe" so prevalent among seekers attracted to the New Age movement (Basil 1988; Gross and Levitt 1994).

The appeal of nonscientific medicine is largely a holdover from popular "counterculture" sentiments of the 1960s and 1970s. Remnants of the rebellious, "back-to-nature" leanings of that era survive as nostalgic yearnings for a return to nineteenth-century-style democratized health care (now wrapped in the banner of patients'rights) and a dislike of bureaucratic, technologic, and specialized treatment of disease (Cassileth and Brown 1988). Likewise, the allure of the "holistic" dogmas of alternative medicine is a descendant of the fascination with Eastern mysticism that emerged in the sixties and seventies. Although the philosophy and the science that underlie these holistic leachings have been severely criticized (Brandon 1985), they retain a strong appeal for those committed to belief in "mind-over-matter" cures, a systemic rather than localized view of pathology, and the all-powerful ability of nutrition to restore health (conceived of as whole-body "balance").

Many dubious health products remain on the market primarily because satisfied customers offer testimonials to their worth. Essentially, they are saying, "I tried it and I got better, so it must be effective." But even when symptoms do improve following a treatment, this, by itself, cannot prove that the therapy was responsible.

THE ILLNESS-DISEASE DISTINCTION

Although the terms disease and illness are often used interchangeably, for present purposes it is worth distinguishing between the two. I shall use disease to refer to a pathological state of the organism due to infection, tissue degeneration, trauma, toxic exposure, carcinogenesis, etc. By illness I mean the feelings of malaise, pain, disorientation, dysfunctionality, or other complaints that might accompany a disease. Our subjective reaction to the raw sensations we call symptoms is molded by cultural and psychological factors such as beliefs, suggestions, expectations, demand characteristics, self-serving biases, and self-deception. The experience of illness is also affected (often unconsciously) by a host of social and psychological payoffs that accrue to those admitted to the "sick role" by society's gatekeeper (i.e., health professionals). For certain individuals, the privileged status and benefits of the sick role are sufficient to perpetuate the experience of illness after a disease has healed, or even to create feelings of illness in the absence of disease (Alcock 1986).

Unless we can tease apart the many factors that contribute to the perception of being ill, personal testimonials offer no basis on which to judge whether a putative therapy has, in fact, cured a disease. That is why controlled clinical trials with objective physical measures are essential in evaluating therapies of any kind.

CORRELATION DOES NOT IMPLY CAUSATION

Mistaking correlation for causation is the basis of most superstitious beliefs, including many in the area of alternative medicine. We have a tendency to assume that when things occur together, they must be causally connected, although obviously they need not be. For example, there is a high correlation between the consumption of diet soft drinks and obesity. Does this mean that artificial sweeteners cause people to become overweight? When we count on personal experience to test the worth of medical treatments, many factors are varying simultaneously, making it extremely difficult to determine what is cause and effect. Personal endorsements supply the bulk of the support for unorthodox health products, but they are a weak currency because of what Gilovich (1997) has called the "compared to what?" problem. Without comparison to a similar group of sufferers, treated identically except that the allegedly curative element is withheld, individual recipients can never know whether they would have recovered just as well without it.

TEN ERRORS AND BIASES

The question is, then: Why might therapists and their clients who rely on anecdotal evidence and uncontrolled observations erroneously conclude that inert therapies work? There are at least ten good reasons.

1. **The Disease May Have Run Its Natural Course.** Many diseases are self-limiting—providing the condition is not chronic or fatal, the body's own recuperative processes usually restore the sufferer to health. Thus, before a therapy can be acknowledged as curative, its proponents must show that the number of patients listed as improved exceeds the proportion expected to recover without any treatment at all (or that they recover reliably faster than if left untreated). Unless an unconventional therapist releases detailed records of successes and failures over a sufficiently large number of patients with the same complaint, he or she cannot claim to have exceeded the published norms for unaided recovery.

2. **Many Diseases Are Cyclical.** Arthritis, multiple sclerosis, allergies, and gastrointestinal complaints are examples of diseases that normally "have their ups and downs." Naturally, sufferers tend to seek therapy during the downturn of any given cycle. In this way, a bogus treatment will have repeated opportunities to coincide with upturns that would have happened anyway. Again, in the absence of appropriate control groups, consumers and vendors alike are prone to misinterpret improvement due to normal cyclical variation as a valid therapeutic effect.

3. **Spontaneous Remission.** Anecdotally reported cures can be due to rare but possible "spontaneous remissions." Even with cancers that are nearly always lethal, tumors occasionally disappear without further treatment. One experienced oncologist reports that he has seen twelve such events in about

six thousand cases he has treated (Silverman 1987). Alternative therapies can receive unearned acclaim for remissions of this sort because many desperate patients turn to them when they feel that they have nothing left to lose. When the "alternatives" assert that they have snatched many hopeless individuals from death's door, they rarely reveal what percentage of their apparently terminal clientele such happy exceptions represent. What is needed is statistical evidence that their "cure rates" exceed the known spontaneous remission rate and the placebo response rate (see below) for the conditions they treat.

The exact mechanisms responsible for spontaneous remissions are not well understood, but much research is being devoted to revealing and possibly harnessing processes in the immune system or elsewhere that are responsible for these unexpected turnarounds. The relatively new field of psychoneuroimmunology studies how psychological variables affect the nervous, glandular, and immune systems in ways that might affect susceptibility to and recovery from disease (Ader and Cohen 1993; Mestel 1994). If thoughts, emotions, desires, beliefs, etc., are physical states of the brain, there is nothing inherently mystical in the notion that these neural processes could affect glandular, immune, and other cellular processes throughout the body. Via the limbic system of the brain, the hypothalamic pituitary axis, and the autonomic nervous system, psychological variables can have widespread physiological effects that can have positive or negative impacts upon health. While research has confirmed that such effects exist, it must be remembered that they are fairly small, accounting for perhaps a few percent of the variance in disease statistics.

4. **The Placebo Effect.** A major reason why bogus remedies are credited with subjective, and occasionally objective, improvements is the ubiquitous placebo effect (Roberts, Kewman, and Hovell 1993; Ulett 1996). The history of medicine is strewn with examples of what, with hindsight, seem like crackpot procedures that were once enthusiastically endorsed by physicians and patients alike (Skrabanek and McCormick 1990; Barrett and Jarvis 1993). Misattributions of this sort arise from the false assumptions that a change in symptoms following a treatment must have been a specific consequence of that procedure. Through a combination of suggestion, belief, expectancy, cognitive reinterpretation, and diversion of attention, patients given biologically useless treatments can often experience measurable relief. Some placebo responses produce actual changes in the physical condition; others are subjective changes that make patients feel better although there has been no objective change in the underlying pathology.

Through repeated contact with valid therapeutic procedures, we all develop, much like Pavlov's dogs, conditioned responses in various physiological systems. Later, these responses can be triggered by the setting, rituals, paraphernalia, and verbal cues that signal the act of "being treated." Among other things, placebos can cause release of the body's own morphinelike pain killers, the endorphins (Ulett 1996, ch. 3). Because these learned responses can be palliative, even when a treatment itself is physiologically unrelated to the source of the complaint, putative therapies must be tested against a placebo control group—similar patients who receive a sham treatment that resembles the "real" one except that the suspected active ingredient is withheld.

It is essential that the patients in such tests be randomly assigned to their respective groups and that they be "blind" with respect to their active versus placebo status. Because the power of what psychologists call expectancy and compliance effects (see below) is so strong, the therapists must also be blind as to individual patients' group membership. Hence the term double blind—the gold standard of outcome research. Such precautions are required because barely perceptible cues, unintentionally conveyed by treatment providers who are not blinded, can bias test results. Likewise, those who assess the treatment's effects must also be blind, for there is a large literature on "experimenter bias" showing that honest and well-trained professionals can unconsciously "read in" the outcomes they expect when they attempt to assess complex phenomena (Rosenthal 1966; Chapman and Chapman 1967).

When the clinical trial is completed, the blinds can be broken to allow statistical comparison of active, placebo, and no-treatment groups. Only if the improvements observed in the active treatment group exceed those in the two control groups by a statistically significant amount can the therapy claim legitimacy.

5. **Some Allegedly Cured Symptoms are Psychosomatic to Begin with.** A constant difficulty in trying to measure therapeutic effectiveness is that many physical complaints can both arise from psychosocial distress and be alleviated by support and reassurance. At first glance, these symptoms (at various times called "psychosomatic," "hysterical," or "neurasthenic") resemble those of recognized medical syndromes (Shorter 1992; Merskey 1995). Although there are many "secondary gains" (psychological, social, and economic) that accrue to those who slip into "the sick role" in this way, we need not accuse them of conscious malingering to point out that their symptoms are nonetheless maintained by subtle psychosocial processes.

"Alternative" healers cater to these members of the "worried well" who are mistakenly convinced that they are ill. Their complaints are instances of somatization, the tendency to express psychological concerns in a language of symptoms like those of organic diseases (Alcock 1986; Shorter 1992). The "alternatives" offer comfort to these individuals who for psychological reasons need others to believe there are organic etiologies for their symptoms. Often with the aid of pseudoscientific diagnostic devices, fringe practitioners reinforce the somatizer's conviction that the cold-hearted, narrow-minded medical establishment, which can find nothing physically amiss, is both incompetent and unfair in refusing to acknowledge a very real organic condition. A large portion of those diagnosed with "chronic fatigue," "environmental sensitivity syndrome," and various stress disorders (not to mention many suing because of the allegedly harmful effects of silicone breast implants) look very much like classic somatizers (Stewart 1990; Huber 1991; Rosenbaum 1997). When, through the role-governed rituals of "delivering treatment," fringe therapists supply the reassurance, sense of belonging and existential support their clients seek, this is obviously worthwhile, but all this need not be foreign to scientific practitioners who have much more to offer besides. The downside is that catering to the desire for medical diagnoses for psychological complaints promotes pseudoscientific and magical thinking while unduly inflating the success rates of medical quacks. Saddest of all, it perpetuates the anachronistic feeling that there is something shameful or illegitimate about psychological problems.

6. **Symptomatic Relief Versus Cure.** Short of an outright cure, alleviating pain and discomfort is what sick people value most. Many allegedly curative treatments offered by alternative practitioners, while unable to affect the disease process itself, do make the illness more bearable, but for psychological reasons. Pain is one example. Much research shows that pain is partly a sensation like seeing or hearing and partly an emotion (Metzack 1973). It has been found repeatly that successfully reducing the emotional component of pain leaves the sensory portion surprisingly tolerable. Thus, suffering can often be reduced by psychological means, even if the underlying pathology is untouched. Anything that can allay anxiety, redirect attention, reduce arousal, foster a sense of control, or lead to cognitive reinterpretation of symptoms can alleviate the agony component of pain. Modern pain clinics put these strategies to good use every day (Smith, Merskey, and Gross 1980). Whenever patients suffer less, this is all to the good, but we must be careful that purely symptomatic relief does not divert people from proven remedies until it is too late for them to be effective.

7. **Many Consumers of Alternative Therapies Hedge Their Bets.** In an attempt to appeal to a wider clientele, many unorthodox healers have begun to refer to themselves as "complementary" rather than "alternative." Instead of ministering primarily to the ideologically committed or those who have been told there is nothing more that conventional medicine can do for them, the "alternatives" have begun to advertise that they can enhance conventional biomedical treatments. They accept that orthodox practitioners can alleviate specific symptoms but contend that alternative medicine treats the real causes of disease—dubious dietary imbalances or environmental sensitivities, disrupted energy fields, or even unresolved conflicts from previous incarnations. If improvement follows the combined delivery of "complementary" and scientifically based treatments, the fringe practice often gets a disproportionate share of the credit.

8. **Misdiagnosis (by Self or by a Physician).** In this era of media obsession with health, many people can be induced to think they have diseases they do not have. When these healthy folk receive the oddly unwelcome news from orthodox physicians that they have no organic signs of disease, they often gravitate to alternative practitioners who can almost always find some kind of "imbalance" to treat. If "recovery" follows, another convert is born.

Of course, scientifically trained physicians are not infallible, and a mistaken diagnosis, followed by a trip to a shrine or an alternative healer, can lead to a glowing testimonial for curing a grave condition that never existed. Other times, the diagnosis may be correct but the time course, which is inherently hard to predict, might prove inaccurate. If a patient with a terminal condition undergoes alternative treatments and succumbs later than the conventional doctor predicted, the alternative procedure may receive credit for prolonging life when, in fact, there was merely an unduly pessimistic prognosis—survival was longer than the expected norm, but within the range of normal statistical variation for the disease.

9. **Derivative Benefits.** Alternative healers often have forceful, charismatic personalities (O'Connor 1987). To the extent that patients are swept up by the messianic aspects of alternative medicine, psychological uplift may ensue. If an enthusiastic, upbeat healer manages to elevate the patient's mood and expectations, this optimism can lead to greater compliance with, and hence effectiveness of, any orthodox treatments he or she may also be receiving. This expectant attitude can also motivate people to eat and sleep better and to exercise and socialize more. These, by themselves, could help speed natural recovery.

Psychological spinoffs of this sort can also reduce stress, which has been shown to have deleterious effects on the immune system (Mestel 1994). Removing this added burden may speed healing, even if it is not a specific effect of the therapy. As with purely symptomatic relief, this is far from a bad thing, unless it diverts the patient from more effective treatments, or the charges are exorbitant.

10. **Psychological Distortion of Reality.** Distortion of reality in the service of strong belief is a common occurrence (Alcock 1995). Even when they derive no objective improvements, devotees who have a strong psychological investment in alternative medicine can convince themselves they have been helped. According to cognitive dissonance theory (Festinger 1957), when experiences contradict existing attitudes, feelings, or knowledge, mental distress is produced. We tend to alleviate this discord by reinterpreting (distorting) the offending information. To have received no relief after committing time, money, and "face" to an alternate course of treatment (and perhaps to the worldview of which it is a part) would create such a state of internal disharmony. Because it would be too psychologically disconcerting to admit to oneself or to others that it has all been a waste, there would be strong psychological pressure to find some redeeming value in the treatment.

Many other self-serving biases help maintain self-esteem and smooth social functioning (Beyerstein and Hadaway 1991). Because core beliefs tend to be vigorously defended by warping perception and memory, fringe practitioners and their clients are prone to misinterpret cues and remember things as they wish they had happened. Similarly, they may be selective in what they recall, overestimating their apparent successes while ignoring, downplaying, or explaining away their failures. The scientific method evolved in large part to reduce the impact of this human penchant for jumping to congenial conclusions.

An illusory feeling that one's symptoms have improved could also be due to a number of so called demand characteristics found in any therapeutic setting. In all societies, there exists the "norm of reciprocity," an implicit rule that obliges people to respond in kind when someone does them a good turn. Therapists, for the most part, sincerely believe they are helping their patients and it is only natural that patients would want to please them in return. Without patients necessarily realizing it, such obligations are sufficient to inflate their perception of how much benefit they have received. Thus, controls for compliance effects must also be built into proper clinical trials (Adair 1973).

Finally, the job of distinguishing real from spurious causal relationships requires not only controlled observations, but also systematized abstractions from large bodies of data. Psychologists interested in judgmental biases have identified many sources of error that plague people who rely on informal reasoning processes to analyze complex events (Gilovich 1991, 1997; Schick and Vaughn 1995). Dean and colleagues (1992) showed, using examples from another popular pseudoscience, handwriting analysis, that without sophisticated statistical aids, human cognitive abilities are simply not up to the task of sifting valid relationships out of masses of interacting data. Similar difficulties would have confronted the pioneers of pre-scientific medicine and their followers, and for that reason, we cannot accept their anecdotal reports as support for their assertions.

SUMMARY

For the reasons I have presented, individual testimonials count for very little in evaluating therapies. Because so many false leads can convince intelligent, honest people that cures have been achieved when they have not, it is essential that any putative treatment be tested under conditions that control for placebo responses, compliance effects, and judgmental errors.

Before anyone agrees to undergo any kind of treatment, he or she should be confident that it has been validated in properly controlled clinical trials. To reduce the probability that supporting evidence has been contaminated by the foregoing biases and errors, consumers should insist that supporting evidence be published in peer-reviewed scientific journals. Any practitioner who cannot supply this kind of backing for his or her procedures is immediately suspect. Potential clients should be wary if, instead, the "evidence" consists merely of testimonials, self-published pamphlets or books, or items from the popular media. Even if supporting articles appear to have come from legitimate scientific periodicals, consumers should check to see that the journals in question are published by reputable scientific organizations. Papers extolling pseudoscience often appear in official-looking periodicals that turn out to be owned by groups with inadequate scientific credentials but with a financial stake in the questionable products. Similarly, one should discount articles from the "vanity press"—journals that accept virtually all submissions and charge the authors for publication. And finally, because any single positive outcome—even from a carefully done experiment published in a reputable journal—could always be a fluke, replication by independent research groups is the ultimate standard of proof.

If the practitioner claims persecutions, is ignorant of or openly hostile to mainstream science, cannot supply a reasonable scientific rationale for his or her methods, and promises results that go well beyond those claimed by orthodox biomedicine, there is strong reason to suspect that one is dealing with a quack. Appeals to other ways of knowing or mysterious-sounding "planes," "energies," "forces," or "vibrations" are other telltale signs, as is any claim to treat the whole person rather than localized pathology.

To people who are unwell, any promise of a cure is especially beguiling. As a result, false hope easily supplants common sense. In this vulnerable state, the need for hard-nosed appraisal is all the more necessary, but so often we see instead an eagerness to abandon any remaining vestiges of skepticism. Erstwhile savvy consumers, felled by disease, often insist upon less evidence to support the claims of alternative healers than they would previously have demanded from someone hawking a used car. Caveat emptor!

References

Adair, J. 1973. *The Human Subject*. Boston: Little, Brown and Co.

Ader, R., and N. Cohen. 1993. Psychoneuroimmunology: Conditioning and stress. *Annual Review of Psychology 44:* 53–85.

Alcock, J. 1986. Chronic pain and the injured worker. *Canadian Psychology 27*(2): 196–203.

———. 1995. The belief engine. *Skeptical Inquirer 19*(3): 14–8.

Barrett, S., and W. Jarvis. 1993. *The Health Robbers: A Close Lock at Quackery in America*. Amherst, N.Y.: Prometheus Books.

Basil, R., ed. 1988. *Not Necessarily the New Age*. Amherst, N.Y.: Prometheus Books.

Beyerstein, B., and P. Hadaway. 1991. On avoiding folly. *Journal of Drug Issues 20*(4): 689–700.

Beyerstein, B., and W. Sampson. 1996. Traditional medicine and pseudoscience in China. *Skeptical Inquirer 20*(4): 18–26.

Brandon, R. 1985. Holism in philosophy of biology. In *Examining Holistic Medicine,* edited by D. Stalker and C. Glymour. Amherst, N.Y.: Prometheus Books, 127–36.

Cassileth, B., and H. Brown. 1988. Unorthodox cancer medicine. *CA-A Cancer Journal for Clinicians 38*(3): 176–86.

Chapman, L., and J. Chapman. 1967. Genesis of popular but erroneous diagnostic observations. *Journal of Abnormal Psychology 72:* 193–204.

Dean, G., I. Ketty, D. Saklofske, and A. Furnham. 1992. Graphology and human judgement. In *The Write Stuff,* edited by B. and D. Beyerstein. Amherst, N.Y.: Prometheus Books, 342–96.

Festinger, L. 1957. *A Theory of Cognitive Dissonance*. Stanford: Stanford University Press.

Gilovich, T. 1991. *How We Know What Isn't so: The Fallibility of Human Reason in Everyday Life*. New York: Free Press/Macmillan.

———. 1997. Some systematic biases of everyday judgment. *Skeptical Inquirer 21*(2): 31–5.

Gross, P., and N. Levitt, 1994. *Higher Superstition*. Baltimore: Johns Hopkins University Press.

Huber, P. 1991. *Galileo's Revenge: Junk Science in the Courtroom*. New York: Basic Books.

Kiernan, V. 1995. Survey plumbs the depths of international ignorance. *The New Scientist* (April 29): 7.

Merskey, H. 1995. *The Analysis of Hysteria: Understanding Conversion and Dissociation.* 2d ed. London: Royal College of Psychiatrists.

Melzack, R. 1973. *The Puzzle of Pain.* New York: Basic Books.

Mestel, R. 1994. Let mind talk unto body. *The New Scientist* (July 23): 26–31.

O'Connor, G. 1987. Confidence trick. *The Medical Journal of Australia 147:* 456–9.

Roberts, A., D. Kewman, and L. Hovell. 1993. The power of nonspecific effects in healing: Implications for psychosocial and biological treatments. *Clinical Psychology Review 13:* 375–91.

Rosenbaum, J. T. 1997. Lessons from litigation over silicone breast implants: A call for activism by scientists. *Science 276* (June 6. 1997): 1524–5.

Rosenthal, R. 1966. *Experimenter Effects in Behavioral Research.* New York: Appleton-Century-Crofts.

Schick, T., and L. Vaughn. 1995. *How to Think About Weird Things: Critical Thinking for a New Age.* Mountain View, Calif: Mayfield Publishing.

Shorter, E. 1992. *From Paralysis to Fatigue: A History of Psychosomatic Illness in the Modern Era.* New York: The Free Press.

Silverman, S. 1987. Medical "miracles": Still mysterious despite claims of believers. *Psientific American.* (July): 5–7. Newsletter of the Sacramento Skeptics Society, Sacramento, Calif.

Skrabanek, P., and J. McCormick. 1990. *Follies and Fallacies in Medicine.* Amherst, N.Y.: Prometheus Books.

Smith, W., H. Merskey, and S. Gross, eds. 1980. *Pain: Meaning and Management.* New York: SP Medical and Scientific Books.

Stalker, D., and C. Glymour, eds. 1985. *Examining Holistic Medicine.* Amherst, N.Y.: Prometheus Books.

Stewart, D. 1990. Emotional disorders misdiagnosed as physical illness: Environmental hypersensitivity, candidiasis hypersensitivity, and chronic fatigue syndrome. *Int. J. Mental Health 19*(3): 56–68.

Ulett, G. A. 1996. *Alternative Medicine or Magical Healing.* St. Louis: Warren H. Green.

About the Author

Barry L. Beyerstein is at the Brain-Behavior Laboratory, Department of Psychology, Simon Fraser University, Burnaby, British Columbia, V5A 1S6 Canada.

Review and Contemplate

1. What is the distinction between a disease and an illness?
2. With respect to assessing the effectiveness of therapies, explain why it is important to understand that correlation does not imply causation.
3. Name and describe 5 of the 10 reasons ineffective treatments might seem to have worked.
4. What is a placebo control group, and why is it important to have such a group in an experiment designed to investigate the effectiveness of a therapy?
5. What are some examples of treatments or therapies that you or your friends believed in that you now suspect are bogus? Explain why you suspect they are bogus.

2.2
The Suggestibility of Young Children /
MAGGIE BRUCK AND STEPHEN CECI

In 1985, a four-year-old boy who was having his temperature taken with a rectal thermometer in a physician's office said to the nurse, "that's what my teacher does to me at nap time at school." The nurse suspected he had been sexually abused at his day care center and notified the authorities. Investigators repeatedly questioned the children at the day care center about possible abuse by a teacher named Kelly Michaels. Initially, most of the children said they liked Kelly and denied that Kelly had abused them. But after repeatedly being asked questions that suggested they had been abused, the children reported that Kelly had abused them in numerous ways. They reported that Kelly made them drink her urine and lick peanut butter off her genitals, and that Kelly forced them to have sex with her. In 1988, Kelly Michaels was convicted of 115 counts of abuse against 20 children, and was sentenced to 47 years in prison. Today the case of Kelly Michaels is used as an example of how faulty interviewing techniques can lead to false reports of abuse. Kelly Michaels served five years in prison before an appellate court set her free after ruling that she did not receive a fair trial due to the way in which the children had been questioned.

In this article, Bruck and Ceci discuss whether the manner in which an interview is conducted can elicit inaccurate information from children, including information about sexual abuse. The article contains valuable advice on what to do and what to avoid when interviewing children and others. The authors also discuss fascinating studies that illustrate the extent to which false information can be obtained from children interviewed in a suggestive manner.

APA Reference

Bruck, M., & Ceci, S. (1997). The suggestibility of young children. *Current Directions in Psychological Science, 6,* 75–79.

Department of Psychology, McGill University, Montreal, Quebec (M.B.), and Family Studies and Human Development, Cornell University, Ithaca, New York (S.J.C.).

Since the beginning of the 1980s, there have been a number of legal cases in which young children have provided uncorroborated testimony involving sexual abuse. Although it seemed from the evidence that the children in many of these cases were subjected to a number of suggestive interviews, the primary issue in deciding guilt or innocence was the degree to which such interviews could actually bring children to make serious allegations.

Until recently, scientific data provided little insight into this forensic issue. Specifically, although there were a number of studies showing that young children are more suggestible than adults (reviewed by Ceci & Bruck, 1993), these studies were limited to examinations of the influence of single misleading suggestions on children's recall of neutral, and often uninteresting, events. In other words, the conditions of the studies were not similar to the conditions that brought children to court. This empirical vacuum forced a new conceptualization of issues related to children's suggestibility, which, in turn, resulted in an outpouring of new research in the area. In general, two features of the newer research make it more relevant to forensic issues. First, the studies are designed to examine children's suggestibility about events that are personally salient, that involve bodily touching, and that involve insinuations of sexual abuse. Second, the concept of suggestive techniques has been expanded from the traditional view of asking a misleading question or planting a piece of misinformation, so that now studies examine the larger structure and the components of suggestive interviews. In this article, we provide an overview of the results of these newer studies of children's suggestibility.

INTERVIEWER BIAS AND SUGGESTIVE INTERVIEWING TECHNIQUES

We have proposed that *interviewer bias* is the central driving force in the creation of suggestive interviews. Interviewer bias characterizes an interviewer who holds a priori beliefs about the occurrence of certain events and, as a result, molds the interview to elicit from the interviewee statements that are consistent with these prior beliefs. One hallmark of interviewer bias is the single-minded attempt to gather only confirmatory evidence and to avoid all avenues that may produce disconfirmatory evidence. Thus, a biased interviewer does not ask questions that might provide alternate explanations for the allegations (e.g., "Did your mommy tell you, or did you see it happen?"). Nor does a biased interviewer ask about events that are inconsistent with the interviewer's hypothesis (e.g., "Who else besides your teacher touched your private parts? Did your mommy touch them, too?"). And a biased interviewer does not challenge the authenticity of the child's report when it is consistent with the interviewer's hypothesis. When a child provides inconsistent or bizarre evidence, it is either ignored or interpreted within the framework of the biased interviewer's initial hypothesis.

A number of studies highlight the effects of interviewer bias on the accuracy of children's reports (reviewed in Ceci & Bruck, 1995). In some studies, children are engaged in a staged event. Later, naive interviewers, who did not witness the event, are given either accurate or false information about the event and then told to question the children. Interviewers who are given false information are unaware of this deliberate deception, which is carried out to create a "bias." In other studies, children are asked to recall a staged event by an experimenter who intentionally conveys a bias that is either consistent or inconsistent with the staged event. In both types of studies, when questioned by interviewers with false beliefs, children make inaccurate reports that are consistent with the interviewers' biases.

According to our model, interviewer bias influences the entire architecture of interviews, and it is revealed through a number of different component features that are suggestive. We briefly describe some of these in this section.

In order to obtain confirmation of their suspicions, biased interviewers may not ask children open-ended questions, such as "What happened?" but instead resort to a barrage of specific questions, many of which are repeated, and many of which are leading. This strategy is problematic because children's responses to open-ended questions are more accurate than their responses to specific questions. This finding has been reported consistently since the beginning of the century (e.g., see Ceci & Bruck, 1995) and is highlighted in a recent study by Peterson and Bell (1996), who interviewed children after they visited an emergency room for a traumatic injury. Children were first asked open-ended questions (e.g., "Tell me what happened"), and then asked more specific questions (e.g., "Where did you hurt yourself?" or "Did you hurt your knee?"). The children were most likely to report the important details accurately in response to open-ended questions (91% accuracy); errors increased when children were asked specific questions (45% accuracy). Forced-choice questions (e.g., "Was it black or white?") also compromise the reliability of children's reports because children tend not to respond, "I don't know" (e.g., see Walker, Lunning, & Eilts, 1996), even when the question is nonsensical (Hughes & Grieve, 1980).

Not only does accuracy decrease when children are asked specific questions, but there is increased risk of taint when young children are repeatedly asked the same specific questions, either within the same interview or across different interviews (e.g., Poole & White, 1991). Under such circumstances, young children tend to change their answers, perhaps to provide the interviewer with the information that they perceive he or she wants.

Some interviewers convey their bias by asking leading questions and providing information about the alleged target events. When these techniques are repeated across multiple interviews, children's reports may become tainted. For example, in one study (Bruck, Ceci, Francoeur, & Barr, 1995), 5-year-old children visited their pediatrician and received an inoculation. One year later, they were interviewed four times about salient details of that visit. Children who were repeatedly interviewed in a neutral, nonleading manner provided accurate reports about the original medical visit. In contrast, children who were repeatedly given misinformation about some of the salient details were very inaccurate; not only did they incorporate the misleading suggestions into their reports (e.g., falsely claiming that a female research assistant, rather than the male pediatrician, inoculated them), but they also reported nonsuggested but inaccurate events (e.g., falsely reporting that the female research assistant had checked their ears and nose).

Interviewers can also use subtle verbal and nonverbal cues to communicate bias. At times, these cues can set the emotional tone of the interview, and they can also convey implicit or explicit threats, bribes, and rewards for the desired answer. Children are attuned to these emotional tones and act accordingly. In one study, for example, children were asked to recall the details of a visit to a university laboratory that had occurred 4 years previously (Goodman, Wilson, Hazan, & Reed, 1989). At the 4-year follow-up interview, the researchers deliberately created an atmosphere of accusation by telling the children that they were to be questioned about an important event and by saying, "Are you afraid to tell? You'll feel better once you've told." Although few children remembered the original event from 4 years earlier, a number of the children assented to suggestive questions implying abuse; some children falsely reported that they had been hugged or kissed, or that they had had their picture taken in the bathroom, or that they had been given a bath. Thus, children may give incorrect information to misleading questions about events for which they have no memory, if the interviewer creates an emotional tone of accusation.

Stereotype induction is another possible component of a suggestive interview. For example, if a child is repeatedly told that a person "does bad things," then the child may begin to incorporate this belief into his or her reports. A study of preschool children illustrates this pattern (Leichtman & Ceci, 1995). On a number of occasions, the experimenters told the children about their "clumsy" friend Sam Stone, whose exploits included accidentally breaking Barbie dolls and ripping sweaters. Later, Sam came to the children's classroom for a short, accident-free visit. The next day, the teacher showed the children a torn book and a soiled teddy bear. Several weeks later, a number of these 3- to 4-year-old children reported that Sam had been responsible for these acts; some even claimed that they had seen him do these things. Children who had not received the stereotype induction rarely made this type of error.

Techniques that have been especially designed for interviewing children about sexual abuse may be potentially suggestive. For example, anatomically detailed dolls are commonly used by professionals when interviewing children about suspected sexual abuse. It is thought that the use of the dolls overcomes language, memory, and motivational (e.g., embarrassment) problems. However, the existing data indicate that the dolls do not facilitate accurate reporting. In some cases, children are more inaccurate with the dolls, especially when asked to demonstrate certain events that never happened (e.g., Gordon et al., 1993). Thus, dolls may be suggestive if children have not made any allegations but are asked by an interviewer who suspects abuse to demonstrate abuse with the dolls.

Our recent studies provide evidence for this hypothesis (Bruck, Ceci, & Francoeur, 1995; Bruck, Ceci, Francoeur, & Renick, 1995). Three- and 4-year-old children had a medical examination during which some of them received a routine genital examination. After the children were interviewed about the examination, they were given an anatomical doll and told, "Show me on the doll how the doctor touched your genitals." Approximately 50% of the children who had not received a genital examination falsely showed touching on the doll.

Furthermore, when the children who had received a genital examination were asked the same question, a number of them incorrectly showed that the doctor had inserted a finger into their genitals; the pediatrician had never done this. Next, when the children in the study were given a stethoscope and a spoon and asked to show what the doctor did or might do with these instruments, some children incorrectly showed that he used the stethoscope to examine their genitals, and some children inserted the spoon into the genital or anal openings or hit the doll's genitals. None of these actions had occurred. We concluded that these false actions were the result of implicit suggestions that it was permissible to show sexualized behaviors. Also, because of the novelty of the dolls, children were drawn to insert fingers and other objects into their cavities.

Guided imagery is another interviewing technique that is potentially suggestive. Interviewers sometimes ask children to try to remember if or pretend that a certain event occurred and then to create a mental picture of the event and to think about its details. Because young children sometimes have difficulty distinguishing between memories of actual events and memories of imagined events (e.g., Parker, 1995; Welch-Ross, 1995), when asked to pretend about or imagine certain events, children may later come to report them as real and believe them to be so. This hypothesis is supported by studies in which young children were repeatedly asked to think about real as well as imaginary events, creating mental images each time they did so. In one of these studies (Ceci, Loftus, Leichtman, & Bruck, 1994), children increasingly assented to false events with each successive interview. When these children were told after 11 sessions that some of the imagined events had not happened, most of the children who had previously assented to false beliefs continued to hold onto their false statements. These data indicate that a number of the children had actually come to believe that they had experienced the false events.

CONCLUSIONS AND QUALIFICATIONS

In summary, interviewer bias is revealed by a number of suggestive techniques, each of which can compromise the accuracy of young children's reports. In this section, we qualify and elaborate on this conclusion by raising several points. First, although most developmental studies have focused on the suggestibility of preschool children, there is still reason for concern about the reliability of older children's testimony when they are subjected to suggestive interviews. There is ample evidence that children older than 6 years of age are suggestible about a wide range of events (e.g., Goodman et al., 1989; Poole & Lindsay, 1996; Warren & Lane, 1995) and that adults' recollections are impaired by suggestive interviewing techniques (e.g., Hyman & Pentland, 1996; Loftus & Pickrell, 1995).

Second, although there are consistent findings of age differences across studies, there are nevertheless individual differences. Some preschoolers are very resistant to interviewers' suggestions, whereas some older children will immediately fall sway to the slightest suggestion. Researchers are a long way from understanding the source of these individual differences but are beginning to

assess the association between suggestibility and a number of cognitive characteristics (e.g., knowledge base, memory), psychosocial factors (e.g., compliance,
self-esteem), and interviewing techniques (e.g., the use of various suggestive
components).

Third, contrary to previous claims that children are suggestible only about peripheral details (e.g., Melton, 1992), the newer studies show that children are also
suggestible about central events. These central events may involve bodily touching
that may have sexual connotations. Thus, in some suggestibility studies, children
falsely claimed that a nurse licked their knees, a scientist put something "yucky" in
their mouths, a pediatrician inserted a spoon into their genitals, and a man kissed
their friends on the lips and removed some of the children's clothes.

Fourth, the number of suggestive interviewing techniques (which reflects
the degree of interviewer bias) can account for variations in suggestibility estimates across and within studies. If a biased interviewer uses more than one suggestive technique, there is a greater chance for taint than if he or she uses just
one technique. For example, we (Bruck, Ceci, & Hembrooke, in press) constructed interviews that combined a variety of suggestive techniques (visualization, repeated questioning, repeated misinformation) to elicit children's reports
of true events (helping a visitor in the school, getting punished) and false events
(helping a woman find her monkey, seeing a thief taking food from the day
care). After two suggestive interviews, most children in this study had assented
to all events, a pattern that continued to the end of the experiment.

Fifth, the procedures used in most studies do not allow one to determine if
the children's false reports reflect false belief (false memory) or merely knowing
compliance to the interviewer's suggestion. There may be a time course for the
emergence of these different states. Children may start out knowingly comply-
ing to suggestions, but with repeated suggestive interviews, they may come to
believe the suggestions and incorporate them into their memories. There are a
few studies that show that when suggestions are repeated to children over time,
a number of the children do develop false beliefs (eg., Ceci et al., 1994; Leichtman
& Ceci, 1995; Poole & Lindsay, 1996). Furthermore, if the suggestive interviews
cease for a period of time, these false memories fade (e.g., Huffman, Crossman,
& Ceci, 1996; Poole & Lindsay, 1996).

Sixth, children who have undergone repeated suggestive interviews appear
highly credible. When highly trained professionals in the fields of child
development, mental health, and forensics view videotaped interviews of these
subjects, they cannot reliably discriminate between children whose reports are accurate and children whose reports are inaccurate as the result of suggestive
interviewing techniques (see Leichtman & Ceci, 1995). We have attempted to iso-
late the linguistic markers that might differentiate true narratives from false narratives that emerge as a result of repeated suggestive interviews (Bruck et al., in
press). We have found that with repeated suggestive interviews, false stories
quickly come to resemble true stories in terms of the number of details, the spon-
taneity of utterance, the number of details not previously reported (reminis-
cences), inconsistency across narratives, the elaborativeness of the details, and the

cohesiveness of the narrative. It is only the greater consistency of narratives of true events that differentiates them from narratives of false events. Thus, suggestive interviewing procedures can result in highly credible but inaccurate witnesses.

Finally, although we have focused here on the conditions that can compromise reliable reporting, it is also important to acknowledge that a large number of studies show that children are capable of providing accurate, detailed, and useful information about actual events, including traumatic ones (for reviews, see, e.g., Fivush, 1993; Goodman, Batterman-Faunce, & Kenney, 1992). What characterizes these studies is the neutral tone of the interviewers, the limited use of leading questions (for the most part, if suggestions are used, they are limited to a single occasion), and the absence of any motive for the children to make false reports. When such conditions are present, it is a common (although not universal) finding that children are relatively immune to suggestive influences, particularly about sexual details. When such conditions are present in actual forensic or therapeutic interviews, one can have greater confidence in the reliability of children's allegations. It is these conditions that one must strive for when eliciting information from young children.

Note

1. Address correspondence to Maggie Bruck, Department of Psychology, McGill University, 1205 Dr. Penfield, Montreal, Quebec H3A 1B1, Canada; e-mail: bruck@hebb. psych.mcgill.ca.

References

Bruck, M., Ceci, S.J., & Francoeur, E. (1995, March). *Anatomically detailed dolls do not facilitate preschoolers' reports of touching*. Paper presented at the biannual meeting of the Society for Research on Child Development. Indianapolis, IN.

Bruck, M., Ceci, S.J., Francoeur, E., & Barr, R.J. (1995). "I hardly cried when I got my shot!": Influencing children's reports about a visit to their pediatrician. *Child Development, 66,* 193–208.

Bruck, M., Ceci, S.J., Francoeur, E., & Renick, A. (1995). Anatomically detailed dolls do not facilitate preschoolers' reports of a pediatric examination involving genital touching. *Journal of Experimental Psychology: Applied, 1,* 95–109.

Bruck, M., Ceci, S.J., & Hembrooke, H. (in press). Children's reports of pleasant and unpleasant events. In D. Read & S. Lindsay (Eds.), *Recollections of trauma: Scientific research and clinical practice*. New York: Plenum Press.

Ceci, S.J., & Bruck, M. (1993). The suggestibility of the child witness: A historical review and synthesis. *Psychological Bulletin, 113,* 403–439.

Ceci, S.J., & Bruck, M. (1995). *Jeopardy in the courtroom: A scientific analysis of children's testimony*. Washington, DC: American Psychological Association.

Ceci, S.J., Loftus, E.W., Leichtman, M., & Bruck, M. (1994). The role of source misattributions in the creation of false beliefs among preschoolers. *International Journal of Clinical and Experimental Hypnosis, 62,* 304–320.

Fivush, R. (1993). Developmental perspectives on autobiographical recall. In G.S. Goodman & B. Bottoms (Eds.), *Child victims and child witnesses: Understanding and improving testimony* (pp. 1–24). New York: Guilford Press.

Goodman, G.S., Batterman-Faunce, J.M., & Kenney, R. (1992). Optimizing children's testimony. Research and social policy issues concerning allegations of child sexual abuse. In D. Cicchetti & S. Toth (Eds.), *Child abuse, child development, and social policy* (pp. 139–166). Norwood, NJ: Ablex.

Goodman, G.S., Wilson, M.E., Hazan, C., & Reed, R.S. (1989, April). *Children's testimony nearly four years after an event.* Paper presented at the annual meeting of the Eastern Psychological Association, Boston.

Gordon, B., Ornstein, P.A., Nida, R., Follmer, A., Creshaw, C., & Albert, G. (1993). Does the use of dolls facilitate children's memory of visits to the doctor? *Applied Cognitive Psychology, 7,* 459–474.

Huffman, M.L., Crossman, A., & Ceci, S. (1996, March). *An investigation of the long-term effects of source misattribution error: Are false memories permanent?* Poster presented at the biannual meeting of the American Psychology-Law Society, Hilton Head, SC.

Hughes, M., & Grieve, R. (1980). On asking children bizarre questions. *First Language, 1,* 149–160.

Hyman, I.E., & Pentland, J. (1996). The role of mental imagery in the creation of false childhood memories. *Journal of Memory and Language, 35,* 101–117.

Leichtman, M.D., & Ceci, S.J. (1995). The effects of stereotypes and suggestions on preschoolers' reports. *Developmental Psychology, 31,* 568–578.

Loftus, E.F., & Pickrell, J.E. (1995). The formation of false memories. *Psychiatric Annals, 25,* 720–725.

Melton, G. (1992). Children as partners for justice: Next steps for developmentalists. *Monographs of the Society for Research in Child Development, 57*(5, Serial No. 229), 153–159.

Parker, J. (1995). Age differences in source monitoring of performed and imagined actions on immediate and delayed tests. *Journal of Experimental Child Psychology, 60,* 84–101.

Peterson, C., & Bell, M. (1996). Children's memory for traumatic injury. *Child Development, 67,* 3045–3070.

Poole, D.A., & Lindsay, D.S. (1996, June). *Effects of parents suggestions, interviewing techniques, and age on young children's event reports.* Paper presented at the NATO Advanced Study Institute, Port de Bourgenay, France.

Poole, D.A., & White, L. (1991). Effects of question repetition on the eyewitness testimony of children and adults. *Developmental Psychology, 27,* 975–986.

Walker, N., Lunning, S., & Eilts, J. (1996, June). *Do children respond accurately to forced choice questions?* Paper presented to the NATO Advanced Study Institute: Recollections of Trauma: Scientific Research and Clinical Practice, Talmont Saint Hilaire, France.

Warren, A.R., & Lane, P. (1995). The effects of timing and type of questioning on eyewitness accuracy and suggestibility. In M. Zaragoza (Ed.), *Memory and testimony in the child witness* (pp. 44–60). Thousand Oaks, CA: Sage Publications.

Welch-Ross, M. (1995). Developmental changes in preschoolers' ability to distinguish memories of performed, pretended, and imagined actions. *Cognitive Development, 10,* 421–441.

Review and Contemplate

1. What is interviewer bias? Explain how such a bias might lead a child to falsely report being sexually abused by an adult.

2. Bruck and Ceci (1997) stated, "Interviewer bias influences the entire architecture of interviews, and it is revealed through a number of different component features that are suggestive." Describe three of these component features.
3. Do anatomically correct dolls help interviewers elicit accurate information about suspected childhood sexual abuse? Cite evidence from Bruck and Ceci (1997) to support your answer.
4. Bruck and Ceci (1997) stated that "children are capable of providing accurate, detailed, and useful information about actual events, including traumatic ones." Under what conditions do children provide such information?

Recommended Reading

Ceci, S. J., & Bruck, M. (1995) (See References)

Poole, D. A., & Lindsay, D. S. (in press). Assessing the accuracy of young children's reports: Lessons from the investigation of child sexual abuse. *Applied and Preventative Psychology.*

2.3
On the Belief That Arthritis Pain Is Related to the Weather /
DONALD REDELMEIER AND AMOS TVERSKY.

My mother used to complain of chronic pain in her legs, and one day she informed me that she could tell when a hurricane was near the United States because she could feel it in her legs. What made her claim even more extraordinary is the fact that she lived in Michigan, which is about 1,000 miles from the gulf coast region where hurricanes often strike! Although it seems unlikely that her claim was true, it's not uncommon for people to develop false beliefs about relationships between events. The tendency of people to see associations or correlations where none exist is well documented by psychologists. For example, some nurses believe that mental patients are more likely to admit themselves to the hospital on evenings in which there is a full moon, but there is no correlation between the phase of the moon and hospital admissions of mental patients.

Beliefs in such nonexistent relationships are called illusory correlations, and they illustrate one difficulty people sometimes have with statistical reasoning. As you read in Chapter 1, normal cognitive processes can lead to pseudoscientific or paranormal beliefs, and our tendency to search for relationships or correlations between events—including our tendency to develop illusory correlations—is one such cognitive process. My mother's belief that her pain was related to the weather is similar to another fairly common belief: some arthritis patients, and some of their doctors, believe that their pain is related to the weather. In this article, Redelmeier and Tversky examine whether this belief reflects an illusory correlation.

APA Reference

Redelmeier, D. A., & Tversky, A. (1996). On the belief that arthritis pain is related to the weather. *Proceedings of the National Academy of the Sciences of the United States of America, 93,* 2895–2896.

[*]Department of Medicine, University of Toronto, Toronto, ON Canada M5S 1A1; [†]Division of Clinical Epidemiology, Wellesley Hospital Research Institute, Toronto, ON Canada M4Y 113; and [‡]Department of Psychology, Stanford University Stanford, CA, 94305

Contributed by Amos Tversky, December 12, 1995

The publication costs of this article were defrayed in part by page charge payment. This article must therefore be hereby marked "*advertisement*" *in* accordance with 18 U.S.C. §1734 solely to indicate this fact.

ABSTRACT: There is a widespread and strongly held belief that arthritis pain is influenced by the weather; however, scientific studies have found no consistent association. We hypothesize that this belief results, in part at least, from people's tendency to perceive patterns where none exist. We studied patients ($n = 18$) for more than 1 year and found no statistically significant associations between their arthritis pain and the weather conditions implicated by each individual. We also found that college students ($n = 97$) tend to perceive correlations between uncorrelated random sequences. This departure of people's intuitive notion of association from the statistical concept of association, we suggest, contributes to the belief that arthritis pain is influenced by the weather.

For thousands of years people have believed that arthritis pain is influenced by the weather. Hippocrates around 400 B.C. discussed the effects of winds and rains on chronic diseases in his book *Air, Water and Places* (1). In the nineteenth century, several authors suggested that variations in barometric pressure, in particular, were partially responsible for variations in the intensity of arthritis pain (2–4). To the current day, such beliefs are common among patients, physicians, and interested observers throughout the world (5–14). Furthermore, these beliefs have led to recommendations that patients move to milder climates or spend time in a climate-controlled chamber to lessen joint pain (15–17).

The research literature, however, has not established a clear association between arthritis pain and the weather. No study using objective measures of inflammation has found positive results (18, 19), and studies using subjective measures of pain have been conflicting. Some find that an increase in barometric pressure tends to increase pain (20), others find that it tends to decrease pain (21), and others find no association (22, 23). Some investigators argue that only a simultaneous change in pressure and humidity influences arthritis pain (24), but others find no such pattern (25). Several studies report that weather effects are immediate (20), whereas others suggest a lag of several days (26). Due to the lack of clear evidence, medical textbooks—which once devoted chapters to the relation of weather and rheumatic disease—now devote less than a page to the topic (27, 28).

The contrast between the strong belief that arthritis pain is related to the weather and the weak evidence found in the research literature is puzzling. How do people acquire and maintain the belief? Research on judgment under uncertainty indicates that both laypeople and experts sometimes detect patterns where none exist. In particular, people often perceive positive serial correlations in random sequences of coin tosses (29), stockmarket prices (30), or basketball shots (31). We hypothesize that a similar bias occurs in the evaluation of correlations between pairs of time series, and that it contributes to the belief that arthritis pain is related to the weather. We explored this hypothesis by testing (*i*) whether arthritis patients' perceptions are consistent with their data and (*ii*) whether people perceive associations between uncorrelated time series.

We obtained data from rheumatoid arthritis patients ($n = 18$) on pain (assessed by the patient), joint tenderness (evaluated by the physician), and functional status (based on a standard index) measured twice a month for 15 months (32). We also obtained local weather reports on barometric pressure, temperature, and humidity for the corresponding time period. Finally, we interviewed patients about their beliefs concerning their arthritis pain. All patients but one believed that their pain was related to the weather, and all but two believed the effects were strong, occurred within a day, and were related to barometric pressure, temperature, or humidity.

We computed the correlations between pain and the specific weather component and lag mentioned by each patient. The mean of these correlations was 0.016 and none was significant at $P < 0.05$. We also computed the correlation between pain and barometric pressure for each patient, using nine different time lags ranging from 2 days forward to 2 days backward in 12-hr increments. The mean of these correlations was 0.003, and only 6% were significant at $P < 0.05$. Similar results were obtained in analyses using the two other measures of arthritis and the two other measures of the weather. Furthermore, we found no consistent pattern among the few statistically significant correlations.

We next presented college students ($n = 97$) with pairs of sequences displayed graphically. The top sequence was said to represent a patient's daily arthritis pain over 1 month, and the bottom sequence was said to represent daily barometric pressure during the same month (Fig. 2.1). Each sequence was generated as a normal random walk and all participants evaluated six pairs of sequences: a positively correlated pair ($r = +0.50$), a negatively correlated pair ($r = -0.50$),

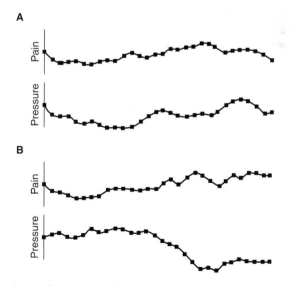

FIGURE 2.1 ▨ Random walk sequences. The upper sequence in each pair represents daily arthritis pain for 30 consecutive observations; the lower sequence represents daily barometric pressure during the same period. For both A and B, the correlation between changes in pain and changes in pressure is 0.00.

and four uncorrelated pairs. Participants were asked to classify each pair of sequences as (*i*) positively related, (*ii*) negatively related, or (*iii*) unrelated. Positively related sequences were defined as follows: "An increase in barometric pressure is more likely to be accompanied by an increase in arthritis pain rather than a decrease on that day (and a decrease in barometric pressure is more likely to be accompanied by a decrease rather than an increase in arthritis pain on that day)." Negatively related sequences and unrelated sequences were defined similarly.

We found that the positively correlated pair and the negatively correlated pair were correctly classified by 89% and 93% of respondents, respectively. However, some uncorrelated pairs were consistently classified as related. For example, the two uncorrelated sequences in Fig. 2.1*A* were judged as positively related by 87%, as negatively related by 2%, and as unrelated by 11% of participants. The two uncorrelated sequences in Fig. 2.1*B* were judged as positively related by 3%, as negatively related by 79%, and as unrelated by 18% of participants. The remaining two pairs of uncorrelated sequences were correctly classified by 59% and 64% of participants. Evidently, the intuitive notion of association differs from the statistical concept of association.

Our results indicate that people tend to perceive an association between uncorrelated time series. We attribute this phenomenon to selective matching, the tendency to focus on salient coincidences, thereby capitalizing on chance and neglecting contrary evidence (33–35). For arthritis, selective matching leads people to look for changes in the weather when they experience increased pain, and pay little attention to the weather when their pain is stable. For graphs, selective matching leads people to focus on segments where the two sequences seem to move together (in the same or opposite direction), with insufficient regard to other aspects of the data. In both cases, a single day of severe pain and extreme weather might sustain a lifetime of belief in a relation between them. The cognitive processes involved in evaluating graphs are different from those involved in evaluating past experiences, yet all intuitive judgments of covariation are vulnerable to selective matching.

Several psychological factors could contribute to the belief that arthritis pain is related to the weather, in addition to general plausibility and traditional popularity. The desire to have an explanation for a worsening of pain may encourage patients to search for confirming evidence and neglect contrary instances (36). This search is facilitated by the availability of multiple components and time lags for linking changes in arthritis to changes in the weather (37). Selective memory may further enhance the belief that arthritis pain is related to the weather if coincidences are more memorable than mismatches (38). Selective matching, therefore, can be enhanced by both motivational and memory effects; our study of graphs, however, suggests that it can operate even in the absence of these effects.

Selective matching can help explain both the prevalent belief that arthritis pain is related to the weather and the failure of medical research to find consistent correlations. Our study, of course, does not imply that arthritis pain and the weather are unrelated for all patients. Furthermore, it is possible that daily measurements over many years of our patients would show a stronger correlation than observed in our data, at least for some patients. However, it is doubtful that sporadic correlations could justify the widespread and strongly held beliefs about arthritis and the weather. The observation that the beliefs are just as prevalent in San Diego (where the weather is mild and stable) as in Boston (where the weather is severe and volatile) casts further doubt on a purely physiological explanation (39). People's beliefs about arthritis pain and the weather may tell more about the workings of the mind than of the body.

References

1. Adams, F. (1991). *The Genuine Works of Hippocrates* (Williams & Wilkins, Baltimore).
2. Webster, J. (1859) *Lancet* i, 588–589.
3. Mitchel, S. W. (1877) *Am. J. Med. Sci.* **73**, 305–329.
4. Everett, J. T. (1879). *Med. J. Exam.* **38**, 253–260.
5. Abdulpatakhov, D. D. (1969) *Vopr. Revm.* **9**, 72–76.
6. Nava, P. & Seda, H. (1964) *Bras. Med.* **78**, 71–74.
7. Pilger, A. (1970) *Med. Klin. Munich* **65**, 1363–1365.
8. Hollander, J. L. (1963) *Arch. Environ. Health* **6**, 527–536.
9. Guedj, D. & Weinberger, A. (1990) *Ann. Rheum. Dis.* **49**, 158–159.
10. Lawrence, J. S. (1977) *Rheumatism in Population* (Heinemann Med. Books, London). pp. 505–517.
11. Rose, M. B. (1974) *Physiotherapy* **60**, 306–309.
12. Rasker, J. J., Peters, H. J. G. & Boon, K. L. (1986) *Scand. J. Rheumatol.* **15**, 27–36.
13. Laborde, J. M., Dando, W. A. & Powers, M. J. (1986) *Soc. Sci. Med.* **23**, 549–554.
14. Shutty, M. S., Cundiff, G. & DeGood, D. E. (1992) *Pain* **49**, 199–204.
15. Hill, D. F. & Holbrook, W. P. (1942) *Clinics* **1**, 577–581.
16. Balfour, W. (1916) *Observations with Cases Illustrative of a New, Simple, and Expeditious Mode of Curing Rheumatism and Sprains* (Muirhead, Edinburgh).
17. Edstrom, G., Lundin, G. & Wramner, T. (1948) *Ann. Rheum. Dis.* **7**, 76–92.
18. Latman, N. S. (1981) *J. Rheumatol.* **8**, 725–729.
19. Latman, N. S. (1980) *N. Engl. J. Med.* **303**, 1178.
20. Rentschler, E. B., Vanzant, F. R. & Rowntree, L. G. (1929) *J. Am. Med. Assoc.* **92**, 1995–2000.
21. Guedj, D. (1990) *Ann. Rheum. Dis.* **49**, 158–159.
22. Dordick, I. (1958) *Weather* **13**, 359–364.
23. Patberg, W. R., Nienhuis, R. I. F. & Veringa, F. (1985) *J. Rheumatol.* **12**, 711–715.
24. Hollander, J. L. & Yeostros, S. J. (1963) *Bull. Am. Meteorol. Soc.* **44**, 489–494.
25. Sibley, J. T. (1985) *J. Rheumatol.* **12**, 707–710.
26. Patberg, W. R. (1989) *Arthritis Rheum.* **32**, 1627–1629.
27. Hollander, J. L., ed. (1960) *Arthritis and Allied Conditions* (Lea & Febiger, Philadelphia), 6th Ed., pp. 577–581.
28. McCarty, D. J., ed. (1989) *Arthritis and Allied Conditions* (Lea & Febiger, Philadelphia), 11th Ed., p. 25.
29. Bar-Hillel, M. & Wagenaar, W. (1991) *Adv. Appl. Math.* **12**, 428–454.
30. Malkiel, B. G. (1990) *A Random Walk Down Wall Street* (Norton, New York).
31. Gilovich, T., Vallone, R. & Tversky, A. (1985) *Cognit. Psychol.* **17**, 295–314.
32. Ward, M. M. (1993) *J. Rheumatol.* **21**, 17–21.

33. Kahneman, D., Slovic, P. & Tversky, A., eds. (1982). *Judgment Under Uncertainty: Heuristics and Biases* (Cambridge Univ. Press, New York).
34. Nisbett, R. & Ross, L. (1980) *Human Inference: Strategies and Shortcomings of Social Judgments* (Prentice-Hall, London), pp. 90–112.
35. Gilovich, T. (1991) *How We Know What Isn't So: The Fallibility of Human Reasoning in Everyday Life* (The Free Press, New York).
36. Chapman, L. J. & Chapman, J. P. (1969) *J. Abnorm. Psychol.* **74,** 271–280.
37. Abelson, R. P. (1995) *Statistics as Principled Argument* (Lawrence Erlbaum, Hillsdale, NJ), pp. 7–8.
38. Tversky, A. & Kahneman, D. (1973) *Cognit. Psychol.* **5,** 207–232.
39. Jamison, R. N., Anderson, K. O. & Slater, M. A. (1995) *Pain* **61,** 309–315.

Review and Contemplate

1. Based on research conducted by scientists other than Redelmeier and Tversky, what general conclusion can be made about the relationship between arthritis pain and the weather?
2. Describe the design and results of the study conducted by Redelmeier and Tversky (1996) with rheumatoid arthritis patients.
3. Explain how "selective matching" may lead arthritis patients to perceive a relationship between the weather and arthritis symptoms.
4. Can you think of other examples of how beliefs in pseudoscientific or paranormal phenomena might be based on illusory correlations?

2.4 The "Mozart Effect": An Example of the Scientific Method in Operation / KENNETH STEELE

Perhaps you have seen all of the music CDs and videos that contain classical music and are marketed to parents as a tool to improve their young child's intelligence. For example, Volume 1 of the "Mozart Effect: Music for Babies" is sold with the following claim: "Studies show that classical music has a powerful effect on the intellectual and creative development of children from the very youngest of ages. This volume aids memory development, enhances auditory and emotional awareness, stimulates rhythmic movement and induces relaxation and sleep." Can listening to classical music really have such a pervasive, powerful effect on a child's development?

The "Mozart Effect" represents both an excellent example of pseudoscience and an important lesson in the central role of replication in science. It started with a research study that found a positive effect of music (i.e., a Mozart sonata) on the spatial reasoning ability of a small group of college students. From there a full-fledged pseudoscientific industry has developed around a much broader "Mozart Effect," and one can buy books and CDs that supposedly utilize this effect to improve the intelligence of children, unlock one's creative spirit, and heal one's body. In this article, Steele discusses the scientific evidence related to the Mozart effect and explains why it's time to bury it. You may recall that I briefly mentioned in Chapter 1 that an important part of the scientific process is for scientists to replicate the results of studies conducted by other scientists. Steele explains how the story of the Mozart effect illustrates this important scientific principle.

APA Reference

Steele, K. M. (2001, November-December). The "Mozart Effect": An example of the scientific method in operation. *Psychology Teacher Network, 11,* 2–3, 5.

TRENDS IN PSYCHOLOGY

Students have difficulty understanding and appreciating the value of the scientific method in dealing with issues in psychology. Typically, students see conclusions from a study or two about a complex question. The problem is that the student must accept or reject these conclusions because they come from a particular source, whether teacher or textbook. This is reasoning by the method of authority, which was not the method used to obtain the original results and is not how research psychologists think about such results.

Some outcomes may be so universal that we can treat them as "facts." Other findings are equivocal or enigmatic. The scientific method is a process of empirical evaluation of all findings. Research on the Mozart effect exemplifies this process for two reasons. First, the effect is relatively simple to understand. Students do not have to learn much about equipment or deep issues of research design. Second, a sequence of experiments appeared in rapid enough order that students can appreciate the process.

THE ORIGINAL FINDING

The original article appeared in Nature (Rauscher, Shaw, & Ky, 1993). It reported that 36 college students showed an increase on spatial reasoning scores from subtests of the Stanford-Binet Scale of Intelligence after listening to a Mozart plano sonata relative to listening to a relaxation tape or silence. The effect occurred only if the subjects were tested immediately. The size of the effect was the equivalent of 8 to 9 IQ points.

The music selection was from the Sonata for Two Pianos in D Major (K. 448). It is lively and emphasizes the virtuosity of the performers. It is not a central place in the Mozart canon.

The spatial reasoning measures consisted of a pattern analysis task, a multiple-choice matrices task, and a multiple-choice paper-folding and cutting task. Figure 2.1 shows an example matrices item. The task is to choose the geometric figure from the lower line which should be inserted in the empty cell to complete

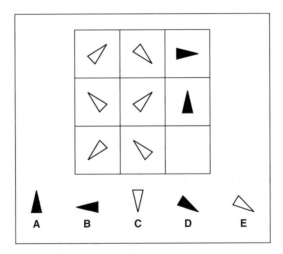

FIGURE 2.1 ▨ Practice Stanford-Binet Matrices item. The correct answers is 'B' for the item illustrated here.

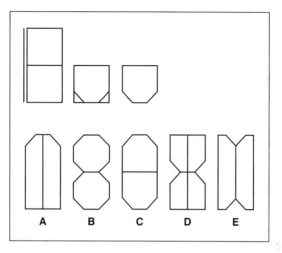

FIGURE 2.2 ■ Practice Stanford-Binet Paper Folding and Cutting item. The correct answer is 'C' for the item illustrated here.

the pattern. Figure 2.2 shows an example paper-folding and cutting item. The top row shows a piece of paper undergoing a fold and a pair of cuts, proceeding from left to right. The task is to pick the illustration in the bottom row that represents the paper when it is unfolded.

Rauscher, Shaw, & Ky (1995) reported a replication of their discovery using only the paper-folding and cutting test.

WHY DID THE EFFECT BECOME FAMOUS?

The authors contended that this was the first experiment to demonstrate that listening to music caused an increase in spatial reasoning. The issue of cause is important. Many people believe there is a positive correlation between academic success (like high school grade point average) and musical experience (like participation in a band) although the research literature is ambiguous.

People often assume that a correlation suggests a causal connection. However no firm conclusion can be drawn as to why this relationship exists. For example, students from wealthy homes may have the added time and opportunity to succeed more than average in both mathematics and music.

The authors' causal interpretation was that exposing a person to that specific sonata was the sole factor that explained the increased reasoning scores. There was no explanation in the original article of why the Mozart effect should have occurred. In later publications, Rauscher and Shaw suggested that this particular sonata was activating brain regions required by the spatial reasoning tasks, and that this overlap of activation could be related to a mathematical model of neural activity by Shaw, a physicist by training.

Later, their interpretation was transformed into the global generalization that participation in music activities would produce increases in mathematical performance and that the existence of the Mozart effect demonstrated the academic necessity of music education in the school curriculum.

Mass marketers sold books and CDs to worried parents with the promise that early exposure to the right music would speed intellectual development. Rauscher and Shaw contributed to the frenzy by adding that listening to this sonata could reverse the effects of senile dementia, epileptic seizures, and improve the maze-learning ability of rats.

HOW TO APPROACH RESEARCH RESULTS

A startling claim is made and repeated widely in the press. How is the claim evaluated? First, one must differentiate between the results of the experiment and the interpretation that was applied to the results. The results were that students showed increased scores on specific problems after hearing a portion of piano sonata relative to their scores after listening to a relaxation tape or sitting in silence. The interpretation was that some property of the music, perhaps a certain pattern of notes, increased the activity of brain regions involved in spatial problems and that this increased brain activity produced increased accuracy of solution of visual puzzles.

One can see a large gap between the results and the interpretation. A purpose of the scientific method is to determine whether the gap can be filled successfully by a series of experiments which successively extend the original finding. To do this researchers needed a description of the critical properties of the music, the means by which the music produced its effect, the range of activities that would be affected, and the expected duration of the effect. But the first step is that you need to be able to produce the effect.

EARLY ATTEMPTS TO PRODUCE A MOZART EFFECT

Several experiments appeared after the initial study and reported negative results. Carstens and colleagues (1995) had students listen to the original Mozart sonata and then answer 64 multiple choice items from the Minnesota Paper Form Board Test. Participants viewed two-dimensional parts and selected the figure that indicated the appearance of the final unit when the parts were assembled.

Carstens and colleagues found no difference in performance between the Mozart group and a control group who meditated in silence. No difference, or a null result, is tricky to interpret. The lack of difference could be due to the lack of effect of listening to the sonata or due to other conditions which interfered with the subjects. Carstens and colleagues found that the subjects' SAT scores predicted Form Board scores but the addition of information of whether the subject listened to Mozart changed the size of the prediction score by a trivial amount. The important point is that the lack of a Mozart effect became meaningful in the context of the other expected finding.

A second study worthy of note was by Newman and colleagues (1995). They increased the number of participants so that detecting the effect would be more likely, and they obtained background information on the musical training and preferences of their subjects. Subjects listened to the Mozart sonata, a relaxation tape, or sat in silence and were tested on items from Ravens Progressive Matrices. The task is very similar to that illustrated in Figure 2.1.

Newman, like Carstens, found no Mozart effect. Additionally, the effect of musical background was not consistent with what would be expected from Mozart-effect advocates. Subjects who had extensive music training (M = 8 years) performed no differently than subjects who had no musical training. Moreover, subjects who indicated a preference for classical music scored significantly worse on the matrices problems compared to those who preferred "other" music.

THE REPLY OF RAUSCHER AND SHAW (1998)

The purpose of Rauscher and Shaw's reply was to explain the difficulties that other researchers were having in producing the Mozart effect. Their major point was that previous experiments did not test the right type of spatial reasoning.

The original 1993 article had reported improvement on the combined measure of the three Stanford-Binet tests because scores on the tasks were well correlated. Rauscher and Shaw (1998) explained that the improvement reported in the 1993 article had occurred only with the paper-folding and cutting task, so the lack of effect observed by Carstens et al. and by Newman et al. with their matrices tasks was not a contradiction.

Second, Rauscher and Shaw suggested that other differences among experiments might interfere with showing the effect. However, they were vague in connecting this suggestion to specific procedures in studies. Finally, they stressed the importance of choice of musical composition. But, five years after the original report, they could be no more specific than "complexly structured music, regardless of style or period."

THE REPLICATIONS BY STEELE AND COLLEAGUES

I had read the Carstens et al. and the Newman et al. experiments in the course of preparing one of my own manuscripts. Their procedures were reasonably similar to Rauscher and Shaw's. Yet there was such a striking difference in outcome. The size of the statistical difference was large in both Rauscher et al. experiments, but was quite miniscule in the Carstens et al. and the Newman et al. experiments. Rauscher and Shaw blamed the problem on the use of the wrong dependent measure.

Perhaps, there was some other aspect of the procedure that explained the difference in results. In this case, the best solution was to replicate the procedure of one of the Rauscher et al. experiments. Like a cook, I would follow her recipe. Having obtained her result then I could vary the recipe to discover what ingredient was causing her bread to rise while everybody else's fell flat.

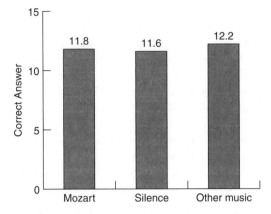

FIGURE 2.3 Steele, Bass, & Crook (1999) Results, The figure shows the mean number of Paper Folding and Cutting items answered correctly by subjects after 10 minutes of hearing either the Mozart piano sonata, a period of silence, or listening to other music.

The Rauscher et al. (1993) report in Nature was very short, and lacked many procedural details. However the 1995 report appeared as a standard length article with the necessary procedural details and had the added bonus of being consistent with the advice of Rauscher and Shaw (1998). The experiment by Steele, Bass, and Crook (1999) replicated the essential details of the 1995 procedure. (*Readers may obtain a copy of this article at <http://www.psych. appstate.edu/Faculty/Steele.htm>*)

Steele, Bass, and Crook (1999) used the same Mozart sonata, the same control condition stimuli, the same paper-folding and cutting task, and the same experimental design. Participants completed a pretest on 16 items. Two days later, subjects were exposed to a treatment condition and then immediately tested on 16 new items. We increased the number of subjects over the Rauscher et al. study to increase the experiment's sensitivity to the effect.

In addition, we used standard variations of design. I was confident that the Mozart effect would be replicated at last, and then the real analysis of discovering the reasons for the contradictory findings would begin. I was shocked with the final results. There was no hint of a Mozart effect. Figure 2.3 shows the average number of items correct for the three groups when tested immediately after the listening condition.

Using Rauscher's own recipe, our bread was as flat at that reported by Carstens, Newman, and others. A complete list of the studies can be found in a summary article by Christopher Chabris.

REQUIEM FOR THE MOZART EFFECT

A requiem is music written to honor the dead. It is odd to speak of a requiem for an effect but it is appropriate in this case. The original report was a startling but isolated claim. The authors provided no testable explanation of why this particular music was endowed with special properties or the nature of those properties. The neurophysiology of the effect and its linkage to mathematical reasoning was fragmented and speculative. The wide-spread endorsements of the effect came from commercial interests and committed advocates instead of the research community.

Yet the effect should be honored because it illustrates the scientific method in operation. The original report was subjected to the same process applied to all scientific claims. The report was followed by a series of studies by independent investigators who sought to verify and understand the effect. Researchers were able to build on the results of earlier investigations and move toward the critical studies, which indicated in this case that the original report could not be verified. The rise and fall of the Mozart effect is a case of effective science in action.

Review and Contemplate

1. What is the Mozart effect?
2. Describe the design and results of the initial study by Rauscher, Shaw, and Ky (1993) that sparked interest in the Mozart effect.
3. Why does Steele imply that the Mozart effect is dead? What evidence does he have to support this assertion?
4. Explain how the Mozart effect is an example of pseudoscience.

3.1

Whence Cometh the Myth That We Only Use 10% of Our Brains? /

BARRY BEYERSTEIN

This selection contains excerpts from a chapter written by Barry Beyerstein about the popular myth that people use only 10% of their brains. This myth has been used to support the argument that the human mind has paranormal abilities that might be tapped in order to unleash extraordinary powers such as telepathy (i.e., mind-to-mind communication) or psychokinesis (i.e., the ability to move objects with one's mind). Beyerstein discusses possible sources of the 10% myth and explains various types of scientific evidence against it.

The belief that we use only 10% of our brains is what social psychologists Anthony Pratkanis and Elliot Aronson call a factoid. A factoid is an assertion that is not supported by evidence, usually because it is false or because it's impossible to obtain evidence to support it. Another example of a factoid was the falsehood spread by Adolf Hitler and his propaganda minister, Joseph Goebbels, that Germany and the rest of Europe were threatened by a Jewish conspiracy.

Chapter 1 explained how normal cognitive and social processes can lead to pseudoscientific and paranormal beliefs, and this reading is a good example of how psychological and social factors contribute to such beliefs. When factoids such as the 10% myth are repeated and spread throughout groups of people, they may become widely treated as true. Factoids may persist for long periods of time because few people attempt to verify their truth or because they satisfy a psychological need. For example, the 10% myth might give people hope that they can become more intelligent or more talented because their brains have so much untapped potential; and those who hear the myth might accept it without researching whether it is true.

APA Reference

Beyerstein, B. L. (1999). Whence commeth the myth that we only use 10% of our brains? In S. Della Sala (Ed.), *Mind myths: Exploring popular assumptions about the mind and brain* (pp. 3–24). New York: John Wiley & Sons.

It ain't the things we don't know that gets us in trouble, it's the things we know that just ain't so —Artemus Ward

Had our esteemed editor decided to offer a prize for the most popular piece of neurononsense in this collection, I believe that I, for once, would be holding the winning ticket. Although the notion that normal people ordinarily use only a tenth of their brains probably ranks as the premier brain-howler of all time, its implausibility has done little to dampen its popularity over generations and continents. I recall it being intoned by teachers in "pep talks" at school, and it remains one of the most likely questions I can expect when I discuss brain matters with community groups on behalf of my university's speakers' bureau. And if I should forget to disabuse them of it beforehand, the 10% myth is sure to be raised by someone each time I teach my freshman "Brain and Behaviour" course. Most often, those who pose the question react with mild dejection when I tell them "it just ain't so"—perhaps a clue as to why this dubious assertion refuses to die. Anything this impervious to evidence must speak to widely felt longings. That is to say, it would be nice if it were true, for, like so many congenial false-hoods, the 10% myth lays open a variety of attractive possibilities.

The most recent luminary to hit me with the "10% solution" was none other than the spoon-bender extraordinaire, Uri Geller. When Geller and I locked horns on Jim Bohannon's national radio programme out of Washington, DC, Geller patiently explained that the reason he could do psychic feats and I could not was that he had discovered how to break through the 10% barrier. It's all a matter of overcoming the crippling doubts spread by crepe-hangers like me. Coincidentally, he just happened to have authored a new self-help book that would share the secret with the rest of us. The magic crystal is included at no extra charge.

In debates with supporters of paranormal or pseudoscientific beliefs, I frequently encounter the claim that "scientists say" we use only 10% of our brains. Curiously, though, none of them has ever been able to tell me which scientists these were or what their reasons were for saying it. Taking the figure as a given, anyway ("Everyone knows that . . ."), proponents usually proceed to argue that if we don't know what that untapped reservoir of brain stuff is doing, it could be harbouring awesome mental powers that only a few adepts have mastered. Members of this enlightened minority could be tapping their latent cerebral potential to accomplish levitation, psychokinesis, clairvoyance, precognition, telepathy or psychic healing, for instance. Or, say other believers, it could be used to achieve voluntary control of bodily functions, perfect learning and recall, transcendence to higher planes of knowledge, or other fantastica scarcely conceivable to mere mortals condemned to subsist on the drudge-like 10%.

Those who passed first-year logic will recognize this as a classic fallacy, the "argument from ignorance". In this gambit, one debater presses the other to concede that in what we (admittedly) don't yet know lies the proof of whatever the first party believes to be true. Lacking solid evidence of their own, those with their backs to the wall often argue that if sceptics cannot prove that something is not the case, this somehow counts as evidence that it is true. The one-tenth figure is, of course, unlikely, but even if it were accurate, it would in no way entail the existence of paranormal powers of mind, which must stand or fall on their own merits. To date, the demonstrations have been less than convincing (Alcock, 1981; Hyman, 1992).

Having been assailed with the 10% myth by teachers, athletic coaches, habitués of the motivational speakers' circuit, hawkers of self-help literature, and a bevy of occultists, I was eventually driven to search for its origins. I had become curious as to why it persists in the face of strong doubts arising from our growing knowledge about the structure and function of the brain. Some preliminary speculations on the topic (Beyerstein, 1987) generated several thoughtful suggestions from readers. Since, as will be apparent by the end of this chapter, much about this question remains unsettled, I would be pleased to hear from present readers as well.

As someone who spends much of his professional life pondering how the brain works, I am quite prepared to admit the enormity of what we do not yet understand about how this kilo-and-a-half of grey matter manages to produce thoughts, feelings, and actions. None the less, I am at a loss to understand how my informants came to know with such pontifical certainty that we normally use only 10% of it. To the best of my knowledge, this alleged "fact" appears nowhere in the literature of neurophysiology or physiological psychology. On the contrary, it is at variance with most of what we do know about the brain; for an overview of the field, see Kolb and Whishaw (1996), Rosenzweig, Leiman and Breedlove (1996) or Kalat (1995).

The "dormant brain" thesis seems to be another of those shibboleths that has insinuated itself into our cultural storehouse of "truths" through mere repetition. Its place in this pantheon of conventional wisdom is made secure by a phenomenon known as "source amnesia" or "cryptomnesia" (Schacter, Harbluk and McLachlan, 1984; Baker, 1992). It seems that the brain stores factual data somewhat differently from the information about where, how and from whom we learned it. Knowledge of the latter sort can fade completely without diminishing our sense of certainty that the facts themselves are true in this way, people often become convinced they are repeating reliable scientific findings when, in reality, they were actually picked up from an issue of *The National Enquirer* or an episode of The X-Files.

SOME SHORTCOMINGS OF THE 10% MYTH

Doubts from the Study of Brain Damage

Certain things they already know should give pause to those who believe in the 10% myth. For instance, when I am asked if the one-tenth figure is true, I often draw the questioner's attention to the well-known consequences of strokes and penetrating head wounds. There is virtually no area of the brain that can be damaged without loss of some mental vegetative or behavioural capacity (Rosner, 1974; Damasio, and Damasio, 1989). If 90% of the brain normally lies unused, there should be many parts of it that could sustain damage without disturbing any of these abilities. Obviously, that is not the case—brain injury just about anywhere has rather specific and lasting effects (Sacks, 1985). Most people are intuitively aware of this, as shown by their answers to the counter-question I sometimes pose: "How well do you think you would cope if you were suddenly to lose the functioning of 90% of your brain?" We all know of stroke victims who have lost relatively small amounts of brain tissue and are severely debilitated. Although there is usually some recovery of function after brain damage, if nine-tenths of the brain were normally held in reserve, we should see far more restoration than we typically do.

DOUBTS FROM THE STUDY OF EVOLUTION

By now, all but the most fervid religious fundamentalists accept that the human brain is the product of millions of years of evolution (Oakley and Plotkin, 1979). Given the conservatism of natural selection, its seems highly improbable that scarce resources would be squandered to produce and maintain such an underutilized organ. Metabolically speaking, the brain is costly to run. For instance, at 2% of total body weight, the brain accounts for 20% of the body's resting oxygen consumption and a similar proportion of the nutrient-bearing bloodflow from the heart. Simply fuelling the sodium–potassium pumps that allow neural membranes to process information consumes a wildly disproportionate chunk of your daily caloric intake. How long would you continue to endure huge power bills to heat all 10 rooms of your home if you never strayed beyond the kitchen?

DOUBTS FROM BRAIN IMAGING RESEARCH

The brain has evolved a certain amount of redundancy in its circuitry as a safety precaution, but little, if any, of it, lies perpetually fallow. Modern imaging techniques soundly refute the notion that there are large areas of the brain that are unused most of the time. The electroencephalogram (EEG), computerized axial tomography (CAT) scans, positron emission tomography (PET) scans, functional magnetic resonance imaging (fMRI), magnetoencephalography (MEG), and regional cerebral bloodflow (rCBF) measures are all tools for inferring the functions of anatomical structures in the living human brain (Roland, 1993; Baranaga, 1997). These imaging techniques show that, even during sleep, there are no completely silent areas in the brain. In fact, such sites of neural tranquillity would be signs of serious pathology.

DOUBTS FROM THE LOCALIZATION
OF FUNCTION IN THE BRAIN

From the foregoing devices, and from observing the consequences of head trauma and the effects of electrically stimulating various sites in the brain, it has become apparent that the cerebrum does not function as a homogeneous unit. Unique psychological processes are handled in different anatomical regions (Figure 3.1). This is known as the doctrine of "localization of function". The history of neurology has witnessed a see-saw battle between the localizationists' and those who preferred the opposing concept of "mass action", the idea that the brain functions holistically in virtually every act (Krech, 1962). Whether they realize it or not, most supporters of the 10% notion implicitly adopt some version of the mass action position. Modern research, on the other hand, has come down firmly on the side of the localizationists, although we now know that the way in which the brain breaks complex chores into subtasks and parcels them out to distributed processing units differs from most common-sense assumptions about how this might be achieved (Gazzaniga, 1989; Petersen et al., 1990).

Clinical neurologists were among the first to recognize that localization of function exists. For instance, from the 1860s on, Aubertin, Broca, Dax and Wernicke began to convert mass action supporters with their demonstrations that the brain mechanisms for language and speech were both lateralized to one hemisphere and localized within the dominant one. Today, we know that specialization for certain mental operations is so precise that small lesions in an area on the underside of the temporal lobe, for example, can leave a patient able to perceive most objects as before, but unable to identify human faces (Damasio, Tranel and Damasio, 1990).

Along the same lines, it was demonstrated in the 19th century that moving a weak electrical probe from site to site on the exposed surface of the brain evokes different psychological phenomena as successive points are stimulated (Young, 1970). The pioneering experiments by Fritsch and Hitzig in Germany and Ferrier in England eventually led Barthelow in the USA and Penfield in Canada to apply this technique with conscious neurosurgical patients, who could report their subjective reactions as their brains were being stimulated. Systematically mapping the cortex in this fashion has confirmed beyond doubt that the brain allocates different tasks to different regions of its anatomy (Krech, 1962; Penfield and Perot, 1963). Understanding the nature of this cortical specialization has permitted the development of technologies such as sensory prostheses for the blind, where patterned electrical stimulation is delivered to the visual areas of the cerebral cortex (Dobelle and Mladejovsky, 1974). The upshot of decades of work, stimulating deep structures as well as the cortex of conscious human patients, is that probing from stem to stem has failed to flush out the freeloading nine-tenths of the brain that some stubbornly contend is lacking an immediate assignment. . . .

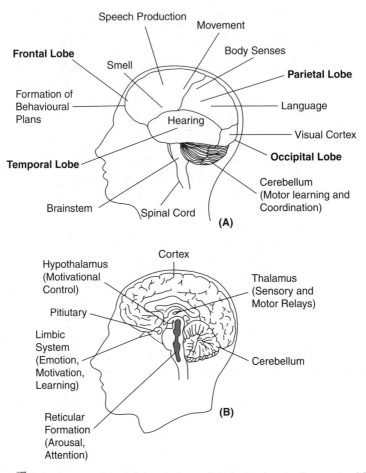

FIGURE 3.1 ▰ (A) Side view of the left hemisphere of the brain, showing (in oversimplified form) its major functional divisions. (B) Midline view of the brain and its functions.

Doubts from the Study of Neural Disuse

The Industrialist Henry Ford once said, "Whatever you have, you must use it or lose it." Bedridden patients and astronauts know that muscles atrophy from disuse and so, apparently, do brain circuits. Much research indicates that neural systems that are underutilized early in life either fail to develop or deteriorate permanently (Hirsch and Jacobson, 1975). If early environmental deprivation results in failure of the deprived brain circuitry to develop, remedial stimulation in later life will not completely overcome the resulting behavioural deficits (Beyerstein and Freeman, 1976). Thus, if the brain really had the idle capacity suggested by the 10% myth, it is likely that the neurons supposedly held in reserve would be useless by the time they were called into service. If 90% of our brains was really idle, the result would probably be large areas of cellular degeneration. No such signs are apparent when normal brains undergo histological examination at autopsy.

Straws for Believers to Grasp

Despite the foregoing objective, diehard supporters of this cherished illusion might attempt a rescue by arguing that the 10% figure refers not simply to neural volume, but rather to underutilized storage capacity or failure to reach peak processing speed, maximal neural interconnectivity, or some other index of brain efficiency. Be that as it may, I know of no way to determine the theoretical limits of such processes in order to estimate the average person's proportional achievements. At any rate, research suggests that it is not lack of storage capacity that hinders performance most; the bottleneck is more likely to arise from difficulty in retrieving what we've safely stored in our brains.

How Might the 10% Myth Have Arisen?

After several years of digging, including much help from friends, colleagues, students, and readers of my earlier efforts, I confess that I have been frustrated in my attempts to unearth the ultimate source of the 10% myth. Perhaps no Boswell was on hand to record the seminal utterance, but some interesting clues have turned up during my search. Although its origins remain obscure, there is little doubt that the primary disseminators (not to mention beneficiaries) of the 10% myth have been the touts and boosters in the ranks of the self-improvement industry, past and present. . . .

Big-Name' Spreaders of the Myth

The 10% myth continued to rattle around the self-improvement industry until mid-century, when it became a staple of courses like those of the Dale Carnegie organization; these days, it resurfaces regularly in the promotional ballyhoo spread by the hawkers of Transcendental Meditation, Scientology, and Neurolinguistic Programming. Motivational speakers still love it and I continue to encounter it in the advertisements for a variety of crackpot "brain-tuner" devices so dear to New Age entrepreneurs. . . .

Although the 10% myth does not appear in the text of the original 1936 version of Dale Carnegie's *How to Win Friends and Influence People*, the popular adventurer, journalist and documentary film narrator, Lowell Thomas, gave it a strong boost in the foreword he wrote for the first edition of that book (which, by the 1956 reprinting, had sold nearly five million copies):

> Professor William James of Harvard used to say that the average man develops only ten percent of his latent mental ability. Dale Carnegie, by helping business men and women to develop their latent possibilities, has created one of the most significant movements in adult education. *(Thomas, in Carnegie, 1936, p. 12)*

Carnegie himself picked up the theme in *How to Stop Worrying and Start Living*, which was published in 1944:

> The renowned William James was speaking of men who had never found themselves when he declared that the average man develops only ten percent of his latent mental abilities. "Compared to what we ought to be," he wrote, "we are only half awake. We are making use of only a small part of our physical and mental resources. Stating the thing broadly, the human individual thus lives far within his limits. He possesses powers of various sorts which he habitually fails to use". *(Carnegie, 1944, p. 123)*

Although Carnegie put quotation marks around the passage he attributed to the pioneering American psychologist William James (1842–1910), he failed to cite a source for this quotation. One of the informants mentioned by Dwight Decker in a 1994 posting to the internet newsgroup, "sci skeptic", thought he remembered James discussing the 10% estimate in his two-volume text. *The Principles of Psychology* (James, 1890). However, both Decker and I were unable to find such a statement in this, James' magnum opus. . . . Trained as a medical doctor, James was too good a physiologist to believe that we literally use only 10% of our brains, but he may well have uttered it metaphorically in his voluminous popular writings, for, as Fellman and Fellman (1981) note, James' speculations about the powers of mind and his advice on human perfectability reached a large audience via his frequent contributions to publications such as the widely read *Popular Science Monthly.*

Hucksters have long known that a reliable way to add instant credibility to almost any assertion is to attribute it to a famous and respected figure. By the mid-20th century, the surest way to appropriate an unassailable mantle of truth for an idea was to attribute it to Albert Einstein. There are instances, in the political sphere for example, where Einstein's enormous public prestige lent disproportionate weight to speculations he made in areas outside his scientific expertise. In what is possibly a myth about a myth, Albert Einstein is supposed to have alluded to the 10% explanation at some time or other in reply to the constant barrage of questions about the source of his brilliance. Prevalent as this tale is, once again its provenance is suspect. Although I have been told dozens of times that Einstein said it, I have been unable to determine when, where, or even if, he did. Neither, apparently, have those who have made an effort to chronicle Einstein's vast accumulation of writings, interviews, and quotations. In a reply to my research assistant, Anouk Crawford, Jeff Mandl, assistant curator of the Albert Einstein Archives, wrote:

> We are not aware that Albert Einstein ever stated that human beings exploit only 10% of the capacity of their brains. Upon receiving your note, we examined our holdings but found no remarks of his on the subject. . . .

WHY DOES THE 10% MYTH REFUSE TO DIE?

If it has been known for ages that the 10% myth makes no sense neurologically, one must wonder about its remarkable longevity. I would suggest that this parable of neural tithing in ordinary folks continues to thrive because it is a soothing allegory for the universal human desire to be more talented, influential, and prosperous. As we have seen, a huge industry has evolved, catering to our noble longing for self-betterment. It is comforting to believe that we all possess huge reserves of untested ability, and if this fantasy can be canonized by reference to brain science, so much the better for would-be profiteers.

Stretching the Facts for Fun and Profit

Pseudoscientists are well aware that a good way to promote a dubious product is to associate it in the public mind with whatever is currently most prestigious in the realm of legitimate science. Even before President Bush declared the 1990s the "decade of the brain" (why only 10 years for such a massive task, one might ask?), it had become common in the self-improvement industrial complex to borrow a patina of scientific respectability for questionable assertions by hitching them to the coattails of reputable findings in neuroscience (Beyerstein, 1990).

Brain researchers themselves have obligingly provided a number of statements over the years that could be innocently misunderstood, or venally stretched, to suit the purposes of the human potential entrepreneurs and their 10% myth. One example of this may have been public misinterpretation of neuroanatomists' pronouncements that the supporting glial cells in the brain ("white matter") outnumber the neurons ("grey matter")—which do the actual mental work — by a factor of 10 to 1.... In this trivial sense, we do, strictly speaking, use less than a tenth of our total brain cells to produce all psychological phenomena, even if the support of that overwhelming mass of glial cells is indispensable to the process. However necessary the glial cells' support functions are for neurons, as far as I know no one has yet begun to market mental exercises or other self-improvement products that promise to transform glial cells into auxiliary "thinking stuff" in order to ensure top grades or a coveted promotion. One hesitates to even mention such an idea, for although this has apparently not yet occurred to the brain hucksters, there is hardly any notion too far-fetched for them to put on the market....

I also believe that the vision of a largely dormant brain acquired some of its unearned scientific gloss from laypersons' misinterpretations of early neurological experiments with lower animals. Pioneering studies by Karl Lashley, for instance, seemed to show that large portions of rat cortex could be removed with apparently little disruption of behaviour (Krech, 1962). These findings led Lashley to become one of the last great proponents of the holistic or "mass action" view of brain function discussed earlier. His notion of equipotentiality suggested that loss of function was proportional to amount of cortex lost, not the site of the loss. The apparent lack of disruption caused by Lashley's lesions was at least consistent with the idea that there is massive redundancy in the brain. Later, more sophisticated behavioural tests did expose functional deficits that weren't obvious with Lashley's testing methods.

In a similar vein, popular confusion regarding certain terms used by early comparative neurologists may have contributed to the misapprehension that we use only 10% of our brains. As depicted in Figure 3.2, research has shown that, with evolutionary advancement, the cerebrum of mammals has enlarged greatly, but that a progressively smaller *proportion* of its mass is concerned with strictly sensory or motor duties. This was demonstrated in the 1930s by studying the cerebral cortex in a variety of species from different levels of the evolutionary tree. Electrical

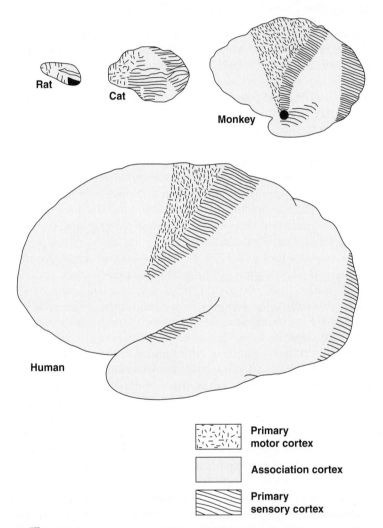

Rat

Cat

Monkey

Human

	Primary motor cortex
	Association cortex
	Primary sensory cortex

FIGURE 3.2 Left-hemisphere views of the brains of various mammalian species (drawn only approximately to scale). The diagrams show the absolute increase in size with evolutionary change, as well as the proportional increase in "association cortex". Because some authors choose to call this association cortex "silent cortex", some readers may have mistakenly thought it was literally "silent".

stimulation of cortical cells and experimentally produced cortical lesions seemed to have minimal effects in these increasingly large nonsensory and nonmotor areas in the brains of the higher species. For that reason, those areas were referred to by some researchers as "silent cortex", although they did not intend this to mean that these regions were literally silent or unused. As we have seen, they are anything but silent — these areas, which today are usually referred to as "association cortex", are responsible for our most uniquely human characteristics, including language, mental imagery, and abstract thought. Areas of maximal activity shift in the brain as we change from one task to another or vary our attention and arousal levels, but there are normally no dormant regions awaiting new assignments.

The term "silent" had a certain allure, however, and its connotations helped some customers of the self-help industry to misconstrue the intent of certain popular works on the brain, published in the 1950s and 1960s, that still leaned toward some aspects of Lashley's concept of mass action. For instance, the influential British neurophysiologist Walter (1963), in *The Living Brain*, a book aimed largely at the intelligent lay person, had the following to say:

> It is true that certain parts of the brain have a regular and recognizable microscopic appearance and respond in a fairly predictable fashion when stimulated electrically, and when diseased or damaged they are associated with certain diagnostic signs or symptoms. But the exceptions to these rules are so numerous and their experimental foundation is so tenuous, that there is now a tendency to support an entirely "holistic" view of brain function, to suppose that all parts are engaged in any sense or any action, and that the location of function is more a probability than a place. That we can conceive of it at all is due to the obscure workings of the brain regions which yield least to experimental probing, the association areas, sometimes called "silent" because their oracles are dumb when threatened by the experimental intruder. These regions make up the greater part of the human brain . . . *(Walter, 1963, p. 71)*.

In this way, however inadvertently, widely read books such as Walter's fostered the mistaken notion that "silent cortex" meant that the brain contains large unused areas. It is no disservice to the memory of truly great researchers such as Karl Lashley and Grey Walter to note that subsequent research overtook their notions of a holistic brain by finding many specific functions in what was previously called "silent cortex". Ironically, though, this later research showed that Lashley and Walter were, in a sense, right after all, but in a somewhat different way than they had intended. Large portions of the brain *are* activated by most mental tasks. It is just that this comes about because the brain breaks complex undertakings into many parallel operations which it then directs to widely dispersed and highly specialized processing modules throughout the cerebrum (Gazzaniga, 1989). This can give the appearance of "mass action" but, in fact, the whole brain is operating more like a symphony orchestra, i.e. a collection of individual sections, each blending its own unique part into the performance of the whole composition. Walter's ideas have also been partially vindicated in that modern views of brain modularity suggest that the task-oriented assemblies of these units are more fluid and temporary than was once thought. Although the modules are indeed highly specialized, different but similar ones might be recruited into temporary networks to accomplish the same task on subsequent occasions. This ability to pick and choose "on the fly" also means that damage to one module leaves open the possibility of substituting another, though perhaps less efficient, assemblage to do the job after trauma to the brain.

It is also possible that what might have given rise to William James' speculation that we only use a small part of our brains (if indeed he said this, as opposed to suggesting that we use only a small part of its *creative potential*) were anecdotal accounts of people who had suffered drastic losses of brain tissue due to accidents or disease, but seemed, none the less, to function more or less normally. Most of these cases were poorly documented and specialists trained to spot more subtle cognitive deficits were typically not consulted. Although they were probably exaggerated for dramatic effect, these stories gained considerable notoriety (Corliss, 1993), especially among mystery-mongers who delight in finding anomalies that science allegedly cannot explain. It seems reasonable to think that they might have lent another bit of credence to the 10% myth.

There have been better-documented cases recently, however, that confirm the remarkable ability of immature brains to reorganize and recover from neural damage. Young children have been known to recover a surprisingly high level of functioning after loss of an entire cerebral hemisphere to injury or disease (Kolb and Whishaw, 1996, Chapter 10). This is far less than 90% of their brains, of course, but because, after birth, dying nerve cells are replaced sparsely if at all, these patients must be making do with whatever neurons remain, raising the possibility at least that there may have been some unused parts lying around. In fact, it seems instead that the functions of the destroyed areas actually "crowd in" alongside those the intact areas were already handling, rather than colonizing previously unused areas. Immediately following the surgical removal of one hemisphere, these children experience devastating disruptions of behaviour and consciousness but, gradually, most abilities, including language, show substantial recovery. Unfortunately, this ability of the remaining neural tissue to assume additional duties when other parts of the brain are decimated wanes with age, as a visit to any neurological ward will quickly convince you.

Even among those who suffer brain damage as young children and regain near-normal functioning, some deficits do remain, although it sometimes requires fairly sophisticated tests to reveal these frailties. The ability to achieve such a high degree of recovery seems to be largely lost by the time of puberty. Much recent research has been devoted to finding ways to suppress certain processes in mature brains that largely prevent adult neural tissue from reestablishing functional connections after brain damage. . . .

CONCLUSION

After much searching, I have come to the conclusion that the 10% myth arose most likely from various attempts to reify popular metaphors about latent powers of the mind. This has been helped along by a combination of honest and self-serving misconstruals of the rightfully modest admissions by neuro-scientists concerning the limits of our current understanding of the brain. Despite the enormous amount that has been learned, it is only honest to confess how much remains to be discovered. Such modesty would have been even more appropriate at the dawn of the 20th century when the myth appears to have taken off. It seems likely that some early investigator's (probably optimistic) estimate that researchers only knew what 10% of the brain does may have been misinterpreted as an assertion that we normally only need or use 10% of it.

In the final analysis, I think that the persistence of this curious assertion is yet another testimonial to the comforting nature of most occult and New Age beliefs. It would be nice if they were true—death would have no sting, merely thinking about desirable outcomes would bring them to pass, and there need be no shortfalls in life, materially or mentally. The 10% myth conveys the welcome message that we could all be Einsteins, Rockefeller's or Uri Gellers if we could just engage that ballast between our ears.

The ubiquity of the 10% myth is reminiscent of the so-called "urban legends" studied by the American folklorist, Jan Harold Brunvand (Brunvand, 1982, 1986). Brunvand has dubbed these mini morality plays "FOAF-lore" (for "Friend-Of-A-Friend") because attempts to verify them invariably lead to an infinite regress. The allegedly true story always seems to have happened to a "friend of a friend", who, upon being approached, says it happened to a "friend of a friend", and so on. Brunvand (1986, p. 165) notes several reasons for the popularity and longevity of urban legends, e.g. they generally have a gripping story line, have a small element of embedded truth, and frequently provide the opportunity to be politically incorrect without incurring social wrath ("Don't blame me, I'm just telling it like it happened," the teller declares). Above all, they offer a vehicle for advancing a warning, incitement or moral lesson that is either stated or implied. Despite the implausibility of many of the story lines in these legends, their underlying messages play on widely held hopes, prejudices and anxieties, and they have an exhortative quality that makes people want to suspend their scepticism. Consequently, people in all walks of life tend to believe and spread these tales, and the media continue to recycle them with minor variations and almost clockwork regularity. As we have seen, variants of the 10% myth exhibit many of these same qualities. I've been told many times about "this guy who went in for an x-ray, and, ya know, they found that his head was full of nothing but water, but he was smart as a whip, anyhow…"

The concept of a trusty "cerebral spare tyre" continues to nourish the clientele of "pop-psychologists" and their many recycling self-improvement schemes. As a metaphor for the fact that few of us fully exploit our talents, who could deny it? As a spur to hope and a source of solace, it is probably done more good than harm, but comfort afforded is not truth implied. As a refuge for occultists and flim-flam artists seeking the neural basis of the miraculous, the probability of its being true is considerably less than 10%.

References

Alcock, J. (1981). *Parapsychology: Science or magic?* New York: Pergamon.

Baker, R. A. (1992). *Hidden memories*. Buffalo: Prometheus Books.

Baranaga, M. (1997). New imaging methods provide a better view into the brain. *Science, 276*, 1974–1976.

Beyerstein, B. L. (1987). The brain and consciousness: Implications for psi phenomena. *Skeptical Inquirer, 12*(2), 163–174.

Beyerstein, B. L. (1990). Brainscams: Neuromythologies of the new age. *International Journal of Mental Health, 19*(3), 27–36.

Beyerstein, B. L., & Freeman, R. D. (1976). Increment sensitivity in humans with abnormal visual experience. *Journal of Physiology (London), 260*, 497–514.

Brunvand, J. H. (1982). *The vanishing hitchhiker: American urban legends and their meaning*. New York: W. W. Norton.

Brunvand, J. H. (1986). *The study of American folklore*. New York: W. W. Norton.

Carnegie, D. (1936). *How to win friends and influence people*. New York: Simon and Schuster.

Carnegie, D. (1944). *How to stop worrying and start living*. New York: Simon and Schuster.

Corliss, W. R. (1993). Remarkable capabilities of badly damaged brains. In *Biological anomalies: Humans II*. Glen Arm, MD: The Sourcebook project.

Damasio, H., & Damasio, A. R. (1989). *Lesion analysis in neuropsychology*. New York: Oxford University.

Damasio, A. R., Tranel, D., & Damasio, H. (1990). Face agnosia and the neural substrates of memory. *Annual Review of Neuroscience, 13*, 89–109.

Dobelle, W. H., & Mladejovsky, M. G. (1974). Phosphines produced by electrical stimulation of the human occipital cortex and their application to the development of a prosthesis for the blind. *Journal of Physiology (London), 243*, 553–576.

Fellman, A. & Fellman, M. (1981). *Making sense of self: Medical advice literature in late nineteenth-century America*. Philadelphia: University of Pennsylvania Press.

Gazzaniga, M. S. (1989). Organization of the human brain. *Science, 245*, 947–952.

Hirsch, H., & Jacobson, M. (1975). The perfectible brain: Principles of neural development. In M. Gazzaniga & C. Blakemore (Eds.), *Handbook of psychobiology*. New York: Academic Press.

Hyman, R. (1992). *The elusive quarry: A scientific appraisal of psychical research*. Amherst, NY: Prometheus Books.

James, W. (1890). *The principles of psychology*. New York: Henry Holt.

Kalat, J. W. (1995). *Biological psychology* (5th ed.). Pacific Grove, CA: Brooks-Cole.

Kolb, B., & Whishaw, I. Q. (1996). *Fundamentals of human neuropsychology* (4th ed.). New York: W. H. Freeman.

Krech, D. (1962). Cortical localization of function. In L. Postman (Ed.), *Psychology in the making: Histories of selected research problems*. New York: Alfred A. Knopf.

Oakley, D. A., & Plotkin, H. C. (Eds). (1979). *Brain, behaviour, and evolution*. London: Methuen.

Penfield, W. & Perot, P. (1963). The brain's record of auditory and visual experience: A final summary and discussion. *Brain, 86*, 595–696.

Petersen, S. E., Fox, P. T., Snyder, A. Z., & Raichle, M. E. (1990). Activation of extrastriate and frontal cortical areas by visual words and word-like stimuli. *Science, 249*, 1041–1044.

Roland, P. E. (1993). *Brain activation*. New York: Wiley-Liss.

Rosenzweig, M. R., Leiman, A. L., & Breedlove, S. M. (1996). *Biological psychology.* Sunderland, MA: Sinauer Associates.

Rosner, B. S. (1974). Recovery of function and localization of function in historical perspective. In D. G. Stein, J. Rosen, & N. Butters (Eds.), *Plasticity and recovery of function in the central nervous system.* New York: Academic Press.

Sacks, O. (1985). *The man who mistook his wife for a hat and other clinical tales.* New York: Summit Books.

Schacter, D. L., Harbluk, J. L., & McLachlan, D. R. (1984). Retrieval without recollection: An experimental analysis of source amnesia. *Journal of Verbal Learning and Verbal Behavior, 23,* 593–611.

Walter, W. G. (1963). *The living brain.* New York: W. W. Norton.

Woodworth, R. S. (1934). *Psychology* (3rd ed.). New York: Henry Holt.

Young, R. M. (1970). *Mind, brain, and adaptation in the nineteenth century: Cerebral localization and its biological context from Gall to Ferrier.* Oxford: Clarendon Press.

Review and Contemplate

1. Explain (a) how the 10% myth has been used to support the argument that the human mind has paranormal abilities and (b) why this argument is not logical.
2. Describe two different types of evidence against the 10% myth.
3. Describe how some of the scientific discoveries (choose two) about the brain might have been misinterpreted as support for the 10% myth.
4. Give one reason the 10% myth refuses to die.

3.2

Can Minds Leave Bodies?
A Cognitive Science Perspective/
D. ALAN BENSLEY

In January 2006, Cincinnati police found the decayed body of 61-year-old Johannas Pope in her home. What was surprising about this case was that Ms. Pope died almost 2½ years earlier, and her daughter, granddaughter, and caretaker continued to live in the house with the deceased woman even though they knew she was dead. They kept her body sitting in a chair in an upstairs room, where they ran an air conditioner to keep her body cool. They also kept the television on in the room for Ms. Pope. Relatives and friends who visited the house were told that Ms. Pope was upstairs and was ill, and none of them went into her room to check on her.

Why would a family keep a dead woman in their house for more than 2 years? The coroner found no evidence of abuse or foul play. It appears that the family kept the deceased Ms. Pope in the room because, before she passed away, she told her family members, "Don't show my body when I'm dead; don't bury me; I'm coming back." Apparently, Ms. Pope believed that her mind or soul would live on after she died, and that it would come back at some later time.

As Bensley points out in this reading, a number of religious and paranormal beliefs rest on the assumption that our minds (or souls) can exist outside of our bodies. This dualistic belief can be traced back to ancient philosophy and religion. Bensley presents a cognitive science perspective on such beliefs and provides a scientific explanation for out-of-body experiences that sometimes occur in people who are near death or people who have taken drugs.

APA Reference

Bensley, D. A. (2003, July/August). Can minds leave bodies? A cognitive science perspective. *Skeptical Inquirer, 27,* 34–39.

Many people believe that the mind can leave the body at death and during out-of-body experiences. Research in cognitive science, however, has shown that this belief is implausible and suggests other explanations—D. Alan Bensley

D. Alan Bensley is a cognitive psychologist and associate professor in the Department of Psychology at Frostburg State University, Frostburg, MD 21532 (e-mail: abeasley@frostburg.edu). He is author of Critical Thinking in Psychology: A Unified Skills Approach and of articles on the improvement of critical thinking and on paranormal topics.

T hirty-nine dead bodies were neatly laid on cots, each dressed in a black robe and Nike sneakers with their heads covered in hoods. Was this some kind of ritual murder? No, this was the 1997 mass suicide of the Heaven's Gate cult resulting from a dangerous combination of belief in dualism, religion, and extrasensory contact with aliens. Cult members believed they were in telepathic contact with extraterrestrials who invited them to a new and better world. To rendezvous with the alien ship, they believed they had to "exit their vehicles." This code expression for killing the body to free the soul reveals a dualistic belief in the separateness of mind and body. For cult members, the body was just a device for temporarily carrying the soul.

This dualistic belief may seem extreme, but other, more common paranormal beliefs (such as belief in ghosts, astral projection, and reincarnation), also imply that the mind or soul can separate from the body. I will examine the dualistic belief from the cognitive science perspective. Cognitive science is an interdisciplinary approach to the study of the mind. It combines the psychological study of mental processes such as consciousness and perception with the study of the brain, philosophy, and other disciplines. Research in cognitive science has shown that mind depends on the functioning of the brain in the physical world. Consequently, the mind cannot "go outside" of the brain.

ORIGINS OF DUALISTIC PARANORMAL BELIEF

The idea that the soul can leave the body is a very old one found in many cultures (Frazer, 1996). A common belief is that when someone dreams of traveling to a place, the soul actually leaves the body and journeys there. The ancient Egyptians believed the soul could leave the body as death. In their burial ceremonies, the Ba, a human-headed bird representing the soul or breath of life, was breathed back into the mummified body to ensure life after death. In the book of Genesis, God breathed the spirit of life into Adam's body formed from the dust of the Earth to make man a living soul. These examples illustrate how the soul or spirit has been commonly associated with air. Like the air we breathe, the soul is ephemeral, essential to life, and can have leave the body. In his detailed study of religious rituals from around the world, Sir James Frazer reported that the Itonamas of South America would close a dying person's mouth and nose to prevent the soul from departing and taking other souls with it. In some cultures, people have used traps to recapture souls that have escaped. Comparing the beliefs of many non-Western cultures, Shiels (1978) found evidence that almost 95 percent of them believed that a soul or spiritual entity could leave the body in some form. The most common occasion for such an experience was during sleep, but some reported the occurrence from illness, use of drugs, and trance states.

Much of the modern dualistic belief in the separability of soul and body had its origins in Greek and Christian thought. Plato, the fifth century B.C. Greek philosopher, believed that the body was a vessel containing the soul and that the mind was the immortal part of the soul that left the body at death to be reincarnated. Over the centuries, many Christians have believed that the soul lives on after physical death, retaining the powers of perception and feeling despite being separated from the body.

René Descartes, the brilliant philosopher-mathematician of the seventeenth century, did much to frame the dualistic position. He began his philosophy by doubting everything. He realized he could doubt the existence of his body and the rest of the physical world, but he could not logically doubt that he was doubting. His famous statement, "I think, therefore I am," exemplifies this reasoning. Because he could doubt the physical world but not his mind, he reasoned that the mind and body must be fundamentally different. In particular, he believed the body was made of physical substance extended in space while the mind or soul was non-physical and not extended. Descartes' position, called substance dualism, has raised fundamental questions about how a non-physical mind could have an effect on a physical body. Nevertheless, many people persist in this belief as if there were no mind-body problem.

CURRENT BELIEF

Belief in dualism is an important part of our commonsense or folk psychology. Intuitively, my mind and body do appear to be different. I can use my mind to imagine. I have no gray hair, but one look in the mirror tells me otherwise. I can imagine I am in California when physically I am sitting at my computer in Maryland. I can decide to move my leg, and it seems as if my mind is causing my body to move. These examples suggest that my mental experience and physical events overlap; but they are not the same. However, it is one thing to imagine that one's mind is separate from one's body and quite another to believe it can *actually* separate from the body. To believe the latter is tantamount to holding a paranormal belief, according to many cognitive neuroscientists who have consistently shown that the mind depends on brain function. Recently, such scientists have paid increasing attention to the dualism found in people's commonsense beliefs because such beliefs are diametrically opposed to their own scientific knowledge of the brain.

Research outside of cognitive science has also shown dualistic, paranormal belief to be prevalent in everyday thinking. The most recent Gallup Poll on paranormal belief in the U.S. found that such beliefs are widespread and may even be on the rise (Newport and Strausberg 2001).

Other research further indicates that mind-body dualism is related to paranormal belief. Cognitive psychologist Keith Stanovich (1989) found that many American college students he tested had high scores on a dualistic belief scale. Moreover, those students with stronger dualistic belief also tended to report stronger belief in ESP, except for Baptists. Another study by Michael Thalbourne (1999) found that dualism in Australian students was significantly correlated with paranormal belief such as belief in life after death and in the possibility of contact with spirits of the dead.

Not surprisingly, many writers in parapsychology, including Lloyd Auerbach (1986), John Beloff (1989), and J.B. Rhine and J.G. Pratt (1957), have made dualistic statements claiming or implying the separation of mind and body. James Alcock (1987) has contended that parapsychology treats mind-body dualism as an essential assumption.

Despite popular belief, many scientists and skeptics doubt the mind can leave the body. The most common opposing view has been materialism or physicalism, a philosophical position maintaining that everything, including mind, is essentially physical. Materialists say the mind only appears to be invisible and not part of the natural physical world. For centuries, scientists have developed physical explanations of many apparently invisible and mysterious phenomena. The wind in the trees is not the movement of some invisible ether, but of many tiny particles of oxygen, nitrogen, and other gases. Along the same lines, materialists have hoped that the soul or mind would be explained in physical terms, much as the wind and air have been. Cognitive scientists, who are rooted in materialism, have sought to explain mental processes in terms of brain activity resulting from physical changes in the environment. So it is not surprising that they and other scientists have pressed for physical evidence that a mind or soul could leave the body.

THE OUT-OF-BODY EXPERIENCE (OBE)

At least initially, the OBE appears to be good evidence that the mind can separate from the body. The term itself, however, is neutral as to whether or not a person has actually left the body and asserts only that a person has had the *ex-perience* of having done so (Palmer 1978). OBEs are fairly common, with estimates ranging from about 10 to 20 percent of the population reporting they have had at least one, depending on the survey (Rogo 1984). OBEs occur in various ways, such as in religious, drug-induced, near-death, meditational, hypnotically induced, or spontaneous experiences (Grosso 1976). Furthermore, OBEs are not associated with any psychological disorder (Tobacyk and Mitchell 1987).

Shortly after college, I had a spontaneous OBE in which it seemed as if some observing part of me had separated from my body. I had lain down on the sofa for a few minutes but had not gone to sleep. Suddenly, it seemed as if I could clearly "see" my entire body lying on the sofa below me for a few seconds before I returned to my usual perspective. Though brief, my OBE had two basic features. First, it seemed as if the experiencing part of me was located at a point outside my physical body. Second, it seemed as though I was consciously perceiving and not dreaming the experience. Like many people who have had an OBE, I have also had lucid dreams, that is, dreams during which I became aware of myself dreaming (Glicksohn 1989). Researchers have found a low but reliable correlation between OBEs and lucid dreaming (Irwin 1988). In fact, sometimes OBEs arise from lucid dreams and may even be indistinguishable from them (Levitan et al. 1999). Yet my experience did not seem like a dream, lucid or otherwise—it seemed like perception. At the time, however, I did not know what it was, and I assumed my OBE was a case of astral projection. Similarly, about this same time I had what I knew was a dream in which I was "flying around" in a kitchen, and I told myself that I was dreaming about astral projection.

The many anecdotal reports of such experiences have sometimes been taken as strong evidence that the mind can actually leave the body (Crookall 1963). However, the usefulness of such anecdotal reports is very limited (Bensley 1998). Although they may provide a rich source of information about the details and "feel" of an experience, OBE descriptions are typically not very well documented, not repeatable, and unverifiable. Often the details of what an OBE experiencer claims to have seen have been found to be inaccurate (Blackmore, 1982).

To obtain better evidence, researchers have used the experimental method, which allows for testing under more controlled conditions to study OBEs. Typically, experimenters have examined the question by testing the accuracy of a subject's perception during an OBE or by looking for some physical sign in the environment that the experiencer has left the body. Despite some strikingly positive results reviewed by Charles Tart (1998), experimental demonstrations have not, in general, shown out-of-body perception to be reliably accurate. Nor has research unambiguously supported the claim that the experiencer can affect the environment when taking an out-of-body excursion (Blackmore 1982, 1992). After reviewing the literature, Blackmore (1982) suggested that adopting a cognitive psychological approach to study OBEs would be more productive.

THE COGNITIVE SCIENCE APPROACH

Traditionally, cognitive scientists have viewed the brain as a kind of complex information processing system, like a computer. The system inputs data through the senses, holds the information in memory, and transforms it into various intermediate states before outputting in the form of behavior. Information processing occurs in the brain as nerve cells send and receive messages using special chemicals called neurotransmitters. Many of these nerve cells are part of processing units and circuits dedicated to processing specific kinds of information. Research with brain scanning has found specific areas of the brain that "light up" or are active when individuals engage in specific mental processes, such as perceiving, attending, remembering, forming mental images, and using language (Posner and Raichle 1994). The brain uses the combined activity of these specific neural processors to form mental representations of the physical world. For example, although perceiving a face depends on the combined activity of multiple brain areas, when one area of the temporal lobe specialized for processing faces is damaged, a person is unable to recognize even his or her own face.

The brain uses its representations to construct an elaborate and usually accurate model of the world—a kind of running simulation. For example, research has shown that the brain has map-like representations of various parts of the body such as the face, arm, and hand. These maps in the brain represent the body in visual and somatic form, carrying detailed information of both how the body looks and feels (Ladavas, Zelon, and Farne 1998). It is important to note, however, that while mental representations, such as visual images, may seem vivid and accurate, they are not exact copies of the physical world in the same way a photograph represents the detail of some object. Moreover, the brain can make a mistake in constructing its model, resulting in misperception of the body or some other part of the world.

The phantom limb experience provides a compelling example of how mental experience of the body depends on the brain's representations of it, and also how perception of the body can be in error. People who have lost a limb, such as a leg, often report they feel the sensation of pain in their missing foot. This, of course, is physically impossible if we assume the pain is originating from the missing foot. However, if we assume that the brain still has a representation of the missing foot, then the perception of pain depends on brain activity (Ramachandran and Hirstein 1998). Could the OBE occur in a similar way, that is, could the brain activate a representation of the body in some unusual way that leads to misperception of the body?

Applying methods from cognitive psychology to study OBEs, Susan Blackmore (1987) found that experiencers used mental imagery differently from those who do not have OBEs. Based on the work of Nigro and Neisser (1983), she found that experiencers were more likely to use an observer or "bird's-eye view" perspective in describing their dreams than others. They were also better able to switch their viewpoint in a mental image, and had clearer and more vivid imagery of their dreams. Blackmore argued that this "bird's-eye view" perspective is like the "over the body" perspective often taken during OBEs. When a person begins to lose normal sensory contact, such as when falling asleep or during sensory deprivation, this unusual perspective may be adopted. The brain seeks to identify which is the best model or interpretation of the incoming sensory data at the time, and this becomes the model of reality that best fits. The system seeks to reestablish sensory contact, and mistakenly picks the wrong model from memory such as the "over the head" perspective and treats it as real. OBE experiencers' greater vividness and clarity of imagery may contribute to the sense of reality they experience during OBEs. Harvey Irwin (1986) has obtained results similar to Blackmore (1987). However, he found that some people had *somatic* OBEs (related to the feeling of the body being outside) while others had *visual* OBEs (related to seeing the body as outside). In these two different cases, the subjects may be paying more or less attention to the visual versus somatic information in the complex representations of their bodies.

Blackmore's research suggests that disturbances in the brain may produce OBEs. Consistent with this prediction, Canadian neurosurgeon Wilder Penfield (1955) was apparently able to produce an OBE by stimulating a patient's brain with minute electrical currents prior to operating on the patient for temporal lobe epilepsy. Before surgical removal of a damaged area that caused the debilitating seizures. Penfield would routinely stimulate different places in the patient's brain, such as in the right temporal lobe shown in Figure 3.3, to prevent the inadvertent removal of healthy brain tissue. Once, after he had electro-stimulated a point in this area, the patient, who had previously had an OBE, exclaimed "I am leaving my body" and then showed a strong fear reaction (Penfield 1955, 458).

Recently, Olaf Blanke and his colleagues (2002) have used electrostimulation of the brain to produce a more convincing OBE in a forty-three-year-old epileptic woman. While trying to find the focus of her brain damage, they stimulated points in the right angular gyrus (shown in Figure 3.3), producing various disturbances in the perception of her body. When stimulated at different intensities, she reported feeling that she was "sinking into the bed," "falling from a height," and seeing parts of her body shortening. (Blanke et al. 2002, 269). At one point she had an OBE in which she saw her trunk and legs from above, the same portion of her body she had felt when stimulated before. However, when they stimulated her epileptic focus in her temporal lobe, over 5 cm away from the angular gyrus, she did not have an OBE Blanke and his colleagues proposed that it was stimulating her angular gyrus that produced the OBE by disrupting the integration of somatosensory and vestibular information—that is, information about the feel and position of her body. These findings support the idea that the brain produces the conscious perception of an embodied self from the coordinated activity of various brain regions.

Drug effects on the brain can also produce OBEs. The drug ketamine, called "Special K" on the street and used as an anaesthetic before surgery, often produces

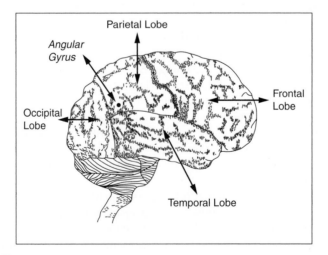

FIGURE 3.3 ▨ A right hemisphere view drawn to show the lobes of the brain and the point in the angular gyrus of the parietal lobe that Blanke and his colleagues (2002) stimulated to produce an OBE.

OBEs. Karl Jansen (1997) has argued that the experience produced by ketamine is very much like the near-death experience (NDE) in which people often report the experience of floating above the body, traveling through a dark tunnel into the light, seeing God, and the conviction that they were actually dead. Although naturally occurring NDEs may result from various causes, ketamine may produce an artificial version of the NDE and an associated OBE by blocking neural transmission in the temporal lobe.

The question arises as to how physical events in the natural environment could produce electrochemical changes in the brain that lead to OBEs. One possibility proposed by Michael Persinger (1995) is that variations in the Earth's magnetic field produced by movement of its tectonic plates could lead to OBEs under the right conditions. Persinger obtained data on the changes in Earth's geomagnetic activity from the National Geophysical Data Center keeping track of the particular level that each subject experienced during testing. First, he externally applied a weak electromagnetic field across large areas of his subjects' brains while depriving them partially of sensory stimulation to enhance awareness of their cognitive processes. Then he had them rate the degree to which they felt detached from their bodies. At a separate session, subjects also answered questions from which he could infer each subject's history of complex, partial epileptic-like experiences. He found that those subjects who had the most epileptic-like experiences also tended to report the most detachment from their bodies on days when geomagnetic activity was at higher levels in general. The geomagnetic disturbance may have destabilized activity in the temporal lobes of those people who had the most epileptic-like experiences. Although this finding may further suggest that cognitive science is moving toward an explanation of the OBE in natural, physical terms, it should be interpreted with caution given the low correlation and our current lack of understanding of how Earth's electromagnetic activity affects brain activity.

Other evidence from evolutionary psychology and the study of consciousness has supported the brain basis of the OBE. It is striking to note that the animals with brains most like our own, the chimpanzee, orangutan, and gorilla, are the only land animals aside from us that can recognize the image of their own bodies in a mirror as belonging to themselves (Gallup 1982). This conscious ability to recognize one's body as an objective part of oneself seems to be related to the brain's ability to form a mental representation of one's body that can be inspected. It also implies the need for the brain to construct a representation of the self as part of its ongoing modeling of the world. Nicholas Humphrey has proposed that it would be adaptive for animals with complex social lives, such as humans and chimps, to include a model of the self in their model of the social world (Humphrey 1978). In this way they could more completely model the possible consequences of their own actions and the responses of others to them. Consistent with this theory, several researchers have found that, like humans, chimpanzees may develop at least the rudiments of a theory of mind allowing them to predict and understand some intentions and behaviors in relation to themselves (Suddendorf and Whitten 2000).

Recently, cognitive scientists have proposed paying more attention to the bodily aspects of experience, challenging traditional views of cognitive science that tend to neglect the body (Johnson 1995). Some argue that the brain's representation of the body is central to its representation of the self (Damasio 1999; Eilan, Marcel, and Bermudez 1995). Some have even challenged traditional cognitive science's emphasis on representation, instead arguing that mental experience is embodied and not due to abstract mental processes distinct from the physical system producing them (Varela, Thompson, and Rosch 1991). Others, like James Gibson, have emphasized the role of the environment in perceiving the self (Neisser 1993). Gibson has made the important point that when we see the environment we almost always see our bodies as well. For example, when I look at the world in front of me I often see part of my leg, arm, or the bridge of my nose.

Supporting an embodied view of conscious experience, Monica Meijsing (2000) has reanalyzed two relevant cases of nervous system damage originally reported by Cole and Pailard (1995). Although these patients have little sensory feedback from their bodies below the neck, they nevertheless have retained their body image. They have retained knowledge of how they look and how much space their bodies occupy while retaining very little control over the movement of their bodies. One of these patients compared her body to a machine saying she felt as if she were a pilot lodged in a ship that was hard to steer.

These striking cases suggest that a person's embodied experience depends on having an intact nervous system. However, whether cognitive scientists adopt the traditional representational view or the newer embodied cognition view, their common conclusion is that conscious experience of the body depends on brain and nervous system function. It follows that anomalous experiences of the body depend on brain and nervous system function as well.

ACKNOWLEDGMENTS

I would like to thank an anonymous reviewer for valuable comments on an earlier draft and Dr. Michael Persinger for providing additional information about his research.

References

Alcock, J.E. 1987. Parapsychology: Science of the anomalous or search for the soul? *Behavioral and Brain Sciences* 10: 553–565.

Auerbach, L. 1986. *ESP, Hauntings, and Poltergeists: A Parapsychologist's Handbook.* New York: Warner Books.

Beloff, J. 1989. Dualism: A parapsychological perspective. In *The Case for Dualism.* Charlottesville: University Press of Virginia.

Bensley, D.A. 1998. *Critical Thinking in Psychology: A Unified Skills Approach.* Pacific Grove, Calif.: Brooks/Cole.

Blackmore, S.J. 1982. Parapsychology—With and without the OBE? *Parapsychology Review* 13: 1–7.

———. 1987. Where am I?: Perspectives in imagery and the out-of-body experience. *Journal of Mental Imagery* 11: 53–66.

———. 1992. *Beyond the Body: An Investigation of Out-of-body Experiences.* (Revised ed.) Chicago: Academy Chicago Publishers.

Blanke, O., S. Ortigue, T. Landis, and M. Seeck. 2002. Stimulating illusory own-body perceptions. *Nature* 419: 269–270.

Cole, J., and J. Pailard 1995. Living without touch and peripheral information about body position and movement: Studies with Deafferented subjects. In J. Bermudez, A. Marcel, and N. Eilan, (Eds.). *The Body and the Self.* Cambridge, Mass.: MIT Press.

Crookall, R. 1963. Only psychological fact? *Light* 83: 17–182.

Damasio, A. 1999. *The Feeling of What Happens: Body and Emotion in the Making of Consciousness.* New York: Harcourt-Brace.

Eilan, N., A. Marcel, and J. Bermudez. 1995. Self-consciousness and the body: An interdisciplinary introduction. In J. Bermudez, A. Marcel, and N. Eilan, (Eds.). *The Body and the Self.* (Pp. 1–28). Cambridge, Mass.: MIT Press.

Frazer, J.G. 1996. *The Illustrated Golden Bough: A Study in Magic and Religion.* New York: Simon and Schuster.

Gallup, G.G. 1982. Self-recognition in primates: Self-awareness and the emergence of mind in primates. *American Journal of Primatology* 2: 237–248.

Glicksohn, J. 1991. The structure of subjective experience: Interdependencies along the sleep-wakefulness continuum. *Journal of Mental Imagery* 13: 99–106.

Grosso, M. 1976. Some varieties of out-of-body experience. *The Journal of the American Society for Psychical Research* 70: 179–193.

Humphrey, N. 1978. Nature's psychologists. *New Scientist* 78: 900–903.

Irwin, H.J. 1986. Perceptual perspective of visual imagery in OBE's, dreams and reminiscence. *Journal of the Society for Psychical Research* 53: 210–217.

———. 1988. Out-of-body experiences and dream lucidity. In J. Gackenbach and S. LaBerge (Eds.). *Conscious Mind, Sleeping Brain,* New York: Plenum Press.

Jansen, K. 1997. The ketamine model of the near-death experience: A central role for the N-Methyl-D-Aspartate receptor. *Journal of Near Death Studies* 16: 5–26.

Johnson, M. L. 1995. Incarnate mind. *Minds and Machines* 5: 533–545.

Ladavas, E., G. Zelon, and A. Farne. 1998. Visual peripersonal space centred on the face in humans. *Brain* 121: 2317–2326.

Levitan, L., S. Laberge, D. DeGracia, and P. Zimbardo. 1999. Out-of-body experiences, dreams, and REM sleep. *Sleep and Hypnosis* 1:186–196.

Meijsing, M. 2000. Self consciousness and the body. *Journal of Consciousness Studies* 7:34–52.

Neisser, U. 1993. The self perceived. In U. Neisser, (Ed.). *The Perceived Self.* Cambridge, UK: Cambridge University Press.

Newport, F., and M. Strausberg. 2001. Americans' belief in psychic and paranormal phenomena is up over last decade. Gallup News Service, 8 June. Online at www.gallup.com/poll/releases/pr010608.asp.

Nigro, G., and U. Neisser 1983. Point of view in personal memories. *Cognitive Psychology* 15:467–482.

Palmer, J. 1978. The out-of-body experience: A psychological theory. *Parapsychology Review* 9: 19–22.

Penfield, W. 1955. The role of the temporal cortex in certain psychic phenomena. *The Journal of Mental Science* 101: 451–465.

Persinger, M. 1995. Out-of-body experiences are more probable in people with elevated complex partial epileptic-like signs during periods of enhanced geomagnetic activity: A nonlinear effect. *Perceptual and Motor Skills* 80: 563–569.

Posner, M.I., and M.E., Raichle. 1994. *Images of Mind.* New York: W.H. Freeman.

Ramachandran, V.S. and W. Hirstein. 1998. The perception of phantom limbs. *Brain* 121: 1603–1630.

Rhine, J.B. and J.G. Pratt. 1957. *Parapsychology: Frontier Science of the Mind.* Springfield, Illinois: Charles C Thomas.

Rogo, D.S. 1984. Researching the out-of-body experience: The state of the art. *Anabiosis: The Journal for Near Death Studies* 4: 21–49.

Shiels, D. 1978. A cross-cultural study of belief in out-of-body experiences, waking and sleeping. *Journal of the Society for Psychical Research* 49: 697–741.

Stanovich, K.E. 1989. Implicit philosophies of mind: The dualism scale and its relation to religiosity and belief in extrasensory perception. *Journal of Psychology* 123: 5–23.

Suddendorf, T., and A. Whitten. 2000. Mental evolution and development: Evidence for secondary representation in children, great apes, and other animals. *Psychological Bulletin* 127: 629–650.

Tart, C.T. 1998. Six studies of out of body experiences. *Journal of Near Death Studies* 17: 73–99.

Thalbourne, M. 1999. Dualism and the sheep goat variable: A replication and extension. *Journal of the Society for Psychical Research* 63: 213–216.

Tobacyk, J., and T. Mitchell. 1987. The out-of-body experience and personality adjustment. *Journal of Nervous and Mental Disease* 175: 367–369.

Varela, F.J., E. Thompson, and E. Rosch. 1991. *The Embodied Mind: Cognitive Science and Human Experience.* Cambridge, Mass.: MIT Press.

Review and Contemplate

1. Explain what Bensley calls the "dualistic belief." Does research in cognitive science support this belief?
2. Explain the philosophical position called materialism.
3. Briefly describe Bensley's own out-of-body experience (OBE). Explain why such anecdotal reports of OBEs do not constitute strong evidence that the mind can actually leave the body.
4. Briefly describe two findings from research involving (a) brain stimulation and (b) drugs which suggest that OBEs may result from physical events in the brain.
5. Describe one major difference between pseudoscientific and scientific approaches to gathering evidence that is illustrated in Bensley's article (see Chapter 1 for a comparison of pseudoscience and science).

3.3   Dream Interpretation and False Beliefs/
GIULIANA MAZZONI, PASQUALE LOMBARDO,
STEFANO MALVAGIA, AND ELIZABETH LOFTUS

Dreams have long fascinated psychologists and laypeople, who ask questions regarding why we dream and what our dreams mean. Sigmund Freud believed that dreams are full of hidden meanings and that a proper interpretation of dreams can provide insights into a person's unconscious mind, past traumatic experiences, and secret desires. This view survives today in the many books and Web sites people can consult to help them interpret their dreams. One can also find professional clinical psychologists who interpret dreams in their clinical work. Some clinicians believe that certain images and symbols in dreams signal the existence of repressed memories of abuse. For example, some claim that a frightening dream about water suggests that you might have been sexually abused in a bathing situation; or a dream involving blood, sacrifice, or torture might indicate repressed memories of ritualistic abuse.

Today most scientists view dream interpretation as a pseudoscience that can produce inaccurate and potentially harmful results. Nevertheless, some clinical psychologists still use dream interpretation. Mazzoni et al. discuss some problems with dream interpretation and present the results of a study they conducted to determine whether people's beliefs about their past can be changed by a therapist's inaccurate interpretation of their dreams.

APA Reference

Mazzoni, G. A. L., Lombardo, P., Malvagia, S., & Loftus, E. F. (1999). Dream interpretation and false beliefs. *Professional psychology: Research and practice,* 30, 45–50.

Dream interpretation is a common practice in psychotherapy. In the research presented in this article, each participant saw a clinician who interpreted a recent dream report to be a sign that the participant had had a mildly traumatic experience before age 3 years, such as being lost for an extended time or feeling abandoned by his or her parents. This dream intervention caused a majority of participants to become more confident that they had had such an experience, even though they had previously denied it. These findings have implications for the use of dream material in clinical settings. In particular, the findings point to the possibility that dream interpretation may have unexpected side effects if it leads to beliefs about the past that may, in fact, be false.

Dream interpretation is a common current clinical tool used more in some therapies than in others (Brenneis, 1997). Although this tool might not necessarily be problematic as an enterprise, what would be the impact and consequence of a clinician imposing an incorrect interpretation on dream material? Could such misinterpretation influence patients' beliefs about their past in ways that might be detrimental? Could patients be led to false beliefs about their past?

Dream material was viewed by Sigmund Freud (1900/1953, 1918/1955) as providing a royal road to the unconscious and as being a vehicle for unearthing specific traumatic experiences from the past. Psychoanalytic theory and technique (including dream interpretation) dominated psychotherapy training well into the 1950s, when behavioral, humanistic, and cognitive approaches, which do not emphasize dream interpretation, began to have greater impact. Dream interpretation, or dream work, holds a far less central position among clinical intervention tools than it did just 30 years ago.

Nonetheless, a sizable percentage of professional psychologists today report using dream interpretation in their clinical work (Brenneis, 1997; Polusny & Follette, 1996; Poole, Lindsay, Memon, & Bull, 1995). Moreover, a subset of clinicians who work in the area of trauma view dreams as being "exact replicas" of the traumatic experiences (van der Kolk, Britz, Burr, Sherry, & Hartmann, 1984, p. 188). For example, one therapist wrote, "Buried memories of abuse intrude into your consciousness through dreams . . . Dreams are often the first sign of emerging memories" (Fredrickson, 1992, p. 44). Another therapist wrote,

> Repressed memory dreams are dreams that contain a partial repressed memory or symbols that provide access to a repressed memory. During sleep, you have a direct link to your unconscious. Because the channel is open, memory fragments or symbols from repressed sexual abuse memories often intrude

GIULIANA A. L. MAZZONI teaches at the University of Florence. She conducted this research as a Fullbright Scholar and a visiting scholar at the University of Washington. She is a clinical and cognitive psychologist whose research interests include human memory.

PASQUALE LOMBARDO is a clinical psychologist. He received his degree in psychology from the University of Padusa. He is currently in the joint doctoral program in psychology at the University of Bologna and the University of Florence. His research interests are in clinical psychology and physiological psychology.

STEFANO MALVAGLA received his degree in psychology from the University of Padua. He is collaborating on a project (Regione Toscana) on health psychology. His research interests are in cognitive and developmental psychology.

ELIZABETH F. LOFTUS received her PhD from Stanford University. She is professor of psychology and adjunct professor of law at the Department of Psychology, University of Washington. She is president of the American Psychological Society and has had a long-standing research interest in human memory.

PART OF THIS STUDY was supported by a MURST Grant.

CORRESPONDENCE CONCERNING THIS ARTICLE should be addressed to Giuliana A. L. Mazzoni, Department of Psychology, University of Florence, via S Niccolo '89/a, 50125 Florence, Italy, or to Elizabeth F. Loftus, Department of Psychology, University of Washington, Seattle, Washington, 98195–1525.

into the dream state. Even though the memory is embedded in the symbolism of the dream world, it is possible to use the dream to retrieve the memory. *(Fredrickson, 1992, p. 125)*

Does this sort of clinical dream interpretation actually lead to the recovery of a genuine traumatic past? Or is it possible that the dream interpretation might be leading people to develop false beliefs, or even false memories, about their past? And if so, is it harmful?

We recently published several studies that may have some relevance to these questions (Mazzoni & Loftus, 1996). We showed that after a single subtle suggestion, participants falsely recognized items from their dreams and thought that these items had been presented in a list that they learned during the waking state. Our participants first learned a key list of words. In a later session, they received a false suggestion that some items from their previously reported dreams had been presented on the key list. Finally, in a third session, they tried to recall the items that had occurred on the initial key list. A major finding was that participants often falsely recognized their dream items and thought they had been presented on the key list, sometimes as often as they accurately recognized true list items. Despite the high rate of false recognition, and the conviction that participants had about these false memories, it is reasonable to question whether the same kind of results would occur with more personally meaningful events.

THE FLORENCE FALSE INTERPRETATION STUDY

We devised a new methodology for exploring whether such activities can lead people to develop false beliefs about the past. We found individuals who reported that it was unlikely that they had had certain critical experiences before the age of 3 years. The age of 3 years is important to shed light on whether changes that resulted from our manipulation were due to the recovery of true experiences or the creation of false ones (Wetzler & Sweeney, 1986). The critical experiences included episodes like being lost in a public place for some extended time. Later, some of these individuals went through a 30-min minitherapy simulation with a clinical psychologist, who interpreted their dream (no matter what the content of the dream) as if it were indicative of having undergone specific critical experiences in the past.

An initial group of 128 undergraduates from the University of Florence filled out an instrument that we called the Life Events Inventory (LEI) on which they reported on the likelihood of various childhood events having happened to them. The LEI has 36 items, 3 of which are critical items. The inventory asks participants to consider how certain (confident) they are that each event did or did not happen to them before the age of 3 years. Participants respond by ranking items on an 8–point Likert-type scale ranging from 1 (*certain it did not happen*) to 8 (*certain it did happen*). Fifty participants who had low scores (below 4) on the 3 critical items were selected and asked to participate in the next phase of the study. The 3 critical items were as follows: "got lost in a public space," "was abandoned by my parents," and "found myself lonely and lost in an unfamiliar place." The cover story associated with the administration of the LEI explained that the study concerned the frequency of rare and common events that happened during early childhood and that the study goal was the validation of an instrument to measure these experiences.

Of the selected 50 participants, half were randomly assigned to a dream condition, where they received suggestive information about the content of their dream. The other half did not receive any suggestive information about their dreams. Of the 25 participants in the dream condition, only 19 completed all three phases of the experiment; all 25 participants in the non-dream condition completed the experiment. (The difference in completion rate appeared to be due to a handful of participants who were randomly assigned to the dream condition but chose not to participate in what they thought was an additional experiment. Whether this choice was due to already having sufficient credits or some other reason was not explored.) The mean age of the final sample of 44 participants was 21 years, and 64% were women.

All 44 participants returned to take the LEI again after 3 to 4 weeks. However, those in the dream condition also participated during that time in what they thought was a completely different experiment but was actually the dream manipulation.

For the participants in the dream condition, dream interpretation was done 10–15 days after the first LEI. Shortly before the dream session, dream condition participants received a phone call from a clinician asking for their participation in a dream and sleep study. Participants were asked to bring in one or more dreams, which could be a recurrent dream, a recent dream, or a vivid dream (no constraints were put on the type of dream). These participants had their dreams individually interpreted by a clinical psychologist. The particular clinician is a trained clinical psychologist with a private practice in Florence, Italy. He also is well known in the community from his radio program on which he gives clinical advice. Moreover, he has a strong, persuasive personality. In the dream session, the clinician welcomed the participants and explained that the purpose of the study was to collect meaningful dreams and to relate those dreams to sleep characteristics. Then the participants read their own dream report aloud. Next, the clinician asked participants for their own interpretation of the dream and for their comments on the dream. Then the clinician offered his own comments. The comments were framed in terms of a clinical interview (i.e., the psychologist followed a predefined script but was free to make some modifications depending on the responses of the participant). Early on, he explained that he had considerable experience in dream interpretation, and he explained that dreams are meaningful and symbolic expressions of human concern.

A key feature of the dream manipulation was to suggest to participants that the dream was the overt manifestation of repressed memories of events that happened before the age of 3 years. To be specific, the dream interpretation suggested to the participants that the dream was indicative of a difficult childhood experience, such as getting lost in a public place, being abandoned by one's parents, or being lonely and lost in an unfamiliar place—the three critical items. No matter what the content of their dreams, all participants received the same suggestion: that one or more of these critical experiences appeared to have happened to them before the age of 3 years.

To appreciate what the clinician did with the specific dream material, it is helpful to use a concrete example. Suppose a participant came in with a dream report about walking up a mountainside alone on a chilly day and commented that the dream must mean that he finds mountain walking appealing. The clinician might then discuss part of the dream, mentioning the mountain, that the participant reported being alone there, and that despite the participant's remark about liking mountain walking, the "chilly day" suggests that the experience might be a "cold" one for the participant. At that point, the clinician would try to induce the participant to agree with this suggestion. The clinician might then move toward a global interpretation, suggesting that in his vast experience with dream interpretation, a dream like this usually means that the participant is not totally happy with himself, he needs challenge, he resists being helped by others, and might have social or interpersonal difficulties. The clinician then might suggest to the participant that the dream content, and the feelings about that dream, are probably due to some past experience that the participant might not even remember. The clinician would then tell the participant that the specific details mentioned are commonly due to having had certain experiences before age 3, like being lost in a public place, being abandoned even temporarily by parents, or finding oneself lonely and lost in an unfamiliar place. Finally, the clinician would ask whether any of the critical events happened to the participant before the age of 3 years. When the participant claimed not to remember these experiences, the clinician explained how childhood experiences are often buried in the unconscious but do get revealed in dreams.

From this example, it is easy to see some of the general steps that the clinician followed during dream interpretation:

1. He commented on specific items in the dream and tried to relate those items to possible feelings that the participant might have. In the example, the specific items of the mountain walking and the chilly day were related to the possible feelings about its being a cold experience.
2. He tried to induce the participant to agree with and expand on his interpretation.
3. He provided a global interpretation of the dream's meaning. In the example, the clinician suggested that possibly the participant was not totally happy with himself, needed challenge, resisted help, and so forth.
4. He suggested the possibility that specific events of childhood are commonly associated with dream reports like the one provided by the participant. In the example, the specific events were getting lost and feeling abandoned—in other words, the critical events used in this study for all participants.

5. He explicitly suggested that such events had happened to the participant, and he asked for the participant's agreement with that suggestion.
6. When the participant did not recall such an event, the clinician explained that unpleasant childhood experiences can be buried and remain unremembered but are often revealed in dreams.

The entire dream session lasted approximately 30 min. At the end of the dream session, the clinician asked the participant to think over the proposed events and to return later for the sleep assessment. These participants eventually returned to participate in a subsequent sleep study that was actually totally unrelated to the current experiment.

The initial experimenter, who had previously administered the LEI (hereafter referred to as LEI-1), then contacted the participants in the dream condition and arranged for them to return for a second administration of the LEI (hereafter referred to as LEI-2). Approximately 10–15 days passed between LEI-1 and dream interpretation, and an additional 10–15 days passed between dream interpretation and LEI-2. For the non-dream condition participants, the LEI administrations were separated by the same amount of time but without any intervening dream interpretation.

After the LEI-2, participants were thoroughly debriefed. At this time, they were asked whether they had linked the two experiments in any way, and no participant reported having done so.

To determine if the false dream interpretation had caused participants to become more confident that the critical events had occurred, we examined whether LEI scores moved up or down for each of the three critical items. We also calculated the percentage of participants whose responses increased, decreased, or did not change from the LEI-1 to the LEI-2. The data for the three critical items (lost in public place, abandoned by parents, and lonely and lost) are shown in Figure 3.4. We predicted that after dream interpretation, participants would be more confident that the events had happened.

First examine what happened without dream interpretation: These participants in the control condition reported no change in score on two target items and a clear decrease on the remaining item ("lonely and lost"). The same was not true for participants in the dream condition. For all three items, their scores were far more likely to increase, and they rarely decreased on the LEI-2. For two of the critical events, about 80% of the scores increased. To analyze these data statistically, we conducted several Mann-Whitney U tests, comparing the dream and non-dream (control) conditions. We found that the two groups differed significantly for two of the critical items: "lost in a public place" and "lonely and lost in an unfamiliar place." Participants in the dream condition were far more likely to increase their confidence that they had had these experiences before the age of 3 years.

The same differences between the dream and non-dream condition groups were found when we analyzed the degree of movement. For each participant, we calculated the numerical difference between the scores assigned to each

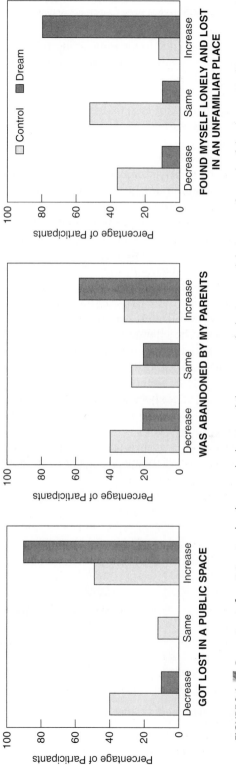

FIGURE 3.4 Percentage of participants who decreased, who stayed the same, and who increased their scores for each of the three critical items on the Life Events Inventory.

item in LEI-2 and the scores assigned to the same items in LEI-1. Figure 3.5 shows the change scores from LEI-1 to LEI-2 for the three critical items for non-dream condition versus dream condition participants.

As Figure 3.5 shows, for control condition participants, the changes in LEI scores were relatively small and not systematic. One item changed in a slightly positive way ("abandoned by parents"), whereas the other two items changed in a slightly negative way.

For the dream condition participants, the picture was completely different. All three items changed in a positive direction. The biggest difference between dream and non-dream condition participants occurred for the item "lonely and lost in an unfamiliar place," where the dream condition participants showed a mean positive change of 2.58 and the control participants showed a mean negative change of −.44. At the right of Figure 3.5, the mean change in LEI is averaged across all critical items and participants, and a strong overall influence of the dream interpretation can be seen. The mean change in the dream condition was 2.26 on the 8-point scale, whereas in the non-dream condition it was −.16.

To analyze these data statistically, we conducted several students' t tests for independent samples on the change scores. We found that the dream and non-dream condition participants differed significantly for two critical items: lost in a public place and lonely and lost. Dream and non-dream participants differed on the last critical item, abandoned by parents, only by a one-tailed test. Thus, the two methods of analysis, one that involved proportions of participants who shifted and one that involved measures of mean shift, produced similar results.

To be sure that our results were not due to inadvertent differences in pretreatment LEI scores, we calculated the mean pretreatment score for each critical

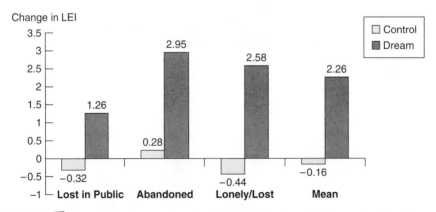

FIGURE 3.5 ■ Mean change in scores on the Life Events Inventory (LEI) for each of the three critical items. At the right is mean change collapsed across the three critical items.

TABLE 3.1 ▰▰▰▰▰▰▰▰▰▰▰▰▰▰▰▰▰▰▰▰▰▰▰▰▰▰▰▰▰▰▰▰▰▰▰▰▰▰

Average Pretreatment (LEI-1) and Posttreatment (LEI-2) Scores in the Non-Dream and the Dream Groups for the Three Critical Events

	Nondream		Dream	
Critical event	**LEI-1**	**LEI-2**	**LEI-1**	**LEI-2**
Lost	2.52	2.20	2.47	3.74
Abandoned	2.24	2.51	2.47	5.42
Lonely and lost	2.92	2.48	2.16	4.74

Note. LEI-1 = first administration (pretreatment) of the Life Events Inventory (LEI); LEI-2 = second administration (posttreatment) of the LEI. Scores are on an 8-point Likert-type scale ranging from 1 (*certain it did not happen*) to 8 (*certain it did happen*).

item. These pretreatment scores are shown in Table 3.1, separately for dream and non-dream participants. The posttreatment mean scores are also shown. Notice that the dream and non-dream participants did not differ in terms of their pretreatment scores, but they showed large differences in their posttreatment scores.

The previous two analyses suggested that the dream manipulation caused participants to become more certain that they had had specific negative experiences in their early childhood. A question then arose as to whether the shifts were localized only to the specific experiences mentioned by the clinician, or whether the clinician's intervention caused a general negative feeling, creating in participants the belief that they were more likely to have experienced a vast array of negative events in their early lives. We assessed this possibility by examining the dream condition versus non-dream condition differences on the negative filler items, such as "witnessed a person dying" or "threatened by a stranger." If the dream manipulation produced general negativity, this negativity might be represented in increased confidence on negative filler items as compared with non-dream conditions response on those negative filler items. In fact, we found that the dream manipulation had no impact on the negative filler items. Rather, the influence of the dream manipulation was very specific to the critical items that were specifically mentioned by the clinician.

Why did the dream interpretation lead to increased confidence that certain suggested events occurred? One possible explanation is that the dream interpretation created a true belief, reminding some participants of a true experience from their past. Such a reminder, if it occurred, probably did not occur during the therapy session itself, because no participant reported a memory for one of the critical events during the therapy. However, in the 10–15 days between the therapy and the final session, some participants might have recalled an actual experience. We deliberately suggested critical events to have occurred before the age of 3 years so that any memory that was produced could be deemed unlikely to be a real memory because of the childhood amnesia problem. However, it is entirely possible that the therapy might have led to ruminations that reminded participants of an event that occurred after the age of 3 years, but they misdated the experience during LEI-2 and mistakenly thought that it occurred before the age of 3. This process would lead to dramatic shifts in the LEI. Our data cannot rule this possibility out completely, and it is possible that these kinds of cases accounted for some of the shift that we observed. However, we would argue that if participants were so ready to conclude after dream interpretation that an experience that they actually had at age 6 or 8 or 12 happened to them before the age of 3, this also would constitute a distortion of belief or memory.

Another possible reason that participants increased their confidence in the suggested events in that the dream interpretation created a false belief. If false beliefs have been constructed, how and why does this process happen? One answer to this question can be found in the large literature on memory distortion that has shown that people are susceptible to suggestion (Gheorghin, Netter, Eysenck, & Rosenthal, 1989). In the current empirical work, we have found a form of suggestion that is both explicit and subtle. It is explicit in that the clinician used his authority to tell the dreamers that their mental products were likely to be revealing particular past experiences. It is subtle in the sense that the dreamers were encouraged to come up with their own specific instances of such experiences.

IMPLICATIONS AND APPLICATIONS

Our findings have important implications for therapists. They show that people are suggestible in a simulation that bears more resemblance to a therapeutic setting than has been used in prior empirical studies. Moreover, the findings hint at the strong influence that a clinician can have in a short period of time. This power may extend to other therapist-client interactions that are characterized by therapist interpretation of information provided by the client.

One might ask whether it is reasonable to generalize from our brief therapy simulation with students to the world of clinicians and their patients. After all, many of the differences between our minitherapy and real-world therapy are relatively easy to point out. Nonetheless, we believe that these very differences are such that we may be underestimating the power and influence that can occur in a clinical setting. We used students, who were presumably reasonably mentally healthy, whereas clinical patients may have a greater need to find an explanation for problems or distress. We had a single short therapy simulation, whereas clinical patients often experience many sessions during which suggested interpretations are offered to them. Our therapy simulation was limited to only a few elements that the participants provided (e.g., the dream and a brief reaction to the dream), whereas clinical patients provide a great many elements (dreams, thoughts, behaviors, feelings) with which the therapist works. Whether these elements are critical for influencing how people reflect on their past experiences is, of course, a matter for further research investigation.

One might ask whether it is even the case that therapists are using dream material to suggest that events occurred in a client's early life. We have found a number of examples that support the contention that some therapists do indeed make these kinds of suggestions from dream material. This conclusion comes not only from surveys of clinicians (e.g., Poole et al., 1995), but also from the writings of specific clinicians. For example, in *Crisis Dreaming*, readers are told, "Recurring dreams, particularly of being chased or attacked, suggest that such events really occurred" (Cartwright & Lamberg, 1992, p. 185). Are the authors of this book communicating this information to their clients? Are therapist-readers of this book taking dream material that involves chases and attacks and telling a client that it means that such events occurred? Although we cannot know that therapist–readers are following the advice implicit in this book, it is worth considering the likelihood that they might do so and might inadvertently create false beliefs or memories.

Could therapists produce similar effects without explicit dream interpretation? We believe the dream interpretation is probably not necessary but might add a bit of influential power. Here is why: Suppose instead of interpreting dreams the clinician simply responds to the comments made by a client during the first 5 min of interaction. If the clinician takes that 5 min of material and interprets the material as being indicative of an early childhood trauma, the client may eventually come to believe that he or she experienced such a trauma. In fact, even in the absence of dream interpretation, such suggestive comments might increase the likelihood of illusory beliefs or memories. According to Lindsay and Read (1995), suggestions from a trusted authority can be especially influential when they communicate a rationale for the plausibility of buried memories of childhood trauma. Moreover, the trusted authority might be especially influential if be or she offers repeated suggestions, giving anecdotes ostensibly from other patients.

However, it is also worth pointing out that working with dream material might be a particularly potent way to influence clients, for better or worse. It certainly might help to enhance the influence process, because people presumably enter therapy with a set of beliefs about the meaning of dreams in their lives and how much dreams can reveal about an individual's past. Given a predisposition on the part of some clients to already believe in the significance of dreams, the trusted authority can capitalize on the a priori beliefs and use them in the service of altering the autobiography.

Are therapists aware of the power they have? Almost by definition therapists must believe that they have the power to change people, because at least some forms of therapy emphasize changing people's beliefs from ones that are nonadaptive to ones that are more adaptive. Even more generally, therapy is about changing people. However, therapists may be appreciating their power to change people primarily when they are thinking about the good it can produce in people or thinking about ways to make their clients change for the better. They may not be appreciating that they also have the power to change people for the worse. This type of change can happen, for example, when a therapist adopts a hypothesis too early and, even when the hypothesis is wrong, presses it on the client. Our data show that even a randomly generated hypothesis can be embraced by individuals and can produce profound changes in the way they view their past. We have demonstrated that these interventions can make people believe that they have had experiences that they previously denied. However, it is also likely that these interventions have the power to make people doubt their true experiences. Our hope is that heightened awareness of this power might enhance the likelihood of cautious use of these sorts of interventions.

References

Brenneis, C. B. (1997). *Recovered memories of trauma: Transferring the present to the past*. Madison, WI: International Universities Press.

Cartwright, R. & Lamberg, L. (1992). *Crisis dreaming—Using your dreams to solve your problems*. New York: HarperCollins.

Fredrickson, R. (1992). *Repressed memories*. New York: Simon & Schuster.

Freud, S. (1953). *The interpretation of dreams* (Standard ed. 4 & 5). London: Hogarth Press. (Original work published 1900)

Freud, S. (1955). *From the history of an infantile neurosis* (standard ed. 17, pp. 1–122). London: Hogarth Press. (Original work published 1918).

Gheorghiu, V. A., Netter, P., Eyesenck, H. J., & Rosenthal, R. (Eds). (1989). *Suggestion and suggestibility*. New York: Springer-Verlag.

Lindsay, D. S., & Read, J. D. (1995). "Memory work" and recovered memories of childhood sexual abuse: Scientific evidence and public, professional, and personal issues. *Psychology, Public Policy, & the Law, 1*, 846–908.

Mazzoni, G. A. L., & Loftus, E. F. (1996). When dreams become reality. *Consciousness & Cognition, 5*, 442–462.

Polusny, M. A., & Follette, V. M. (1996). Remembering childhood sexual abuse. *Professional Psychology: Research and Practice, 27*, 41–52.

Poole, D. A., Lindsay, D. S., Memon, A., & Bull, R. (1995). Psychotherapy and the recovery of memories of childhood sexual abuse: U.S. and British practitioners' opinions, practices, and experiences. *Journal of Consulting and Clinical Psychology, 63*, 426–437.

van der Kolk, B., Britz, R., Burr, W., Sherry, S., & Hartmann, E. (1984). Nightmares and trauma: A comparison of nightmares after combat with life-long nightmares in veterans. *American Journal of Psychiatry, 141*, 187–190.

Wetzler, S. E., & Sweeney, J. A. (1986). Childhood amnesia: An empirical demonstration. In D. C. Rubin (Ed.), *Autobiographical memory* (pp. 191–201). Cambridge, MA: Cambridge University Press.

Received July 25, 1997
Revision received April 3, 1998
Accepted April 20, 1998

Review and Contemplate

1. Why do some clinicians engage in dream interpretation with their clients; what do they hope to discover?
2. What are the central findings of the study conducted by Mazzoni et al. (1999)?
3. Describe one of the important implications of Mazzoni et al.'s findings for practicing therapists.
4. How is this article related to the topic of pseudoscience?

CHAPTER 4
Child Development

4.1   *Common Myths of Children's Behavior/*
CATHERINE FIORELLO

As Catherine Fiorello notes, parenting is generally not considered a pseudoscience. However, parents may take a pseudoscientific approach to determining which factors influence their child's behavior. For example, parents may notice that their child seems more hyperactive after eating dessert and conclude that sugar increases hyperactivity. I know several parents who restrict their children's sugar intake based on this belief. Children in this situation may not be allowed to eat cake at birthday parties, go trick-or-treating on Halloween, or eat pancakes or applesauce in a restaurant. Such restrictions on children's behavior may be unnecessary if, in fact, ingesting sugar does not make them more hyperactive. This article focuses on the scientific evidence related to this myth and several others that parents believe.

Chapter 1 described how the difficulties people sometimes have with methodological and statistical reasoning contribute to the development of pseudoscientific beliefs. Fiorello discusses several of these difficulties, including failures to consider base rates, covariates, regression toward the mean, or missing control groups. Overcoming these difficulties and understanding the important principles of scientific thinking discussed in this article may go a long way toward helping us think straight about children's behavior and parenting; it may also help parents avoid falling victim to pseudoscientists who dole out faulty parenting advice in books, videos, Web sites, and talk shows.

APA Reference

Fiorello, C. A. (2001, May/June). Common myths of children's behavior. *Skeptical Inquirer, 25,* 37–39, 44.

A number of false beliefs about children's behavior are very common among parents and the lay public. This article summarizes scientific findings and applies critical thinking to show what's tripped up so many of us.

No one considers parenting a pseudoscience, but many of the "truths" that parents believe are contradicted by scientific knowledge. Discussion of these myths can shed light on our knowledge of children's behavior. In addition, the discussion illustrates some basic scientific principles that can also be applied elsewhere.

1. "Don't give Sheldon that candy—sugar makes him so hyper!" Many parents and teachers report that children's consumption of sugar results in hyperactivity. But the empirical research is clear: consumption of sugar has no effect on children's behavior as rated by objective observers (Milich, Wolraich, and Lindgren 1986). So why are parents and teachers convinced it has such devastating effects? They are not aware of the need to *control for covariates*. A covariate is another variable that is associated with the variable of interest, in this case sugar consumption, but that might not be as noticeable. What variables might be overlooked by parents and teachers in judging the effects of sugar? Well, think about the situations in which children eat a lot of sugar, like birthday parties and Halloween—these are situations that are likely to excite children.

There's another possible covariate, too. Children whose parents don't restrict sugar at all, letting their children eat whatever they want whenever they want it, are also more likely to let their children run wild in other ways. And parents who restrict sugar (it is bad for your teeth, after all) are also more likely to teach self-restraint and obedience. But we often see the child without seeing the parenting. So we see an association between the sugar and the behavior, instead of an association between parenting style and behavior.

2. "She's writing her letters backward—it must be dyslexia." Many parents and teachers become concerned when a child is reversing letters, afraid that this is a sign of dyslexia. But the empirical research indicates that the primary indicator of reading disabilities such as dyslexia is difficulty with auditory processing and phonemic awareness—breaking words down into their component sounds (Beitchman and Young 1997; Shaywitz 1996). Dyslexia isn't a visual disability at all, but an auditory one. Parents and teachers should be concerned about a child who can't generate rhyming words, not one who is reversing letters.

Catherine A. Fiorello is an assistant professor of school psychology as Temple University. She is a licensed psychologist in Pennsylvania and Kentucky and a nationally certified school psychologist. Fiorello can be contacted at the School Psychology Program, Temple University (004-00), 1301 Cecil B. Moore Ave. RA-260, Philadelphia, PA 19122-6091 or by e-mail at cfiorello@nimbus.temple.edu.

So why are people so concerned about reversals? They are not aware of the effect of *base rate* in interpreting behavior. The base rate is the percentage of the general population that has a given characteristic. In this case, all children start out making reversals. After all, letters and numbers are the only things that we draw where the direction the figure is facing makes a difference in its name. (A dog facing right instead of left is still a dog; a 'd' facing right instead of left is now a 'b'.) Children gradually learn which way the letters face and by second or third grade they are no longer making reversals. The same percentage of children make reversals, whether they are having difficulty with reading or not (Black 1973; Pemberton et al. 1993), although children with reading disabilities may keep it up a little longer. But people only notice with the kids who are having trouble—and never compare it to the base rate.

3. "Tanisha is just immature. If we have her repeat first grade, she'll do better in school." Many parents and teachers are convinced that some children are too young or too immature for their grade placement, and that retention will help them catch up. But the empirical research indicates the opposite—retention not only has no long-term benefits, it can actually harm children emotionally (Jimerson, et al. 1997). In fact, children rate retention as the third most horrible thing they can imagine happening to them—after losing a parent and going blind (Yamamoto, et al. 1987). So why are parents and teachers convinced that it is helpful? Lack of long-term followup and lack of a control group. In most cases, a teacher judges the outcome of retention the next year, when the child is actually repeating the same grade. At that point, the child may be doing well academically. But the following year, when the child starts to fall behind again, the teacher isn't following up any more. And the parent says, "Well, the retention helped for a while, but now we need to try something else." And without a comparison to children who weren't retained, it's hard to see the benefits of promotion—and the costs of retention.

4. "Praise doesn't work. After I compliment John, his performance goes downhill. It's yelling whenever he messes up that really gets results!" Many parents and teachers are convinced that punishment is more effective in changing behavior than praise. But the empirical research indicates that positive reinforcement is more effective than punishment in changing behavior and especially in teaching new skills (Alberto and Troutman 1999). So why are parents and teachers convinced that punishment is better? They aren't familiar with the statistical concept of *regression to the mean*. When you are first learning something, there is a large element of random chance in how good your performance will be. Statistically, this random variation causes an interesting effect. After a particularly good performance, the chances are the next one will be worse, no matter what happens. And after a particularly bad one, the chances are the next one will be better, no matter what happens. So it looks like the praise caused your performance to deteriorate, and the yelling caused you to do better. But really, it was just random variation bringing you closer to the average. (For more on the regression effect, see "Superstition and the Regression Effect," by Kruger, Savitsky, and Gilovich, SI 23[2] March/April 1999.)

5. "I was spanked as a kid and I turned out okay." Many parents and teachers are convinced that occasional spanking is necessary, or at least not harmful. But the empirical research indicates that, while most children who are spanked do turn out all right, children who are not spanked do better, and for a significant minority of children, spanking is harmful and abusive (Hyman 1990; Straus, Sugarman and Giles-Sims 1997). So why are parents and teachers convinced? They aren't aware of the necessity of an appropriate comparison group. They look at their own experience without considering, "what would I have been like if I hadn't been spanked as a child?" Of course, children can't be exactly equated. But when you randomly select large groups of children, you can compare the groups and draw some conclusions. As a group, children who are never spanked are in better shape psychologically—they are less likely to be aggressive or depressed later in life. There is even some evidence that they may be smarter (Straus and Paschall undated). Of course, we don't know if parents who spank are different in other ways from parents who don't—they might reason verbally with their children instead of spanking, or be more educated overall. The only way to directly test the effects of just spanking, would be to randomly assign children to be spanked—and we couldn't ethically do that.

  6. **"Attention Deficit Hyperactivity Disorder doesn't really exist. After all, we're all fidgety and inattentive sometimes."** Many parents and teachers are convinced that ADHD isn't a "real" disorder, but an excuse for bad behavior or poor parenting, or just a way to label normal kids as having a problem. ADHD may, indeed, be overdiagnosed in this country. But the empirical research indicates that 3 to 5 percent of children have such severe symptoms that it affects their functioning in almost every area, including school performance, making friends, and getting along in the family and community (Barkley 1998).

  So why are parents and teachers convinced? They're not familiar with the process of diagnosis and the importance of norms. Parents and teachers may have read an article or heard a speaker that presented a list of symptoms, including items such as that the child "often does not seem to listen when spoken to directly" and "often fidgets with hands or feet or squirms in seat." The part that seldom gets presented, though, is the fact that diagnosticians must determine that the symptoms "have persisted for at least six months to a degree that is maladaptive and inconsistent with developmental level" and cause "clinically significant impairment" in functioning (American Psychiatric Association 1994). In other words, we are not diagnosing children who are normally fidgety; we are comparing children to others of the same age and gender and diagnosing those who have very extreme symptoms (often the most extreme 2 percent). We only diagnose children whose functioning (usually in school, with peers, and at home) is significantly impaired by their inattention, impulsivity, and hyperactivity. And in addition we rule out other causes of the symptoms—such as reactions to grief, trauma, or abuse; hearing difficulties; or physical illness.

  7. **"We're in the middle of an ADHD epidemic! Ten to twenty percent of all children should be on Ritalin!"** This myth is the converse of the above. Because there is no objective test for ADHD, actually diagnosing it can be tricky. Many pediatricians diagnose ADHD based on a short office visit and good response to a trial of Ritalin (Copeland, et al. 1987). This process overlooks many

common problems that can mimic ADHD, including depression, anxiety, medication side effects, abuse, lead poisoning, hearing impairment, and more. True, ADHD isn't caused by bad parenting, but children from a chaotic home may never have learned to focus and pay attention. Making the diagnosis based on a good response to Ritalin can be especially dangerous, since some of the disorders that mimic ADHD can be made worse (including tic disorders and anxiety disorders).

In addition, since Ritalin is a stimulant, it can improve performance in *anyone* who takes it, and up to 30 percent of children properly diagnosed with ADHD do not have a positive response (Barkley 1998). The diagnosis of ADHD is as much a process of ruling everything else out as it is a process of identifying ADHD. We don't really know if there is a physical difference in the brain wiring or chemical makeup of a child with ADHD; we just rule out every other possible cause of the inattention, impulsivity, and hyperactivity. So if a child gets a diagnosis of ADHD from a professional who has only seen the child briefly, or if a physician suggests trying Ritalin "just to see if it works," or if a well-meaning teacher says that she "knows" a child has ADHD because she's seen it so many times, a parent should remain skeptical and request a comprehensive evaluation. And even if a full evaluation identifies a child as having ADHD, a rush to Ritalin isn't necessarily called for.

The benefits of scientific thinking are not limited to questions that *seem* scientific. Many aspects of parenting are intuitive, but an awareness of what science says about children's behavior can still be helpful. In addition, the principles of scientific thinking illustrated in these examples may be useful elsewhere in daily life. Remembering regression to the mean the next time you are teaching your spouse to drive a standard transmission car may save some wear and tear!

References

Alberto, Paul A., and Anne C. Troutman. 1999. Applied behavior analysis for teachers (5th ed.). Upper Saddle River, NJ: Prentice-Hall.

American Psychiatric Association. 1994. Diagnostic and statistical manual of mental disorders (4th ed.). Washington, D.C.

Barkley, Russell A. 1998. Attention-Deficit Hyperactivity Disorder: A handbook for diagnosis and treatment. New York, NY: Guilford Press.

Beitchman, Joseph H., and Arlene R. Young. 1997. Learning disorders with a special emphasis on reading disorders: A review of the past 10 years. *Journal of the Academy of Child and Adolescent Psychiatry* 36, no. 8 (August): 1020–32.

Black, F. William, 1973. Reversal and rotation errors by normal and retarded readers. *Perceptual and Motor Skills* 36, no. 3: 895–98, 3.

Copeland, L., et al. 1987. Pediatricians' reported practices in the assessment and treatment of attention deficit disorders. *Journal of Developmental and Behavioral Disorders* 8, no. 4: 191–97.

Hyman, Irwin. 1990. *Reading, Writing and the Hickory Stick*. Lexington, MA: Lexington Books.

Jimerson, Shane, et al. 1997. A prospective, longitudinal study of the correlates and consequences of early grade retention. *Journal of School Psychology* 35, no. 1: 3–25.

Milich, Richard, Mark L. Wolraich, and Scott Lindgren. 1986. Sugar and hyperactivity: A critical review of empirical findings. *Clinical Psychology Review* 6, no. 6: 493–513

Pemberton, Elizabeth, et al. 1993. Letter reversals produced and recognized by dyslexic and nondyslexic children. Biennial Meeting of the Society for Research in Child Development. New Orleans, LA, March.

Shaywitz, Sally E. 1996. Dyslexia. *Scientific American* November, 98–104.

Straus, Murray A., and Mallie J. Paschall. Corporal punishment by mothers and child's cognitive development: A longitudinal study. www.unh.edu/ftl/cp51japa.htm. undated.

Straus, Murray A., D. B. Sugarman, and J. Giles-Sims. 1997. Spanking by parents and subsequent antisocial behavior of children *Archives of Pediatric and Adolescent Medicine* 151: 761–67.

Yamamoto, Kaoru, et al. 1987. Voices in unison! Stressful events in the lives of children in six countries. *Journal of Child Psychology and Psychiatry* 28, no. 6: 855–64.

Review and Contemplate

1. What is a covariate? Explain how covariates might lead parents to perceive a causal relationship between sugar consumption and hyperactivity when, in fact, no such relationship exists.

2. Do parents tend to believe that (a) punishment or (b) positive reinforcement is more effective for changing their child's behavior? Which consequence is actually more effective?

3. What does research suggest about the effects of spanking on children?

4. Fiorello implied that diagnosing ADHD based on a good response to Ritalin is not an effective strategy. Explain why.

4.2 Separating Fact from Fiction in the Etiology and Treatment of Autism: A Scientific Review of the Evidence/

JAMES HERBERT, IAN SHARP, AND BRANDON GAUDIANO

Autism is considered a pervasive developmental disorder that impacts most areas of functioning in children, including their language ability, cognitive functioning, and social skills. The sharp increase in the number of children diagnosed with autism in the past two decades has led to media reports about baffling outbreaks or a full-blown epidemic of autism. However, in an article published in the journal *Current Directions in Psychological Science,* Gernsbacher, Dawson, and Goldsmith (2005) explained that the increase in diagnosed cases of autism is most likely due to changes in the criteria for diagnosing autism, increased public awareness of the disorder, and increased reporting of autism by schools due to changes in federal reporting requirements. Thus, there is no mysterious autism epidemic.

The increased number of children diagnosed with autism, and the fact that scientists have yet to pinpoint the exact causes of autism, make it a prime target for pseudoscience. As Gernsbacher, Dawson, and Goldsmith (2005) noted, "false epidemics solicit false causes." For example, one popular pseudoscientific theory is that childhood vaccinations are responsible for the autism "epidemic." As you can imagine, such a theory might scare parents into avoiding vaccinations for their children, increasing the risk that their children will be exposed a variety of preventable diseases. The following reading is an excerpt from a scientific article by Herbert, Sharp, and Gaudiano that focuses on pseudoscientific theories of the causes of autism. Their discussion of treatments of autism was excluded in order to reduce the length of the article, but interested readers should consult the original article for this discussion.

APA Reference

Herbert, J. D., Sharp, I. R., & Gaudiano, B. A. (2002). Separating fact from fiction in the etiology and treatment of autism: A scientific review of the evidence. *The Scientific Review of Mental Health Practice, 1,* 23–43.

Autistic-spectrum disorders are among the most enigmatic forms of developmental disability. Although the cause of autism is largely unknown, recent advances point to the importance of genetic factors and early environmental insults, and several promising behavioral, educational, and psychopharmacologic interventions have been developed. Nevertheless, several factors render autism especially vulnerable to pseudoscientific theories of etiology and to intervention approaches with grossly exaggerated claims of effectiveness. Despite scientific data to the contrary, popular theories of etiology focus on maternal rejection, candida infections, and childhood vaccinations. Likewise, a variety of popular treatments are promoted as producing dramatic results, despite scientific evidence suggesting that they are of little benefit and in some cases may actually be harmful. Even the most promising treatments for autism rest on an insufficient research base, and are sometimes inappropriately and irresponsibly promoted as "cures." We argue for the importance of healthy skepticism in considering etiological theories and treatments for autism.

James D. Herbert, Ian R. Sharp, and Brandon A. Gaudiano, Department of Clinical and Health Psychology, MCP Hahnemann University, Philadelphia, Pennsylvania.

Correspondence concerning this article should be addressed to James D. Herbert, Department of Clinical and Health Psychology, MCP Hahnemann University, Mail Stop 988, 245 N. 15th Street, Philadelphia, PA 19102-1192; E-mail: james_herbert@drexel.edu.

Autism is a pervasive developmental disorder marked by profound deficits in social, language, and cognitive abilities. Prevalence rates range from 7 to 13 cases per 10,000 (Bryson, 1997; Bryson, Clark, & Smith, 1988; Steffenberg & Gillberg, 1986; Sugiyama & Abe, 1989). It is not clear if the actual prevalence of autism is increasing, or if the increased frequency of diagnosis has resulted from wider recognition of the disorder and especially recognition of the full range of pervasive developmental disorders, often referred to as "autistic-spectrum disorders."[1] Either way, autism is no longer considered rare, occurring more commonly than Down's syndrome, cystic fibrosis, and several childhood cancers (Fombonne, 1998; Gillberg, 1996).

The degree of impairment associated with autism varies widely, with approximately 75% of autistic individuals also meeting criteria for mental retardation (American Psychiatric Association [APA], 1994). Autism occurs three to four times more frequently in males than females (Bryson et al., 1988; Steffenberg, & Gillberg, 1986; Volkmar, Szatmari, & Sparrow, 1993). Although recent advances have been made with respect to possible causal factors (Rodier, 2000), the exact etiology of autism remains unknown. Moreover, although certain behavioral, educational, and pharmacological interventions have been demonstrated to be helpful for many individuals with autism, there is currently no cure for the disorder.

---

[1]We use the term "autism" throughout this paper to refer not only to classic autistic disorder (American Psychiatric Association, 1994), but in some cases to the full range of autistic-spectrum disorders. The vast majority of the research reviewed in this paper does not distinguish among the various subtypes of autistic-spectrum disorders. It is therefore often impossible to judge the degree to which research findings are unique to autistic disorder per se, or are generalizable to other pervasive developmental disorders.

WHY AUTISM IS FERTILE GROUND FOR PSEUDOSCIENCE

Several factors render autism especially vulnerable to etiological ideas and intervention approaches that make bold claims, yet are inconsistent with established scientific theories and unsupported by research (Herbert & Sharp, 2001). Despite their absence of grounding in science, such theories and techniques are often passionately promoted by their advocates. The diagnosis of autism is typically made during the preschool years and, quite understandably, is often devastating news for parents and families. Unlike most other physical or mental disabilities that affect a limited sphere of functioning while leaving other areas intact, the effects of autism are pervasive, generally affecting most domains of functioning. Parents are typically highly motivated to attempt any promising treatment, rendering them vulnerable to promising "cures." The unremarkable physical appearance of autistic children may contribute to the proliferation of pseudoscientific treatments and theories of etiology. Autistic children typically appear entirely normal; in fact, many of these children are strikingly attractive. This is in stark contrast to most conditions associated with mental retardation (e.g., Down's syndrome), which are typically accompanied by facially dysmorphic features or other superficially evident abnormalities. The normal appearance of autistic children may lead parents, caretakers, and teachers to become convinced that there must be a completely "normal" or "intact" child lurking inside the normal exterior. In addition, as discussed above, autism comprises a heterogeneous spectrum of disorders, and the course can vary considerably among individuals. This fact makes it difficult to identify potentially effective treatments for two reasons. First, there is a great deal of variability in response to treatments. A given psychotropic medication, for example, may improve certain symptoms in one individual, while actually exacerbating those same symptoms in another. Second, as with all other developmental problems and psychopathology, persons with autism sometimes show apparently spontaneous developmental gains or symptom improvement in a particular area for unidentified reasons. If any intervention has recently been implemented, such improvement can be erroneously attributed to the treatment, even when the treatment is actually ineffective. In sum, autism's pervasive impact on development and functioning, heterogeneity with respect to course and treatment response, and current lack of curative treatments render the disorder fertile ground for quackery.

A number of contemporary treatments for autism can be characterized as pseudoscientific. Most scientists agree that there are no hard-and-fast criteria that distinguish science from pseudoscience; the differences are in degree, rather than kind (Bunge, 1994; Herbert et al., 2000; Lilienfeld, 1998). Although a detailed treatment of pseudoscience in mental health is beyond the scope of this paper, a brief discussion of the features that distinguish it from legitimate science is important in order to provide a context for considering currently popular etiological theories and treatments for autism. In general, pseudoscience is characterized by claims presented as being scientifically verified even though in reality they lack empirical support (Shermer, 1997). Pseudoscientific treatments tend to be associated with exaggerated claims of effectiveness that are well outside the range of established procedures. They are often based on implausible theories that cannot be proven false. They tend to rely on anecdotal evidence and testimonials, rather than controlled studies, for support. When quantitative data are considered, they are considered selectively. That is, confirmatory results are highlighted, whereas unsupportive results are either dismissed or ignored. They tend to be promoted through proprietary publications or Internet Web sites rather than refereed scientific journals. Finally, pseudoscientific treatments are often associated with individuals or organizations with a direct and substantial financial stake in the treatments. The more of these features that characterize a given theory or technique, the more scientifically suspect is becomes.

A number of popular etiological theories and treatment approaches to autism are characterized by many of the features of pseudoscience described above (Green, 1996a; Green, 2001; Herbert & Sharp, 2001; Smith, 1996). Still other treatments, although grounded on a sound theoretical basis and supported by some research, are nonetheless subject to exaggerated claims of efficacy. What follows is a review of the most popular dubious theories and questionable intervention approaches for autism. We also review promising etiologic theories and treatments. Some intervention programs are designed specifically for young children, whereas others are applied across a wider age range.

THE ETIOLOGY OF AUTISM: SEPARATING FACT FROM FICTION

Psychoanalytic Explanations

Although modern theories of autism posit the strong influence of biological factors in the etiology of the disorder, psychoanalytic theories have abounded traditionally. Kanner (1946) was the first to describe the parents of children with autism as interpersonally distant. For example, he concluded that the autistic children he observed were "kept neatly in refrigerators which did not defrost" (Kanner, 1973, p. 61). However, Kanner also stressed that the disorder had a considerable biological component that produced disturbances in the formation of normal emotional context. It was Bruno Bettelheim who was perhaps the most influential theorist promoting psychoanlytic interpretations of autism. Bettelheim rose to prominence as director of the University of Chicago's Orthogenic School for disturbed children from 1944 to 1978. He rejected Kanner's conclusions positing a biological role in the etiology in autism and was convinced that autism was caused by "refrigerator" mothers. According to Bettelheim, autistic symptoms are viewed as defensive reactions against cold and detached mothers. These unloving mothers were sometimes assumed to be harboring "murderous impulses" toward their children. For example, in his book *The Empty Fortress*, Bettelheim (1967) wrote that one autistic girl's obsession with the weather could be explained by dissecting the word to form "we/eat/her," indicating that she was convinced that her mother, and later others, would "devour her." Based on his conceptualization of autism, Bettelheim promoted a policy of "parentectomy" that entailed separation of children from their parents for extended periods of time (Gardner, 2000). Other psychoanalytic therapists such as Mahler (1968) and Tustin (1981) promoted similar theories positing problems in the mother-child relationship as causing autism (see Rosner, 1996, for a review of psychoanalytic theories of autism).

After his suicide in 1990, stories began to emerge that tarnished Bettelheim's reputation (Darnton, 1990). Several individuals claimed abuse at the hands of the famous doctor when they were at the Orthogenic School. Furthermore, information emerged that Bettelheim often lied about his background and training. For example, although he frequently claimed to have studied under Freud in Vienna, Bettelheim possessed no formal training in psychoanalysis whatsoever, and instead held a degree in philosophy. Also, Bettelheim claimed that 85% of his patients at the Orthogenic School were cured after treatment; however, most of the children were not autistic and the case reports he presented in his books were often fabrications (Pollak, 1997). Despite the continued acceptance of Bettelheim's theories in some circles, no controlled research has been produced to support the refrigerator mother theory of autism. For example, Allen, DeMeyer, Norton, Pontus, and Yang (1971) did not find differences between parents of autistic and mentally retarded children and matched comparison children on personality measures. Despite the complete absence of controlled evidence, even today some psychoanalytic theorists continue in the tradition of Bettelheim by highlighting the putative role of early mother-child attachment dysfunctions in causing autism (Rosner, 1996).

Candida Infection

Candida albicans is a yeastlike fungus found naturally in humans that aids in the destruction of dangerous bacteria. Candidiasis is an infection caused by an overgrowth of candida in the body. Women often contract yeast infections during their childbearing years. In addition, antibiotic medication can disrupt the natural balance among microorganisms in the body, resulting in an overgrowth of candida (Adams & Conn, 1997). In the 1980s, anecdotal reports began to emerge suggesting that some children with candidiasis later developed symptoms of autism. Supporters of this theory point to animal studies in which candida was shown to produce toxins that disrupted the immune system, leading to the possibility of brain damage (Rimland, 1988). Furthermore, Rimland speculated that perhaps 5 to 10% of autistic children could show improved functioning if treated for candida infection. Proponents often recommend that Nystatin, a medication used to treat women with yeast infections, be given to children whose mothers had candidiasis during pregnancy, whether or not the children show signs of infection. However, there is no evidence that mothers of autistic children have a higher incidence of candidiasis than mothers in the general population and only uncontrolled case reports are presented as evidence for the etiological role of candida infection in autism (Siegel, 1996).

Adams and Conn (1997) presented the case study of a 3-year-old autistic boy who reportedly showed improved functioning following a vitamin treatment for candida infection. However, the boy was never medically diagnosed with candidiasis and was only reported to meet criteria based on questionnaire data. In addition, reports of the child's functioning were mostly based on parental report (especially concerning functioning prior to the course of vitamin treatment) and not on standardized assessment instruments. Although interesting, such presentations provide no probative data on the possible role of candidiasis in causing autism. Without reliable and valid evidence to the contrary, case reports cannot rule out a host of confounding variables, including any natural remission or change in symptoms due to developmental maturation or even merely to the passage of time. It is important to remember that many people, especially women, contract candida infections at different points in their lives, sometimes without even knowing that they are infected because the symptoms are so mild (Siegel, 1996). However, there is no evidence that even severe candidiasis in humans can produce brain damage that leads to the profound deficits in functioning found in autism.

MMR Vaccination

There has recently been much public concern that the mumps, measles, and rubella (MMR) vaccine is causing an increased incidence of autism. As evidence of the link between the MMR vaccine and autism, proponents point to the fact that reported cases of autism have increased dramatically over the past two decades, which appear to coincide with the widespread use of the MMR vaccine starting in 1979. In fact, Dales, Hammer, and Smith (2001) found in their analyses of California Department of Developmental Services records that the number of autistic disorder caseloads increase approximately 572% from 1980 to 1994. Indicating a similar trend in Europe, Kaye, Melero-Montes, and Jick (2001) reported that the yearly incidence of children diagnosed with autism increased sevenfold from 1988 to 1999 in the United Kingdom. Fears that the MMR vaccine may be responsible for this rise in the increasing incidence of autism have been picked up in the media and some parents have decided to decline vaccinations for their children in an effort to protect them from developing autism (Manning, 1999).

Rimland (2000) saw "medical overexuberance" as producing a tradeoff in which vaccinations protect children against acute diseases while simultaneously increasing their susceptibility to more chronic disorders, including autism, asthma, arthritis, allergies, learning disabilities, Crohn's disease, and attention deficit hyperactivity disorder. Pointing out that the average number of vaccines school-age children receive is now at 33, Rimland blamed the "vaccine industry" for making products that have not been properly tested before their widespread usage. He concluded by stating that research on this problem should be of the "highest priority."

In fact, it was preliminary research findings that initially raised the possibility that the MMR vaccine might be related to the apparent increase in the incidence of autism. The British researcher Andrew Wakefield and colleagues (1998) reported 12 case studies of children who were diagnosed with particular forms of intestinal abnormalities (e.g., ileal-lymphoid-nodular hyperplasia). Eight out of the 12 children demonstrated behavioral disorders diagnosed as representing autism, which reportedly occurred after MMR vaccination. The authors concluded that "the uniformity of the intestinal pathological changes and the fact that previous studies have found intestinal dysfunction in children with autistic-spectrum disorders, suggests that the connection is real and reflects a unique disease process" (p. 639). However, Wakefield et al. made it clear in their report that they did not prove an actual causal connection between the MMR vaccine and autism.

Although the Wakefield et al. (1998) case reports suggested that the MMR vaccine may be associated with autism, recent epidemiological research has provided strong evidence against any such connection. Kaye et al. (2001) conducted a time trend analysis on data taken from the UK general practice research database. As discussed earlier, they found that the yearly incidence of diagnosed autism increased dramatically over the last decade (0.3 per 10,000 persons in 1988 to 2.1 per 10,000 persons in 1999). However, the prevalence of MMR vaccination among children remained virtually constant during the analyzed time period (97% of the sample). If the MMR vaccine were the major cause of the increased reported incidence of autism, then the risk of being diagnosed with autism would be expected to stop rising shortly after the vaccine was instated at its current usage. However, this was clearly not the case in the Kaye study, and therefore no time correlation existed between MMR vaccination and the incidence of autism in each birth order cohort from 1988 to 1993.

In an analogue study in the United States, Dales et al. (2001) found the same results when using California Department of Developmental Services autism caseload data from the period 1980 to 1994. Once again, the time trend analysis did not show a significant correlation between MMR vaccine usage and the number of autism cases. Although MMR vaccine usage remained fairly constant over the observed period, there was a steady increase of autism caseloads over the time studied. It is important to note that the increased incidence of autism found in these two studies most likely reflects an increased awareness of autism-spectrum disorders by professionals and the public in general, along with changes in diagnostic criteria, rather than a true increase in the incidence of the disorder (Kaye et al., 2001). Most recently, the U.S. government's Institute of Medicine, in a comprehensive report cosponsored by the National Institutes of Health and the Centers for Disease Control and Prevention, recently concluded that there exists no good evidence linking the MMR vaccine and autism (Stratton, Gable, Shetty, & McCormick, 2001).

The MMR hypothesis reveals several important lessons for the student of autism. First, parents and professionals alike can easily misinterpret events that co-occur temporally as being causally related. The fact that the MMR vaccine is routinely given at around the same age that autism is first diagnosed reinforces the appearance of a link between the two. Second, the MMR-autism link reveals nicely the self-correcting nature of science. Like many hypotheses in science, the MMR-autism hypothesis, although reasonable when initially proposed, turned out to be incorrect or at best incomplete. Third, the issue illustrates the persistence of incorrect ideas concerning the etiology and treatment of autism even in the face of convincing evidence to the contrary. For example, Rimland (2000) purported to warn the public of the dangers of child vaccinations because of their link to autism and begins his article with the decree: "First, do no harm." However, recent research indicates that the MMR vaccine cannot be responsible for the sharp increases in diagnosed autism, and the real harm is the public health concern raised by encouraging parents to avoid vaccinating their children from serious diseases that can easily be prevented.

Current Scientific Findings

Research has implicated genetic factors, in utero insults, brain abnormalities, neurochemical imbalances, and immunological dysfunctions as contributing to autism. Siblings of individuals with autism have about a 3% chance of having the disorder, which is 50 times greater than the risk in the general population. In monozygotic twins, if one twin has autism, the second has a 36% chance of being diagnosed with the disorder and an 82% chance of developing some autistic symptoms (Trottier, Srivastava, & Walker, 1999). Although not definitive, the higher concordance rates in monozygotic twins relative to fraternal siblings suggests a genetic contribution to the etiology of autism. Nevertheless, the lack of 100% concordance for monozygotic twins suggests that the disorder probably develops as the result of combined effects of genetic and environmental factors.

Genetic disorders that have been identified as producing an increased risk of developing autism or pervasive developmental disorders include tuberous sclerosis, phenylketonuria, neurofibromatosis, fragile X syndrome, and Rett syndrome (Folstein, 1999; Trottier et al., 1999). Recent findings have also implicated a variation of the gene labeled HOXA1 on chromosome 7 as doubling the risk of autism, although this is only one of the many possible genes linked to the disorder (Rodier, 2000). Nevertheless, although some gene variants may increase the risk of developing autism, other variants may act to decrease the risk, explaining the large variability in the expression of autism.

Rubella infection of the mother during pregnancy and birth defects resulting from ethanol, valproic acid, and thalidomide exposure are also known in utero risk factors (Rodier, 2000). However, these factors can only explain the development of autism in a small subset of individuals. Regarding time for increased vulnerability, evidence from individuals exposed to thalidomide now points to the conclusion that the in utero insults that increase the risk of the autism probably occur quite early, within the first trimester of gestation (Stromland, Nordin, Miller, Akerstrom, & Gillberg, 1994). Other research that has compared individuals with autism with those without the disorder found differences in brain wave activity, brain (e.g., cerebellar) structures, and neurotransmitter levels (Trottier et al., 1999).

Scientific evidence supports the conclusion that autism is a behavioral manifestation of various brain abnormalities that likely develop as the result of a combination of genetic predispositions and early environmental (probably in utero) insults. Although recent scientific discoveries provide important clues to the development of the disorder, the etiology of autism is complex and the specific causes are still largely unknown.

Summary of Etiologic Theories and Research

There is currently no empirical support for theories that implicate unloving mothers, yeast infections, or childhood vaccinations as the cause of autism. The evidence invoked in support of these claims involves uncontrolled case studies and anecdotal reports. The confusion about the causes of autism appears to stem largely from illusory temporal correlations between the diagnosis of the disorder and normal events occurring in early childhood. No research has demonstrated a differential risk for autism due to maternal personality characteristics, the presence of candidiasis, or the use of the MMR vaccine. Scientific evidence points to genetic predispositions and various early environmental insults to the developing fetus as responsible for the development of the disorder.

References

Adams, L., & Conn, S. (1997). Nutrition and its relationship to autism. *Focus on Autism & Other Developmental Disabilities, 12,* 53–58.

Allen, J., DeMeyer, M. K., Norton, J. A., Pontus, W., & Yang, E. (1971). Intellectuality in parents of psychotic, subnormal, and normal children. *Journal of Autism & Childhood Schizophrenia, 3,* 311–326.

American Psychiatric Association (1994). *Diagnostic and statistical manual of mental disorders* (4th ed.). Washington, DC: Author.

Bettelheim, B. (1967). *The empty fortress.* New York: Free Press.

Bettison, S. (1996). The long-term effects of auditory training on children with autism. *Journal of Autism & Developmental Disorders, 26,* 361–374.

Bryson, S. (1997). Epidemiology of autism: Overview and issues outstanding. In D. J. Cohen & F. R. Volkmar (Eds.), *Handbook of autism and pervasive developmental disorders* (2nd ed., pp. 41–46). New York: Wiley.

Bryson, S. E., Clark, B. S., & Smith, I. M. (1988). First report of a Canadian epidemiological study of autistic syndromes. *Journal of Child Psychology and Psychiatry, 29,* 433–445.

Bunge, M. (1984). What is pseudoscience? *Skeptical Inquirer, 9,* 36–46.

Dales, L., Hammer, S. J., & Smith, N. J. (2001). Time trends in autism and in MMR immunization coverage in California. *Journal of the American Medical Association, 285,* 1183–1185.

Darnton, N. (1990, September 10). Beno Brutalheim? *Newsweek, 111*(11), 59–60.

Folstein, S. E. (1999). Autism. *International Review of Psychiatry, 11,* 269–278.

Fombonne, E. (1998). Epidemiology of autism and related conditions. In F. R. Volkmar (Ed.), *Autism and pervasive developmental disorders* (pp. 32–63). New York: Cambridge University Press.

Gardner, M. (2000). The brutality of Dr. Bettelheim. *Skeptical Inquirer, 24*(6), 12–14.

Gardner, M. (2001). Facilitated communication: A cruel farce. *Skeptical Inquirer, 25,* 17–19.

Gillberg, C. (1996). The psychopharmacology of autism and related disorders. *Journal of Psychopharmacology, 10,* 54–63.

Green, D. (2001). Autism and "voodoo science" treatments. *Priorities for Health, 13*(1), 27–32, 69.

Green, G. (1996a). Evaluating claims about treatments for autism. In C. Maurice, G. Green, & S. C. Luce (Eds.), *Behavioral intervention for young children with autism: A manual for parents and professionals* (pp. 15–28). Austin, TX: PRO-ED.

Herbert, J. D. Lilienfeld, S. O., Lohr, J. M., Montgomery, R. W., O'Donohue, W. T., Rosen, R. M., & Tolin, D. F. (2000). Science and pseudoscience in the development of eye movement desensitization and reprocessing: Implications for clinical psychology. *Clinical Psychology Review, 20,* 945–971.

Herbert, J. D., & Sharp, I. R. (2001). Pseudoscientific treatments for autism. *Priorities for Health, 13*(1), 23–26, 59.

Kanner, L. (1946). Autistic disturbances of affective contact. *American Journal of Psychiatry, 103,* 242–246.

Kanner, L. (1973). *Childhood psychosis: Initial studies and new insights.* Washington, DC: V. H. Winston & Sons.

Kaye, J. A., Melero-Montes, M., & Jick, H. (2001). Mumps, measles, and rubella vaccine and the incidence of autism recorded by general practitioners: A time trend analysis. *British Medical Journal, 322,* 460–463.

Lilienfeld, S. O. (1998). Pseudoscience is contemporary clinical psychology: What it is and what we can do about it. *The Clinical Psychologist, 51,* 3–9.

Mahler, M. (1968). *On human symbiosis and the vicissitudes of individuation.* New York: International Universities Press.

Manning, A. (1999, August 16). Vaccine-autism link feared. *USA Today.*

Pollak, R. (1997). *Creation of Dr. Bettelheim: A biography of Brauo Bettelheim.* New York: Simon & Schuster.

Rimland, B. (1988). Candida-caused autism? *Autism Research Review International Newsletter.* Retrieved December 6, 2001, from http://www.autism.com/ari/editorials/candida.html.

Rimland, B. (2000, April 26). Do children's shots invite autism? *Los Angeles Times.* Retrieved from http://www.latimes.com/archives.

Rodier, P. M. (2000). The early origins of autism. *Scientific American, 282,* 56–63.

Roser, K. (1996). A review of psychoanalytic theory and treatment of childhood autism. *Psychoanalytic Review, 83,* 325–341.

Siegel, B. (1996). *The world of the autistic child: Understanding and treating autistic spectrum disorders.* New York: Oxford University Press.

Shermer, M. (1997). *Why people believe weird things: Pseudoscience, superstition, and other confusions of our time.* New York: W. H. Freeman.

Smith, T. (1996). Are other treatments effective? In C. Maurice, G. Green, & S. C. Luce (Eds.), *Behavioral intervention for young children with autism: A manual for parents and professionals* (pp. 45–59). Austin, TX: PRO-ED.

Steffenburg, S., & Gillberg, C. (1986). Autism and autistic-like conditions in Swedish rural and urban areas: A population study. *British Journal of Psychiatry, 149,* 81–87.

Stratton, K., Gable, A., Shetty, P., & McCormick, M. (Eds.) (2001). *Immunization safety review: Measles-mumps-rubella vaccine and autism.* Washington, DC: National Academy Press.

Stromland, K., Nordin, V., Miller, M., Akerstrom, B., & Gillberg, C. (1994). Autism in thalidomide embryopathy: A population study. *Developmental Medicine and Child Neurology, 36,* 351–356.

Sugiyama, T., & Abe, T. (1989). The prevalence of autism in Nagoya, Japan: A total population study. *Journal of Autism & Developmental Disorders, 19,* 87–96.

Trottier, G., Srivastava, L., & Walker, C. D. (1999). Etiology of infantile autism: A review of recent advancements in genetic and neurobiological research. *Journal of Psychiatry & Neuroscience, 24,* 103–115.

Tustin, F. (1981). *Autistic states in children.* Boston: Routledge.

Volkmar, F. R., Szatmari, P., & Sparrow, S. S. (1993). Sex differences in pervasive developmental disorders. *Journal of Autism & Developmental Disorders, 23,* 579–591.

Wakefield, A. J., Murch, S. H., Anthony, A., Linnell, J., Casson, D. M., Malik, M., Berelowitz, M., Dhillon, A. P., Thomson, M. A., Harvey, P., Valentine, A., Davies, S. E., & Walker-Smith, J. A. (1998). Ileal-lymphoid-nodalar hyperplasia, non-specific colitis, and pervasive developmental disorder in children. *Lancet, 351,* 637–641.

Review and Contemplate

1. Describe two reasons autism is fertile ground for pseudoscience.
2. According to the psychoanalytic perspective, what is the main cause of autism? What does the scientific evidence suggest about this theory?
3. Briefly describe the "candida infection" theory of autism and why the theory is problematic.
4. Explain why the timing of the MMR vaccination might lead parents to believe that it causes autism. Briefly describe the evidence against this belief.

4.3

Project DARE: No Effects at 10-Year Follow-Up/

DONALD LYNAM, RICHARD MILICH, RICK ZIMMERMAN, SCOTT NOVAK, T. K. LOGAN, CATHERINE MARTIN, CARL LEUKEFELD, AND RICHARD CLAYTON

The Drug Abuse Resistance Education (DARE) program is very popular in public school systems across the country. My daughter completed this program when she was in the fifth grade, and perhaps you or your child completed this progam as well. The program utilizes police officers who teach children—typically in the fifth or sixth grade—information about drugs, skills to resist social pressures to use drugs, decision-making skills, and self-esteem. The Web site for DARE explains that it "was founded in 1983 in Los Angeles and has proven so successful that it is now being implemented in nearly 80 percent of our nation's school districts and in more than 54 countries around the world." DARE has received high praise from government officials, including Congress members, governors, and presidents. In fact, each year the president of the United States declares one day a national DARE day.

Prevention of illegal drug use among children is certainly a goal that many parents, police officers, and government officials desire, and this may be a major reason for the widespread acceptance and support of the DARE program. However, a crucial question is whether the DARE program actually decreases students' use of illegal drugs. The DARE Web site presents "research and evaulations" of the program, but most of the information listed there is not scientific research that has been published in scientific journals. Also, the published scientific research on DARE that has failed to find positive effects of the program is not mentioned on the Web site. You may recall from Chapter 1 that an emphasis on confirmation rather than refutation is one of the characteristics of pseudoscience.

In this article, Lynam et al. discuss the research evidence on the effectiveness of DARE. If you find the authors' statistical analysis difficult to understand, focus on the authors' verbal description of the results. Although the terminology the authors use to describe the analysis may sound complex, the analysis simply examines the effects of the DARE program while controlling for the influence of factors such as students' prior use of cigarettes or alcohol. Table 4.1 presents numbers called beta coefficients that indicate the size of each effect. Larger numbers mean a larger effect, and those numbers with asterisks beside them mean that the effect is greater than what one would expect by chance.

APA Reference

Lynam, D. R., Milich, R., Zimmerman, R., Novak, S. P., Logan, T. K., Martin, C., Leukefeld, C., & Clayton, R. (1999). Project DARE: No effects at 10-year follow-up. *Journal of Consulting and Clinical Psychology, 67,* 590–593.

The present study examined the impact of Project DARE (Drug Abuse Resistance Education), a widespread drug-prevention program, 10 years after administration. A total of 1,002 individuals who in 6th grade had either received DARE or a standard drug-education curriculum, were reevaluated at age 20. Few differences were found between the 2 groups in terms of actual drug use, drug attitudes, or self-esteem, and in no case did the DARE group have a more successful outcome than the comparison group. Possible reasons why DARE remains so popular, despite the lack of documented efficacy, are offered.

The use of illegal substances in childhood and adolescence occurs at an alarming rate. In response to this problem, there has been a widespread proliferation of schoolwide intervention programs designed to curb, if not eliminate, substance use in this population. Project DARE (Drug Abuse Resistance Education) is one of the most widely disseminated of these programs (Clayton, Cattarello, & Johnstone, 1996).

The widespread popularity of DARE is especially noteworthy, given the lack of evidence for its efficacy. Although few long-term studies have been conducted, the preponderance of evidence suggests that DARE has no long-term effect on drug use (Dukes, Ullman, & Stein, 1996; McNeal & Hansen, 1995; Rosenbaum, Flewelling, Bailey, Ringwalt, & Wilkinson, 1994). For example, Clayton et al. (1996) examined the efficacy of DARE among over 2,000 sixth-grade students in a city school system. The students' attitudes toward drugs, as well as actual use, were assessed before and after the intervention and then for the next 4 years through 10th grade. Although the DARE intervention produced a few initial improvements in the students' attitudes toward drug use, these changes did not persist over time. More importantly, there

Donald R. Lynam and Richard Milich, Department of Psychology, University of Kentucky; **Rick Zimmerman and Scott P. Novak,** Department of Behavioral Science, College of Medicine, University of Kentucky; **T. K. Logan and Carl Leukefeld,** Center on Drug and Alcohol Research, University of Kentucky; **Catherine Martin,** Department of Psychiatry, University of Kentucky; **Richard Clayton,** Center for Prevention Research, University of Kentucky.

This research was supported by Grant DA05312-10 from the National Institute on Drug Abuse and by General Clinical Research Center Grant M01 RR026202 from the National Institutes of Health.

Correspondence concerning this article should be addressed to Donald R. Lynam, Department of Psychology, University of Kentucky, Lexington, Kentucky 40506. Electronic mail may be sent to DLYNA1@POP.UKY.EDU.

were no effects in actual drug use initially or during the follow-up period. Further, results from shorter term studies are no more encouraging: these studies suggest that the short-term effects of DARE on drug use are, at best, small. In a meta-analysis of eight evaluations of the short-term efficacy of DARE, Ennett, Tobler, Ringwalt, and Flewelling (1994) found that the average effect size produced by DARE on drug use was .06, an effect size that does not differ significantly from zero.

Given the continued popularity of DARE, the limited number of long-term follow-ups, and the possibility of "sleeper effects" (effects showing up years after program participation), it seems important to continue to evaluate the long-term outcomes of DARE. The present study followed up the Clayton et al. (1996) sample through the age of 20. As far as we know, this 10-year follow-up is the longest reported on the efficacy of DARE. The original study, although presenting 5-year follow-up data, assessed adolescents during a developmental period when experimentation with drugs is quite prevalent and even considered normative by some authors (Moffitt, 1993; Shedler & Block, 1990). The prevalence of minor drug use during this period may suppress the effects of DARE. However, by the age of 20, experimentation with drugs has reached its peak and begun to decline: it may be during this period that the effects of DARE will become evident. In fact, Dukes, Stein, and Ullman (1997) reported a 6-year follow-up that demonstrated an effect for DARE on the use of harder drugs when participants were in the 12th grade; this effect was not present 3 years earlier.

METHOD

Participants

The initial sample for this study consisted of sixth graders in the 1987–1988 academic year in a Midwestern metropolitan area of 230,000. An overwhelming majority of the sample came from urban or suburban areas. With regard to socioeconomic status (SES), the area is considered one of the more prosperous counties is a state known for its pockets of extreme poverty. Although actual SES measures were not collected, given the size and inclusiveness of the sample, the sample can be assumed to represent all economic strata. Of the initial sample, 51% were male and 75% were White.

Data were collected before and after the administration of DARE. Follow-up questionnaire data were collected from the students over a 5-year period from 6th through 10th grade. Of the original participants, completed questionnaires were obtained on at least three occasions (once in 6th grade, once in 7th or 8th grade, and once in 9th or 10th grade) for 1,429 students. This became the sample targeted for the present young adult follow-up study. Completed mailed surveys were received from 1,002 participants between the ages of 19 and 21.

The final sample of 1,002 consisted of 431 (43%) men and 571 (57%) women. The average age of the participants was 20.1 (*SD* = 0.78). The racial composition of the sample was as follows: 748 (75.1%) were White, 204 (20.4%)

were African American, and 44 (0.4%) were of other race or ethnicity. Seventy-six percent of the final sample had received DARE, which corresponds almost exactly to the 75% of sixth graders who were originally exposed to DARE.

We conducted attrition analyses to determine whether the 1,002 participants differed from those 427 individuals who were eligible for the mailed survey study but from whom no survey was obtained.... Participants who were missing completed surveys tended to be older males who reported using cigarettes in the sixth grade. In general, attrition seemed to have little effect on the results that are reported here.

Procedures

Those individuals who could be located were sent a letter and a consent form requesting their participation in a follow-up to their earlier participation in the DARE evaluation. Those individuals who returned the signed consent form were mailed a questionnaire that took approximately 30 to 45 min to complete. Of the available sample, 5 had died, 176 refused to participate, 83 could not be located, and 163 were contacted but did not return the survey. For their time and effort, participants were paid $15 to $50.

Measures

Similar to the earlier data collection, participants were asked questions about their use of alcohol, tobacco, marijuana, and other illegal drugs. For each drug category, participants were asked to report how often they had used the substance in their lifetime, during the past year, and during the past month. In addition, participants were asked a variety of questions concerning their expectancies about drug use. For each drug, respondents reported how likely they believed using that drug would lead to five negative consequences (e.g., "get in trouble with the law" and "do poorly at school or work") as well as how likely they believed using that drug would lead to eight positive consequences (e.g., "feel good" and "get away from problems"). Negative and positive expectancy scores were formed for each drug at each age. Two potential mediators of the DARE intervention, peer-pressure resistance and self-esteem, were also assessed. Participants responded to nine items designed to assess the ability to resist negative peer pressure (e.g., "If one of your best friends is skipping class or calling in sick to work, would you skip too?"). Finally, participants responded to the 10-item Rosenberg Self-Esteem Scale (Rosenberg, 1965). All scale scores had acceptable reliabilities (alphas ranged from .73 to .93, with an average of .84).

Initial DARE Intervention

A complete description of the experimental and comparison interventions is contained in the Clayton et al. (1996) study. Twenty-three elementary schools were randomly assigned to receive the DARE intervention, whereas the remaining 8 schools received a standard drug-education curriculum. The DARE intervention was delivered by police officers in 1-hr sessions over 17 weeks. The focus of the DARE curriculum is on teaching students the skills needed to recognize and resist social pressures to use drugs. Additionally, the curriculum focuses on providing information about drugs, teaching decision-making skills, building self-esteem, and choosing healthy alternatives to drug use. The control condition was not a strict no-treatment condition but instead consisted of whatever the health teachers decided to cover concerning drug education in their classes. The drug education received by students in the control condition cannot be described in detail because of the considerable latitude on the part of teachers and schools in what was taught. Nonetheless, in many instances, emphasis was placed on the identification and harmful effects of drugs, peer pressure was frequently discussed, and videos using scare tactics were often shown. These drug education units lasted approximately 30 to 45 min over a period of 2 to 4 weeks.

RESULTS AND DISCUSSION

Because the school, and not the individual, was the unit of randomization in the present study, we used hierarchical linear modeling, with its ability to model the effect of organizational context on individual outcomes. For each of the substances (cigarettes, alcohol, and marijuana), we constructed three hierarchical linear models (HLMs) that examined amount of use, positive expectancies, and negative expectancies. We conducted additional analyses on peer-pressure resistance, self-esteem, and the variety of past-year illicit drug use. An HLM was used to model the effect of DARE on the school mean of each dependent variable (drug use and expectancies) while controlling for pre-DARE factors. This allowed for the comparison of how each school mean varied with the effect of DARE. We conducted preliminary analyses in which the effect of DARE was also modeled on the relationship between pre-DARE baseline and the substantive outcomes. Significant effects would suggest that DARE affected the relation between pre- and post-DARE outcomes. These effects were not significant and were thus fixed across schools. Respondents' sixth-grade reports of lifetime use served as baseline measures, whereas age-20 reports of past-month use of cigarettes, alcohol, and marijuana served as outcome measures.[1] The results of the full HLMs are presented in Table 4.1.

Cigarettes

Pre-DARE levels of use and negative expectancies about cigarette use were significantly related to their counterparts 10 years later. There were no relations between DARE status and cigarette use and expectancies, suggesting that DARE had no effect on either student behavior or expectancies.

---

[1]Results were unchanged when prevalence of use or heavy use, rather than frequency of use, was used as the outcome variable.

TABLE 4.1

Hierarchical Linear Models Examining the Influence of Project DARE on Age-20 Levels of Drug Use, Drug Expectancies, Peer-Pressure Resistance, and Self-Esteem

Variable	Fixed effect[a]
Frequency of past-month cigarette use	
Intercept (γ_0)	−.076
Level 1: Pre-DARE lifetime cigarette use (β_1)	.240***
Level 2: DARE status (γ_1)	.101
Negative expectancies toward cigarettes	
Intercept (γ_0)	.108
Level 1: Pre-DARE expectancies (β_1)	.145***
Level 2: DARE status (γ_1)	−.152
Positive expectancies toward cigarettes	
Intercept (γ_0)	−.071
Level 1: Pre-DARE expectancies (β_1)	.009
Level 2: DARE status (γ_1)	.053
Frequency of past-month alcohol use	
Intercept (γ_0)	−.034
Level 1: Pre-DARE lifetime alcohol use (β_1)	.115**
Level 2: DARE status (γ_1)	−.018
Negative expectancies toward alcohol	
Intercept (γ_0)	.075
Level 1: Pre-DARE expectancies (β_1)	.105**
Level 2: DARE status (γ_1)	−.034
Positive expectancies toward alcohol	
Intercept (γ_0)	−.052
Level 1: Pre-DARE expectancies (β_1)	.085*
Level 2: DARE status (γ_1)	.048
Frequency of past-month marijuana use	
Intercept (γ_0)	.033
Level 1: Pre-DARE lifetime marijuana use (β_1)	.098**
Level 2: DARE status (γ_1)	−.044
Negative expectancies toward marijuana	
Intercept (γ_0)	−.013
Level 1: Pre-DARE expectancies (β_1)	.123***
Level 2: DARE status (γ_1)	.039
Positive expectancies toward marijuana	
Intercept (γ_0)	−.021
Level 1: Pre-DARE expectancies (β_1)	.045
Level 2: DARE status (γ_1)	.011
Variety of illegal drugs used in past year[b]	
Intercept (γ_0)	−.081
Level 2: DARE status (γ_1)	.080
Peer-pressure resistance	
Intercept (γ_0)	.058
Level 1: Pre-DARE peer-pressure resistance (β_1)	.118**
Level 2: DARE status (γ_1)	−.139

Variable	effect[a]
Self-esteem	
Intercept (γ_0)	.133
Level 1: Pre-DARE self-esteem (β_1)	.129[**]
Level 2: DARE status (γ_1)	−.181[*]

Note. DARE status is coded 0 = control, 1 = DARE intervention.
[a]All beta coefficients presented are group-mean-centered, standardized effect sizes. [b]There were no base-line measures for this model; thus, a means-as-outcomes model was estimated.
[*]$p < .05$; [**]$p < .01$; [***]$p < .001$.

Alcohol

Pre-DARE levels of lifetime alcohol use and positive and negative expectancies about alcohol use were significantly related to their counterparts 10 years later. DARE status was unrelated to alcohol use or either kind of alcohol expectancy at age 20.

Marijuana

Pre-DARE levels of past-month marijuana use and negative expectancies about use were significantly related to their counterparts 10 years later. Similar to the findings for cigarettes, respondents' sixth-grade positive expectancies about marijuana use were not significantly related to marijuana expectancies at age 20. DARE status was unrelated to marijuana use or either kind of marijuana expectancy at age 20.

Illicit Drug Use

Finally, the number of illicit drugs (except marijuana) used in the past year was examined. Because no measures for these items were obtained during the initial baseline measurement, we estimated a means-as-outcomes HLM using no Level 1 predictors and only DARE status as a predictor at Level 2. The results show that DARE had no statistically significant effect on the variety of illicit drugs used.

Peer-Pressure Resistance

The results for peer-pressure resistance were similar to previous results. Pre-DARE levels of peer-pressure resistance were significantly related to peer-pressure resistance levels 10 years later, whereas DARE status was unrelated to peer-pressure resistance levels.

Self-Esteem

Finally, pre-DARE levels of self-esteem were significantly related to self-esteem levels at age 20. Surprisingly, DARE status in the sixth grade was negatively related to self-esteem at age 20, indicating that individuals who were exposed to DARE in the sixth grade had lower levels of self-esteem 10 years later. This results was clearly unexpected and cannot be accounted for theoretically; as such, it would seem best to regard this as a chance finding that is unlikely to be replicated.

Our results are consistent in documenting the absence of beneficial effects associated with the DARE program. This was true whether the outcome consisted of actual drug use or merely attitudes toward drug use. In addition, we examined processes that are the focus of intervention and purportedly mediate the impact of DARE (e.g., self-esteem and peer resistance), and these also failed to differentiate DARE participants from nonparticipants. Thus, consistent with the earlier Clayton et al. (1996) study, there appear to be no reliable short-term, long-term, early adolescent, or young adult positive outcomes associated with receiving the DARE intervention.

Although one can never prove the null hypothesis, the present study appears to overcome some troublesome threats to internal validity (i.e., unreliable measures and low power). Specifically, the outcome measures collected exhibited good internal consistencies at each age and significant stability over the 10-year follow-up period. For all but two measures (positive expectancies for cigarettes and marijuana), measurements taken in sixth grade, before the administration of DARE, were significantly related to measurements taken 10 years later, with coefficients ranging from small ($\beta = 0.09$ for positive expectancies about alcohol) to moderate ($\beta = 0.24$ for cigarette use). Second, it is extremely unlikely that we failed to find effects for DARE that actually existed because of a lack of power. Thus, it appears that one can be fairly confident that DARE created no lasting changes in the outcomes examined here.

Advocates of DARE may argue against our findings. First, they may argue that we have evaluated an out-of-date version of the program and that a newer version would have fared better. Admittedly, we evaluated the original DARE curriculum, which was created 3 years before the beginning of this study. This is an unavoidable difficulty in any long-term follow-up study; the important question becomes, How much change has there been? To the best of our knowledge, the goals (i.e., "to keep kids off drugs") and foci of DARE (e.g., resisting peer pressure) have remained the same across time as has the method of delivery (e.g., police officers). We believe that any changes in DARE have been more cosmetic than substantive, but this is difficult to evaluate until DARE America shares the current content of the curriculum with the broader prevention community.

One could also argue that the officers responsible for delivering DARE in the present study failed to execute the program as intended. This alternative seems unlikely. DARE officers receive a structured, 80-hr training course that covers a number of topics, including specific knowledge about drug use and consequences of drug use, as well as teaching techniques and classroom-management skills. Considerable emphasis is given to practice teaching and to following the lesson plans. Although we did not collect systematic data on treatment fidelity in the present study, a process evaluation by Clayton, Cattarello, Day, and Walden (1991) attested to the fidelity to the curriculum and to the quality of teaching by the DARE officers.

Finally, advocates of DARE might correctly point out that the present study did not compare DARE with a no-intervention condition but rather with a control condition in which health teachers did their usual drug-education programs. Thus, technically, we cannot say that DARE was not efficacious but instead that it was no more efficacious than whatever the teachers had been doing previously. Although this is a valid point, it is unreasonable to argue that a more expensive and longer running treatment (DARE) should be preferred over a less expensive and less time-consuming one (health education) in the absence of differential effectiveness (Kazdin & Wilson, 1978).

This report adds to the accumulating literature on DARE's lack of efficacy in preventing or reducing substance use. This lack of efficacy has been noted by other investigators in other samples (e.g., Dukes et al., 1996; Ennett et al., 1994; Wysong, Aniskiewicz, & Wright, 1994). Yet DARE continues to be offered in a majority of the nation's public schools at great cost to the public (Clayton et al., 1996). This raises the obvious question, why does DARE continue to be valued by parents and school personnel (Donanermeyer & Wurschmidt, 1997) despite its lack of demonstrated efficacy? There appear to be at least two possible answers to this question. First, teaching children to refrain from drug use is a widely accepted approach with which few individuals would argue. Thus, similar to other such interventions, such as the "good touch/bad touch" programs to prevent sexual abuse (Reppucci & Haugaard, 1989), these "feel-good" programs are ones that everyone can support, and critical examination of their effectiveness may not be perceived as necessary.

A second possible explanation for the popularity of programs such as DARE is that they *appear* to work. Parents and supporters of DARE may be engaging in an odd kind of normative comparison (Kendall & Grove, 1988), comparing children who go through DARE with children who do not. The adults rightly perceive that most children who go through DARE do not engage in problematic drug use. Unfortunately, these individuals may not realize that the vast majority of children, even without any intervention, do not engage in problematic drug use. In fact, even given the somewhat alarming rates of marijuana experimentation in high school (e.g., 40%; Johnston, O'Malley, & Bachman, 1996), the *majority* of students do not engage in any drug use. That is, adults may believe that drug use among adolescents is much more frequent than it actually is. When the children who go through DARE are compared with this "normative" group of drug-using teens, DARE appears effective.

References

Clayton, R. R., Cattarello, A. M., Day, L. E., & Walden, K. P. (1991). Persuasive communication and drug abuse prevention: As evaluation of the DARE program. In L. Donobew, H. Sypher, & W. Bukowski (Eds.), *Persuasive communication and drug abuse prevention* (pp. 295–313). Hillsdale, NJ: Erlbaum.

Clayton, R. R., Cattarello, A. M., & Johnstone, B. M. (1996). The effectiveness of Drug Abuse Resistance Education (Project DARE): 5-year follow-up results. *Preventive Medicine, 25,* 307–318.

Donnermeyer, J. F., & Wurschmidt, T. N. (1997). Educators' perceptions of the D.A.R.E. program. *Journal of Drug Education, 27*, 259–276.

Dukes, R. L., Stein, J. A., & Ullman, J. B. (1997). Long-term impact of Drug Abuse Resistance Education (D.A.R.E.). *Evaluation Review, 21*, 483–500.

Dukes, R. L., Ullman, J. B., & Stein, J. A. (1996). A three-year follow-up of Drug Abuse Resistance Education (D.A.R.E.). *Evaluation Review, 20*, 49–66.

Ennett, S. T., Tobler, N. S., Ringwalt, C. L., & Flewelling, R. L. (1994). How effective is drug abuse resistance education? A meta-analysis of Project DARE outcome evaluations. *American Journal of Public Health, 84*, 1394–1401.

Johnston, L. D., O'Malley, P. M., & Bachman, J. G. (1996). *National survey results on drug use from the Monitoring the Future Study, 1975–1994.* Rockville, MD: National Institute on Drug Abuse.

Kazdin, A. E., & Wilson, G. T. (1978). Criteria for evaluating psychotherapy. *Archives of General Psychiatry, 35*, 407–416.

Kendall, P. C., & Grove, W. M. (1988). Normative comparisons in therapy outcomes. *Behavioral Assessment, 10*, 147–158.

McNeal, R. B., & Hansen, W. B. (1995). An examination of strategies for gaining convergent validity in natural experiments. *Evaluation Review, 19*, 141–158.

Moffitt, T. E. (1993). Adolescence-limited and life-course persistent antisocial behavior: A developmental taxonomy. *Psychological Review, 100*, 674–701.

Reppucci, N. D., & Haugaard, J. J. (1989). Prevention of child sexual abuse: Myth or reality. *American Psychologist, 44*, 1266–1275.

Rosenbaum, D. P., Flewelling, R. P., Bailey, S. L., Ringwalt, C. L., & Wilkinson, D. L. (1994). Cops in the classroom: A longitudinal evaluation of Drug Abuse Resistance Education (D.A.R.E.). *Journal of Research in Crime and Delinquency, 31*, 3–31.

Rosenberg, M. (1965). *Society and the adolescent self-image.* Princeton, NJ: Princeton University Press.

Shedler, J., & Block, J. (1990). Adolescent drug use and psychological health: A longitudinal inquiry. *American Psychologist, 45*, 612–630.

Wysong, E., Aniskiewicz, R., & Wright, D. (1994). Truth and DARE: Tracking drug education to graduation and as symbolic politics. *Social Problems, 41*, 448–472.

Received March 12, 1998
Revision received November 10, 1998
Accepted November 12, 1998

Review and Contemplate

1. Briefly describe the DARE program.
2. Briefly describe the design of the study conducted by Lynam et al. (1999). What impact did DARE have on students' use of cigarettes, alcohol, and marijuana? What effect did it have on their resistance to peer pressure and their self-esteem?
3. What have research studies, other than the one by Lynam et al. (1999), found about the effectiveness of DARE?
4. Why does DARE continue to be valued by parents and school personnel?
5. Why might the DARE program be considered pseudoscientific? Which of the six characteristics of pseudoscience, discussed in Chapter 1, seem most relevant to the DARE program?

5.1

What's That I Smell?
The Claims of Aromatherapy/
LYNN MCCUTCHEON

Aromatherapy is defined by the National Association for Holistic Aromatherapy as "the art and science of utilizing naturally extracted aromatic essences from plants to balance, harmonize and promote the health of body, mind and spirit." They claim that aromatherapy has "proven, therapeutic benefits for a variety of conditions," including depression, poor memory, fear, wounds, motion sickness, asthma, varicose veins, wrinkles, and sprains.

Psychologists have long known that odors influence our memories and emotions. For example, pleasant odors, such as those of chocolate chip cookies or cinnamon rolls, may evoke pleasant memories and emotions. Some research even suggests that the presence of pleasant odors can boost the likelihood that people will help others in need of a favor. However, the claims of aromatherapists go well beyond the documented effects of odors. For example, an aromatherapist might claim that chamomile is good for insomnia or that jasmine promotes sexual arousal. As mentioned in the previous paragraph, the National Association for Holistic Aromatherapy lists a wide variety of serious ailments that supposedly benefit from aromatherapy. In this article, McCutcheon discusses the problems with such claims.

Chapter 1 pointed out that normal cognitive and social processes—such as the difficulties people have with methodological reasoning—may lead to pseudoscientific beliefs. One aspect of methodological reasoning that is relevant to this article is the need to consider how confounding variables—that is, variables other than aromatherapy that were present at the same time as the therapy—may explain changes in a person's health following a treatment. For example, if a person put a few drops of an aromatic oil into a warm bath in order to relieve stress, was it the aromatic oil or the warm bath that produced the decrease in stress? In this situation the warm bath is confounded with the aromatherapy, and we cannot determine what caused the improvement. McCutcheon refers to this problem as "confused causation."

APA Reference

McCutcheon, L. (1996, May/June). What's that I smell? The claims of aromatherapy. *Skeptical Inquirer, 20,* 35–37.

A small dose of aromatic oil may make for a pleasant experience, but the claims of aromatherapy go way beyond that.

Aromatherapy typically involves putting a few drops of some pleasant-smelling, plant-derived oil in your bath water, sniffing it from an inhaler, or massaging it directly into your skin. I sampled a number of these "essential oils," as they are called, and I was impressed with their unique aromas. So what's the problem with smelling something fragrant while you are bathing or while you are getting massaged? According to John Meisenheimer, who practices dermatology in Orlando, Florida, a tiny percentage of the population is allergic to some essential oils. But for the rest of us, the answer is, "nothing." A small dose of aromatic oil probably won't hurt you a bit, and if you enjoy the smell, that's fine!

The problem lies with the claims made by aromatherapy's most widely known practitioners—claims that are causally confused, ambiguous, dubious, and unsupported by scientific evidence. After reading several books and articles written by the enthusiastic supporters of aromatherapy, I believe that there are some recurrent themes that are worth a closer look.

One such theme is what I call "confused causation." Virtually all aromatherapists claim that if you relax for several minutes in warm bath water to which has been added a few drops of essential oil, you will get out of the tub feeling pleasant. I agree, but what causes the pleasantness? Is it the warmth, the water, the minutes spent resting, the few drops of oil, or some combination thereof? It would be easy to conduct an experiment in order to find out, but for some strange reason aromatherapists haven't seen fit to do this. Instead, they imply that the essential oil is the main cause. Says Meisenheimer: "The amount of essential oil from a few drops placed in your bath that might actually penetrate the stratum corneum [skin] is probably too small to have any meaningful, systemic, physiologic effect."

Other examples of confused causation permeate aromatherapists' writings. Hoffmann (1987, p. 94) claims that chamomile is good for insomnia *if* taken in a late bath. Is it the lateness or the chamomile that makes you sleepy? For stress, Lavabre (1990, p. 108) recommends relaxation, a better diet, nutritional supplements, more exercise, and a few drops of an oil blend. Heinerman informs us (1988, p. 197) that jasmine oil massaged into the abdomen and groin promotes sexual stimulation. I'll bet it does, with or without the jasmine. On page 301 he suggests that to make unsafe water safe, boil it and add rosemary, sage, or thyme before drinking. The heat probably kills most of the germs. Edwards (1994, p. 135) mentions that many patients in hospitals in England receive massages with essential oils. According to her, "the relaxing and uplifting effect of the oils helps boost the morale of the patients." Isn't it possible that the massage did as much to boost morale as the oils did?

One of the favorite tactics employed by aromatherapists is the use of ambiguous claims. Any good psychic can tell you that you *never* make a specific prediction. You always leave yourself enough room so that whatever the outcome, you can claim success. Judging from what I read, the aromatherapists have mastered this strategy. Here are some of my favorites, followed by my brief commentary.

According to Frawley (1992, p. 155), incense "cleanses the air of negative energies." What are negative energies? The reader is encouraged to get massaged with oil regularly (p. 155) because this "keeps the nerves in balance." How would we know an unbalanced nerve if we saw one? Hoffmann tells us (p. 95) that ylang ylang is "supposedly an aphrodisiac." Is it or or isn't it? Lavabre declares (p. 114) that benzoin resinoid will "drive our evil spirits." I'd love to see that. Presumably spruce oil is an even better essence because it is recommended (p. 64) "for any type of psychic work." Why limit yourself to evil spirits? Edwards (p. 134) quotes Visant Lad as saying that "life energy enters the body through breath taken through the nose." Is life energy the same thing as oxygen, and if so, why can't it enter through the mouth? About tea tree oil, Edwards opines (p. 135), "There is hope [it] may play a role in the successful treatment of AIDS." Is it hope or is it evidence? On the same page she tells readers that aromatherapy is good for "restoring harmony and balance between the mind and body." Such a phrase can mean almost anything you wish.

Not all of the claims are hopelessly ambiguous or unlikely to be true. I did a computer search of the psychological literature back to 1967, using the terms *essential oils, aromatherapy,* and the names of 23 common essences. I found that chamomile (Roberts and Williams 1992) can put people in a better mood, and lavender sometimes causes mistakes in arithmetic (Ludvigson and Rottman 1989). Furthermore, several of the odors used by aromatherapists are capable of producing physiological arousal as measured by electroencephalogram (EEG) recordings (Klemm et al. 1992); and emotional changes, as measured by self-report (Kikuchi et al. 1992; Nakano et al. 1992). Peppermint odor appears to be capable of causing very small EEG, electromyogram (EMG), and heart rare changes during sleep (Badia et al. 1990); and some odors can modify artificially induced sleep time in mice (Tsuchiya et al. 1991). There is evidence that specific odors can better enable one to recall information that was learned in the presence of that odor (Smith et al. 1992).

As a whole, these findings stretched to the limit would support only small craft, sailing cautiously near the shores of the aromatic sea. Unfortunately, some aromatherapists have been more than willing to sail boldly into uncharted waters. Consider these claims about specific essential oils, with my comments.

"A few drops of jasmine (Tisserand 1988, p. 87) cures postnatal depression." I didn't find any olfactory research that mentions postnatal depression. "Marjoram oil (Tisserand, p. 37) turns off sexual desire." The few studies I found that mentioned marjoram had nothing to do with sex. Price (1991, p. 93) tells us that juniper berry is "relaxing" and "stimulating" (both?), and she (p. 48) and Valner (1982, p. 87) recommend lavender for insomnia. The Klemm study showed that lavender was both arousing and unpleasant. Hoffmann (p. 94) claims that patchouli is good for anxiety. My computer search of the word *patchouli* turned up nothing. Valnet (p. 70) claims that ylang ylang is good for one's sex drive. *Ylang ylang* didn't turn up anything either.

Other claims of dubious validity are common to the writings of aromatherapists—broad claims that are related to the practice of aromatherapy in general. The following claims are my words, but they represent a synthesis of views expressed by the authors listed.

- *Smell is the most direct route to the brain.* (Avery 1992; Edwards 1994; Green 1992; Raphael 1994). The implication is that smell is superior to the other senses because olfactory information gets to the brain quickest, and since aromatherapy is concerned with smell, it is a superior method of treatment. Olfactory information gets to the brain very quickly, but so does auditory, tactile, and visual information. The differences would certainly be measured in milliseconds, and it would have no practical consequence. The olfactory sense is directly linked to the limbic system—a portion of the brain concerned with emotionality and memories. The aromatherapists make much of this—the smell of ginger evokes memories of grandma's cookies, etc. What they don't tell you is that the sight of grandma's photo or hearing her voice can do the same. All the senses are part of a massive network that links all parts of the brain. Smell enjoys no particular advantage when it comes to access to or speed of access to various parts of the brain.
- *Natural oils are better than synthetic ones.* (Avery 1992; Edwards 1994; Hillyer 1994; Lavabre 1990; Price 1991; Raphael 1994; Rose 1988). Most of these authors felt it unnecessary to explain such a statement, but Lavabre told readers that "natural" molecules work better because they have memory (p. 49). It is possible to make a synthetic preparation identical on a molecular level to the most important compound in an essential oil. John Renner, who has heard many of the bizarre claims made by aromatherapists, told me that if the molecules are the same, "I doubt seriously that your body could tell the difference." Given that essential oils contain several compounds, it seems possible that a natural oil might have more than one active agent. If that is so, then aromatherapists should be spearheading the research effort to determine which chemical compounds are inducing the changes they claim are taking place. Instead, most of them seem all too willing to assume that natural oils are better, and that there is no need to defend this assertion with any rationale or research evidence.

■ *Essential oils can help your memory.* (Hoffmann 1987; Lavabre 1990; Price 1991; Valnet 1982). I found no evidence to support this, and none of these authors provided a hint about how they arrived at that conclusion. Psychologist Elizabeth Loftus, a world-renowned human memory expert, told me in a personal communication that she knows "of no cogent scientific evidence that smells cure amnesia, or that they strengthen memory." There is such a phenomenon as context-dependent learning. It has been shown that it is easier to remember X when you can return to the environment or context in which you learned X. Presumably, the context provides cues that make it easier to recall X. It has further been shown that at least one essential oil can serve as a contextual cue (Smith et al. 1992). If this is the basis for the above-mentioned claim, it is highly misleading. The essence itself is not important, only the fact that it was a significant part of the context in which the original learning took place. In other words, if the essence wasn't present when you learned X, then it won't help you recall it later.

■ *Scientists are doing a lot of research on essential oils.* (Avery 1992; Price 1991; Rose 1988; Valner 1982). Statements like this are usually followed by specific claims. The implication is that these claims are supported by scientific research. As we saw earlier, that isn't necessarily true. Whether or not scientists really *are* doing a lot of research on essential oils is debatable. By comparison with 50 years ago, there is probably more research on essential oils today. By comparison with hearing and vision, research on the consequences of smelling essential oils lags way behind. If there really is a lot of research on the effects of essential oils, why is it that these authors are so reluctant to cite it? Their books and articles rarely list or mention any scientific journal articles. Instead, if there are any references at all they are to books written by other aromatherapists.

All of this sounds as though I am strongly opposed to the use of essential oils. I'm not! If it pleases you to put some in your bath water or have a little rubbed on your back once in a while, by all means, go ahead. It is not the odor that arises from these fragrances that is troubling, it is the stench arising from the unwarranted claims made about them.

References

Avery, A. 1992. *Aromatherapy and You.* Kailua, HI: Blue Heron Hill Press.

Badia, P., et al. 1990. Responsiveness to olfactory stimuli presented in sleep. *Physiology and Behavior* 48: 87–90.

Edwards, L. 1994. Aromatherapy and essential oils. *Healthy and Naural Journal.* October, pp. 134–137.

Frawley, D. 1992. Herbs and the mind. In *American Herbalism; Essays on Herbs and Herbalism*, ed. by M. Tierra. Freedom, Calif.: Crossing Press.

Green, M. 1992. Simpler scents: The combined use of herbs and essential oils. In *American Herbalism: Essays on Herbs and Herbalism*, ed. by M. Tierra. Freedom, Calif.: Crossing Press.

Heinerman, J. 1988. *Heinerman's Encyclopedia of Fruits, Vegetables, and Herbs*, West Nyack, N.Y.: Parker Publishing.

Hillyer, P. 1994. "Making $cents with Aromatherapy." *Whole Foods*, February, pp. 26–35.

Hoffmann, D. 1987. Aromatherapy. In *The Herbal Handbook*. Rochester, Vt.: Healing Arts Press.

Kikuchi, A., et al. 1992. Effects of odors on cardiac response patterns and subjective states in a reaction time task. *Psychological Folia* 51: 74–82.

Klemm, W. R. et al. 1992. Topographical EEG maps of human response to odors. *Chemical Senses* 17: 347–361.

Lavabre, M. 1990. *Aromatherapy Workbook*. Rochester, Vt.: Healing Arts Press.

Ludvigson, H., and T. Rottman. 1989. Effects of ambient odors of lavender and cloves on cognition, memory, affect and mood. *Chemical Sense* 14: 525–536.

Nakano, Y., et al. 1992. A study of fragrance impressions, evaluation and categorization. *Psychologica Folia* 51: 83–90.

Price, S. 1991. *Aromatherapy for Common Ailments*. New York: Simon and Schuster.

Raphael, A. 1994. "Ahh! Aromatherapy." *Delicious*, December pp. 47–48.

Roberts, A., and J. Williams, 1992. The effect of olfactory stimulation on fluency, vividness of imagery and associated mood: A preliminary study. *British Journal of Medical Psychology* 65: 197–199.

Rose, J. 1988. Healing scents from herbs: Aromatherapy. In *Herbal Handbook*. Escondido, Calif.: Bernard Jensen Enterprises.

Smith, D. G., et al. 1992. Verbal memory elicited by ambient odor. *Perceptual and Motor Skills* 74: 339–343.

Tisserand, M. 1988. *Aromatherapy for Women*. Rochester, Vt.: Healing Arts Press.

Tsuchiya, T., et al. 1991. Effects of olfactory stimulation on the sleep time induced by pentobarbital administration in mice. *Brain Research Bulletin* 26: 397–401.

Valnet, J. 1982. *The Practice of Aromatherapy*. London: C. W. Daniel.

Review and Contemplate

1. Explain and give two examples of the problem of "confused causation" with respect to claims made for the effects of aromatherapy.

2. Give three examples of how aromatherapists make ambiguous claims about aromatherapy, making it difficult to determine if the claims are accurate.

3. If there is some scientific evidence that odors can influence our mood and memory, why would aromatherapy be considered a pseudoscience?

4. Explain how odors might improve memory recall through context-dependent learning. How is this different from aromatherapists' claim that "essential oils can help your memory"?

5.2   *What You Expect is What You Believe (But Not Necessarily What You Get):* A Test of the Effectiveness of Subliminal Self-Help Audiotapes/

ANTHONY PRATKANIS, JAY ESKENAZI, AND ANTHONY GREENWALD

Subliminal messages are those that are so faint or fast that people are unaware that they have been exposed to them. The public's fear over the potential power of subliminal messages to influence our behavior was prompted by a report by James Vicary in the late 1950s. Vicary claimed that he used subliminal messages to persuade people to buy more popcorn and Coke while they were watching a movie. The subliminal messages were the words "EAT POPCORN" and "DRINK COKE," which were flashed on the movie screen so fast that moviegoers could not detect the words. Today marketers sell subliminal messages for a variety of purposes, including self-improvement. You can purchase subliminal tapes designed to help you lose weight, improve your self-esteem, quit smoking or drinking, restore sexual urges, and improve your memory.

This selection contains excerpts from an article by Pratkanis et al. in which they examined the effectiveness of self-help subliminal tapes. Their article nicely illustrates the difference between scientific and pseudoscientific approaches to evaluating subliminal self-help tapes. A pseudoscientist might simply point to the testimonials of satisfied users of subliminal tapes; for example, people who use subliminal tapes designed to improve their memory might report memory improvements after using the tapes. One problem with this evidence is that people's reports of memory improvement might be due more to their expectations that these tapes would work than to an actual effect of the subliminal tapes. Pratkanis et al. describe a scientific study designed to investigate this possibility.

APA Reference

Pratkanis, A. R., Eskenazi, J., & Greenwald, A. G. (1994). What you expect is what you believe (but not necessarily what you get): A test of the effectiveness of subliminal self-help audiotapes. *Basic and Applied Social Psychology, 15,* 251–276.

Seventy-eight subjects, ranging in age from 18 to 60 years, participated in an experiment on the effectiveness of commercially produced subliminal self-help audiotapes. Upon completing pretest memory and self-esteem tests, subjects randomly received either a subliminal self-help tape designed to improve memory or increase self-esteem and were told that they had received either a memory or a self-esteem tape. After listening to the tape for 5 weeks in a home environment, subjects returned to the laboratory for memory and self-esteem tests. The results showed that the subliminal self-help tapes did not affect any of the performance measures in a manner consistent with manufacturer claims. However, subjects' perceptions of personal improvement were consistent with their expectations. Specifically, subjects who thought they had listened to a self-esteem tape were more likely to indicate that their self-esteem had improved and subjects who thought they had listened to a memory tape were more likely to indicate their memory had improved regardless of the actual subliminal content.

In 1987 Americans spent over $50 million on subliminal tapes and materials designed for therapeutic purposes—a 10% increase over 1986 sales (Natale, 1988). In their search for better self and health, consumers purchased subliminal tapes designed to accomplish such goals as improving self-esteem, increasing memory abilities, reducing weight, controlling anger and temper, and increasing sexual responsiveness. The tapes supposedly work, according to manufacturers, because they contain inaudible messages directed at the subconscious. The purpose of this study is to evaluate the effectiveness of one set of mass-marketed subliminal tapes.[1]

CLAIMS FOR THE POWER OF SUBLIMINAL INFLUENCE

The supposed power of subliminal messages was first brought to the public's attention in the late 1950s by James Vicary (for history, see Pratkanis, 1992; Rogers, 1992–1993). During a showing of the movie *Picnic*, Vicary claimed to have flashed the words *EAT POPCORN* and *DRINK COKE* at one third of a millisecond. As a result, lobby sales of popcorn increased by 57.7% and Coke by 18.1% (for reports of Vicary's study, see Cousins, 1957; "Psychologists Hit use," 1958). Later, Vicary admitted that he had actually done little research and that his data base was "too small to be meaningful" (Danzig, 1962, p. 73; see Weir, 1984).

Many Americans believe in the power of subliminal influence. A public opinion poll shows that almost 81% of the respondents who had heard of subliminal advertising believed that it was a current practice; over 68% believed it to be successful in selling products (Zanot, Pincus, & Lamp, 1983). The public's belief in the power of subliminal persuasion has been reinforced by numerous news articles (e.g., Cousins, 1957) and by Wilson Bryan Key's best-selling books (1973, 1976, 1980, 1989; see also Bornstein, 1989). In response to public concern, subliminal advertising has been banned in Australia

---

[1]Requests for reprints should be sent to Anthony R. Pratkanis, Board of Psychology, University of California, Santa Cruz, CA 95064.

and Britain, results in the loss of a broadcast license in the United States, and has been ruled to be speech not protected by the First Amendment to the U.S. Constitution.

More recently, the proponents of subliminal influence have attempted to use the technique for prosocial goals such as reducing crime and theft in stores (see "Words Whispered," 1980) and realizing therapeutic benefits and human potential. For example, the sales catalog of a leading manufacturer of subliminal self-help audiotapes states:

> The secret [of our audiotapes] is really simple: they allow you to *directly* access the subconscious mind. And in order to make lasting improvements in your life, you must make changes at a subconscious level. Subliminal tapes permit you to do just that, by working directly with that portion of your mind which actually maintains ongoing control of your life. There is still another reason why subliminal tapes are so effective: they permit positive messages to reach the subconscious without interference from the conscious mind. This is important, because often your conscious mind will question or reject certain statements . . . But subliminal messages bypass the conscious mind, and imprint directly on the subconscious mind, where they create the basis for the kind of life you want.

Some recent studies have been conducted to support the tape manufacturers' claims. In a survey of subliminal tape customers, VandenBoogert (1984) found that the more times a customer reported listening to a tape, the more likely they would answer yes to the question, "Did the tape provide the benefit expected?" Borgeat and Chaloult (1985) broadcast subliminal relaxation tapes for 6 years on CIME-FM radio in Canada. A listener survey found widespread belief in the value of the broadcast with the tapes becoming a commercial success, selling over 50,000 copies (a "Gold Record"). In other research, Borgeat, Elie, Chaloult, and Chabot (1985) reported that auditory subliminal stimuli were capable of evoking psychophysiological responses. Both the Vanden Boogert and Borgeat lines of research can be criticized on several grounds, including low response rate (15.5% in the VandenBoogert study), lack of a control group in the Borgeat and Chaloult report, and only one of seven patterns of data in the Borgeat et al. study supporting their claims (see Pratkanis, 1990). Nevertheless, this and similar research is often cited as evidence for the effectiveness of subliminal self-help audiotapes (Shulman, Shuiman, & Rafferty, 1990; Taylor, 1988) and for the effectiveness of subliminal auditory stimulation in general (Shevrin, 1990).

A SKEPTICAL APPRAISAL OF SUBLIMINAL INFLUENCE CLAIMS

Research on subliminal stimulation began before the turn of the century (Suslowa, 1863). The accumulated research has shed light on two important issues: (a) When is a presentation subliminal? and (b) What effects are likely to occur as a result of a subliminal presentation? (For reviews, see Cheesman & Merikle, 1985;

Dixon, 1981; Greenwald, 1992; Holender, 1986; Marcel, 1983; Pratkanis & Greenwald, 1988).

When is a Presentation Subliminal?

Cheesman and Merikle (1985) introduced a distinction between objective and subjective thresholds of awareness. An *objective threshold* is a level of stimulus presentation at which forced-choice responding indicates that a stimulus is undetectable. A *subjective threshold* is a level of presentation of greater intensity at which subjects can objectively discriminate a stimulus but have no subjective confidence as to the correctness of their decisions. The distinction is important because, when subliminal effects occur, they are most likely to be obtained with stimuli presented below the subjective, but not the objective threshold. Various operations and manipulation checks have been developed (i.e., pattern masking, shadowing the attended channel, repeated forced-choice assessment of stimuli identification) that enable a researcher to assess whether the presentation is above or below the objective or subjective threshold of awareness. . . .

What Subliminal Effects Are Reliable?

In a review of the literature and a survey of researchers interested in subliminal perception, Greenwald (1992; see also Pratkanis & Greenwald, 1988) found a growing consensus concerning subliminal effects. In general, research on subliminal stimulation has demonstrated subliminal perception (i.e., minimal information processing outside of awareness) of stimuli presented at the subjective (but not objective) threshold, but little evidence for subliminal influence or persuasion (i.e., motivational or behavioral changes as a result of subliminal stimulation) at any threshold. Further, subliminal perception effects are very simple in type, involving minor cognitive feats such as identifying simple word meaning, stimulus intensity, or the spatial location of a subliminal presentation. The best evidence to date for subliminal perception comes from dichotic listening research (i.e., the cocktail party effect) and subliminal semantic activation (i.e., subliminally presented primes facilitating the recognition of related words).

In contrast, little evidence has been obtained that complex multiword propositions can be unconsciously analyzed, much less that subliminal commands are capable of influencing motivation and behavior (for reviews, see McConnell, Cutler, & McNeil, 1958; Moore, 1982, 1988, 1993; Pratkanis & Greenwald, 1988). Studies supporting subliminal claims often were not actually conducted (as in the case of the Vicary study), failed to replicate, produced internally inconsistent findings, or were subject to multiple methodological criticisms including missing control groups, inadequate specification of subliminal thresholds, inconsistency of findings, and a host of experimental confounds (see Balay & Shevrin, 1988; Cheesman & Merikle, 1985; Holender, 1986; Merikle, 1988; Synodinos, 1988). Further, many researchers have failed to obtain predicted subliminal effects (see, e.g., Beatty & Hawkins, 1989; Manro & Washburn, 1908; Severance & Dyer, 1973; Titchener & Pyle, 1907; Vokey & Read, 1985).

Summary

A skeptical appraisal of subliminal self-help tapes would conclude: (a) There is no evidence that subliminal messages exist on the tape; (b) if they are on the tape, they are below the objective threshold and thus likely not to have an effect; and (c) the types of effects expected from subliminal tapes (motivation and behavior change) have yet to be demonstrated in the laboratory.

Such skepticism has been rebutted by subliminal tape manufacturers. In response to (a), they would argue that subliminal messages exist on tapes because they put them there (indeed, their advertisements often describe special recording procedures that make their own tapes special). To (b), they would say that subliminal messages work by bypassing the conscious mind; therefore, the distinction between objective and subjective thresholds is not useful (indeed, subliminal messages are superior to supraliminal messages because they bypass the potential counterarguing of the conscious mind). To rebut (c), they would point to much evidence claiming that subliminal therapy works, including evaluation studies conducted by tape manufacturers, the *EAT POPCORN/DRINK COKE* study, research on subliminal perception, research on subliminal psychodynamic activation (Hardaway, 1990; Silverman & Weinberger, 1985), studies demonstrating the effectiveness of subliminal auditory stimulation (Borgeat & Chaloult, 1985; Borgeat et al., 1985; Swingle, 1992), and the testimony of clinicians concerning the effectiveness of subliminal tapes (Shulman et al., 1990; Swingle, 1992).

DO SUBLIMINAL MESSAGES WORK, AND IF SO, HOW?

One possible mechanism for reconciling the proponents and critics of subliminal persuasion is based on the concept of an expectancy or placebo effect. An expectancy effect occurs when subjects' expectations (in this case, about what will occur as a result of listening to the subliminal audiotape) affect what does occur and their perceptions as to whether it did, in fact, occur.

A study conducted by the Canadian Broadcast Corporation ("Phone now," 1958) illustrates the potential power of expectations. During a popular Sunday night television show, viewers were told about the Vicary *EAT POPCORN/ DRINK COKE* study and were informed that the station would do a test of subliminal persuasion (although the content of the message was not revealed). The message *Phone Now* was then flashed subliminally on the screen 352 times. Telephone company records indicated that phone usage did not increase, nor did local television stations report an increase in calls. However, almost half of the nearly 500 letters sent in by viewers indicated that they felt compelled to "do something" and many felt an urge to eat or drink. It appears that expectations created by the Vicary study influenced what people believed had happened.

In sum, the purpose of our study is to evaluate the therapeutic claims made by proponents of subliminal self-help audiotapes and to investigate the viability of an expectancy interpretation of their effects. In our study, subjects listened to subliminal tapes designed to improve either self-esteem or memory. To test for placebo effects, some tapes were mislabeled so that some subjects with a self-esteem tape thought they had a memory tape and some subjects with a memory tape thought they had a self-esteem tape. We took measures of self-esteem and memory improvement via standard tests and via self-perception. One original hypothesis of the study was that placebo effects would be easier to obtain on verbal measures of self-esteem than on less voluntary measures of memory. Our design is similar to one used by the Royal Commission of 1784 (which included such scientists as Benjamin Franklin and Antoine Lavoisier) to evaluate and later dismiss the claims of mesmerism (see Gould, 1991, Chap. 12).

METHOD

Subjects

Seventy-eight subjects, ranging in age from 18 to 60 years, served as voluntary participants.[1] Fifty-five subjects participated in partial fulfillment of their requirements for introductory psychology courses. Twenty-three subjects were recruited from the Santa Cruz community through classified ads in community newspapers. Before beginning the study, all subjects were told of the time commitment involved. Subjects from the community were not paid for their participation and student subjects could find easier means of obtaining their experimental credit hours. This recruitment procedure was designed to insure that subjects were interested in the therapeutic value of subliminal tapes at least to an extent similar to those who might purchase subliminal tapes.

Subjects were randomly assigned to a 2 (Tape: Self-Esteem vs. Memory) × 2 (Expectation: Expect Self-Esteem Tape vs. Expect Memory Tape) × 2 (Time of Test: Pretest vs. Posttest) design with time of test as a within-subject factor. Note that, in such designs, subjects serve as their own control and a traditional no-tape-control treatment is not needed. All experimental materials were coded in a manner to prevent experimenters from identifying the treatment to which a subject was assigned until the completion of the study.

Procedure

All data collections took place on the University of California, Santa Cruz, campus. In designing the procedures, we attempted to follow all manufacturer

---

[1] Ten additional subjects were unable to complete the experiment. Two subjects could not be reached during the course of the experiment (1 subject had no phone, 1 subject's phone became disconnected), 1 subject developed salmonella poisoning, and the other 7 reported that they were unable to return to a posttest session.

guidelines. For example, subjects were told to use the audiotapes daily, to use them anytime they liked, and to simply play the tape in the background as they went about their daily activities. The procedures used in the study were developed under the advice of two tape company representatives. The experiment consisted of two laboratory sessions with an intervening period of 5 weeks.

Pretest session. On arrival at the first session, subjects received information about subliminal audiotapes and the experimental procedures. Specifically, the experimenter explained that the audiotapes used in the study had been obtained from a prominent supplier of subliminal audiotapes and that typewritten labels had been provided to maintain the company's anonymity during the experiment. Subjects were asked to listen to their cassette at least once per day, preferably more, for the duration of the 5-week experiment. The experimenter explained that the experiment was to last 5 weeks because the subliminal tape company indicated that it would take 4 to 5 weeks of daily listening for the tapes to work. We selected this interval because the manufacturer claimed that positive results would occur immediately, but that dramatic results should appear in 4 to 5 weeks.

Subjects were then given a listening log to keep track of the number of hours they listened to their cassettes. Subjects were told that one purpose of the study was to determine whether the amount and time of listening were related to the effectiveness of the tapes. Subjects were told to discontinue their participation in the experiment if they felt (at any time) that they could not maintain a daily listening schedule. To insure continued listening, subjects were also asked to call each week to reports their progress. Subjects that failed to do so were contacted by the experimenters. . . .

The next part of the session consisted of a pretest assessment of self-esteem and memory abilities. Subjects were given a questionnaire that began with a page of background items assessing demographic variables (age, sex, occupation) as well as subjects' beliefs about, and experience with, subliminal tapes.

After everyone had completed the first page, the subjects were asked to turn the page to begin the three timed memory tasks. For each memory test, the experimenter began by instructing subjects to memorize the material. After 3 min had elapsed, subjects were told to stop and turn the page. As a filler task to disrupt short-term memory and to prevent rehearsal of information, subjects then rated how difficult it was to learn the material and how well they expected to perform on a subsequent memory test. After responding to these two questions, subjects were given 1 min to answer (or guess the answer) to a set of four trivia questions (taken from Pratkanis, 1984/1985; e.g., "In 1917, the first woman was elected to the U.S. Congress. What was this Congresswoman's name?").

After completing the three memory tests, subjects worked on the remaining measures at their own pace. These measures included three measures of self-esteem, an agreement rating with the self-esteem and memory affirmations implanted on the tape, the Crowne-Marlowe Social Desirability Scale (Crowne & Marlowe, 1964), and the Rotter (1966) Internal-External (I-E) Locus of Control Scale.

On completing the questionnaire, subjects received their tape. As the tape was given to the subject, the experimenter pointed to the tape's label and verbally noted the title of the tape. Subjects were also given a copy of materials normally provided by the subliminal tape manufacturer to its customers.

Posttest session. The second laboratory session was conducted 5 weeks later. Subjects were asked to complete another questionnaire (similar to the one used in the pretest session). The first set of questions asked subjects about their listening patterns and the perceived effectiveness of their tape. Subjects next completed the timed memory measures followed by measures of self-esteem, endorsement of the self-esteem and memory implants, the Crowne-Marlowe Social Desirability and Rotter Locus of Control scales. On the last page subjects were asked for feedback about the experiment. After subjects finished the questionnaire, they were fully debriefed concerning the details and purpose of the study. All subjects were given a surprise gift of their subliminal audiotape as a reward for their participation.

Independent Variables

Audiotapes. The subliminal tapes were commercially available audiotapes designed to improve either self-esteem or memory abilities, supplied free for purposes of testing by a major subliminal tape manufacturer.[2] All tapes were original and factory-fresh; no experimenter-duplicated tapes were used. The supraliminal content of both tapes was identical and featured classical music. The tapes differed in their subliminal content. According to the manufacturer, the self-esteem tape contained subliminal self-affirmations such as, "I have high self-worth and high self-esteem" whereas the memory tape contained subliminal self-affirmations such as, "My ability to remember and recall is increasing daily." According to the manufacturer, the subliminal content of the two tapes differed dramatically with the self-esteem tape emphasizing self-worth and confidence and the memory tape emphasizing memory abilities.

Tape expectations. Expectations about the subliminal tape were manipulated by placing a label on the tape which read either "Subliminal Building Self-Esteem" or "Subliminal Memory Improvement."

Dependent Variables

Self-Esteem measures. Three standardized self-esteem scales were used to assess changes in self-esteem. These measures were the Revised Janis-Field

---

[2]To remove the possibility of conflict of interest on the part of researchers and to eliminate any possibility that the results might be interpreted as either an endorsement or criticism of any specific brands, we have elected not to include the tape manufacturer's name in the report of this research.

Feelings of Inadequacy Scale (Eagly, 1973), the Rosenberg Self-Esteem Scale (Rosenberg, 1965), and the Coopersmith Self-Esteem Inventory (Coopersmith, 1967). Each scale was given at the pretest and posttest sessions to enable calculation of a change score.

Memory tests. Four memory tests were used to assess various facets of memory. The tests consisted of two versions of a person-memory test, a paired-associate learning test, and a passage recall test and a single version of an incidental memory measure. The two versions of the person-memory, paired associate, and passage recall tests were given at the pretest and posttest sessions (with versions counterbalanced across subjects) whereas the incidental test was given only at the posttest session.

The person-memory task consisted of a list of 20 statements connecting one of five 6-letter surnames with a trait word (e.g., "Duncan is responsible" or "Parker is inefficient"). . . . At time of recall, subjects were given a list of the surnames followed by four blanks and were asked to recall the trait words that went with each name. Recall was scored as total words recalled and matched with the correct name. . . .

The paired-associate task consisted of 12 pairs of nonsense syllables (e.g., *QES-CEH, TEV-GID, GAW-MPA*) taken from Greeno, James, DaPalito, and Polson (1978). (The two versions of this test consisted of the same nonsense syllables paired with different prefixes.) At time of recall, subjects were given the first half of each nonsense pair and were asked to recall the second half. Recall was scored as total nonsense syllables recalled and matched with the correct prefix. . . .

The passage recall task used the balloon and laundry stories taken from Bransford and Johnson (1972). The passages were a paragraph in length and consisted of a series of disjoined sentences describing either a young man attempting to communicate with a young woman (balloon story) or procedures on how to do a load of wash (laundry story). At time of recall, subjects were given blank sheets of paper and asked to recall as much of the passage as they could. The passage recall task was scored using a gist criterion (i.e., did the subject's response capture the gist of the sentence?). The passage recall test was intended to assess memory for text and prose.[3]

The incidental recall task employed procedures similar to those used in levels of processing research (Cermak & Craik, 1979). For this task, subjects were first given 90 sec to rate 18 adjectives (e.g., merciful, jealous, blunt) in terms of likability using a 7-point scale. At time of recall, subjects were given a blank

---

[3]All memory tests were scored by two coders. When scoring discrepancies occurred, the coders examined the subject's answers together and agreed on the correct score. In additions to the scoring procedure described, we also coded the total number of person-memory adjectives and nonsense syllables recalled and scored the passage task using a verbatim criterion. These alternative scoring procedures produced results similar to the main analyses with one exception noted later (see results for memory measures).

sheet and 90 sec to recall the adjectives. Recall was scored as the total of correctly recalled adjectives. The purpose of the incidental recall task was to assess memory of items for which subjects were unaware that they would be tested.

Subliminal self-affirmation ratings. The subliminal self-affirmation task consisted of rating the self-descriptiveness of 16 memory statements and 32 self-esteem statements that were (according to the tape manufacturer) subliminally embedded on the tape. Subjects were asked to rate their agreement with each statement using a 7-point scale of agreement. The responses to the individual items were summed to form a memory and self-esteem self-affirmation scale. The affirmation tasks were designed to assess the proposition that the listener will come to agree with the subliminal self-affirmations, so that the affirmations replace one's unconscious programming and thereby effect change.

Self-perceived improvement measures. Subject's perceptions of the effectiveness of the subliminal tapes were assessed via five questions asking subjects to respond (yes or no) to: "Do you feel that the tape has improved your. . . ?" with the words "memory," "self-confidence," "concentration," "self-esteem," and "relaxation" completing each question.

Ancillary measures. At the beginning of the pretest questionnaire, we asked the following questions to assess subjects' beliefs about subliminal tapes and their motivation for improvement: "Do you believe subliminal tapes are effective (yes, no, or unsure)?" "Have you used subliminal tapes in the past (yes or no)?" "How motivated are you to increase your self-esteem?" "How motivated are you to improve your memory?" Responses to the last two questions were made on 9-point scales ranging from *not very motivated* (1) to *strongly motivated* (9).

At the beginning of the posttest questionnaire, we asked subjects, "What is the total number of times you listened to the tape? (1) 1–15 times, (2) 16–30 times, (3) 31–45 times, (4) 46–60 times, (5) 61–75 times, (6) 76–90 times, and (7) 91 times or more." This question is similar to one asked by VandenBoogert (1984) and was meant to replicate her results as well as to serve as another measure of listening frequency. . . .

RESULTS

User Characteristics and Listening Frequency

For the most part, our subjects expressed considerable belief in the effectiveness of subliminal tapes and a strong desire to improve their self-esteem and memory. At the pretest session, only 1 of 78 subjects doubted the effectiveness of subliminal tapes, with the rest of the sample stating their confidence in the tape's effectiveness (19.7%) or their feeling that the issue of effectiveness was still open (78.9%). A portion of the sample (18.4%) had used subliminal tapes in the past. At the beginning of the study, the majority of subjects indicated that they were highly motivated to increase their self-esteem (75.3% of the sample answering at the midpoint or higher to the question, "How motivated are you to increase your self-esteem?") and to improve their memory (79.2% answering at the midpoint or higher to the question, "How motivated are you to improve your memory?").

The listening logs and self-reported listening frequency at the posttest indicate that, for the most part, subjects followed the instructions to listen to their hour-long tape at least once a day. . . .

Performance Measures

Self-esteem. The self-esteem data were analyzed using a 2 (Tape: Self-Esteem vs. Memory) × 2 (Expectation: Self-Esteem vs. Memory) × 2 (Time of Test: Pretest vs. Posttest) × 3 (Type of Self-Esteem Test: Rosenberg, Coopersmith, or Janis-Field) ANOVA with the latter two factors as within-subject variables. The results showed three significant procedural effects indicating that: the self-esteem tests differed in terms of their range and average score, $F(2, 148) = 1088.20, p < .01$; subjects increased their self-esteem at posttest regardless of treatment, $F(1, 74) = 30.26$, $p < .01$; and this increase in self-esteem varied as a function of type of test, $F(2, 148) = 10.77, p < .01$. Given that this increase in self-esteem did not vary as a function of treatment, it is best interpreted as a practice effect or a general fluctuation in self-esteem as a function of the academic term.

The critical Tape × Time of Test interaction was marginally significant, $F(1, 74) = 3.63, p = .06$. A series of ANOVAs performed on each self-esteem measure revealed that subjects who received a subliminal memory tape improved their self-esteem more over time (compared to those receiving a self-esteem tape) as measured by the Coopersmith scale, $F(1, 74) = 3.94, p < .05$. This effect did not occur with the Rosenberg scale ($F < 1$), but was marginally significant with the Janis-Field scale, $F(1, 74) = 3.47, p < .1$. This finding is, of course, opposite to that expected on the basis of the claims made by the tape manufacturer. It is best interpreted as a Type I error, although it does suggest that our self-esteem measures are sensitive enough to detect actual change should such change occur.

Memory. The memory data were analyzed with an ANOVA like the one used for the self-esteem data except that type of self-esteem test was replaced with type of memory test (either person-memory, nonsense syllables, or passage recall) as the last variable. As with the self-esteem measures, the results showed three significant procedural effects indicating that: the memory tests differed in terms of their range and average score, $F(2, 146) = 69.35, p < .01$; subjects improved their memory at posttest regardless of treatment, $F(1, 73) = 28.96$, $p < .01$; and this improvement varied as a function of type of test, $F(2, 146) = 6.90, p < .01$. Given that this improvement in memory did not vary as a function of treatment, it is best interpreted as a practice effect.

The critical Tape × Time of Test interaction did not approach significance ($F < 1$). However, there was one significant three-way interaction involving expectation, type of memory test, and time of test, $F(2, 146) = 3.38$, $p < .05$. Subjects who thought they had a memory tape showed more improvement on the passage recall scored using a gist criterion (an improvement of 4.5) compared to subjects expecting a self-esteem tape (an improvement of 1.4), with a univariate $F(1, 73) = 3.83, p = .06$. This effect was not obtained for measures of person-memory, nonsense syllables, or the passage recall scored using a verbatim criteria (all univariate $ps > .25$). Given the inconsistency of this result across measures, it is difficult to interpret as a reliable finding.

The incidental recall task was given at the posttest measure only and was thus analyzed separately using a 2 (Tape) × 2 (Expectation) ANOVA. No significant effects were obtained ($Fs < 1$).

Self-Affirmations. According to the tape manufacturer, subliminal tapes work because the tapes direct positive messages (affirmations) to the subconscious mind. Thus, personal endorsement of the affirmations on the tapes appears critical for therapeutic value. The self-esteem and memory affirmations were analyzed separately using 2 (Tape) × 2 (Expectation) × 2 (Time of Test) ANOVAs. Only one significant effect was obtained: Consistent with the self-esteem measures, subjects in all treatments endorsed more self-esteem affirmations at posttest than they did at pretest, $F(1, 74) = 22.78, p < .01$. This effect did not occur with the memory self-affirmations. . . .

In sum, subliminal self-help audiotapes did not affect any of the nine performance measures in a manner consistent with manufacturer's claims. Similarly, tape expectations did not systematically influence performance.

Self-Perceived Improvement

Expectations created by the experimental manipulations did influence subjects' perceptions of the tapes' effectiveness. . . . Subjects who received a tape labeled *self-esteem* were almost three times as likely to answer yes to the question "Did the tape improve your self-esteem?" than did subjects who received a tape labeled *memory* (48.57% vs. 17.65%), $\chi^2(1, N = 69) = 7.42, p < .01$. A similar pattern was obtained for the question "Did the tape improve your self-confidence?" (44.12% vs. 21.21%), $\chi^2(1, N = 67) = 3.98, p < .05$.

In contrast, subjects who received a tape labeled *memory* were more likely to report that it was effective in improving their memory. Specifically, 48.48% of those subjects who thought they had a memory tape answered "yes" to the question, "Did the tape improve your memory?" compared to none of the subjects who thought they had a self-esteem tape, $\chi^2(1, N = 70) = 23.25, p < .01$. A similar pattern was obtained for the question "Did the tape improve your concentration?" (47.22% vs. 13.51%), $\chi^2(1, N = 73) = 9.85, p < .01$.

The subjects' self-perceptions of self-esteem and memory improvement were unaffected by whether they had actually listened to the self-esteem or the memory tape. In addition, the independent variables did not systematically influence self-perceptions of relaxation. . . .

DISCUSSION

Our findings can best be described as: What you expect is what you believe, but not necessarily what you get. In other words, expectations about the therapeutic value of subliminal self-help tapes led subjects to believe that listening to such tapes had indeed improved either their memory capabilities or increased their self-esteem. In fact, objective measures showed that no such improvement had occurred. We call this result an *illusory placebo effect*—expectations (as opposed to the actual therapy) created the illusion of improvement that did not, in fact, occur.

Comparison with Other Studies Evaluating Subliminal Audiotapes

After completing our study, eight additional studies evaluating the therapeutic value of subliminal self-help tapes appeared in the literature. For the most part, these studies differed procedurally from ours and thus can be used to strengthen our conclusions. Lenz (1989/1990) had 270 Los Angeles police trainees listen to background music with or without subliminal messages during a regular class for a total of 30 hr over an 8-week period. The subliminal messages were designed to improve either learning of the law or marksmanship. The tapes did not improve either. Russell, Rowe, and Smouse (1991) had students listen (for 10 weeks) to two tapes designed to improve study skills, two tapes with just ocean sounds, or a no-tape control. The tapes improved neither grade-point average nor final exam scores. Auday, Mellett, and Williams (1991) conducted three studies using subliminal tapes designed to improve memory, reduce anxiety and stress, and increase self-confidence. In each study, subjects listened (for about a month) to either a subliminal tape or another tape without subliminals but with identical sounds. The subliminal tapes proved ineffective on all three fronts. Merikle and Skanes (1992) had subjects listen (for 5 weeks) to either a weight-loss subliminal tape, a dental anxiety tape labeled as a weight-loss tape (a placebo control treatment), or a no-tape control treatment. The three groups of subjects did not differ in weight loss. Finally, Spangenberg (1990/1991) conducted two studies that used a design identical to ours, but used tapes from different manufacturers and different dependent measures. He found no therapeutic value attributable to the tapes.

There have now been nine empirical studies conducted by non-tape-company researchers investigating the effectiveness of subliminal tapes. These nine studies have employed tapes from different manufacturers, studied a wide range of dependent variables, used both forced (in-class) and free (in-home) listening formats, manipulated or held constant expectancies about the tapes, and employed a variety of experimental designs. All nine studies failed to find an effect consistent with the manufacturer's claims, prompting the National Academy of

Sciences to conclude, "there is neither theoretical foundation nor experimental evidence to support claims that subliminal self-help audiotapes enhance human performance" (Eich & Hyman, 1991, p. 116). . . .

Implications of the Research

***Methodological implications.* . . .** [T]he study raises the possibility that expectancy effects (Rosenthal, 1966) can serve as an alternative explanation of subliminal findings. Expectancy effects can be controlled by directly manipulating subjects' expectations or by using a double-blind procedure. Finally, the study provides a reminder that testimonials can be biased (Werkmeister, 1948) and thus serve as an inadequate means of evaluating subliminal therapies. In our study, subjects' claims for what happened did not, in fact, match what did (or, more precisely, did not) occur.

Why didn't we obtain a placebo effect?   One of the original hypotheses of the study was that expectations about the efficacy of subliminal therapy could possibly result in actual therapeutic gain independent of the benefit that might accrue from subliminal messages. This placebo effect did not occur and has not occurred in other studies that either manipulated or reinforced expectations concerning the therapeutic value of subliminal tapes. The literature suggests three reasons why we did not obtain a placebo effect (Ross & Olson, 1981; White, Tursky & Schwartz, 1985).

First, the power of placebo effects may themselves be illusory. For example, consider the famous study by Storms and Nisbett (1970) in which insomniacs were put to bed with a placebo pill and the expectation that the pill would create arousal. The primary dependent variable in this (and many subsequent studies) was a self-report of the latency of sleep onset. Such a measure corresponds to our measures of self-perceived improvement (i.e., an illusory placebo effect) as opposed to our direct assessments of memory and self-esteem. Shapiro (1981) argued that placebos primarily influence subjective reports and "that the amount of variance accounted for by the placebo on organic clinical conditions is minimal" (p. 97).

Second, in pharmacological studies, one reliable finding concerning the efficacy of placebos is that placebo effects mirror the efficacy of the actual treatment. In such studies, there are usually three treatments: no treatment, placebo control, and drug treatment. Regardless of the actual drug treatment, the placebo subjects act like the drug treatment subjects. The direction of effects are similar, subjects report similar side effects, and drug and placebo groups follow the same short-term time-effect curves. Perhaps most interesting, placebo effects are usually 50% to 60% as effective as the treatment regardless of the treatment. For example, Evans (1985) found that in reducing postoperative pain a placebo was 56% as effective as morphine (a very effective pain reduction agent), 56% as effective as codeine, and 54% as effective as aspirin (a much less effective agent). Similar results have been obtained in studies of drug treatment of depression (Evans, 1985) and insomnia (Bootzin, 1985). Our study did not include an actual treatment control group receiving an effective treatment such as social skills training or a course in the use of memory mnemonics.

Third, as the pharmacological studies indicate, the role of specific expectations (created by a specific drug treatment) are very important for producing placebo effects. For placebo effects to occur, it is often necessary for the specific expectation to change a mediating variable that then produces the effect. For example, Evans (1985) found that placebos are effective in reducing pain if they are successful in reducing anxiety about the upcoming experience of pain. In Darley and Fazio's (1980) model of the self-fulfilling prophecy, the perceiver believes the target to possess a certain attribute (say, low intelligence) and then engages in behavior (talking down to the person, asking stupid questions, looking for stupid behavior) that then causes the target to act as expected. It may be that expectations about the effectiveness of subliminal self-help tapes are too broad to influence behavior (i.e., "I will improve my memory" vs. "I will use a mnemonic strategy") and do not influence specific mediators such as the frequency of using mnemonic and self-referencing memory strategies (see Vallacher & Wegner's, 1985, action identification model for elaboration of this point).

In sum, the results of our study (and those of other researchers) cast doubt on the placebo value of subliminal therapy. Further, the literature on placebos indicates that it would be difficult to design a subliminal therapy that created expectations capable of producing placebo effects. Placebos work when they generate specific expectations similar to those generated by an effective intervention. In all likelihood, it would be easier (and more effective) to administer the effective therapy than to try to engineer such effects with subliminal tapes.

Why do people purchase subliminal self-help tapes? The results of this study help explain a paradox. Much prior research finds little evidence for motivational and behavioral effects of subliminal stimulation. Indeed, this study adds another null result to that body of literature. Despite this lack of evidence, many Americans believe in subliminal influence. This belief may be based, not on an objective assessment of the merits of subliminal stimuli, but on the expectations created, in part, by the mass media and subliminal tape manufacturers (see Pratkanis, 1992). Tape users may bias their interpretation and recall of daily events in support of their expectations of a successful treatment (Conway & Ross, 1984; Ross, 1989) or may provide glowing testimonials in justification of 5 weeks of effortful listening (Aronson & Mills, 1959).

In sum, the study reminds us that, when it comes to subliminal tapes, "Let the buyer beware." We know of no published independent study that has demonstrated convincingly the effectiveness of subliminal self-help audiotapes. Consumers should expect the same testing and evaluation of subliminal self-help tapes as they would of any other pharmaceutical or therapeutic product.

ACKNOWLEDGMENTS

This research is based on Jay Eskenazi's senior honors thesis conducted at the University of California, Santa Cruz. The results were originally presented at the Western Psychological Association Meeting, Los Angeles, April 26, 1990.

The research was supported in part by a William P. Massaro Thesis Award to Eskenazi.

We thank Leslie Smith for assistance in data collection, and Marlene B. Turner and Mary Sue Weldon for helpful comments.

References

Anday, B. C., McBett, J. L., & Wiliams, P. M. (1991, April). *Self-improvement using subliminal self-help audiotapes: Consumer benefit or consumer fraud?* Paper presented at the meeting of the Western Psychological Association, San Francisco.

Balay, J., & Shevrin, H. (1988). The subliminal psychodynamic activation method: A critical review. *American Psychologist, 43,* 161–174.

Beatty, S. E., & Hawkins, D. I. (1989). Subliminal stimulation: Some new data and interpretation. *Journal of Advertising, 18,* 4–8.

Bootzin, R. R. (1985). The role of expectancy in behavior change. In L. White, B. Tursky, & G. E. Schwartz (Eds.), *Placebo: Theory, research, and mechanisms* (pp. 196–210). New York: Guilford.

Borgeat, F., and Chaloult, L. (1985). A relaxation experiment using radio broadcasts. *Canada's Mental Health, 33,* 11–13.

Borgeat, F., Elie, R., Chaloult, L., & Chabot, R. (1985). Psychophysiological responses to masked auditory stimuli. *Canadian Journal of Psychiatry, 30,* 22–27.

Bornstein, R. F. (1989). Subliminal techniques as propaganda tools: Review and critique. *Journal of Mind and Behavior, 10,* 231–262.

Bransford, J. D., & Johnson, M. (1972). Contextual prerequisites for understanding: Some investigations of comprehension and recall. *Journal of Verbal Learning and Verbal Behavior, 11,* 717–726.

Cermak, L. S., & Craik, F. I. M. (Eds.). (1979). *Levels of processing in human memory.* Hillsdale, NJ: Lawrence Eribaum Associates, Inc.

Cheesman, J., & Merikle, P. M. (1985). Word recognition and consciousness. In D. Besner, T. G. Waller, & G. E. MacKinnon (Eds.), *Reading research: Advances in theory and practice* (Vol. 5, pp. 311–352). New York: Academic.

Coppersmith, S. (1967). *The antecedents of self-esteem.* San Francisco: Freeman.

Cousins, N. (1957, October 5). Smudging the subconscious. *Saturday Review,* p. 20.

Crowne, D., & Marlowe, D. (1964). *The approval motive.* New York: Wiley.

Danzig, F. (1962, September 17). Subliminal advertising—Today it's just an historical flashback for researcher Vicary. *Advertising Age,* pp. 73–74.

Darley, J. M., & Fazio, R. H. (1980). Expectancy confirmation processes arising in the social interaction sequence. *American Psychologist, 35,* 867–881.

Dixon, N. F. (1981). *Preconscious processing.* New York: Wiley.

Eagly, A. H. (1973). Revised Janis-Field Feelings of Inadequacy Scale. In J. P. Robinson & P. R. Shaver (Eds.), *Measures of social psychological attitudes* (pp. 143–147). Ann Arbor: University of Michigan, Institute for Social Research.

Eich, E., & Hyman, R. (1991). Subliminal self-help. In D. Druckman & R. A. Bjork (Eds.). *In the mind's eye: Enhancing human performance* (pp. 107–119). Washington, DC: National Academy Press.

Evans, F. J. (1985). Expectancy, therapeutic instructions, and the placebo response. In L. White, B. Tursky, & G. E. Schwartz (Eds.), *Placebo: Theory, research, and mechanisms* (pp. 215–228). New York: Guilford.

Gould, S. J. (1991). *Bully for brontosaurus.* New York: Norton.

Greeno, J. G., James, C. T., DaPolito, F., & Polson, P. G. (1978). *Associative learning: A cognitive analysis.* Englewood Cliffs, NJ: Prentice-Hall.

Greenwald, A. G. (1992). New Look 3: Unconscious cognition reclaimed. *American Psychologist, 47,* 766–779.

Hardaway, R. A. (1990), Subliminally activated symbiotic fantasies: Facts and artifacts. *Psychological Bulletin, 107,* 177–195.

Holender, D. (1986). Semantic activation without conscious identification in dichotic listening, parafoveal vision, and visual masking: A survey and appraisal. *Behavior and Brain Sciences, 9,* 1–66.

Key, W. B. (1973). *Subliminal seduction,* Englewood Cliffs, NJ: Signet.

Key, W. B. (1976). *Media sexploitation.* Englewood Cliffs, NJ: Signet.

Key, W. B. (1980). *The clam-plate orgy.* Englewood Cliffs, NJ: Signet.

Key, W. B. (1989). *The age of manipulation.* New York: Holt.

Lenz, S. (1990). The effects of subliminal auditory stimuli on academic learning and motor skills performance among police recruits. (Doctoral dissertation, California School of Professional Psychology, 1989). *Dissertation Abstracts International, 50,* 3165B.

Manro, H. M., & Washburn, M. F. (1908). The effect of imperceptible line on the judgment of distance. *American Journal of Psychology, 19,* 242.

Marcel, A. J. (1983). Conscious and unconscious perception: Experiments on visual masking and word recognition. *Cognitive Psychology, 15,* 197–237.

McConnell, J. V., Cutler, R. I., & McNell, E. B. (1958). Subliminal stimulation: An overview. *American Psychologist, 13,* 229–242.

Merikle, P. M.(1998). Subliminal auditory messages: An evaluation. *Psychology & Marketing, 5,* 352–372.

Merikle, P. M., & Skanes, H. E. (1992). Subliminal self-help audiotapes: A search for placebo effects. *Journal of Applied Psychology, 77,* 772–776.

Moore, T. E. (1982). Subliminal advertising: What you see is what you get. *Journal of Marketing, 46,* 38–47.

Moore, T. E. (1988). The case against subliminal manipulation. *Psychology & Marketing, 5,* 297–316.

Moore, T. E. (1992). Subliminal perception: Facts and fallacies. *Skeptical Inquirer, 16,* 273–281.

Natale, J. A. (1988, September). Are you open to suggestion? *Psychology Today,* pp. 28–30.

"Phone now," said CBC subliminally—but nobody did. (1958, February 10). *Advertising Age,* p. 8.

Pratkanis, A. R. (1985). *Attitudes and memory: The heuristic and schematic functions of attitudes* (Doctoral dissertation, Ohio State University, Columbus, 1984). *Dissertation Abstracts International, 45,* 3657B.

Pratkanis, A. R. (1990, July 31—August 1), [Testimony given before Judge Jerry Carr Whitehead in the trial of Vance and Robertson v. Judas Priest and CBS Records, Reno, NV].

Pratkanis, A. R. (1992). The cargo-cult science of subliminal persuasion. *Skeptical Inquirer, 16,* 260–272.

Pratkanis, A. R., & Greenwald, A. G. (1988). Recent perspectives on unconscious processing: Still no marketing applications. *Psychology & Marketing, 5,* 339–355.

Psychologists hit use of subliminal methods in ads as "unprofessional." (1958, June 16). *Advertising Age,* p. 85.

Rogers, S. (1992–1993). How a publicity blitz created the myth of subliminal advertising. *Public Relations Quarterly, 37,* 12–17.

Rosenberg, M. (1965). *Society and the adolescent self-image.* Princeton, NJ: Princeton University Press.

Rosenthal, R. (1966). *Experimenter effects in behavioral research.* New York: Appleton-Century-Crofts.

Ross, M., & Olson, J. M. (1981). An expectancy-attribution model of the effects of placebos. *Psychological Review, 88,* 408–437.

Rotter, J. B. (1966). Generalized expectations for internal versus external control of reinforcement. *Psychological Monographs, 80*(1, Whole No. 609).

Russell, T. G., Rowe, W., & Smouse, A. D. (1991). Subliminal self-help tapes and academic achievement: An evaluation. *Journal of Counseling & Development, 69,* 359–362.

Severance, L. J., & Dyer, F. N. (1973). Failure of subliminal word presentations to generate interference to color naming. *Journal of Experimental Psychology, 101,* 186–189.

Shapiro, A. K. (1981). [Review of Brody's *Placebos and the philosophy of medicine*]. *Social Science and Medicine, 15E,* 96–97.

Shevrin, H. (1990, July 24). [Testimony given before Judge Jerry Carz Whitehead in the trial of Vance and Robertson v. Judas Priest and CBS Records, Reno, NV].

Shulman, L. M., Shulman, J., & Rafferty, G. P. (1990). *Subliminal: The new channel to personal power.* Santa Monica, CA: InfoBooks.

Silverman, L. H., & Weinberger, J. (1985). Mommy and I are one: Implications for psychotherapy. *American Psychologist, 40,* 1296–1308.

Spangenberg, E. R. (1991). *An empirical test of subliminal self-help audiotapes: Are expectancies the active ingredient?* (Doctoral dissertation, University of Washington, 1990). *Dissertation Abstracts International, 52,* 233A.

Storms, M. D., & Nisbett, R. E. (1970). Insomnia and the attribution process. *Journal of Personality and Social Psychology, 16,* 319–328.

Suslowa, M. (1863). Veranderungen der hautgefule unter dem einfluses electrischer reizung. *Zeitschrift für Rationelle Medicin, 18,* 155–160.

Swingle, P. G. (1992). *Subliminal treatment procedures: A clinician's guide.* Sarasota, FL: Professional Resource Press.

Synodinos, N. E. (1988). Review and appraisal of subliminal perception within the context of signal detection theory. *Psychology & Marketing, 5,* 317–336.

Taylor, E. (1988). *Subliminal learning: An eclectic approach.* Salt Lake City, UT: Just Another Reality Publishing.

Titchener, E. B., & Pyle, W. H. (1970). The effect of imperceptible shadows on the judgment of distance. *Proceedings of the American Philosophical Society, 46,* 94–109.

Vallacher, R., & Wegner, D. M. (1985). *A theory of action identification.* Hillsdale, NJ: Lawrence Eribsum Associates, Inc.

VandenBoogert, C. (1984). *A study of Potentials Unlimited subliminal persuasion self-hypnosis tapes.* Grand Rapids, MI: Potentials Unlimited.

Vokey, J. R., & Read, J. D. (1985). Subliminal messages: Between the devil and the media. *American Psychologist, 40,* 1231–1239.

Weir, W. (1984, October 15). Another look at subliminal "facts". *Advertising Age,* p. 46.

Werkmeister, W. H. (1948). *An introduction to critical thinking.* Lincoln, NE: Johnsen.

White, L., Tursky, B., & Schwartz, G. E. (Eds.). (1985). *Placebo: Theory, research, and mechanisms.* New York: Guilford.

Words whispered to subconscious supposedly deter thefts, fainting. (1980, November 25). *Wall Street Journal.*

Zanot, E. J., Pincus, J. D., & Lamp, E. J. (1983). Public perceptions of subliminal advertising. *Journal of Advertising, 12,* 37–45.

Review and Contemplate

1. Explain the difference between subliminal perception and subliminal persuasion. Is there any reliable evidence for either phenomenon?

2. Briefly describe the design and main results of the study by Pratkanis et al. (1994).

3. What is an illusory placebo effect? Explain how the findings of Pratkanis et al. (1994) are an example of such an effect.

4. Briefly describe the results of studies on subliminal audiotapes other than the study by Pratkanis et al. (1994). (e.g., Studies on tapes designed to improve marksmanship, study skills, etc.).

5.3

Psychic Crime Detectives: A New Test for Measuring Their Successes and Failures/
RICHARD WISEMAN, DONALD WEST, AND ROY STEMMAN

In May 2004, Charles Capel, a retired Miami University professor who had Alzheimer's disease, wandered away from his home in Oxford, Ohio. Despite extensive searches by police and volunteers, Capel was missing for months. In October, the police decided to hire self-proclaimed psychic detective Noreen Renier to assist in the search. Police sent Renier some of Capel's tootbrushes and shoes. From Virginia, Renier used visions she received from Capel's personal items to help her determine the location of Capel. According to Sgt. Jim Squance of the Oxford police, Renier said that Capel was approximately 8 miles from his house, and she mentioned seeing a stone, a wooded area, a creek, a fence, and a tower with an antenna on top of it. After the remains of Capel were found, news reports indicated that Renier's information was accurate and that she had helped the police find Capel's body. Sgt. Squance said, "When you see the results, you've got to be in awe."

Psychic crime detectives have been credited with helping police identify and locate criminals, find the bodies of murder victims, and fill in the missing details of a crime. Although television shows and news reporters sometimes make it appear as though psychics are amazingly accurate at such tasks, they typically do not test the psychics' abilities in a scientific manner. We should not rely on after-the-fact reports of a psychic detective's apparent success to determine the psychic's accuracy. One problem with relying on these reports is that people have a tendency to make the psychic's statements fit the details of the crime after the fact, even if the psychic gave vague or inaccurate information. For example, near the location of Charles Capel's body was a subdivision named Stone Creek. This was interpreted as being consistent with Renier's statement about a "stone," but Renier did not say that Capel was near the Stone Creek subdivision. If you think about it, mentioning a "stone" is quite vague, and it could be considered consistent with a wide variety of scenarios. What if there had been a large stone near Capel's body, a stone in his shoe, or he had been hit with a stone; would we interpret these facts as being consistent with Renier's statement?

We also tend to remember information the psychic provided that was consistent with the facts and overlook information that was inconsistent. For example, Capel was found near a wooded area, but he was not 8 miles from his home; he was less than a mile away. How much of the information provided by Renier was inaccurate? It's difficult to answer this question without a full transcript of what Renier told the police. Finally, we don't know whether Renier's statements were "accurate" simply by chance. Psychic detectives often say that bodies will be found near water or near wooded areas because killers typically hide bodies in such areas. Another interesting fact about the Capel case is that although the police credited Renier with helping them solve this case, the police did not find Capel's body. In fact, the police searched for two months after they received Renier's advice, and they still could not find Capel. His body was actually discovered by a hunter who saw the body while walking through the area.

If we cannot rely on anectdotal reports, such as the one involving Noreen Renier, to determine the accuracy of psychic detectives, how might we test these detectives in a more scientific manner? In this article, Wiseman et al. (1996) describe their efforts to test several psychic detectives' ability to determine the details of crimes after being given items related to those crimes.

APA Reference

Wiseman, R., West, D., & Stemman, R. (1996). Psychic crime detectives: A new test for measuring their successes and failures. *Skeptical Inquirer, 20,* 38–40, 58.

A controlled test of 'psychic detectives,' using a novel method, found that they were no more accurate than college students. Yet the psychics all thought they had been successful.

Many psychics claim to be able to help the police solve serious crime. Recent surveys suggest that approximately 35 percent of urban United States police departments and 19 percent of rural departments (Sweat and Durm 1993) admit to having used a psychic at least once in their investigations. In addition, Lyons and Truzzi (1991) report the widespread use of psychic detectives in several other countries including Britain, Holland, Germany, and France.

Most of these psychics' claims are supported only by anecdotal evidence. This is unfortunate because it is often extremely difficult to rule out nonpsychic explanations. For example, Hoebens (1985) described how some psychics have made several (often conflicting) predictions relating to an unsolved crime. Once the crime was solved, the incorrect predictions were forgotten while the correct ones were exhibited as evidence of paranormal ability. Rowe (1993) cites examples of psychics making vague and ambiguous predictions that later were interpreted to fit the facts of the crime. Lyons and Truzzi (1991) noted that it is often difficult to obtain "baseline" information for many of these predictions. For example, a psychic may state that a murder weapon will be discovered "near, or in, a large body of water." Although this may later prove to be accurate, it is difficult to know how many criminals dump incriminating objects in areas that could be seen as "large bodies of water" (e.g., streams, lakes, rivers, the ocean, etc.) and therefore establish a statistical baseline for the prediction.

Some investigators have overcome these problems by carrying out controlled tests of psychic detection abilities. One of the earliest controlled studies was conducted by a Dutch police officer, Filippus Brink. Brink carried out a one-year study using four psychics. These psychics were shown various photographs and objects and asked to describe the crimes that had taken place. Some of the photographs and objects were connected with actual crimes; others were not. In a report to INTERPOL, Brink (1960) noted that the psychics had failed to provide any information that would have been of any use to an investigating officer. However, this report is brief and, as noted by Lyons and Truzzi (1991, p. 51): "Because Brink gives us few details of his method and analysis in this report, the strength, if not the value, of his conclusions cannot really be evaluated."

Studies have been carried out by Martin Reiser of the Los Angeles Police Department. An initial study by Reiser, Ludwig, Saxe, and Wagner (1979) involved twelve psychics. Each psychic was presented with several sealed envelopes containing physical evidence from four crimes (two solved, two unsolved). The psychics were asked to describe the crimes that had taken place. They were then allowed to open the envelopes and describe any additional impressions they received from the object. The study was double-blind, as neither the psychics nor the experimenters had any prior knowledge of the details of the crimes.

The psychics' statements were then coded into several categories (e.g., crime committed, victim, suspect, etc.) and compared with the information known about the crime. For each of the psychics' predictions that matched the actual information, they were awarded one point. The psychics' performances were less than impressive. For example, the experimenters knew that 21 key facts were true of the first crime. The psychics identified an average of only 4. Similarly, of the 33 known facts concerning the second crime, the psychics correctly identified an average of only 1.8. This data caused Reiser et al. to conclude: "The research data does not support the contention that psychics can provide significant additional information leading to the solution of major crime" (pp. 21–22).

Reiser and Klyver (1982) also carried out a follow-up study that used three groups of participants: psychic detectives, students, and police homicide detectives. Four crimes were used (two solved and two unsolved) and again physical evidence from each crime was presented to participants in sealed envelopes. Reiser and Klyver report that the data produced by the three groups was quite different in quantity and character. The psychic detectives produced descriptions that were, on average, six times the length of the student descriptions. In addition, the psychic detectives' statements sounded more confident and dramatic than those produced by either the students or the homicide detectives.

Parts of the descriptions were separated into several categories (e.g., sex of criminal, age, height, etc.) and, if correct, assigned one point. A comparison between the three groups showed that although the psychics produced the greatest number of predictions, they were not any more accurate than either the students or the homicide detectives.

In August 1994 the authors of this article were contacted by a British television company involved in making a major documentary series on the paranormal (Arthur C. Clarke's "Mysterious Universe"). One of their programs was to be devoted to psychic detectives, and the producers were eager to film a well-controlled test of three British psychics. The company approached the authors and asked if we would design and carry out these tests. We agreed.

This was the first test of its type in Britain and one of only a handful carried out anywhere in the would. In addition, the methods used during previous studies have been the subject of some criticism (see Lyons and Truzzi 1991) so the authors throught it worthwhile to devise a new method for testing the claims of psychic detection.

This test compared the performance of two groups of participants: psychic detectives and a "control" groups of college students. Two of the psychics were professional while the third (who will be referred to as "Psychic 1") was not, but had recently received a great deal of attention from the British media. The psychic's local police force (Herefordshire Police Force) described him as follows:

> When [psychic's name] comes to the police with his dreams, he is taken seriously and the information that he passes on to his established contact, Sgt. Richard Mac-Gregor, is acted upon immediately (*Psychic News*, November 26, 1994, p. 1)[1]

None of the students claimed to be psychic or had any special interest in criminology.

Each participant was shown three items that had been involved in one of three crimes: a bullet, a scarf, and a shoe. They were asked to handle each of the objects and speak aloud any ideas, images, or thoughts that might be related to these crimes. Participants were told that they were free to take as long as they wished and to say as little or as much as they thought necessary. During the test they were left alone in the room, but everything they said and did was filmed.

After they had finished commenting on all three objects, the participants were given three response sheets (one for each object), each containing 18 statements. Six of each of the 18 statements were true of each crime. The participants were then asked to mark the 6 statements that they believed were true about the crime in question.

Table 5.1 presents the individual scores for each of the six participants. None of the scores of any of the individuals was statistically significant or impressive.

It could be argued that the above method of testing might *underestimate* participants' psychic ability. For example, a participant may have made several accurate comments describing the crime in question but, nevertheless, obtained

TABLE 5.1

Individual/Group Means, Standard Deviations (in Brackets), Z-Scores, and P-Values.

	Individual scores (min = 0, max = 6)	Group scores (min = 0, max = 6)	Z-score	P-value (2 tailed)
Psychic 1	2.3 (1.15)		.24	.8
Psychic 2	2.66 (0.57)	2.09 (0.68)	.73	.46
Psychic 3	1.33 (0.57)		.73	.46
Student 1	2 (0.5)		0	1
Student 2	2 (0.5)	2.33 (0.57)	0	1
Student 3	3 (1.73)		1.21	.22

a low score if this information was not included on the list of 18 statements. For this reason, a judge not involved in the test transcribed and separated all of the comments made by the participants as the participants handled the objects. The order of these statements was then randomized within each crime and presented to two additional judges. These judges were asked to read about each crime and rate the accuracy of each statement from 1 (very inaccurate) to 7 (very accurate). Table 5.2 contains the average of the two judges' ratings (inter-rater reliability = .77).

Overall, the psychics made a total of 39 statements while the students made 20 statements. A paired *t*-test showed no significant differences for the accuracy ratings of students and psychics (t = 2.38, df = 4, p[2 tailed] = .074). This supports Reiser and Klyver's finding that even though psychics tend to make more predictions than students, they are no more accurate.

After their predictions had been recorded, the participants were told about the crimes associated with each of the target objects. This debriefing was filmed, and it is interesting to review the way in which the participants reacted to finding out the truth about each crime:

TABLE 5.2

Individual/Group Accuracy Means, Standard Deviations (in Brackets), and Number of Statements.

	Accuracy rating (min = 0, max = 7)	Number of statements	Group scores (min = 0, max = 7)
Psychic 1	3.87 (2.57)	15	
Psychic 2	3.65 (1.83)	16	3.83 (0.17)
Psychic 3	4.00 (1.96)	8	
Student 1	6.37 (0.64)	8	
Student 2	4.14 (2.62)	7	5.63 (1.28)
Student 3	5.10 (2.13)	5	

Crime 1. The Moat Farm murder, 1889–1903. In 1889 an army sergeant major named Samuel Herbert Dougal wished to have an affair with his maid but first needed to dispose of his wife. On May 16, 1889, he and his wife went out for a horse-and-trap ride into the town. During the trip Dougal shot his wife in the head and buried her in a ditch. The body remained buried for four years before the police eventually discovered it. The shoes worn by the corpse were identified by a cobbler as belonging to the dead woman, and Dougal was hung for the murder in 1903.

Crime 2. The murder of Constable Gutteride, 1927. In 1927 a police officer (Constable George William Gutteridge from the Essex Police Force) stopped a stolen car. The driver suddenly pulled out a gun and fired two shots—one into each of Constable Gutteridge's eyes. The car was later found abandoned in Brixton, London. A six-month-long investigation resulted in two men having been caught and hanged. An important part of the incriminating evidence was the bullet removed from the scene of the crime.

Crime 3. The killing of Margery Pattison, 1962. Margery Pattison, a 71-year-old widow, returned to her flat and disturbed her milkman who had entered through an unlocked door and had started to look for money. An argument ensued and the man grabbed the scarf around her neck, pulled it tight, and strangled her. The man was later caught and charged with murder.

All three psychics thought that they had been successful. On hearing that Crime 2 involved the killing of a police officer, Psychic 1 noted that one of his precognitive dreams involved Police Constable Keith Blakelock (who had been killed on duty in London a few years earlier). This participant noted that he thought at the time the dream was related to Blakelock's murder, but that he now believed it related to the killing of Constable Gutteridge. The same participant remarked that he felt he had given a successful description of Crime 1, as he had said it involved a woman having been raped and murdered and that "that is the fundamental theme of the crime." Psychic 1 failed to recall that he had also said the woman was murdered by a black man and that it happened on Tottenham Court Road. Both of these statements were incorrect. This lends support to the notion that some psychic detection may appear to work, in part, because inaccurate predictions may be forgotten about later, whereas successful ones are recalled and elaborated on.

Psychic 2 remarked that he believed that the experiment showed a "good conclusion all round" and that "my colleagues and I have put the jigsaw puzzle together." He emphasized that all three psychics believed that the scarf was involved in suffocation, had had trouble with Crime 2, but had predicted that the shoe-related crime involved some form of burial.

Psychic 3 also thought that there had been a consensus on the scarf and shoe. Remarking on the lack of information forthcoming on Crime 2, the psychic noted that "sometimes access to information is not appropriate at certain times." Despite this, he said that he was "relatively pleased with the outcome."

In short, this study provided no evidence to support the claims of psychic detection and, as such, the results are in accordance with other controlled studies. The study utilized a novel method of evaluating psychic detection. The way in which the participants responded to being told the true nature of the crimes gives some insight into some of the mechanisms that might cause individuals to believe erroneously that they are able to solve crimes by psychic means.

Notes

This research was carried out with support from the Committee for the Scientific Investigation of Claims of the Paranormal.

The authors would like to thank Granite Television, London, Melvin Harris, and Sergeant Fred Feather for helping to set up our study described in this paper. Thanks also to Matthew Smith for helping to run the experiment, and Carol Hurst for carrying out the qualitative analysis of the data. Finally, our thanks to the psychics and students who kindly gave up their time to act as subjects. Correspondence regarding this article should be addressed to Richard Wiseman.

1. Richard Wiseman contacted Sgt. Richard MacGregor of the Herefordshire Police Force concerning this matter and received confirmation that the above statement was correct (personal communication, December 19, 1994).

References

Brink, F. 1960. Parapsychology and criminal investigations. *International Criminal Police Reviews*, 134, 3–9.

Hoebens, P. H. 1985. Reflections on psychic sleuths. Edited by Marcello Truzzi in *A Skeptic's Handbook of Parapsychology*, ed. by P. Kurtz, part 6, pp. 631–643. Amherst, N.Y.: Prometheus Books.

Lyons, A. and M. Truzzi. 1991. *The Blue Sense*. New York: Warner Books.

Herts police admit to using psychic help. 1994. *Psychic News*, Nov. 26, 3259:1.

Reiser, M., L. Ludwig, S. Saxe, and C. Wagner. 1979. An evaluation of the use of psychics in the investigation of major crimes. *Journal of Police Science and Administration*, 7(1): 1825. (Reprinted in Nickel, J. [Ed.], *Psychic Sleuths*, Prometheus Books, Amherst, N.Y., 1994).

Reiser, M., and N. Klyver. 1982. A comparison of psychics, detectives, and students in the investigation of major crimes. In *Police Psychology: Collected Papers* by M. Reiser, Los Angeles, Calif.: Lehi.

Rowe, W. F. 1993. Psychic detectives: A critical examination. SKEPTICAL INQUIRER, 17(2): 159–165.

Sweat, J. A., and M. W. Durm. 1993. Psychics: Do police departments really use them? SKEPTICAL INQUIRER, 17(2): 148–158.

Review and Contemplate

1. Wiseman, West, and Stemman (1996) explained that most psychic detectives' claims are supported only by anecdotal evidence. Explain the problem with such evidence.
2. Briefly describe the design and results of the study conducted by Reiser and Klyver (1982).

3. Briefly describe the design and results of the study conducted by Wiseman, West, and Stemman (1996).
4. Explain how the psychics' comments—after they learned the true nature of the crimes—provide some insight into why individuals may believe incorrectly that they can solve crimes by psychic means.

About the Authors

Lynn McCutcheon taught psychology full-time for 23 years and currently teaches as an adjunct at Florida Southern College. Home address: 240 Harbor Drive, Winter Garden, FL 34787.

Richard Wiseman (to whom correspondence should be addressed) is the Perrott-Warrick Senior Research Fellow as the University of Hertfordshire, College Lane, Hatfield, Herts, AL10 9AB, U.K. Donald West is at Cambridge University. Roy Stemman is editor of *Reincarnation Magazine.*

CHAPTER 6
Learning and Memory

6.1

Different Strokes for Different Folks? A Critique of Learning Styles /
STEVEN STAHL

My wife often tells me that she learns best by listening to an instructor's oral presentation, and she believes that I learn best by reading information. Would that make her an auditory learner and me a visual learner? The basic idea behind the notion of learning styles is that people have different styles or ways of learning, and they learn best when information is provided to them in a manner that best suits their learning style. According to supporters of learning styles, visual learners learn best by seeing pictures, maps, illustrated textbooks, videos, or other visual media. Auditory learners, on the other hand, prefer to hear sound; thus, they may learn best by hearing a lecture or reading a book aloud.

To many people, the notion of learning styles sounds reasonable. In fact, if you search the Web, you will find a variety of sites that help you assess your learning style and give advice on how to increase your ability to learn given your style of learning. In this article, Steven Stahl points out that although the notion of learning styles has intuitive appeal, it doesn't fare well under scientific scrutiny.

While reading this selection, notice how it illustrates some of the differences between scientific and pseudoscientific approaches to gathering evidence discussed in Chapter 1. For example, Chapter 1 discussed the fact that high-quality scientific evidence typically consists of peer-reviewed, scientific journal articles. Stahl points out that the evidence cited to support learning styles typically does not meet this scientific standard for evidence.

APA Reference

Stahl, S. A. (1999). Different strokes for different folks? A critique of learning styles. *American Educator, 23*(3), 27–31.

I work with a lot of different schools and listen to a lot of teachers talk. Nowhere have I seen a greater conflict between "craft knowledge" or what teachers know (or at least think they know) and "academic knowledge" or what researchers know (or at least think they know) than in the area of learning styles. Over the years, my experience has told me to trust teachers; it has also taught me that teachers' craft knowledge is generally on target. I don't mean to say that teachers are always right, but they have learned a great deal from their thousands of observations of children learning in classrooms. So, when teachers talk about the need to take into account children's learning styles when teaching, and researchers roll their eyes at the sound of the term "learning styles," there is more to it than meets the eye.

The whole notion seems fairly intuitive. People are different. Certainly different people might learn differently from each other. It makes sense. Consider the following from the Web site of the National Reading Styles Institute, a major proponent of the application of learning styles to the teaching of reading:

> We all have personal styles that influence the way we work, play, and make decisions. Some people are very analytical, and they think in a logical, sequential way. Some students are visual or auditory learners; they learn best by seeing or hearing. These students are likely to conform well to traditional methods of study.
>
> Some people (we call them "global learners") need an idea of the whole picture before they can understand it, while "analytic learners" proceed more easily from the parts to the whole. Global learners also tend to learn best when they can touch what they are learning or move around while they learn. We call these styles of learning "tactile" and "kinesthetic." In a strictly traditional classroom, these students are often a problem for the teacher. She has trouble keeping them still or quiet. They seem unable to learn to read. (http://www.nrsi.com/about.html)

This all seems reasonable, but it isn't.

RESEARCH AND LEARNING STYLES

The reason researchers roll their eyes at learning styles is the utter failure to find that assessing children's learning styles and matching to instructional methods has any effect on their learning. The area with the most research has been the

Steven A. Stahl is professor of reading education at the University of Georgia and co-director of the Center for Improvement of Early Reading Achievement. His research interests are in beginning reading and vocabulary instruction.

global and analytic styles referred to in the NRSI blurb above. Over the past 30 years, the names of these styles have changed—from "visual" to "global" and from "auditory" to "analytic"—but the research results have not changed.

In 1978, Tarver and Dawson reviewed 15 studies that matched visual learners to sight word approaches and auditory learners to phonics. Thirteen of the studies failed to find an effect, and the two that found the effect used unusual methodology. They concluded:

> Modality preference has not been demonstrated to interact significantly with the method of teaching reading.[1]

One year later, Arter and Jenkins reviewed 14 studies (some of these are overlapping), all of which failed to find that matching children to reading methods by preferred modalities did any good. They concluded:

> [The assumption that one can improve instruction by matching materials to children's modality strengths] appears to lack even minimal empirical support.[2]

Kampwirth and Bates, in 1980, found 24 studies that looked at this issue. Again, they concluded:

> Matching children's modality strengths to reading materials has not been found to be effective.[3]

In 1987, Kavale and Forness reviewed 39 studies, using a meta-analysis technique that would be more sensitive to these effects. They found that matching children by reading styles had nearly no effect on achievement. They concluded:

> Although the presumption of matching instructional strategies to individual modality preferences has great intuitive appeal, little empirical support for this proposition was found. . . . Neither modality testing nor modality teaching were shown to be [effective].[4]

A fifth review, in 1992, by Snider found difficulties in reliably assessing learning styles and a lack of convincing research that such assessment leads to improvement in reading.

> Recognition of individuals' strengths and weaknesses is good practice, using this information, however, to categorize children and prescribe methods can be detrimental to low-performing students. Although the idea of reading style is superficially appealing, critical examination should cause educators to be skeptical of this current educational fad.[5]

These five research reviews, all published in well-regarded journals, found the same thing: One cannot reliably measure children's reading styles and even if one could, matching children to reading programs by learning styles does not improve their learning. In other words, it is difficult to accurately identify children who are "global" and "analytic." So-called global children do not do better in whole language programs than they would in more phonics-based programs. And so-called analytic children do not do better in phonics programs than they do in whole language programs. In short, time after time, this notion of reading styles does not work.

This is an area that has been well researched. Many other approaches to matching teaching approaches to learning styles have not been well researched, if at all. I could not find studies in refereed journals, for example, documenting whether the use of Howard Gardner's Multiple Intelligences Model[6] improved instruction. This does not mean, of course, that the use of the model does not improve achievement, only that I could not find studies validating its use. The same is true of other learning style models.

One cannot prove a negative. Even if all of these studies failed to find that matching children by learning styles helps them read better, it is always possible that another study or another measure or another something will find that matching children to their preferred learning modality will produce results. But in the meantime, we have other things that we *know* will improve children's reading achievement. We should look elsewhere for solutions to reading problems.

Yet, the notion of reading styles (or learning styles) lingers on. This is true not only in my talks with teachers, but also in the literature that teachers read. The most recent issue of *Educational Leadership* included, as part of a themed issue on innovations, several articles on learning styles. *Phi Delta Kappan* also regularly contains articles on learning styles, as do other publications intended for teachers.

RESEARCH INTO LEARNING STYLES

Among others, Marie Carbo claims that her learning styles work is based on research. [I discuss Carbo because she publishes extensively on her model and is very prominent on the workshop circuit. In the references for this article, I cite a few examples of her numerous writings on the topic.[7]] But given the overwhelmingly negative findings in the published research, I wondered what she was citing, and about a decade ago, I thought it would be interesting to take a look. Reviewing her articles, I found that out of 17 studies she had cited, only one was published.[8] Fifteen were doctoral dissertations and 13 of these came out of one university—St. John's University in New York, Carbo's alma mater. None of these had been in a peer-refereed journal. When I looked closely at the dissertations and other materials, I found that 13 of the 17 studies that supposedly support her claim had to do with learning styles based on something other than modality. In 1997, I found 11 additional citations. None of these was published, eight were dissertations, and six of these came from St. John's. In short, the research cited would not cause anyone to change his or her mind about learning styles.

WHAT DO PEOPLE MEAN BY LEARNING STYLES?

Modality refers to one of the main avenues of sensation such as vision and hearing. I have only talked about modality-based reading styles because these are both the best researched and the most heavily promoted. The National Reading Styles Institute claims that it has worked with "over 150,000 teachers," and its advertisements seem to be everywhere. Furthermore, these notions of "visual" and "auditory" learners or "global" and "analytic" learners have been around for a long time and have found their way into a number of different programs, not just the NRSI programs.

There are other ways of looking at learning styles. People have proposed that children vary not only in perceptual styles, but on a host of different dimensions. To name a few, people have suggested that children are either two-dimensional/three-dimensional, simultaneous/sequential, connecting/compartmentalizing, inventing/reproducing, reflective/impulsive, field dependent/field independent, and so on.

Some of these are *learning preferences,* or how an individual chooses to work. These might include whether a person prefers to work in silence or with music playing, in bright light or dim light, with a partner or alone, in a warm room or a cool room, etc.

Some of these are *cognitive styles,* such as whether a person tends to reflect before making a choice or makes it impulsively, or whether a person tends to focus on details or sees the big picture.

Some of these are *personality types,* such as whether a person is introverted or extroverted.

Some of these are *aptitudes,* like many of Howard Gardner's multiple intelligences. Gardner suggests that people vary along at least seven different dimensions—*linguistic* or the ability to use language, *logico-mathematical* or the ability to use reasoning especially in mathematics, *spatial* or the ability to use images or pictures, *bodily-kinesthetic* or the ability to control movement, *musical, interpersonal* or the ability to work with people, and *intrapersonal* or the thinking done inside oneself. The last two are more like personality types, rather than aptitudes or even learning styles. The others are Gardner's attempt to expand the notion of what we think is intelligent behavior to people who are skilled in music, or dance, or even in interpersonal relations. In contrast to the traditional vision of learning styles as either/or categories (either a person is visual or he or she is auditory), multiple intelligences are put forth by Gardner as separate abilities. A child may be strong in a few of these areas, or none of these areas.

What is a teacher to do with all this? If there are children who prefer to work with music, then the teacher might either provide Walkmans for those who prefer music or play music openly and provide earplugs for those who don't. If there are children who prefer to work in bright light, the teacher might seat those children over by the window. Children who like to snack while reading can be allowed to eat during class (healthy foods, of course). It would be easy to see how accommodating all of these preferences in a class could lead to chaos. How would a teacher lecture, give assignments, or even call to order a class in which a sizable proportion of the students was wearing earplugs? Or how does one regulate the temperature so part of the room is warm and part cool?

Others have used learning styles theory as a way of making sure that all the needs of diverse learners are being met. Marguerite Radenich used Gardner's model to examine literature study guides.[9] Her ideal was one that incorporated all of these ways of knowing into an integrated whole to be used to study adolescent literature. Thus, Gardner's model was used here to create more multidimensional instruction. This is very different from using these different styles to segregate children into groups where they would receive fairly one-dimensional instruction.

Thoughtful educators have tried to make this work, and perhaps it is workable, but trying to meet all of the preferences of a group of children would seem to take energy that would be better spent on other things. This is especially true since no one has proven that it works.

LEARNING STYLES AND FORTUNE TELLING

Why does the notion of "learning styles" have such enduring popularity—despite the lack of supporting evidence? I believe that this phenomenon has a lot in common with fortune telling.

You go to see a fortune teller at a circus. She looks you over and makes some quick judgments—how young or old you are, how nicely you are dressed, whether you appear anxious or sad or lonely—and based on these judgments, tells your fortune. The fortune she tells may be full of simple and ambiguous statements—"you will be successful at your next venture," "you will be lucky at love," or may be more complex—"you are successful at home, but someone is jealous; make sure you watch yourself." Either way, the statements are specific enough so that they sound predictive, but ambiguous enough that they could apply to a number of situations.

When we read the statements on a Learning Style Inventory, they sound enough like us that we have a flash of recognition. These inventories typically consist of a series of forced choices, such as these from Marie Carbo's *Reading Style Inventory, Intermediate,* 1995.[10]

A. I always like to be told exactly how I should do my reading work.
B. Sometimes I like to be told exactly how I should do my reading work.
C. I like to decide how to do my reading work by myself.

Or

A. I like to read in the morning.
B. I don't like to read in the morning.

A. I like to read after lunch.
B. I don't like to read after lunch.

A. I like to read at night.
B. I don't like to read at night.

Or

A. I read best where it's quiet with no music playing.
B. I read best where there is music playing.
C. I read about the same where it's quiet or where there is music playing.

Since all of us have some preferences (my experience is that adults have clear preferences about music during reading, especially), these items tend to ring true. Like the fortunes told by the fortune teller, these statements at first light seem specific enough to capture real distinctions among people. But the problem with choices like these is that people tend to make the same choices. Nearly everybody would prefer a demonstration in science class to an uninterrupted lecture. This does not mean that such individuals have a visual style, but that good science teaching involves demonstrations. Similarly, nearly everybody would agree that one learns more about playing tennis from playing than from watching someone else play. Again, this does not mean that people are tactile/kinesthetic, but that this is how one learns to play sports. Many of these "learning styles" are not really choices, since common sense would suggest that there would not be much variance among people. In the class sample provided with the Reading Style Inventory above, for example, 96 percent of the fifth-graders assessed preferred quiet to working while other people were talking, 88 percent preferred quiet to music, 79 percent picked at least two times of day when they preferred to work, 71 percent had no preference about temperature, and so on. Virtually all of the questions had one answer preferred by a majority of the students.

The questions are just specific enough to sound like they mean something, but vague enough to allow different interpretations. For example, does "music" refer to Mozart or Rap? Obviously, one's choices would be different for different types of music. A more serious question would arise over the "teacher direction" item. Doesn't the amount of teacher direction needed depend on the difficulty of the assignment? There are some assignments that are self-evident and do not need much teacher direction, but when work gets complex, students need more direction. This is not a matter of preference.

The other major problem with these inventories is that there are no questions about a child's reading ability. So children with reading problems are given the same measure as children who are doing well in reading. This has two effects. First, there is a bias on some items for children with different abilities. Consider these two items, also from the Carbo inventory:

A. It's easy for me to remember rules about sounding out words.
B. It's hard for me to remember rules about sounding out words.

Or

 A.   When I write words, I sometimes mix up the letters.
 B.   When I write words, I almost never mix up the letters.

Children with reading problems are more likely to answer that they do not remember phonics rules and that they sometimes mix up the letters. According to the learning styles research reports, such children are likely to be considered as having a global (or visual) preference.[11] Actually, this may not be a preference at all, but a reflection of the child's current level of reading ability. The potential for harm occurs when children with reading problems are classified as "global" (visual) learners and thereby miss out on important instruction in decoding, or are classified as "analytic" (auditory) learners and miss out on opportunities to practice reading in connected text.

Not including information about reading ability also leads to some strange prescriptions. Adults attending learning styles workshops often get prescriptions for beginning reading instruction methods, such as the language experience approach or phonics/linguistic approaches, certainly not needed by competent readers. And for children, too, some of the approaches may be inappropriate. The language experience approach, for example, is best suited for children at the emergent literacy stage, when they need to learn about basic print concepts, one-to-one matching, letter identification, and so on.[12] For a second-grader, or even a newly literate adult, language experience may be appropriate (if they still have not mastered basic print concepts) or highly inappropriate (if they are already reading fluently). It depends on the readers' skill, not their learning styles.

RELIABILITY

If you are to use a test, even an inventory like the one cited above, it should be reliable. If a test is reliable, that means you are going to get the same (or close to the same) results every time you administer it. If a test is 100 percent reliable (or has a reliability coefficient of 1.0), then a person will score exactly the same on Thursday as on Tuesday. Perfection is tough to come by, so we generally want a reliability coefficient to be .90 or higher.[13] If a test is not reliable, or trustworthy, then it is difficult to believe the results. This is a problem, not only with inventories, but with any measure that asks subjects to report about themselves.

Reliabilities of these measures are relatively low. The self-reported reliabilities of Carbo's Reading Style Inventory and Dunn and Dunn's Learning Style Inventories are moderate, especially for a measure of this kind—in the neighborhood of the .60s and the .70s. Similar reliabilities are reported for the Myers-Briggs Inventory, another learning styles assessment.[14] These are lower than one would want for a diagnostic measure. And, these scores are inflated, since for many items there is generally one answer that nearly everybody chooses. This would tend to make the reliabilities higher.

The vagueness in the items may tend to make the reliabilities low. Again, how a child interprets each item will influence how it is answered, as with the "teacher direction" and "music" examples discussed earlier.

Test-retest reliabilities are particularly important for a measure of learning styles. These moderate reliabilities could be interpreted in two ways. The test itself may not be a reliable measure of what it is supposed to measure—that is, a person has a stable learning style, but the test is not getting at it. If the test is not reliable, then the information it gives is not trustworthy.

The other possibility is that learning styles may change, from month to month, or even week to week. This is also problematic. If we are talking about matching a person to a situation using this instrument, this is a relatively long-term (semester or academic year) matching. If a person's style changes, then one either must measure learning styles frequently, or allow for more flexible assignments.

How Reading Develops

The Learning Style model assumes that different children need different approaches to learn to read. Children are different. They come to us with different personalities, preferences, ways of doing things. However, the research so far shows that this has little to do with how successful they will be as readers and writers. Children also come to us with different amounts of exposure to written text, with different skills and abilities, with different exposure to oral language. The research shows that these differences *are* important.

Rather than different methods being appropriate for different children, we ought to think about different methods being appropriate for children at different stages in their development. Children differ in their phonemic abilities, in their ability to recognize words automatically, in their ability to comprehend and learn from text, and in their motivation and appreciation of literature.[15] Different methods are appropriate for different goals. For example, approaches that involve the children in reading books of their own choice are important to develop motivated readers.[16] But whole language approaches, which rely largely on children to choose the materials they read, tend not to be as effective as more teacher-directed approaches for developing children's word recognition or comprehension.[17]

A language experience approach may be appropriate to help a kindergarten child learn basic print concepts. The child may learn some words using visual cues, such as might be taught through a whole word method. With some degree of phonological awareness, the child is ready to learn letters and sounds, as through a phonic approach. Learning about letters and sounds, in combination with practice with increasingly challenging texts, will develop children's ability to use phonetic cues in reading, and to cross-check using context. With additional practice in wide reading, children will develop fluent and automatic word recognition. None of this has anything to do with learning styles; it has to do with the children's current abilities and the demands of the task they have to master next.

WHAT DO TEACHERS GET OUT OF LEARNING STYLES WORKSHOPS?

I have interviewed a number of teachers who have attended learning styles workshops. These were meetings of 200 to 300 teachers and principals, who paid $129 or so to attend a one-day workshop or up to $500 to attend a longer conference. They have found them to be pleasant experiences, with professional presenters. The teachers also feel that they learned something from the workshops. After I pressed them, what it seemed that they learned is a wide variety of reading methods, a respect for individual differences among children, and a sense of possibilities of how to teach reading. This is no small thing. However, the same information, and much more, can be gotten from a graduate class in the teaching of reading.

These teachers have another thing in common—after one year, they had all stopped trying to match children by learning styles.

References

[1]Tarver, Sara, and M.M. Dawson. 1978. Modality preference and the teaching of reading. *Journal of Learning Disabilities* 11:17–29.

[2]Arter, J.A., and Joseph A. Jenkins. 1979. Differential diagnosis prescriptive teaching: A critical appraisal. *Review of Educational Research* 49:517–555.

[3]Kampwirh, T.J., and M. Bates. 1980. Modality preference and teaching method. A review of the research. *Academic Therapy* 15:597–605.

[4]Kavale, Kenneth, A., and Steven R. Forness. 1987. Substance over style: Assessing the efficacy of modality testing and teaching. *Exceptional Children* 54:228–239.

[5]Snider, Vicki. E. 1992. Learning styles and learning to read: A critique. *Remedial and Special Education* 13:6–18.

[6]Gardner, Howard. 1993. *Frames of mind: The theory of multiple intelligences.* New York: Basic Books.

[7]For example, Carbo. Marie. 1997. Reading styles times twenty. *Educational Leadership* 54 (6):38–42; Carbo, Marie, Rita Dunn, and Kenneth Dunn. 1986. *Teaching students to read through their individual learning styles.* Englewood Cliffs, NJ.: Prentice-Hall.

[8]See Stahl, Steven A. 1988. Is there evidence to support matching reading styles and initial reading methods? A reply to Carbo. *Phi Delta Kappan* 70 (4):317–322.

[9]Radenich, Marguerite Cogorno. 1997. Separating the wheat from the chaff in middle school literature study guides. *Journal of Adolescent and Adult Literacy* 41 (1):46–57.

[10]All examples are from Carbo, Marie, 1995. *Reading Style Inventory Intermediate (RSI-I):* Author.

[11]Carbo, M. 1988. Debunking the great phonics myth. *Phi Delta Kappan* 70:226–240.

[12]Stahl, Steven A., and Patricia D. Miller. 1989. Whole language and language experience approaches for beginning reading. A quantitative research synthesis. *Review of Educational Research* 59 (1):87–116.

[13]Harris, Albert J., and Edward Sipay. 1990. *How to increase reading ability.* 10th ed. White Plains, N.Y.: Longman.

[14]Pittenger, David, J. 1993. The utility of the Myers-Briggs Type Indicator. *Review of Educational Research* 63:467–488.

[15]Stahl, Steven A. 1998. Understanding shifts in reading and its instruction, *Peabody Journal of Education* 73(3–4):31–67.

[16]Morrow, Lesley M., and Diane Tracey, 1998. Motivating contexts for young children's literacy development: Implications for word recognition development. In *Word recognition in beginning literacy*, edited by J. Metsala and L. Ehri. Mahwah, N.J.: Erlbaum; Turner, Julianne, and Scott G. Paris. 1995. How literacy tasks influence children's motivation for literacy. *The Reading Teacher* 48:662–673.

[17]Stahl and Miller, op cit., Stahl, Steven A., C. William Suttles, and Joan R. Pagnucco. 1996. The effects of traditional and process literacy instruction on first-graders' reading and writing achievement and orientation toward reading. *Journal of Educational Research* 89:131–144.

Review and Contemplate

1. What are some examples of learning styles that are thought to influence how children learn to read?
2. Give two examples of research evidence on whether matching method of instruction to children's learning styles improves learning. What does Stahl conclude about the effectiveness of such an approach?
3. What does it mean to say that a test is reliable? Do reading styles inventories tend to be reliable measures? What does this imply about the usefulness of these measures?
4. According to Stahl (1999), how might the practice of fortune telling help us understand why the notion of learning styles continues to be popular despite the lack of supporting evidence?

6.2

Past-life Identities, UFO Abductions, and Satanic Ritual Abuse: The Social Reconstruction of Memories /
NICHOLAS SPANOS, CHERYL BURGESS, AND MELISSA FAITH BURGESS

In her book, titled *Abducted,* Dr. Susan Clancy discussed how people come to believe they were abducted by aliens. She told the story of Will Andrews, a 42-year-old chiropractor. Dr. Clancy stated, "For the past ten years he has had vivid memories of having been repeatedly taken away by 'beings' and medically, psychologically, and sexually experimented on. During his abductions, he became close to his 'alien guide'—a streamlined, sylph-like creature. Although they didn't communicate verbally, he feels they became 'spiritually connected' and their connection resulted in a number of hybrid babies. He never sees his children, but he feels their presence. 'I know they're out there, and they know who I am.'"

Although some believe that anecdotal reports of alien abductions are evidence that aliens have actually visited our planet and abducted people, you read in Chapter 1 that scientists do not rely on anecdotes or testimonials for evidence. One problem with anecdotal reports of alien abductions is that although the people who give such reports may truly believe the abduction occurred, it is possible that they are remembering events that never actually took place.

Spanos, Burgess, and Burgess discuss fascinating stories of people who believe they (a) lived a past life, (b) have many different personalities living within them, (c) were abducted by aliens, or (d) participated in ritualized satanic abuse involving the rape and murder of children. Although these beliefs and memories are very real to many people who experience them, the authors present evidence that suggests that socially influenced, false memories underlie these amazing beliefs.

APA Reference

Spanos, N. P., Burgess, C. A., and Burgess, M. F. (1994). Past-life identities, UFO abductions, and satanic ritual abuse: The social reconstruction of memories. *The International Journal of Clinical and Experimental Hypnosis, 42,* 433–446.

Carleton University, Ottawa, Ontario, Canada

ABSTRACT: People sometimes fantasize entire complex scenarios and later define these experiences as memories of actual events rather than as imaginings.

This article examines research associated with three such phenomena: past-life experiences, UFO alien contact and abduction, and memory reports of childhood ritual satanic abuse. In each case, elicitation of the fantasy events is frequently associated with hypnotic procedures and structured interviews which prov ide strong and repeated demands for the requisite experiences, and which then legitimate the experiences as "real memories." Research associated with these phenomena supports the hypothesis that recall is reconstructive and organized in terms of current expectations and beliefs.

It is now generally acknowledged that recall involves reconstructive processes and is strongly influenced by current beliefs and expectations (Bower, 1990; Loftus, 1979). As pointed out by Bartlett (1932) many years ago, people typically organize their recall of past events in a way that makes sense of their present situation and is congruent with their current expectations. What they recall frequently involves a mixture of correctly remembered and misremembered information that is often impossible to disentangle. Often there is little or no correlation between the accuracy of recall and the confidence that people place in their recall. It is not unusual for people to be convinced about the accuracy of a remembrance that turns out to be false (Loftus, 1979; Wells, Ferguson, & Lindsay, 1981). Contrary to popular belief, hypnotic procedures do not reliably enhance the accuracy of recall and, at least under some circumstances, may lead subjects to become even more overconfident than usual in their inaccurate recall (Smith, 1983; Spanos, Quigley, Gwynn, Glatt, & Perlin, 1991). Leading questions and other suggestive interview procedures, whether or not they are administered in a hypnotic context, can produce a very substantial deterioration in recall accuracy even when subjects remain highly confident in their inaccurate remembrances (Spanos, Gwynn, Comer, Baltruweit, & deGroh, 1989).

To a large extent, these ideas about memory have been developed and refined in the context of studying eyewitness testimony. The implications of these ideas have been particularly influential at shaping the critical attitudes taken by many psychologists toward the reliability of eyewitness testimony, and toward the usefulness of hypnotic and other procedures that are touted as "refreshing" such testimony (Loftus, 1979; Orne, 1979; Smith, 1983; Wagstaff, 1989). In the typical eyewitness situation, however, the memory distortions under consideration involve inaccuracies in detail (e.g., identifying the wrong suspect of real crime) rather than fabrications of entire complex scenarios (e.g., detailed descriptions of an entire gun battle that never occurred). Little systematic research is available that examines the applications of reconstructive and expectancy-guided views of memory to situations in which people "remember" entire scenarios that never happened. This article describes research of this kind conducted in our laboratory and examines the implications of our findings for three phenomena that appear to involve the wholesale "remembering" of fictitious events; past-life identities (Warnbach, 1979), UFO alien contact and abduction reports (Jacobs, 1992), and reports of satanic ritual child abuse from patients diagnosed with multiple personality disorder (Fraser, 1990; Young, Sachs, Braun, & Watkins, 1991).

EXPERIMENTAL CREATION
OF PAST-LIFE PERSONALITIES

Several studies have examined factors that influence the formation of false memories by employing the phenomenon of past-life hypnotic regression. Some believers in reincarnation contend that people can be hypnotically regressed back to a time before their birth when they led previous lives (e.g., Wambach, 1979). The available evidence does not support this hypothesis and suggests instead that "memories" of having lived a past life are fantasy constructions (Baker, 1992; Spanos, Menary, Gabora, DuBreuil, & Dewhirst, 1991; Wilson, 1982). These fantasy constructions are important, however, because they can shed light on the processes by which people come to treat their fantasies as real, and because past-life identities are similar in many respects to the secondary or alter identities of multiple personality disorder patients. Like multiple personality disorder patients, subjects who report past lives behave as if they are inhabited by secondary selves. These selves display moods and personality characteristics that are different from the person's primary self, have a different name than the primary self, and report memories of which the primary self was previously unaware. Just as multiple personality disorder patients come to believe that their alter identities are real personalities rather than self-generated fantasies, many of the subjects who remember past lives continue to believe in the reality of their past lives after termination of the hypnotic session.

Kampman (1976) found that 41% of highly hypnotizable subjects reported a past-life identity and called themselves by different names when given hypnotic suggestions to regress back before their birth. Contrary to the notion that multiple identity experiences are a sign of mental illness, Kampman's (1976) past-life responders scored higher on measures of psychological health than did subjects who failed to report a past life.

In a series of experiments, Spanos, Menary, et al. (1991) also obtained past-life identity reports following hypnotic regression suggestions. Frequently the past-life identities were quite elaborate. They had their own names and frequently described their lives in great detail. Subjects who reported past-life experiences scored higher on measures of hypnotizablity and fantasy proneness, but no higher on measures of psychopathology than those who did not exhibit a past life.

The social nature of past-life identities was demonstrated by showing that the characteristics that subjects attributed to these identities were influenced by expectations transmitted by the experimenter (Spanos, Menary, et al, 1991; Experiment 2). Subjects provided with prehypnotic information about the characteristics of their identities (e.g., information about the identities' expected race and sex) were much more likely than those who did not receive such information to incorporate these characteristics into their descriptions of their past-life selves.

A different study (Spanos, Menary, et al., 1991, Experiment 3) tested the hypothesis that experimenter expectations influence the extent to which past-life identities describe themselves as having been abused during childhood. Before past-life regression, subjects were informed that their past-life identities would be questioned about their childhoods to obtain information about child-rearing practices in earlier historical times. Those in one condition were further told that children in past times had frequently been abused. Those in the other condition were given no information about abuse. The past-life identities of subjects given abuse information reported significantly higher levels of abuse during childhood than did the past-life identities of control subjects. In summary, these studies indicate that both the personal attributes and memory reports elicited from subjects during past-life identity enactments are influenced by the beliefs and expectations conveyed by the experimenter/hypnotist. When constructing their past lives, subjects shape the attributes and biographies attributed to these identities to correspond to their understandings of what significant others believe these characteristics to be.

After termination of the hypnotic regression procedure, some past-life reporters believed that their past-life experiences were memories of actual, reincarnated personalities, whereas others believed that their past-life identities were imaginary creations. Hypnotizability did not predict the extent to which subjects assigned credibility to their past-life identities. Instead, the degree of credibility assigned to these experiences correlated significantly with the degree to which subjects believed in reincarnation before the experiment, and the extent to which they expected to experience a real past life.

In a final study Spanos, Menary, et al. (1991; Experiment 4) manipulated prehypnotic information that concerned the reality of past-life experiences. Subjects in one condition were informed that past-life experiences were interesting fantasies rather than evidence of real past-life memories. Those in another condition were provided with background information which suggested that reincarnation was a scientifically credible notion, and that past-life identities were real people who had lived earlier lives. Subjects in the two conditions were equally likely to construct past-life experiences, but those assigned to the imaginary creation condition assigned significantly less credibility to these identities than did those told that reincarnation was scientifically credible.

Taken together these findings indicate that experiences of having lived a past life are social creations that can be elicited easily from many normal people, and that are determined by the understandings that subjects develop about such experiences from the information to which they are exposed. Past-life identities can be quite complex and detailed, and subjects draw from a wide array of sources outside of the immediate situation (e.g., television shows, historical novels, aspects of their own past, wish-fulfilling daydreams) to flesh out their newly constructed identity and to provide it with the history and characteristics that are called for by their understanding of the current task demands. The most important factor in influencing the extent to which past-life experiences are defined as real memories appears to be the extent to which subjects hold a belief system that is congruent with this interpretation (i.e., a belief in reincarnation). Information from an authoritative source which legitimates or delegitimates reincarnation beliefs also influences the extent to which subjects define their experiences as real memories rather than imaginings.

All of these past-life experiments either tested only highly hypnotizable subjects or found that the reporting of past lives was correlated significantly with hypnotizablity. Hypnotizablity refers to the extent to which subjects respond to hypnotic suggestions, and it correlates significantly with such dimensions as fantasy proneness and an openness to unusual experiences (see deGroh, 1989, for a review). One interpretation suggests that hypnotizablity or its imaginal correlates may constitute cognitive abilities which predispose individuals to construct secondary identities when such experiences are called for by contextual demands, and when these subjects are motivated to respond to those demands.

However, an alternative hypothesis suggests that hypnotizablity is correlated with the development of past-life identities because the suggestions that called for these experiences were administered in a hypnotic context and therefore were likely to call up the same attitudes and expectations as the hypnotizablity test situation. Whether circumstances can be created that will elicit multiple identity enactments from low hypnotizables remains to be determined.

ENCOUNTERS WITH UFO ALIENS

Reports of seeing unidentified flying objects (UFOs) and belief that such objects are extraterrestrial spacecraft have increased dramatically since World War II. Nevertheless, the available scientific evidence fails to support the hypothesis that these reports reflect the sighting of alien spacecraft (Sheaffer, 1986). Initially, UFO reports focused on the purported sightings of the crafts themselves. However, by the mid-1960s purportedly true accounts of people who claimed to have been abducted by UFO aliens began to appear (e.g., Fuller, 1966). Some of these accounts gained a great deal of notoriety. In addition, uncritical and sensationalistic documentary-type television shows and movies that featured alien contact became popular (Sheaffer, 1986). At the same time, reports of contact and abduction by aliens mushroomed, and such reports appear to be increasing in frequency (Klass, 1989).

Recently, Spanos, Cross, Dickson, and DuBreuil (1993) interviewed subjects who claimed UFO experiences. One group of these subjects simply reported distant lights or shapes in the night sky that appeared to move in erratic patterns and that they interpreted as UFOs. However, a second group of 20 subjects reported more elaborate experiences that included close contact with alien spaceships and/or alien beings, and occasionally, abduction by the aliens. Subjects in both UFO groups failed to differ in hypnotizablity or fantasy proneness from comparison subjects, and either failed to differ, or scored higher, than comparison subjects on indexes of mental health and IQ. However, subjects in both UFO groups believed more strongly in the reality of UFOs than did comparison subjects, and those with elaborate UFO experiences also held other esoteric beliefs (e.g., reincarnation) more strongly than comparison subjects.

Subjects who reported elaborate UFO experiences were much more likely to report their experience was sleep related than were those who reported more mundane (i.e., lights in the sky) experiences. Many of the elaborate experiences were clearly night dreams or hypnagogic imagery. In addition, almost a quarter of those in the elaborate UFO group reported frightening experiences that included full body paralysis and, frequently, vivid multisensorial hallucinations. For example, one subject reported:

> I was lying in bed facing the wall, and suddenly my heart started to race. I could feel the presence of three entities standing beside me. I was unable to move my body but could move my eyes. One of the entities, a male, was laughing at me, not verbally but with his mind. *(Spanos et al., 1993, p. 627)*

Experiences of this kind are most probably explicable as sleep paralysis; a phenomenon that is usually estimated as occurring in approximately 15% to 25% of the population, and that is commonly associated with feelings of suffocation, the sense of a presence, and hallucinations (Bell et al., 1984; Hufford, 1982). These findings suggest that at least some of the characteristics common to many elaborate UFO reports (e.g., being paralyzed by the aliens) may be grounded in the physiological changes that underlie sleep paralysis experiences.

Not all elaborate UFO experiences were sleep related. Moreover, the elaborateness of UFO experiences was positively correlated with questionnaire variables that assessed propensities toward experiencing unusual body sensations, and fantasy proneness. Hypnotizablity, however, failed to correlate significantly with elaborateness.

Taken together, the findings of Spanos et al. (1993) indicate that elaborate UFO experiences that are later described as memories are particularly likely to occur in people who believe in alien visitation, and who also interpret unusual sensory and imaginal experiences in terms of the alien hypothesis.

People who believe that they might have been abducted by aliens but cannot remember, or who dream of aliens or experience gaps in memory that they are unable to explain, sometimes undergo hypnotic (or non-hypnotic) interviews aimed at uncovering, "hidden memories" of their alien abduction (Jacobs, 1992; Klass, 1989). Frequently, the interviews include two phases. In the first phase background information is obtained and clients are asked about unusual or inexplicable experiences that have occurred during their life. These include "missing time" experiences, unusual or bizarre dreams, and experiences that suggest hypnagogic imagery or sleep paralysis (e.g., having seen a ghost, strange lights, or a monster). Such experiences are defined as distorted memories of alien abduction that call for further probing (Jacobs & Hopkins, 1992). Moreover, making such experiences salient enhances the likelihood that some of their characteristics (e.g., paralysis, feelings of suffocation) will be incorporated into any abduction memories that are recalled in Phase 2. Phase 2 typically involves hypnotic or nonhypnotic guided imagery employed to facilitate recall. This may involve leading questions (Baker, 1992), or the subject may be pressed repeatedly for more details (Jacobs, 1992). In addition, subjects may be informed that some material is so deeply hidden that several such interviews are required, Subjects who have difficulty "remembering" some or all of their abduction are defined as "blocking" and are provided with strategies for facilitating recall. These include asking subjects to imagine a curtain and then to peek behind it to view their abduction, or to imagine a movie screen on which they see their abduction replayed (Jacobs & Hopkins, 1992).

Given that subjects in past-life experiments frequently reported elaborate past-life identities on the basis of much less prodding, it is not surprising that such interviewing procedures lead clients to generate imaginative scenarios in which they are abducted by aliens. It is also not surprising that clients typically interpret their abduction fantasies as memories rather than as fantasies. After all, they usually sought help because they believed that they might have been abducted. In other words, they already possessed a set of background beliefs and current expectations that facilitated the interpretation of such fantasies as memories. In addition, their abduction fantasies are legitimated as memories by the interviewers who treat them as such and who do not provide alternative explanations. Finally, it is worth noting that people who believe that they have been abducted frequently join support groups that include other abductees (Jacobs, 1992). The sharing of abduction experiences in such groups can only serve to enhance their uniformity and further legitimate them as real memories.

RITUAL SATANIC ABUSE AND MULTIPLE PERSONALITY DISORDER

The large majority of patients who eventually receive a multiple personality disorder diagnosis do not display symptoms of multiplicity and are unaware that they have alter identities before they enter treatment with the therapist who "discovers" their multiplicity (Kluft, 1985). Moreover, this "discovery" frequently involves the use of highly leading hypnotic interviews in which patients are explicitly informed that they have alter personalities and attempts are made to communicate directly with these alters, learn their names, their functions, and so on (Bliss, 1986; Spanos, Weekes, & Bertrand, 1985; Wilbur, 1984).

Most studies find that multiple personality disorder patients report extremely high rates of childhood sexual and/or physical abuse (e.g., Ross, Miller, Bjornson, Reagor, & Fraser, 1991). Contrary to the majority opinion in the multiple personality disorder literature, however, these data do not demonstrate that child abuse causes multiplicity. At least three noncausal factors appear to influence the high rates of reported child abuse obtained from multiple personality disorder patients: (a) high base rates of reported child abuse in the clinical samples from which patients who will be diagnosed with multiple personality disorder are drawn, (b) use of a child abuse history to justify implementing leading "diagnostic" interviews that generate displays of multiplicity, and (c) confabulation of abuse in patients who generate such "memories" only after exposure to leading interviews that call for and legitimate such reports (Spanos, in press).

The strong connection between child abuse and multiple personality disorder is of recent origin. Early cases (i.e., pre-1920) were much less likely than modern ones to be associated with reports of child abuse (Bowman, 1990;

Kenny, 1986), and the abuse that was reported in these early cases lacked the lurid ritualistic satanic elements that are becoming increasingly prominent in the abuse memories proffered by modern multiple personality disorder patients.

Although controversy remains concerning its actual rate of occurrence (Wakefield & Underwager, 1992), there is general agreement that the sexual abuse of children in our society is a good deal more common than was once believed (Finkelhor, 1987). Frequently, people who were sexually abused as children retain their memories of these experiences (Femina, Yeager, & Lewis, 1990). In some cases, however, adults in psychotherapy report for the first time remembering early child abuse. According to many multiple personality disorder therapists (e.g., Bliss, 1986), these reports reflect memories of actual abuse that was repressed at the time of its occurrence and recovered later during the therapeutic process. However, an alternative hypothesis suggests that these reports may frequently reflect confabulations induced by the unwitting suggestions of therapists (Loftus, 1993; Spanos, in press). Unfortunately, in such cases it is usually difficult or impossible to either corroborate or disconfirm the validity of these memory reports (Wakefield & Underwager, 1992). Reported memories of ritual satanic child abuse are an exception. These reports are of theoretical importance for memory researchers because the available data indicate that they are almost always believed-in fantasy constructions rather than memories of actual events (Jenkins & Maier-Katkin, 1991; Mulhern, 1991b; Spanos, in press).

By 1980 the idea of a relationship between child abuse and multiple personality disorder was well established. In that year a book titled *Michelle Remembers* (Smith & Pazdec, 1980) reported on ritual satanic tortures that a woman had purportedly experienced during childhood and then forgotten until they were recovered during therapy. Michelle's story became a part of the propaganda used by the Evangelical Christian movement that became increasingly prominent in American social and political life during the 1980s. This movement reinvigorated the mythology of satanism—the idea that there exists a powerful but secret international satanic conspiracy that carries out heinous crimes. These crimes supposedly include the kidnapping, torture, and sexual abuse of countless children as well as mass murder, forced pregnancies, and cannibalism (Bromley, 1991; Hicks, 1991; Lyons, 1989).

Large numbers of therapists who identified themselves as active Christians joined the multiple personality disorder movement in the 1980s (Mulhern, 1993), and soon accounts like those of Michelle began to be reported by the alters of multiple personality disorder patients during therapy (Frazer, 1990; Young et al., 1991). By the mid-1980s, 25% of multiple personality disorder patients in therapy had recovered memories of ritual satanic abuse, and by 1992 the percentage of patients recovering such memories was as high as 80% in some treatment facilities (Mulhern, 1993).

If they were real, the ritual satanic crimes "remembered" by multiple personality disorder patients would require a monumental criminal conspiracy that has been in existence for at least 50 years and that has been responsible for the murder of thousands of people (Hicks, 1991). The FBI and other law enforcement agencies throughout North America have investigated many satanic abuse allegations made by multiple personality disorder patients but have been unable to substantiate the existence of the requisite criminal conspiracy (Lanning, 1992). These repeated failures to find evidence of satanic ritual abuse strongly indicate that the vast majority of these allegations are false, and that the "memories" on which they are based are fantasies rather than remembrances of actual events (Hicks, 1991).

Bottoms, Shaver, and Goodman (1991) surveyed psychotherapists across the United States about the frequency with which they had seen patients who reported ritual abuse memories. Seventy percent of the therapists who responded indicated no contact with such patients. A small minority, however, reported having seen large numbers of patients who reported ritual abuse. This pattern of findings suggests that therapists who regularly obtain such reports play an active role in shaping the ritual abuse "memories" of their patients.

Frequently, satanic abuse memories are elicited during hypnotic interviews that explicitly suggest such abuse. In such cases it is common for the therapist to explicitly describe satanic rituals and possibly to show the patient pictures of satanic symbols or photographs of possible cult leaders. The therapist then addresses the patient's alters and asks if any of them recognize the material or remember similar experiences (Mulberry, 1991a).

Multiple personality disorder patients are often chronically unhappy people with well-developed imaginations, who become strongly attached to and dependent on their therapists. Consequently, they are motivated to use the information from such interviews to construct an autobiography that will make sense of their lives and their symptoms, and that will win approval and validation from their therapist (Spanos, in press). In this context it is worth recalling the ease with which highly hypnotizable college students were induced to report past life personalities who "remembered" that they had been abused as children, when the expectation of such abuse had been conveyed to them before their hypnotic regression (Spanos, Menary, et al., 1991).

Recently, Ofshe (1992) described the case of a fundamentalist Christian man named Paul Ingram who, after highly leading interrogations confessed to having participated in the satanic ritual abuse of his own children. The case provides a "real life" example of the ease with which false memories can be generated in people who hold a belief system that is congruent with the false information. Ingram was initially accused of incest by one of his daughters after she had attended a church-sponsored retreat intended to reveal sexual abuse. Ingram initially denied the charges, but after being convinced that his children would not lie, he agreed that Satan may have hidden from him his own crimes. Many of the events to which Ingram eventually confessed were suggested to him by the police officers and psychologist who interrogated him, and he was supported in his confessions by his minister. Along with repeatedly raping his children, Ingram confessed to belonging to a satanic cult and participating in the murder of 25 babies. Although Ingram had no history of mental illness before his arrest, he was diagnosed as suffering from multiple personality disorder by at least one psychologist.

Ofshe (1992) demonstrated Ingram's willingness to accept suggested fantasies as real memories by concocting a set of ritual abuse events that had not been alleged against Ingram. When Ofshe questioned Ingram about these false events using guided imagery and other interrogative procedures employed by the police, Ingram readily confessed to them. Later Ingram insisted that the false events had really happened and had not been suggested to him during the interrogation.

Some patients report memory fragments or dreams with satanic content and only after are exposed to hypnotic interviews aimed at confirming such abuse. However, since many multiple personality disorder patients are enmeshed in a social network where they hear about satanic abuse from other patients, therapists, and shared newsletters, and where they or their fellow patients attend workshops devoted to such abuse, "spontaneous" dreams and memories do not provide serious evidence of actual ritual abuse (Mulhern, 1991b).

CONCLUSION

The findings reviewed above are consistent with the view that recall is reconstructive and guided by current motivations and expectations. In addition, these findings indicate that social factors can lead people to generate complex fantasy scenarios and to define such experiences as actual memories of real events. In many cases some elements in these fantasies are memories. For instance, past-life reporters frequently incorporate information from their own past, or events and plots recalled from books and movies into their past-life identities, and UFO reporters sometimes experience abduction dreams or complex sleep paralysis episodes. The memory of these experiences can then form the core of their abduction fantasies and help to legitimate these fantasies as memories. Some multiple personality disorder patients may use memories of actual abuse around which they add elaborate satanic elements. Despite the inclusion of real memory elements, however, past-life, UFO and satanic ritual abuse "memories" are primarily fantasy constructions. Typically they are organized around expectations derived from external sources, embedded in a belief system that is congruent with their classification as memories, and legitimated as memories by significant others. In short, whether experiences are counted as memories of actual happenings or as fantasies may, under some circumstances, have less to do with characteristics intrinsic to these experiences than to the internal context (i.e., supportive belief structures) in which they are embedded and the external context (i.e., social legitimation) in which they are validated (Johnson, 1988).

Manuscript submitted March 23, 1993; final revision received January 27, 1994.

1. The writing of this article was supported by a grant to the first author from the Soscial Sciences and Humanities Research Council of Canada.
2. Requests for reprints should be addressed to Cheryl A. Burgess, Department of Psychology, 8550 Loeb Building, 1125 Colonel By Drive, Carleton University, Ottawa, Ontario K1S 3B6, Canada.

The International Journal of Clinical and Experimental Hypnosis, Vol. XLII. No. 4, October 1994, 433–446 (c) 1994 The International Journal of Clinical and Experimental Hypnosis.

References

Baker, R.A. (1992), *Hidden memories,* Buffalo, NY, Prometheus.

Bartlett, E.C. (1032), *Remembering,* Cambridge, Cambridge University Press.

Bell, C.C., Shakoor, B., Thompson, B., Dew, D., Hughley, E., Mays, R., and Shorter-Gooden, K. (1984). Prevalence of isolated sleep paralysis in Black subjects. *Journal of the National Medical Association, 76,* 501–508.

Bliss, E.I. (1986) *Multiple personality, allied disorders and hypnosis,* New York, Oxford.

Bottoms, B. L., Shaver, P.R., & Goodman, G.S. (1991, August). *Profile of ritual and religion related abuse allegations reported to clinical psychologists in the United States.* Paper presented at the 99th annual convention of the American Psychological Association, San Francisco.

Bower, G. (1990). Awareness, the unconscious and repression: An experimental psychologist's perspective. In J.L. Singer (Ed.), *Repression and dissociation: Implications for personality, theory, psychopathology, and health* (pp. 209–222). Chicago, University of Chicago Press.

Bowman, E.S. (1990). Adolescent multiple personality disorder in the nineteenth and early twentieth centuries, *Dissociation, 3,* 179–187.

Bromley, D.G. (1991). Satanism: The new cult scare. In J.T. Richardson, J. Best, & D.G. Bromley (Eds.), *The satanism scare* (pp. 49–72). New York: Aldine deGruyter.

DeGroh, M. (1989). Correlates of hypnotic susceptibility. In N.P. Spanos & J.F. Chaves (Eds.), *Hypnosis the cognitive behavioral perspective.* Buffalo, NY, Prometheus.

Femina, D.D., Yeager, C.A., & Lewis, D.O. (1990). Child abuse: Adolescent records vs. adult recall. *Child Abuse and Neglect, 14,* 227–231.

Finkelhor, D. (1987). The sexual abuse of children: Current research reviewed. *Psychiatric Annals, 17,* 233–241.

Fraser, G.A. (1990). Satanic ritual abuse: A cause of multiple personality disorder. *Journal of Child and Youth Care,* pp. 55–66.

Fuller, J.G. (1966). *The interrupted journey,* New York: Dell.

Hicks, R.D. (1991). *In pursuit of Satan,* Buffalo, NY: Prometheus.

Hufford, D. (1992). *The terror that comes in the night.* Philadelphia University of Pennsylvania Press.

Jacobs, D.M. (1992), *Secret life: Firsthand accounts of UFO abductions.* New York: Simon & Schuster.

Jacobs, D.M., & Hopkins, B. (1992). *Suggested techniques for hypnosis and therapy of abductees.* Unpublished manuscript, Department of History, Temple University, Philadelphia, PA.

Jenkins, P., & Maier-Katkin, D. (1991). Occult survivors: The making of a myth. In J.T. Richardson, K. Best, & D.G. Bromley (Eds.), *The satanism scare* (pp. 49–72). New York: Aldine deGryter.

Johnson, M.K. (1988). Discriminating the origin of information. In T.F. Oltmanns & B.A. Maher (eds.), *Delusional beliefs* (pp. 34–65). New York: Wiley.

Kampman, R. (1976). Hypnotically induced multiple personality: An experimental study. *International Journal of Clinical and Experimental Hypnosis, 24,* 215–217.

Kenny, M.G. (1981), Multiple personality and spirit possession. *Psychiatry, 44,* 337–356.

Kenny, M.G. (1986). *The passion of Ansel Bourne: Multiple personality and American culture.* Washington, DC: Smithsonian Institution Press.

Klass, P.J. (1989). *UFO abductions: A dangerous game.* Buffalo, NY: Prometheus.

Kluft, R.P. (1985). The natural history of multiple personality disorder. In R.P. Kluft (Ed.), *Childhood antecedents of multiple personality* (pp. 197–238). Washington, DC: American Psychiatric Press.

Lanning, K.V. (1992). A law enforcement perspective on allegations of ritual abuse. In D.K. Sakheim & S.E. Devine (eds.), *Out of darkness: Exploring satanism and ritual abuse* (pp. 109–146). New York: Lexington.

Loftus, E.F. (1979). *Eyewitness testimony.* Cambridge, MA: Harvard University Press.

Loftus, E.F. (1993). The reality of repressed memories. *American Psychologist 48,* 518–537.

Lyons, A. (1989). *Satan wants you: The cult of devil worship in America.* New York: Mysterious Press.

Merskey, H. (1992). The manufacture of personalities: The production of multiple personality disorder. *British Journal of Psychiatry, 160,* 327–340.

Mulhern, S. (1991a). Letter to the editor. *Child Abuse and Neglect, 14,* 609–611.

Mulhern, S. (1991b). Satanism and psychotherapy: A rumor in search of an inquisition. In J.T. Richardson, J. Best, & D.G. Bromley (eds.), *The satanism scare* (pp. 145–172) New York: Aldine de Gruyter.

Mulhern, S. (1993). *Le trouble de la personnalite multiple a la recherche du trauma perdu* [The trouble of multiple personality in the research of lost trauma]. Unpublished manuscript, Laboratorie des Rumeurs des Mythes du Futur et des Sectes, U.F.R. Anthropologie, Ethnologie, Science des Relgions, Universite de Paris, France.

Ofshe, R.J. (1992). Inadvertent hypnosis during interrogation: False confession due to dissociative state; mis-identified multiple personality and the satanic cult hypothesis. *International Journal of Clinical and Experimental Hypnosis, 40,* 125–156.

Orne, M.T. (1979). The use and misuse of hypnosis in court. *International Journal of Clinical and Experimental Hypnosis, 27,* 311–341.

Ross, C.A., Miller, S.D., Bjornson, L., Reagor, P., & Fraser, G.A. (1991). Abuše histories in 102 cases of multiple personality disorder. *Canadian Journal of Psychiatry, 36,* 97–101.

Sheaffer, R. (1986). *The UFO verdict.* Buffalo, NY: Prometheus.

Smith, M. & Pazder, L. (1980). *Michelle remembers.* New York: Pocket Books.

Smith, M.C. (1983). Hypnotic memory enhancement of witnesses: Does it work? *Psychological Bulletin, 94,* 387–407.

Spanos, N.P. (1989). Hypnosis, demonic possession and multiple personality: Strategic enactments and disavowals of responsibility for actions. In C.A. Ward (ed.), *Altered states of consciousness and mental health: Theoretical and methodological issues* (pp. 96–124). Newbury Park, CA: Sage.

Spanos, N.P. (in press). Multiple identity enactments and multiple personality disorder: A sociocognitive perspective. *Psychological Bulletin.*

Spanos, N.P., Cross, P., Dickson, K., & DuBreuil, S.C. (1993). Close encounters: An examination of UFO experiences. *Journal of Abnormal Psychology, 102,* 624–632.

Spanos, N.P., Gwynn, M.I., Comer, S.L., Baltruweit, W.J., & deGroh, M. (1989). Are hypnotically induced pseudomemories resistant to cross-examination? *Law and Human Behavior, 13,* 271–289.

Spanos, N.P., Menary, E., Gabora, N.J., DuBreuil, S.C., & Dewhirst, B. (1991). Secondary identity enactments during hypnotic past-life regression: A sociocognitive perspective. *Journal of Personality and Social Psychology, 61,* 308–320.

Spanos, N.P., Quigley, C.A., Gwynn, M.I., Glatt, R.L., & Perlini, A.H. (1991). Hypnotic interrogation, pretrial preparation, and witness testimony during direct and cross-examination. *Law and Human Behavior, 15,* 639–653.

Wagstaff, G.F. (1989). Forensic aspects of hypnosis. In N.P. Spanos & J.F. Chaves (Eds.), *Hypnosis: The cognitive-behavioral perspective* (pp. 340–357). Buffalo, NY: Prometheus.

Wakefield, H., & Underwager, R. (1992). Recovered memories of alleged sexual abuse: Lawsuits against parents. *Behavioral Sciences and the Law, 10,* 483–507.

Wambach, H. (1979). *Life before life.* New York: Bantam.

Wells, G.L., Ferguson, T.J., & Lindsay, R.C.L. (1981). The tractability of eyewitness confidence and its implications for triers of fact. *Journal of Applied Psychology, 66,* 688–696.

Wilbur, C.B. (1984). Treatment of multiple personality. *Psychiatric Annals, 14,* 27–31.

Wilson, I. (1982). *Reincarnation? The claims investigated.* Harmondsworth, Middlesex, England: Penguin.

Young, W.C., Sachs, R.G., Braun, G.G., & Watkins, R.T. (1991). Patients reporting ritual abuse in childhood: A clinical syndrome. Report of 37 cases. *Child Abuse and Neglect, 15,* 181–189.

Review and Contemplate

1. Describe the research findings that suggest memories of past-life identities are fantasy constructions rather than real memories. How might people come to mistakenly believe they have led a past life?

2. Explain two different ways that people might come to believe they were visited or abducted by aliens. (HINT: One way is sleep related, the other is not).

3. What evidence suggests that multiple personality disorder (also known as Dissociative Identity Disorder) is socially constructed (i.e., people learn to exhibit the disorder rather than developing it spontaneously or as a result of abuse)?

4. What evidence suggests that memories of satanic ritual abuse are false memories (cite at least two types of evidence)?

6.3

Memory Recovery Techniques in Psychotherapy: Problems and Pitfalls / STEVEN JAY LYNN, ELIZABETH LOFTUS, SCOTT LILIENFELD, AND TIMOTHY LOCK

After experiencing severe postpartum depression, Patricia Burgess sought in-patient psychiatric care in a large Chicago hospital in 1986. Patricia's therapists helped her uncover previously hidden memories of her role as the high priestess of a satanic cult. She recalled participating in satanic rituals, being abused by numerous men, abusing her own children, murdering adults and babies, and engaging in cannibalism. After her condition worsened, she was transferred to another psychiatric unit where she began to doubt the reality of her new memories. Patricia eventually realized that none of the events her therapists helped her "remember" actually happened. She was not the high priestess of a satanic cult, and she had not abused or murdered anyone. Her therapists had used a mixture of psychiatric drugs, hypnotism, and highly suggestive questioning to bring out these false memories. Patricia eventually won a $10.6 million lawsuit against the hospital and the psychiatrists.

Patricia's story is a rather extreme example of the destructive power of various pseudoscientific techniques for unearthing supposedly repressed memories. Sigmund Freud believed that some of our thoughts, wishes, and memories—especially those that may cause us psychological distress—get pushed back into our unconscious minds so we are no longer consciously aware of them. He called this phenomenon repression. Although reliable scientific evidence for repressed memories is lacking, a substantial number of mental health professionals believe they exist and use a variety of memory recovery techniques to help patients remember traumatic memories. Lynn, Loftus, Lilienfeld, and Lock describe these memory recovery techniques and discuss scientific evidence that suggests they may result in the creation rather than the recovery of traumatic memories.

APA Reference

Lynn, S. J., Loftus, E. F., Lilienfeld, S. O., & Lock, T. (2003, July/August). Memory recovery techniques in psychotherapy: Problems and pitfalls. *Skeptical Inquirer, 27,* 40–46.

Memory recovery techniques that are widely used in psychotherapy including hypnosis, age regression, guided imagery, dream interpretation, bibliotherapy, and symptom interpretation can distort or create—rather than reveal— allegedly repressed traumatic memories.

In 1997, Nadean Cool won a $2.4 million malpractice settlement against her therapist in which she alleged that he used a variety of suggestive memory recovery procedures to persuade her that she had suffered horrific abuse and harbored more than 130 personalities including demons, angels, children, and a duck. Prior to therapy, Nadean recounted problems typical of many women including a history of bulimia, substance abuse, and mild depression. During her five-year treatment, Nadean's therapist allegedly maintained that she could not improve unless she uncovered repressed traumatic memories. To do so, Nadean participated in repeated hypnotic age regression and guided imagery sessions, and was subjected to an exorcism and fifteen-hour marathon therapy sessions. Nadean recalled frightening images of participating in a satanic cult, eating babies, being raped, having sex with animals, and being forced to watch the murder of her eight-year-old friend after these interventions, and her psychological health deteriorated apace. Eventually Nadean came to doubt that the recovered memories were "real," terminated treatment with her therapist, and recouped much of the ground she had lost.

Although Nadean Cool's therapy strayed far beyond conventional practice, her therapist is in the company of many professionals who perform so-called "memory work" to help clients retrieve memories of ostensibly repressed

Steven Jay Lynn is a professor of psychology at the State University of New York at Binghamton. He is a past president of the Division of Psychological Hypnosis of the American Psychological Association and author of twelve books and more than 200 scientific articles. E-mail: slynn@binghamton.edu. **Elizabeth F. Loftus** is distinguished professor of psychology and social behavior, criminology, law and society at the University of California at Irvine. She is past president of the American Psychological Society, a CSICOP Fellow, and author of twenty books and more than 250 articles. **Scott O. Lilienfeld** is associate professor of psychology at Emory University. He is president of the Society for a Science of Clinical Psychology, a CSICOP Fellow, and editor of *The Scientific Review of Mental Health Practice*. **Timothy Lock** is the Coordinator of Adults Sexual Offender Treatment at the Westchester Jewish Community Services. He has published articles and chapters on the topic of memory recovery techniques and false memories.

This article is a substantially revised and abbreviated version of a chapter entitled, "The remembrance of things past: Problematic memory recovery techniques in psychotherapy," which appeared in S.O. Lilienfeld, S.J. Lynn, and J.M. Lobr (Eds.), *Science and Pseudoscience in Clinical Psychology,* New York: Guilford. The article is published with the permission of the publisher, Portions of this article were included in a talk entitled, "Problematic memory recovery techniques in psychotherapy," by Steven Jay Lynn, presented at the Fourth International Skeptics Conference, Burbank, California.

abuse. Poole, Lindsay, Mcmon, and Bull (1995) reported that 25 percent of licensed doctoral level psychologists surveyed in the United States and Great Britain indicated that they: (a) use two or more techniques such as hypnosis and guided imagery to facilitate recall of repressed memories; (b) consider memory recovery an important part of treatment; and (c) can identify patients with repressed or otherwise unavailable memories as early as the first session (see Polousny and Follecte 1996 for similar findings). In addition, over three-quarters of the U.S. doctoral-level psychotherapists reported using at least one memory recovery technique to "help clients remember childhood sexual abuse." In this article we consider a number of widely used memory recovery procedures, and whether they can distort or create, rather than reveal, traumatic memories.

CLINICAL TECHNIQUES

Guided Imagery

One important class of techniques relies on guided imagery, in which patients imagine scenarios described by the therapist. So long as imagery techniques focus on current problems, as in visualizing pleasant scenes to develop relaxation skills, there is probably little cause for concern about false memory creation. However, the use of imagery to uncover allegedly repressed memories is controversial and warrants concern because people frequently confuse real and imagined memories, particularly when memories are initially hazy or unavailable. Roland (1993), for example, proposed using visualization to jog "blocked" memories of sexual abuse, and a "reconstruction" technique for recovering repressed memories of abuse. According to Poole et al. (1995), 32 percent of U.S. therapists report using "imagery related to the abuse."

Suggesting False Memories

Memory errors are not random. What is recalled depends on current beliefs, inferences, guesses, expectancies, and suggestions. People can clearly be led by suggestions to integrate a fabricated event into their personal histories. In Loftus's research (Loftus, Coan, and Pickrell 1996; Loftus and Pickrell 1995), twenty-four participants were asked by an older sibling to remember real and fictitious events (e.g., getting lost in a shopping mall). The older sibling initially provided a few details about the false event, such as where the event allegedly occurred, after which the subjects were interviewed one to two weeks apart. A quarter of the subjects claimed to remember the false event; some provided surprisingly detailed accounts of the event that they came to believe had actually occurred. Similar studies with college students have shown that approximately 20–25 percent report experiencing such fictitious events as: (a) an overnight hospitalization for a high fever and a possible ear infection, accidentally spilling a bowl of punch on the parents of the bride at a wedding reception, and evacuating a grocery store when the overhead sprinkler systems erroneously activated (Hyman et al. 1995); and (b) a serious animal attack, serious indoor accident, serious outdoor accident, a serious medical procedure, and being injured by another child (Porter, Yuille, and Lehman 1998).

Hypnosis

Many therapists endorse popular yet mistaken beliefs about hypnosis. Yapko's (1994) survey revealed that 47 percent of a sample composed of professionals had greater faith in the accuracy of hypnotic than non-hypnotic memories, 54 percent believed to some degree that hypnosis is effective for recovering memories as far back as birth, and 28 percent believed that hypnosis is an effective means of recovering past life memories. If hypnosis were able to accurately retrieve forgotten memories, confidence in its use for recovering memories would be warranted. But this is not the case. The following conclusions are based on major reviews of the literature[1]:

1. Hypnosis increases the sheer volume of recall, resulting in both more incorrect and correct information. When the number of responses is statistically controlled, hypnotic recall is no more accurate than nonhypnotic recall.

2. Hypnosis produces more recall errors and higher levels of memories for false information.

3. False memories are associated with subjects' levels of hypnotic suggestibility. However, even relatively non-suggestible participants report false memories.

4. Hypnotized persons sometimes exhibit less accurate recall in response to misleading questions compared with nonhypnotized participants.

5. In general, hypnotized individuals are more confident about their recall accuracy than are nonhypnotized individuals, and an association between hypnotizability and confidence has been well documented.

6. Even when participants are warned about possible memory problems associated with hypnosis, they continue to report false memories during and after hypnosis, although some studies indicate that warnings decrease pseudomemories.

7. Contrary to the claim that hypnosis facilitates the recall of emotional or traumatic memories, hypnosis does not improve recall of emotionally arousing events (e.g., films of shop accidents, depictions of fatal stabbings, a mock assassination, an actual murder videotaped serendipitously), and arousal level is not associated with hypnotic recall.

8. Hypnosis does not necessarily produce more false memories or unwarranted confidence in memories than highly suggestive nonhypnotic procedures. However, simply asking participants to focus on the task at hand and to do their best to recall specific events yields accurate recall comparable to hypnosis, but with fewer or comparable recall errors.

Our dour assessment of hypnosis for recovering memories has been echoed by professional societies, including divisions and task forces of the American Psychological Association and the Canadian Psychiatric Association. The American Medical Association (1994) has asserted that hypnosis be used only for investigative purposes in forensic contexts. However, even when hypnosis is used solely for investigative purposes, there are attendant risks. Early in an investigation, the information obtained through hypnosis could lead investigators to pursue erroneous leads and even to interpret subsequent leads as consistent with initial and perhaps mistaken hypnotically generated evidence.

Searching for Early Memories

According to Adler (1931), "The first memory will show the individual's fundamental view of life. . . . I would never investigate a personality without asking for the first memory (p. 75)." More recently, Olson (1979) articulated a belief shared by many therapists (Papanek 1979) that "[Early memories] when correctly interpreted often reveal very quickly the basic core of one's personality . . . and suggest . . . bedrock themes with which the therapist must currently deal in treating the client" (p. xvii).

Most adults' earliest reported memories date back to between 36 and 60 months of age. Virtually all contemporary memory researchers agree that accurate memory reports of events that occur before 24 months of age are extremely rare (see Malinoski, Lynn, and Sivec 1998), due to developmental changes that influence how children process, retrieve, and share information. Adults' memory reports from 24 months of age or earlier are likely to represent confabulations, condensations, and constructions of early events, as well as current concerns and stories heard about early events (Spanos 1996). Although certain early memories might well have special significance,[2] such memories are highly malleable. Malinoski, Lynn, and Green (1999) examined early memories in a study in which interviewers probed for increasingly early memories until participants twice denied any earlier memories. Participants then received "memory recovery techniques" similar to those advocated by some therapists (e.g., Farmer 1989, Meiselman 1990). Interviewers asked participants to see themselves "in their mind's eye" as a toddler or infant, and "get in touch" with memories of long ago. Participants were informed that most young adults can retrieve memories of very early events—including their second birthday—if they "let themselves go" and try hard to visualize and concentrate. Interviewers then asked for subjects' memories of their second birthdays and reinforced increasingly early memory reports.

The average age of the initial reported memory was 3.7 years: Only 11 percent of individuals reported memories at or before age 24 months, and 3 percent reported a memory from age 12 months or younger. However, after receiving the visualization instructions, 59 percent of the participants reported a memory of their second birthday. After interviewers pressed for even earlier memories, the earliest memory reported was 1.6 years, on average. Fully 78.2 percent of the sample reported at least one memory that occurred at or earlier than 2 years, outside the boundary of infantile amnesia. More than half (56 percent) of the participants reported a memory between birth and 18 months of life; a third (33 percent) reported a memory that occurred at age 12 months or earlier, and 18 percent reported memories dated from six months or earlier. Remarkably, 4 percent of the sample reported memories from the first week of life!

Age-regression

Age-regression involves "regressing" a person back through time to an earlier life period. Subjects are typically asked to mentally re-create events that occurred at successively earlier periods in life, or to focus on a particular event at a specific age, with suggestions to fully relive the event. A televised documentary (*Frontline* 1995) showed a group therapy session in which a woman was age-regressed through childhood, to the womb, and eventually to being trapped in her mother's Fallopian tube. The woman provided a convincing demonstration of the emotional and physical discomfort that one would experience if one were indeed stuck in such an uncomfortable position. Although the woman may have believed in the veracity of her experience, research indicates that her regression experiences were not memory-based. Instead, age-regressed subjects behave according to situational cues and their knowledge, beliefs, and assumptions about age-relevant behaviors. According to Nash (1987), age-regressed adults do not show the expected patterns on many indices of development, including brain activity (EEGs) and visual illusions. No matter how compelling, "age-regressed experiences" do not represent literal reinstatements of childhood experiences, behaviors, and feelings.

Hypnotic Age-regression

Although hypnosis is often used to facilitate the experience of age-regression, it can distort memories of early life events. Nash, Drake, Wiley, Khalsa, and Lynn (1986) attempted to corroborate the memories of subjects who had participated in an earlier age-regression experiment. This experiment involved age-regressing hypnotized and role-playing (control) subjects to age three to a scene in which they were in the soothing presence of their mothers. During the experiment, subjects reported the identity of their transitional objects (e.g., blankets, teddy bears). Third-party verification (parent report) of the accuracy of recall was obtained for fourteen hypnotized subjects and ten control subjects. Hypnotic subjects were less able than were control subjects to identify the transitional objects actually used. Hypnotic subjects' hypnotic recollections matched their parent's reports only 21 percent of the time, whereas control subjects' reports were corroborated by their parents 70 percent of the time.

Sivec and Lynn (1997) age-regressed participants to the age of five and suggested that they played with a Cabbage Patch Doll (if a girl) or a He-Man toy (if a boy). These toys were not released until two or three years after the target time of the age-regression suggestion. Half of the subjects received hypnotic age-regression instructions and half received suggestions to age-regress that were not administered in a hypnotic context. While none of the nonhypnotized persons was influenced by the suggestion, 20 percent of the hypnotized subjects rated the memory as real and were confident that the event occurred at the age to which they were regressed.

Past Life Regression

The search for traumatic memories can extend to well before birth (see Mills and Lynn 2000). "Past life regression therapy" is based on the premise that traumas that occurred in previous lives contribute to current psychological and physical symptoms. For example, psychiatrist Brian Weiss (1988) published a widely publicized series of cases focusing on patients who were hypnotized and age-regressed to "go back to" the origin of a present-day problem. When patients were regressed, they reported events that Weiss interpreted as having their source in previous lives.

Vivid and realistic experiences during age-regression can seem very convincing to both patient and therapist. However, Spanos, Menary, Gabora, DuBreuil, and Dewhirst (1991) determined that the information participants provided about specific time periods during their hypnotic age-regression was almost "invariably incorrect" (p. 137). For example, one participant who was regressed to ancient times claimed to be Julius Caesar, emperor of Rome, in 50 B.C., even though the designations of B.C. and A.D. were not adopted until centuries later, and even though Julius Caesar died decades prior to the first Roman emperor. Spanos et al. (1991) informed some participants that past life identities were likely to be of a different gender, culture, and race from that of the present personality, whereas other participants received no prehypnotic information about past life identities. Participants' past life experiences were elaborate, conformed to induced expectancies about past life identities (e.g., gender, race), and varied in terms of the pre-hypnotic information participants received about the frequency of child abuse during past historical periods. In summary, hypnotically-induced past life experiences are fantasies constructed from available cultural narratives about past lives and known or surmised facts regarding specific historical periods, as well as cues present in the hypnotic situation (Spanos 1996).

Symptom Interpretation

Therapists often inform suspected abuse victims that their symptoms suggest a history of abuse (Blume 1990, Fredrickson 1992). Examples of symptom interpretation can be found in many popular psychology and self-help sources (e.g., Bass and Davis 1992). Some popular self-help books on the topic of incest include lists of symptoms (e.g., "Do you use work or achievements to compensate for inadequate feelings in other parts of your life?") that are presented as possible or probable correlates of childhood incest. Blume's "Incest Survivors' After-effects Checklist" consists of thirty-four such correlates. The scale instructions read: "Do you find many characteristics of yourself on this list? If so, you could be a survivor of incest." Blume also indicates that "clusters" of these items predict childhood sexual abuse, and that "the more items endorsed by an individual the more likely that there is a history of incest." Many of the characteristics on such checklists are vague and applicable to many non-abused individuals. Much of the seeming "accuracy" of such checklists could stem from "P.T. Barnum effects"—the tendency to believe that highly general statements true of many individuals in the population apply specifically to oneself (Emery 2002).

Although there may be numerous psychological correlates of sexual abuse (but see Rind, Tromovitch, and Bauserman 1998, for a competing view), no known constellation of specific symptoms, let alone diagnosis, is indicative of a history of abuse. Some genuine victims of childhood incest experience many symptoms, others only some, and still others none. Moreover, nonvictims experience many of the same symptoms often associated with sexual abuse (Tavris 1993). Nevertheless, Poole et al. (1995) found that more than one-third of the U.S. practitioners surveyed reported that they used symptom interpretation to recover suspected memories of abuse.

Bogus Personality Interpretation

For ethical reasons, researchers have not directly tested the hypothesis that false memories of childhood abuse can be elicited by informing individuals that their personality characteristics are suggestive of such a history. However, studies have shown that personality interpretation can create highly implausible or false memories. Spanos and his colleagues (Spanos, Burgess, Burgess, Samuels, and Blois 1999) informed participants that their personality indicated that they had a certain experience during the first week of life. After participants completed a questionnaire, they were told that a computer-generated personality profile based on their responses indicated they were "High Perceptual Cognitive Monitors," and that people with this profile had experienced special visual stimulation by a mobile within the first week of life. Participants were falsely told that the study was designed to recover memories to confirm the personality test scores. The participants were age-regressed to the crib; half of the participants were hypnotized and half received non-hypnotic age-regression instructions. In the non-hypnotic group, 95 percent of the participants reported infant memories and 56 percent reported the target mobile. However, all of these participants indicated that the memories were fantasy constructions or they were unsure if the memories were real. In the hypnotic group, 79 percent of the participants reported infant memories, and 46 percent reported the target mobile. Forty-nine percent of these participants believed the memories were real, and only 16 percent classified the memories as fantasies.

DuBreuil, Garry, and Loftus (1998) used the bogus personality interpretation paradigm and non-hypnotic age-regression to implant memories of the second day of life (crib group) or the first day of kindergarten (kindergarten group). College students were administered a test that purportedly measured personality and were told that, based on their scores, they were likely to have participated in a nationwide program designed to enhance the development of personality and cognitive abilities by means of red and green moving mobiles. The crib group was told that this enrichment occurred in the hospital immediately after birth, and the kindergarten group was told that the mobiles were placed in kindergarten classrooms. Participants were given the false information that memory functions "like a videotape recorder" and that age-regression can access otherwise inaccessible memories. Participants were age-regressed (nonhypnotically) to the appropriate time period and given suggestions to visualize themselves at the target age. Twenty-five percent of the kindergarten group and 55 percent of the crib group reported the target memory. All kindergarten participants believed that their memories corresponded to real events. In the crib group, 33 percent believed in the reality of their memories, 50 percent were unsure, and 17 percent of participants did not believe in the reality of their memories.

Dream Interpretation

Viewed by Freud as the "royal road to the unconscious," dreams have been used to provide a window on past experiences, including repressed traumatic events. For example, van der Kolk, Britz, Burr, Sherry, and Hartmann (1984) claimed that dreams can represent "exact replicas" of traumatic experiences (p. 188), a view not unlike that propounded by Fredrickson (1992), who argued that dreams are a vehicle by which "Buried memories of abuse intrude into . . . consciousness" (p. 44).

The popularity of dream interpretation has waned in recent years. However, survey research indicates that at least a third of U.S. psychotherapists (37–44 percent) still use this technique (see also Brenneis 1997, Polusny and Follette 1996). These statistics are noteworthy given that no data exist to support the idea that dreams can be interpreted as indicative of a history of child abuse (Lindsay and Read 1994). When dreams are interpreted in this manner by an authority figure such as a therapist, rather than as reflecting the residues of the day's events or as the day's concerns seeping into dreams, it can constitute a strong suggestion to the patient that abuse actually occurred.

Mazzoni and her colleagues simulated the effects of dream interpretation of stressful yet non-abuse-related life events. Mazzoni, Lombardo, Malvagia, and Loftus (1997) had participants report on their childhood experiences on two occasions, three to four weeks apart. Between sessions, some subjects were exposed to a brief (half hour) therapy simulation in which an expert clinician analyzed a dream report that they had brought to the session. No matter what participants dreamed, they received the suggestion that their dream was indicative of having experienced certain events (e.g., being lost in a public place or abandoned by parents) before the age of three. Although subjects had indicated that they had not experienced these events before age three, many individuals revised their accounts of their past. Relative to controls who had not received the personalized suggestion, "therapy" participants were far more likely to develop false beliefs that before age three they had been lost in a public place, had felt lonely and lost in an unfamiliar place, and had been abandoned by their parents.

Mazzoni, Loftus, Seitz, and Lynn (1999) extended this paradigm to a memory of having been bullied as a child; dream interpretation increased participants' confidence that the event (being bullied or getting lost) had occurred, compared with control participants who were given a brief lecture about dreams. Six of the twenty-two participants in the dream interpretation condition recalled the bullying event and four of the five participants in the dream interpretation condition recalled getting lost. In conclusion, it is possible to implant childhood memories using personality and dream interpretation.

Bibliotherapy

Many therapists who treat patients with suspected abuse histories prescribe "survivor books" or self-help books written specifically for survivors of childhood abuse to provide "confirmation" that the individual's symptoms are due to past abuse and to provide a means of gaining access to memories. The books typically provide imaginative exercises and stories of other survivors' struggles, as well as potential support for actual abuse survivors. However, the fact that the writers interpret current symptoms as indicative of an abuse history and include suggestive stories of abuse survivors may increase the risk that readers will develop false memories of abuse. Some of the most influential popular books of this genre include Bass and Davis' (1988) *Courage to Heal,* Fredrickson's (1992) *Repressed Memories,* and Blume's (1990) *Secret Survivors: Uncovering Incest and Aftereffects in Women.*

Mazzoni, Loftus, and Kirsch (2001) provided a dramatic illustration of how reading material and psychological symptom interpretation can increase the plausibility of an initially implausible memory of witnessing a demonic possession. The study was conducted in Italy, where demonic possession is viewed as a more plausible occurrence than in America. However, in an initial testing session, all of the participants indicated that demonic possession was not only implausible, but that it was very unlikely that they had personally witnessed an occurrence of possession as children. A month after the first session, participants in one group read three short articles indicating that demonic possession is more common than is generally believed and that many children have witnessed such an event. Participants were compared with individuals who read three short articles about choking and with individuals who received no manipulation. Participants exposed to one of the manipulations returned the following week and, based on their responses to a fear questionnaire they completed, were informed (regardless of their actual responses) that their fear profile indicated that they had probably either witnessed a possession or had almost choked during early childhood.

When the original questionnaire was completed in a final session, 18 percent of the students indicated that they had probably witnessed possession. No changes in memories were evident in the control condition. In summary, events that were not experienced during childhood and initially thought to be highly implausible can, with sufficient credibility-enhancing information, come to be viewed as having occurred in real life.

HYPOTHESIZED PATH OF FALSE MEMORY CREATION

Imaginative narratives of sexual abuse that never occurred and past life reports arise when patients come to believe that the narrative provides a plausible explanation for current life difficulties. The narrative can achieve a high degree of plausibility due to many factors:

> (1) the prevalent belief that abuse and psychopathology are associated; (2) the therapist's support or suggestion of this interpretation; (3) the failure to consider alternative explanations for everyday problems; (4) the search for confirmatory data; (5) the use of suggestive memory recovery techniques that increase the plausibility of abuse and yield remembrances consistent with the assumption that abuse occurred; (6) increasing commitment to the narrative on the part of the client and therapist, escalating dependence on the therapist, and anxiety reduction associated with ambiguity reduction; (7) the encouragement of a "conversion" or "coming out" experience by the therapist or supportive community (e.g., therapy group), which solidifies the role of "abuse victim," and which is accompanied by reinforcing feelings of empowerment; and (8) the narrative's provision of continuity to the past and the future, as well as a sense of comfort and identity.

People are not equally vulnerable to the potentially suggestive influences of memory recovery procedures. At the very least it is necessary to believe that at least some memories remain intact indefinitely so that they can be retrieved, and that memory recovery techniques can retrieve these stored memories. In addition, fantasy prone, imaginative, compliant, as well as highly hypnotically suggestible people appear to be especially vulnerable to suggestive influences and to the development of false memories.

The evidence provides little support for the use of memory recovery techniques in psychotherapy. Contrary to the idea that people repress memories in the face of trauma, traumatic events are highly memorable (Shobe and Kihlstrom 1997). Even if a small percentage of accurate memories can be recovered in psychotherapy, there is no evidence for a causal connection between non-remembered abuse and psychopathology. In addition, the mere experience of painful emotions, when not tied to attempts to bolster positive coping and mastery, can be harmful (Littrell 1998). Indeed, there is no empirically supported psychotherapy that relies on the recovery of traumatic memories to achieve a positive therapeutic outcome. Adshead (1997) argued that if memory work with trauma patients is not effective, then "it would therefore be just as unethical to use memory work for patients who could not use it or benefit by it, as it would be to prescribe the wrong medication, or employ a useless surgical technique" (p. 437).

Before concluding, let us be clear about what the findings reviewed do not mean as well as what they do mean. First, all memory recovery techniques are not necessarily problematic. For example, the "cognitive interview" (Fisher and Geiselman 1992), which incorporates a variety of techniques derived from experimental research on memory (e.g., providing subjects with retrieval cues, searching for additional memorial details), holds promise as a method of enhancing memory in eyewitness contexts. Second, we do not wish to imply that all uses of hypnosis in psychotherapy are problematic. Controlled research evidence suggests that hypnosis may be useful in treating pain, medical conditions, and habit disorders (e.g., smoking cessation), and as an adjunct to cognitive-behavioral therapy (e.g., anxiety, obesity). Nevertheless, the extent to which hypnosis provides benefits above and beyond relaxation in such cases remains unclear (Lynn, Kirsch, Barabasz, Cardena, and Patterson 2001). The questionable scientific status of hypnosis as a memory recovery technique has no bearing on the therapeutic efficacy of hypnosis, which must ultimately be investigated and judged on its own merits. Finally, we do not wish to claim that all memories recovered after years or decades of forgetting are necessarily false. We remain open to the possibility that certain recovered childhood memories are veridical, although further research is needed to document their existence and possible prevalence. These important and unresolved issues notwithstanding, the conclusion that certain suggestive therapeutic practices can foster false memories in some clients appears indisputable.

Notes

1. The following reviews were used as sources: Erdelyi 1994; Lynn, Lock, Myers, and Payne 1997; Lynn, Neuschatz, Fite, and Rhue 2001; Nash 1987; Spanos 1996; Steblay & Bothwell 1994; Witehouse, Dinges, E. C. Orne, and M.T. Orne 1988.

2. Some therapists do not assume that early memories reports are necessarily accurate but posit that such memories nevertheless provide a window into clients' personalities; the claim of these therapists is not of concern to us here.

References

Adler, A. 1927. *Understanding Human Nature*. New York: Greenberg.

Adshead, G. 1997. Seekers after truth: Ethical issues raised by the discussion of "false" and "recovered" memories. In J.D. Read and D.S. Lindsay (Eds.), *Recollections of Trauma: Scientific Evidence and Clinical Practice*. New York: Plenum Press.

American Medical Association. 1994. Council on Scientific Affairs. *Memories of Childhood Abuse*. CSA Report 5-A-94.

American Psychological Association. 1995. *Psychotherapy guidelines for working with clients who may have an abuse or trauma history*. Division 17 Committee on Women, Division 42 Trauma and Gender Issues Committee.

Bass, E., and L. Davis. 1988. *The Courage to Heal*. New York: Harper & Row.

Blume, E.S. 1990. *Secret Survivors: Uncovering Incest and Its Aftereffects in Women*. New York: John Wiley and Sons.

Canadian Psychiatric Association. 1996, March 25. Position statement: Adult recovered memories of childhood sexual abuse. *Canadian Journal of Psychiatry* 41: 305–306.

DuBreuil, S.C., M. Garry, and E.F. Loftus. 1998. Tales from the crib: Age-regression and the creation of unlikely memories. In S.J. Lynn and K.M. McConkey (Eds.), *Truth in Memory*. Washington, D.C.: American Psychological Association.

Emery, C.L. 2002. The validity of childhood sexual abuse victim checklists in popular psychology literature: A Barnum effect. Unpublished honors thesis, Emory University, Atlanta.

Erdelyr, M. 1994. Hypnotic hypermnesia: The empty set of hypermnesia. *International Journal of Clinical and Experimental Hypnosis* 42: 379–390.

Fisher, R.P., and R.E. Griselman. 1992. *Memory Enhancement Techniques for Investigative Interviewing*. Springfield, Illinois: Charles C. Thomas.

Frederickson, R. 1992. *Repressed Memories*. New York: Fireside/Parkside. *Frontline*. 1995. Divided memories. Producer, Ofra Bikel.

Hyman, J.E. Jr., T.H. Husband, and F.J. Billings. 1995. False memories of childhood experiences. *Applied Cognitive Psychology* 9: 181–197.

Lindsay, D. S., and D. Read. 1994. Psychotherapy and memories of childhood sexual abuse: A cognitive perspective. *Applied Cognitive Psychology* 8: 281–338.

Littrell, J. 1998. Is the experience of painful emotion therapeutic? *Clinical Psychology Review* 18: 71–102.

Loftus, E.F. 1993. The reality of repressed memories. *American Psychologist* 48: 518–537.

Loftus, E.F., and G. Mazzoni. 1998. Using imagination and personalized suggestion to change behavior. *Behavior Therapy* 29: 691–708.

Loftus, E.F., and J.E. Pickrell. 1995. The formation of false memories. *Psychiatric Annals* 25: 720–725.

Lynn, S.J., I. Kirsch, A. Barabasz, E. Cardena, and D. Patterson. 2000. Hypnosis as an empirically supported adjunctive technique: The state of the evidence. *International Journal of Clinical and Experimental Hypnosis* 48: 343–361

Lynn, S.J., T.G. Lock, B. Myers, and D.G. Payne. 1997. Recalling the unrecallable: Should hypnosis be used to recover memories in psychotherapy? *Current Directions in Psychological Science* 6: 79–83.

Lynn, S.J., B. Myers, and P. Malinoski. 1997. Hypnosis, pseudomemories, and clinical guidelines: A sociocognitive perspective. In D. Read and S. Lindsay (Eds.), *Recollections of Trauma: Scientific Research and Clinical Practice*. New York: Plenum Press.

Lynn, S.J., J. Neuschatz, R. Fire, and J.W. Rhue. 2001. Hypnosis and memory: Implications for the courtroom and psychotherapy. In M. Eisen, and G. Goodman (Eds.), *Memory, Suggestion, and the Forensic Interview*. New York: Guilford.

Malinoski, P., and S.J. Lynn. 1999. The plasticity of very early memory reports: Social pressure, hypnotizability, compliance, and interrogative suggestibility. *International Journal of Clinical and Experimental Hypnosis* 47: 320–345.

Malinoski, P., S.J. Lynn, and H. Sivec. 1998. The assessment, validity, and determinants of early memory reports: A critical review. In S.J. Lynn and K. McConkey (Eds.), *Truth in Memory*. New York: Guilford.

Mazzoni, G.A., E.F. Loftus, and I. Kirsch. 2001. Changing beliefs about implausible autobiographical memories. *Journal of Experimental Psychology: Applied* 7: 51–59.

Mazzoni, G.A., E.F. Loftus, A. Seitz, and S.J. Lynn. 1999. Creating a new childhood: Changing beliefs and memories through dream interpretation. *Applied Cognitive Psychology* 13: 125–144.

Mazzoni, G.A., P. Lombardo, S. Malvagia, and E.F. Loftus. 1997. Dream Interpretation and False Beliefs. Unpublished manuscript, University of Florence and University of Washington.

Meiselman, K. 1990. *Resolving the Trauma of Incest: Reintegration Therapy with Survivors.* San Francisco: Jossey-Bass.

Mills, A., and S.J. Lynn. 2000. Past-life experiences. In E. Cardena, S.J. Lynn, and S. Krippner (Eds.), *The Varieties of Anomalous Experience.* New York: Guilford.

Nash, M.R. 1987. What, if anything, is regressed about hypnotic age regression? A review of the empirical literature. *Psychological Bulletin* 102: 42–52.

Nash, M.J., M. Drake, R. Wiley, S. Khalsa, and S.J. Lynn. 1986. The accuracy of recall of hypnotically age regressed subjects. *Journal of Abnormal Psychology* 95: 298–300.

Olson, H.A. 1979. The hypnotic retrieval of early recollections. In H.A. Olson (Ed.), *Early Recollections: Their Use in Diagnosis and Psychotherapy.* Springfield, Illinois: Charles C. Thomas.

Papanek, H. 1979. The use of early recollections in psychotherapy. In H.A. Olson (Ed.), *Early Recollections: Their Use in Diagnosis and Psychotherapy.* Springfield Illinois: Charles C. Thomas.

Polusny, M.A., and V.M. Follene. 1996. Remembering childhood sexual abuse: A national survey of psychologists' clinical practices, beliefs, and personal experiences. *Professional Psychology: Research and Practice* 27: 41–52.

Poole, D.A., D.S. Lindsay, A. Memon, and R. Bull. 1995. Psychotherapists' opinions, practices, and experiences with recovery of memories of incestuous abuse. *Journal of Consulting and Clinical Psychology* 68: 426–437.

Porter, S., J.C. Yuille, and D.R. Lehman. 1999. The nature of real, implanted, and fabricated childhood emotional events: Implications for the recovered memory debate. *Law and Human Behavior* 23: 517–537.

Roland, C.B. 1993. Exploring childhood memories with adult survivors of sexual abuse: Concrete reconstruction and visualization techniques. *Journal of Mental Health Counseling* 15: 363–372.

Shobe, K.K., and J.F. Kihlstrom. 1997. Is traumatic memory special? *Current Directions in Psychological Science* 6: 70–74.

Sivec, H.J., S.J. Lynn, and P.T. Malinoski. 1997. Hypnosis in the cabbage patch: Age regression with verifiable events. Unpublished manuscript, State University of New York at Binghamton.

Spanos, N.P. 1996. *Multiple Identities and False Memories: A Sociocognitive Perspective.* Washington, D.C.: American Psychological Association.

Spanos, N.P., C.A. Burgess, M.F. Burgess, C. Samuels, and W.O. Blois. 1999. Creating false memories of infancy with hypnotic and nonhypnotic procedures. *Applied Cognitive Psychology* 13: 201–218.

Spanos, N.P., E. Menary, M.J. Gabota, S.C. DuBreuil, and B. Dewhirst. 1991. Secondary identity enactments during hypnotic past-life regression: A sociocognitive perspective. *Journal of Personality and Social Psychology* 61: 308–320.

Steblay, N.M., and R.K. Bothwell. 1994. Evidence for hypnotically refreshed testimony: The view from the laboratory. *Law and Human Behavior* 18: 635–651.

Tavris, C. 1993. Beware the incest survivor machine. *New York Times Book Review,* January 3, pp. 1, 16–17.

Van der Kolk, B.A. 1994. The body keeps the score: Memory and the evolving psychobiology of posttraumatic stress. *Harvard Review of Psychiatry* 1: 253–265.

Weiss, B.L. 1988. *Many Lives, Many Masters*. New York: Simon & Schuster.

Yapko, M.D. 1994. Suggestibility and repressed memories of abuse: A survey of psychotherapists' beliefs. *American Journal of Clinical Hypnosis* 36: 163–171.

Review and Contemplate

1. Briefly describe the clinical techniques of guided imagery and hypnosis, and explain why they are problematic with respect to memory recovery.
2. Describe one study that suggests hypnotic age-regression can distort people's memories.
3. Explain the problem with using a person's dreams to determine if the person has a history of child abuse.
4. Describe five of the eight factors that lead patients to perceive a high degree of plausibility in imaginative narratives of sexual abuse that never occurred.

7.1 Nostradamus's Clever 'Clairvoyance': The Power of Ambiguous Specificity /
MAZIAR YAFEH AND CHIP HEATH

Perhaps you've heard of Michel Nostradamus. He's the famous 16th-century French astrologer who apparently predicted, hundreds of years in advance, such events as the assassination of President John F. Kennedy, the atrocities committed by Adolf Hitler, and the September 11, 2001, terrorist attacks in the United States. More recently, some believe that Nostradamus predicted Hurricane Katrina, a Category 4 hurricane that hit New Orleans in 2005, causing billions of dollars in damage and more than a thousand deaths. Could the "shaking of land and sea" in the city of "Orleans" mentioned in the quote below from Nostradamus refer to Hurricane Katrina?

> The cities of Tours, Orleans, Blois, Angers, Reims and Nantes are troubled by sudden change.
>   Tents will be pitched by [people] of foreign tongues; rivers, darts at Rennes, shaking of land and sea.

Did Nostradamus have amazing psychic abilities, or do people's interpretations of his prophecies tell us more about the psychology of living individuals than about the psychic abilities of a man who died hundreds of years ago? Yafeh and Heath discuss how some of the common cognitive strategies we use may lead us to perceive Nostradamus as an amazing prophet, even when his prophecies are scrambled in a random fashion. Thus, this article is an excellent example of the point made in Chapter 1 that normal cognitive processes can lead to paranormal beliefs. One cognitive tendency that is particularly relevant to this article is called confirmation bias, or our tendency to search for information that confirms (rather than disconfirms) our hypotheses or beliefs.

APA Reference
Yafeh, M., & Heath, C. (2003, September/October). Nostradamus's clever 'clairvoyance': The power of ambiguous specificity. *Skeptical Inquirer, 27,* 36–40.

How did a French astrologer, dead for over 400 years, become a premier commentator on world events in 2001? The authors' research shows that Nostradamus's dark prophecies are ambiguous enough to "work" for events selected at random and even when they are scrambled.

Amidst the chaos and confusion after the September 11 terrorist attacks, anxious people flocked to the Internet for any information that would shed light on the horrific event and its implications. In the weeks after the attack, Google, the most widely used World Wide Web search engine, predictably reported sharp increases in searches for "Osama Bin Laden" and "Al Qaeda."

Yet Google also reported that in the two weeks following the attacks, searches for a sixteenth-century astrologer surpassed those for Bin Laden and his organization (Grossman 2001). In fact, "Nostradamus" became one of Google's top searches, surpassing even the perennial favorite topic of "sex"! (See Figure 7.1 for converging results from the "Buzz Index" on Yahoo, another popular search engine.) How did a French astrologer, dead for over 400 years, become a premier commentator on world events in 2001?

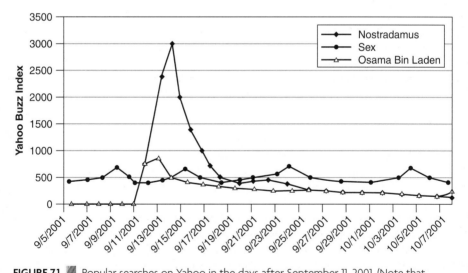

FIGURE 7.1 ▨ Popular searches on Yahoo in the days after September 11, 2001. (Note that "Nostradamus" beats out "Osama Bin Laden" and even perennial favorite "sex.")

Maziar Yafeh is a senior at Stanford University majoring in economics and psychology, and **Chip Heath** is an associate professor, of organizational behavior. This project began during a sophomore research seminar that Heath teaches on Urban Legends, Conspiracy Theories, and Other Distortions in the Marketplace of Ideas. Correspondence may be addressed to Heath at GSB-Stanford University, 518 Memorial Way," Stanford, CA 94305. E-mail: chip-heath@stanford.edu.

Michel Nostradamus was a sixteenth-century French physicist and astrologer who gained fame in the Renaissance for *Centuries,* his ten-volume collection of 942 four-line poetic prophecies, which he published in 1555. These prophecies have been eagerly studied for centuries.

In the tumult after tragic events, people over the last 400 years may have turned to Nostradamus to understand their world, just as modern citizens did right after the September 11 attacks. If so, then Nostradamus doesn't really have to predict events before they occur, he just has to look as though he predicted them *after* they have already occurred. That in itself is a pretty clever accomplishment: How could Nostradamus do it?

After spending a year researching his work and running controlled experiments, we suggest a combination of two factors: ambiguously specific prophecies that focus on dark, foreboding events.

AMBIGUOUSLY SPECIFIC PROPHECIES

Anyone who has visited a card reader or psychic knows that the lifeblood of the fortune-telling trade is vagueness (such as "You will face an important decision soon"). In part, Nostradamus's prophecies seem to match this vagueness test. He used a famously cryptic, poetic style, interspersing his original French with selected Hebrew, Latin, and Spanish words and phrases, to create an aura of vagueness around each prophecy. Hence, each prophecy is difficult to attribute to an exact event.

But is vagueness enough? Clearly, it is not vagueness that drew Internet searchers to the following Nostradamus prophecy in the days after September 11:

At forty-five degrees the sky will burn,
Fire to approach the great new city,
In an instant a great scattered flame will leap up,
When one will want to demand proof of the Normans.

On the contrary, it is the prophecy's unnerving similarities to the attacks; it seems written specifically for our time.

Or was it? The art of Nostradamus, our research shows, is that what appears to be specific is in fact generalizable. Nostradamus's gift is that he writes poetry that is apparently specific (at least when someone examines it with a specific historical event in mind), but that is in fact ambiguous—which we use in the dictionary sense of "allowing for multiple meanings." Indeed, it may be ambiguous enough that it could apply to many different tragic events.

But how could we test the hypothesis that this ambiguity contributes to Nostradamus's ability to appear prophetic? One way might be to choose two different events and see whether a particular prophecy could be equally well applied to each. If the same prophecy seems equally prophetic for two very different events, this indicates that Nostradamus is appealing at least in part because of his ambiguity.

With this test in mind, we chose two events for comparison: the September 11 attack on World Trade Center and the London Blitz (the fifty-seven consecutive nights during World War II in which Germany bombarded London). We selected these two events because they both took place in a specific city and are characterized in pictures, videos, and people's minds by explosions and vivid images of fire.

We concentrated on the words *city* and *fire* because these were key words in the Nostradamus prophecy we mentioned previously that circulated widely on the Internet after the World Trade Center attacks. We found eleven prophecies that contained these key words, and randomly picked ten to use in our experiment. We presented these ten prophecies to two groups of participants; one group was asked to say whether each prophecy indicated that Nostradamus might have predicted the events of September 11, the other whether each prophecy predicted the London Blitz.

Our participants were eighty Stanford University undergraduates, who are typically quite skeptical of notions of prophecy, so any results we find might underestimate the actual success of the prophecies with a less skeptical audience. For each of the ten prophecies, we asked our participants whether the prophecy predicted either September 11 or the Blitz, and gave them three choices: yes, no, and maybe. The "yes" option was almost never used, and the "no" option was used frequently. However, across the ten prophecies, the "maybe" option was chosen a surprising amount. Participants who were asked to think about the September 11 attacks on average thought that 3.2 of the prophecies may have predicted the attacks, and participants asked to think about the Blitz thought that 2.8 may have predicted those attacks. This overall difference was not statistically significant, so our participants in effect said that Nostradamus's prophecies were equally foresightful about (and relevant to) September 11 and the Blitz.

This level of "maybe" responses could suggest that Nostradamus was a pretty good prophet—about a third of his prophecies seemed at least somewhat prophetic about events that occurred 400 years after his death. However this interpretation is disputed by one key fact: participants in both groups were impressed by the *same* prophecies, regardless of whether they considered September 11 or the Blitz. For example, 68 percent of participants thought that the following prophecy might have predicted the September 11 attacks:

> Earthshaking fire from the centre of the earth,
> Will cause tremors around the new city,
> Two great rocks will war for a long time,
> Then arethusa will redden a new river.

Here, the "earthshaking fire" causing "tremors around the new city" might have seemed very applicable; the "new city" seems a good code word for "New York," and the "two great rocks" a good analogy for the twin towers.

However, 61 percent of our participants thought this same prophecy might also refer to the events of the Blitz; the "earthshaking fire" causing "tremors" seemed applicable to the Blitz as well. The word "new" seems to have been ignored since London is not one of Europe's newest cities, but in the case of the Blitz the "two great rocks" warring may have been seen as emblematic of the two strongest European armies—Germany and England—facing off across the English Channel. This "successful" prophecy is thus ambiguous enough that it seems almost equally applicable to two very different events, yet it contains enough specific detail that it looks as though Nostradamus is on to something.

Our results here are consistent with research in psychology on individual decision making. Research on "confirmation bias" and related topics has shown that individuals don't naturally consider alternative hypotheses for a particular pattern of data (see Klayman 1995; Nisbett and Ross 1980). Our participants, though smart and skeptical, fell into this same well-documented trap. Implicitly they were asking "Did Nostradamus predict the event I'm considering?" As they searched for evidence that confirmed or disconfirmed whether he did so, they probably weren't paying attention to the ambiguity of his prose, and they almost certainly weren't asking themselves whether the same prophecy could have predicted *other* events. Yet by neglecting competing hypotheses, our participants left themselves open to be fooled by the ambiguous predictions. Those participants thinking about the Blitz and its connection to the "two great rocks" probably did not consider that the same "evidence" would look equally prescient if they had been considering the New York City attacks instead.

In contrast to the ambiguity of the "successful" prophecies, the least successful prophecies contained imagery that was less ambiguous and offered concrete evidence that could be historically verified. Only 12 percent of our participants thought the following prophecy might fit September 11 and 17 percent thought it fit the Blitz:

> The great city will be thoroughly desolated,
> Of the inhabitants not a single one will remain there,
> Wall, sex, temple and virgin violated,
> Through sword, fire, plague, cannon people will die.

This prophecy is partially applicable to both events because it evokes a "great city" where some people die by fire. However, it is less convincing than the first because it is more specific: New York and London were not "thoroughly" destroyed and neither event prominently featured sex, temples, virgins, or swords.

Across the ten different prophecies, we found a high correlation between the prophecies that supposedly predicted the two events—events that were separated by half a century, different geographies, and different political contexts. True, both events involved "fire" and a "city," but so did most other wars in the last 2,000 years. These results suggest that Nostradamus's true genius was his ability to write descriptions of crises that are sufficiently ambiguous that they could describe almost any crisis.

But how far could we push the ambiguity hypothesis? Nostradamus's prophecies frequently predict "war"—indeed, war is featured in a conspicuous 104 of his 942 prophecies. Are his prophecies ambiguous enough that any of those 104 prophecies could be applied to *any* war? We asked a group of Stanford undergrads to list all the wars they could think of, and we took the top thirteen mentions. Because our students were at an American university, there was an American bias to the wars they remembered, but that did not affect the test we wanted to run. We randomly selected thirteen from 104 war prophecies and assigned them at random to the thirteen different wars; then we asked seventy-four students to indicate whether the prophecy might have predicted the war.

Because we're assigning prophecies to wars at random, we might expect the overall success to be quite low: historical accounts of various wars could not be interchanged at random. If the prophecies had any (unambiguous) content, they shouldn't be interchangeable either.

However, the prophecies were ambiguous enough that on average 29 percent of our participants said any prophecy selected at random "may have" predicted a war selected at random. When the same prophecy can apply equally well to the French Revolution, World War II, and the war on terrorism, this makes Nostradamus a relatively imprecise prophet but a very clever wartime poet—able to capture the overall atmosphere of war in a seemingly specific way, yet speaking ambiguously enough that this prophecies are for the most part not limited in time or location.

To take the poet-versus-prophet test a step further, we thought about how to preserve the poetry while destroying any potential prophecy. Nostradamus's poetry is ambiguous enough that we thought it could be largely preserved even if we scrambled the lines from different prophecies. If Nostradamus had any prophetic ability, this scrambling procedure should destroy any coherent aspects of his prophecies—certainly reducing historical accounts or news stories to gibberish.

We randomly scrambled the lines of our thirteen prophecies, and matched one scrambled prophecy with each of the thirteen wars. Then we asked a second group of seventy-two participants to assess whether the prophecy predicted the war.

With the *original* prophecies, 29 percent had said maybe. With our *scrambled* prophecies, 34 percent said maybe. Thus, if anything, our scrambled prophecies impressed people as *more prophetic* than Nostradamus's originals. (The difference wasn't statistically significant.)

DARK PROPHECIES

While ambiguity is probably the most important feature of Nostradamus's prophecies, another notable feature is their dark, foreboding quality. People are more likely to discuss and try to explain negative events than positive ones. When we're upset or surprised in a negative way, we look for explanations; when we're satisfied or things are proceeding according to our expectations, we don't (Wong and Weiner 1981; for more general discussion, Weiner 1985; Taylor 1995). By writing many prophecies involving negative events, Nostradamus maximized the chances

CAN YOU FIND THE ORIGINAL NOSTRADAMUS PROPHECIES?

Three of the prophecies in this table are from Nostradamus. The other three are versions we created by scrambling the lines of his original prophecies. Can you tell which is which?

1. Arms will be heard clashing in the sky. That very same year the divine one's enemies. They will want unjustly to discuss the holy laws. Through lightning and war the complacent one put to death.

2. The two nephews brought up in diverse places,
He assembles the pardoned before the gods,
They will come to be elevated very high in making war,
Far away where their prince and rector will die.

3. The great younger son will make an end of the war,
Will have carried off the prize from one greater than he,
He holds a flowering branch in this beak,
Without armor he will be surprised suddenly.

4. Two royal brothers will wage war so fiercely,
That between them the war will be so mortal,
That both will occupy the strong places,
Then great quarrel will fill realm and life.

5. The two nephews brought up in diverse places,
Naval battle, land, fathers fallen,
They will come to be elevated very high in making war,
To avenge the injury, enemies succumbed.

6. Through long war all the army exhausted,
To great a faith will betray the monarch instead of gold or silver
they will come to coin leather,
To avenge the injury enemies succumbed.

(#1,4,5 are original and 2,3,6 are our scrambled versions)
Prophecies taken from www.ebooks3.com/ebooks/nostradamus_centuries.html

The top thirteen wars recalled by our participants. We used these to test whether any of Nostradamus's "war" prophecies could be randomly assigned to any randomly selected war.

American Revolution
World War
War on Terrorism
American Civil War
Vietnam War

World War 1
French Revolution
Gulf War
Korean War
Spanish Civil War
French-Indian War
War of 1812
Thirty Years War

that someone confronted with a crisis might look for—and find—something in his prophecies that would remind them of their own current crisis.

To test how much Nostradamus focused on the negative, we randomly sampled 100 of his prophecies and asked a group of students to assess whether they concerned positive or negative events. More than three times as many prophecies discussed negative events as positive ones. We also asked a group of students to list words associated with events of good fortune and misfortune. The top examples of good fortune were *birth* and *discovery,* while *war* and *death* topped the misfortune list. Searching through all of Nostradamus's prophecies, we found that while less than five of them dealt with either *birth* or *discovery,* 104 mentioned *war* and ninety-four mentioned *death.* We're not sure that this focus on the negative makes Nostradamus a good prophet—after all, prophecies of great discoveries and the births of great people might come in handy. On the other hand, when people search for explanations after a tragic event, Nostradamus allows himself many opportunities to provide them with an "answer."

Nostradamus, a clever poet, offers pronouncements of ambiguous doom—so ambiguous, in fact, that his war prophecies can apply to *any* war, and appear equally prophetic even when scrambled.

HOW EFFECTIVELY DOES THE FOLLOWING PROPHECY PREDICT WWII?

For a long time a gray bird will be seen in the sky,

They will be thoroughly devastated by sea and by land

Those (actions) started in France will end there

Captured, dead, bound, pillaged without law of war

58% of our participants thought that Nostradamus may have predicted WWII with this prophecy but it's actually one of our scrambled versions.

Our results show that there is about a 30 percent chance that any randomly selected war prophecy will remind some readers of any randomly selected war. But Nostradamus was sufficiently prolific that his readers don't have to stop with just one prophecy. Imagine someone who was sufficiently intrigued to read all 942 prophecies; wouldn't at least one of the 104 prophecies about "war" seemingly provide an even better match than one selected at random? By writing many prophecies, Nostradamus could take advantage of people's natural tendency to search longer and harder for explanations at times of crisis.

We offer a recipe for a modern prophet: Write a lot of prophecies, focusing on the negative. Take care to keep your prophecies as dark and ambiguous as possible—lots of doom and gloom, very few unambiguous specifics. And someday you too might be invoked as a commentator on world events.

Now if someone could only figure out how to collect royalties from beyond the grave. . . .

References

Grossman, L. 2001. In search of . . . *Time,* October 29, 2001, p. 92.

Klayman, J. 1995. Varieties of confirmation bias. *The Psychology of Learning and Motivation,* 32: 385–418.

Nisbett, R., and L. Ross. 1980. *Human Inference: Strategies and Shortcomings of Social Judgment.* Englewood Cliffs, New Jersey: Prentice-Hall.

Taylor, S.E. 1991. Asymmetrical effects of positive and negative events: The mobilization/minimization hypothesis. *Psychological Bulletin* 110: 67–85.

Weiner, B. 1985. "Spontaneous" causal thinking. *Psychological Bulletin* 97: 74–84.

Wong, P.T., and B. Weiner. 1981. When people ask "Why" questions and the heuristics of attributional search. *Journal of Personality and Social Psychology* 40: 650–663.

Review and Contemplate

1. Who is Michel Nostradamus, and for what is he famous?
2. Briefly describe the evidence that suggests the predictions of Nostradamus appear accurate because they are ambiguous enough to apply to many different tragic events.
3. Define "confirmation bias" and describe how it explains people's tendency to see ambiguous predictions as related to specific events.
4. What "recipe" does the article offer for those who want to be "modern prophets"?
5. Collect the daily horoscope for your astrological sign and three other astrological signs. How are the statements used in horoscopes similar to those used by Nostradamus?

7.2

Like Goes with Like: The Role of Representativeness in Erroneous and Pseudoscientific Beliefs /
THOMAS GILOVICH AND KENNETH SAVITSKY

One early theory of medicine, popularized in the 1600s, was the Doctrine of Signatures. This doctrine stated that natural substances such as plants have well-marked signs that indicate the maladies for which they may be used as treatments. For example, the spotted leaves of the lungwort plant resemble a diseased lung and could, therefore, be used to treat lung ailments. Goldenrod (which has yellow flowers) could be used to treat jaundice (a condition in which the skin appears yellow); bloodroot (the root of which contains a red liquid) could be used to treat blood disorders; toothwort (which has a white root) was thought to be useful for treating toothaches; and the maidenhair fern (which has fine hairs on its roots) could be used to treat baldness.

This early medical thinking relies on a common cognitive shortcut—called the representativeness heuristic—that people use to simplify everyday decisions and judgments. As mentioned in Chapter 1, heuristics are normal cognitive strategies that can sometimes lead to paranormal and pseudoscientific beliefs. The representativeness heuristic is one of several such heuristics. One way we use this heuristic is to estimate the likelihood that a substance can be used to treat a disease based on how similar the substance is to the symptoms of the disease. Thus, goldenrod might have been used to treat jaundice because its yellow flowers resembled the yellow skin of those who had jaundice.

Although early medical beliefs guided by the Doctrine of Signatures may seem obviously faulty to you, similar reasoning is behind a number of more recent practices and beliefs. Gilovich and Savitsky discuss how the representativeness heuristic may underlie faulty medical beliefs, pseudoscientific beliefs, and the popularity of psychoanalytic theory and projective tests.

The misguided premise that effects should resemble their causes underlies a host of erroneous beliefs, from folk wisdom about health and the human body to elaborate pseudoscientific belief systems.

APA Reference

Gilovich, T., & Savitsky, K. (1996, March/April). Like goes with like: The role of representativeness in erroneous and pseudoscientific beliefs. *Skeptical Inquirer, 20,* 34–40.

It was in 1983, at an infectious-disease conference in Brussells, that Barry Marshall, an internal-medicine resident from Perth, Australia, first staked his startling claim. He argued that the peptic ulcer, a painful crater in the lining of the stomach or duodenum, was not caused by a stressful lifestyle as everyone had thought. Instead, the malady that afflicts millions of adults in the United States alone was caused by a simple bacterium, and thus could be cured using antibiotics (Hunter 1993; Monmaney 1993; Peterson 1991; Wandycz 1993).

Although subsequent investigations have substantiated Marshall's claim (e.g., Hentschel et al. 1993), his colleagues initially were highly skeptical. Martin Blaser, director of the Division of Infectious Diseases at the Vanderbilt University School of Medicine, described Marshall's thesis as "the most preposterous thing I'd ever heard" (Monmaney 1993).

What made the idea so preposterous? Why were the experts so resistant to Marshall's suggestion? There were undoubtedly many reasons. For one, the claim contradicted what most physicians, psychiatrists, and psychologists knew (or thought they knew): Ulcers were caused by stress. As one author noted, "No physical ailment has ever been more closely tied to psychological turbulence" (Monmaney 1993, p. 64). In addition, science is necessarily and appropriately a rather conservative enterprise. Although insight, creativity, and even leaps of faith are vital to the endeavor, sound empirical evidence is the true coin of the realm. Much of the medical establishment's hesitation doubtless stemmed from the same healthy skepticism that readers of the SKEPTICAL INQUIRER have learned to treasure. After all, Marshall's results at the time were suggestive at best—no cause-effect relationship had yet been established.

But there may have been a third reason for the reluctance to embrace Marshall's contention, a reason we explore in this article. The belief that ulcers derive from stress is particularly seductive—for physicians and laypersons alike—because it flows from a general tendency of human judgment, a tendency to employ what psychologists Amos Tversky and Daniel Kahneman have called the "representativeness heuristic" (Kahneman and Tversky 1972, 1973; Tversky and Kahneman 1974, 1982). Indeed, we believe that judgment by representativeness plays a role in a host of erroneous beliefs, from beliefs about health and the human body to handwriting analysis and astrology (Gilovich 1991). We consider a sample of these beliefs in this article.

THE REPRESENTATIVENESS HEURISTIC

Representativeness is but one of a number of heuristics that people use to render complex problems manageable. Heuristics are often described as judgmental shortcuts that generally get us where we need to go—and quickly—but at

Thomas Gilovich, professor of psychology at Cornell University and a Fellow of CSICOP, is the author of How We Know What Isn't So: The Fallibility of Human Reason in Everyday Life. **Kenneth Savitsky** is a doctoral student in social psychology at Cornell University.

the cost of occasionally sending us off course. Kahneman and Tversky liken them to perceptual cues, which generally enable us to perceive the world accurately, but occasionally give rise to misperception and illusion. Consider their example of using clarity as a cue for distance. The clarity of an object is one cue people use to decide how far away it is. The cue typically works well because the farther away something is, the less distinct it appears. On a particularly clear day, however, objects can appear closer than they are, and on hazy days they can appear farther away. In some circumstances, then, this normally accurate cue can lead to error.

Representativeness works much the same way. The representativeness heuristic involves a reflexive tendency to assess the similarity of objects and events along salient dimensions and to organize them on the basis of one overarching rule: "Like goes with like." Among other things, the representativeness heuristic reflects the belief that a member of a given category ought to resemble the category prototype, and that an effect ought to resemble the cause that produced it. Thus, the representativeness heuristic is often used to assess whether a given instance belongs to a particular category, such as whether an individual is likely to be an accountant or a comedian. It is also used in assigning causes to effects, as when deciding whether a meal of spicy food caused a case of heartburn or determining whether an assassination was the product of a conspiracy.[1]

Note that judgment by representativeness often works well. Instances often resemble their category prototypes and causes frequently resemble their effects. Members of various occupational groups, for example, frequently do resemble the group prototype. Likewise, "big" effects (such as the development of the atomic bomb) are often brought about by "big" causes (such as the Manhattan Project).

Still, the representativeness heuristic is only that—a heuristic or shortcut. As with all shortcuts, the representativeness heuristic should be used with caution. Although it can help us to make some judgments with accuracy and case, it can also lead us astray. Not all members fit the category prototype. Some comedians are shy or taciturn, and some accountants are wild and crazy. And although causes are frequently representative of their effects, this relationship does not always hold: Tiny viruses give rise to devastating epidemics like malaria or AIDS; and splitting the nucleus of an atom releases an awesome amount of energy. In some cases, then, representativeness yields inaccuracy and error. Or even superstition. A nice example is provided by craps shooters, who roll the dice gently to coax a low number, and more vigorously to encourage a high one (Hanslin 1967). A small effect (low number) requires a small cause (gentle roll), and a big effect (high number) requires a big cause (vigorous roll).

How might the belief in a stress-ulcer link derive from the conviction that like goes with like? Because the burning feeling of an ulcerated stomach is not unlike the gut-wrenching, stomach-churning feeling of extreme stress (albeit more severe), the link seems natural: Stress is a representative cause of an ulcer.[2] But as Marshall suggested (and subsequent research has borne out), the link may be overblown. Stress alone does not appear to cause ulcers (Glavin and Szabo 1992; Soll 1990).

REPRESENTATIVENESS AND THE CONJUNCTION FALLACY

One of the most compelling demonstrations of how the representativeness heuristic can interfere with sound judgment comes from a much-discussed experiment in which participants were asked to consider the following description (Tversky and Kahneman 1982, 1983):

> Linda is 31 years old, single, outspoken, and very bright. She majored in philosophy. As a student, she was deeply concerned with issues of discrimination and social justice, and also participated in anti-nuclear demonstrations.
>
> Now, based on the above description, rank the following statements about Linda, from most to least likely:
>
> a. Linda is an insurance salesperson.
> b. Linda is a bank teller.
> c. Linda is a bank teller and is active in the feminist movement.

If you are like most people, you probably thought it was more likely that "Linda is a bank teller and is active in the feminist movement" than that "Linda is a bank teller." It is easy to see why: A feminist bank teller is much more representative of the description of Linda than is "just" a bank teller. It reflects the political activism, social-consciousness, and left-of-center politics implied in the description.

It may make sense, but it cannot be. The category "bank teller" subsumes the category "is a bank teller and is active in the feminist movement." The latter therefore cannot be more likely than the former. Anyone who is a bank teller and is active in the feminist movement is automatically also a bank teller. Indeed, even if one thinks it is impossible for someone with Linda's description to be solely a bank teller (that is, one who is not a feminist), being a bank teller is still *as* likely as being both. This error is referred to as the "conjunction fallacy" because the probability of two events co-occurring (i.e., their conjunction) can never exceed the individual probability of either of the constituents (Tversky and Kahneman 1982, 1983; Dawes and Mulford 1993).

Such is the logic of the situation. The psychology we bring to bear on it is something else. If we start with an unrepresentative outcome (being a bank teller) and then add a representative element (being active in the feminist movement), we create a description that is at once more psychologically compelling but objectively less likely. The rules of representativeness do not follow the laws of probability. A detailed description can seem compelling precisely because of the very details that, objectively speaking, actually make it less likely. Thus, someone may be less concerned about dying during a trip to the Middle East than about dying in a terrorist attack while there, even though the probability of death due to a *particular* cause is obviously lower than the probability of death due to the set of all possible causes. Likewise, the probability of global economic collapse can seem remote until one sketches a detailed scenario in which such a collapse follows, say, the destruction of the oil fields in the Persian Gulf. Once again, the additional details make the outcome less likely at the same time that they make it more psychologically compelling.

REPRESENTATIVENESS AND CAUSAL JUDGMENTS

Most of the empirical research on the representativeness heuristic is similar to the work on the conjunction fallacy in that the judgments people make are compared to a normative standard—in this case, to the laws of probability. The deleterious effect of judgment by representativeness is thereby established by the failure to meet such a standard. Previous work conducted in this fashion has shown, for example, that judgment by representativeness leads people to commit the "gambler's fallacy," to overestimate the reliability of small samples of data, and to be insufficiently "regressive" in making predictions under conditions of uncertainty.

The ulcer example with which we began this article does not have this property of being obviously at variance with a clear-cut normative standard. The same is true of nearly all examples of the impact of representativeness on causal judgments: It can be difficult to establish with certainty that a judgmental error has been made. Partly for this reason, there has been less empirical research on representativeness and causal judgments than on other areas, such as representativeness and the conjunction fallacy. This is not because representativeness is thought to have little impact on causal judgments, but because without a clear-cut normative standard it is simply more difficult to conduct research in this domain. The research that has been conducted, furthermore, is more suggestive than definitive. Nonetheless, the suggestive evidence is rather striking, and it points to the possibility that representativeness may exert at least as much influence over causal judgments as it does over other, more exhaustively researched types of judgments. To see how much, we discuss some examples of representativeness-thinking in medicine, in pseudoscientific systems, and in psychoanalysis.

REPRESENTATIVENESS AND MEDICAL BELIEFS

One area in which the impact of representativeness on causal judgments is particularly striking is the domain of health and medicine. Historically, people have often assumed that the symptoms of a disease should resemble either its cause or its cure (or both). In ancient Chinese medicine, for example, people with vision problems were fed ground bat in the mistaken belief that bats had particularly keen vision and that some of this ability might be transferred to the recipient (Deutsch 1977). Evans-Pritchard (1937) noted many examples of the influence of representativeness among the African Azande (although he discussed them in the context of magical-thinking, not representativeness). For instance, the Azande used the ground skull of the red bush monkey to cure epilepsy. Why? The cure should resemble the disease, so the herky-jerky movements of the monkey make the essence of monkey appear to be a promising candidate to settle the violent movements of an epileptic seizure. As Evans-Pritchard (quoted in Nisbett and Ross 1980, p. 116) put it:

> Generally the logic of therapeutic treatment consists in the selection of the most prominent external symptoms, the naming of the disease after some object in nature it resembles, and the utilization of the object as the principal ingredient in the drug administered to cure the disease. The circle may even be completed by belief that the external symptoms not only yield to treatment by the object which resembles them but are caused by it as well.

Western medical practice has likewise been guided by the representativeness heuristic. For instance, early Western medicine was strongly influenced by what was known as the "doctrine of signatures," or the belief that "every natural substance which possesses any medicinal virtue indicates by an obvious and well-marked external character the disease for which it is a remedy, or the object for which it should be employed" (quoted in Nisbett and Ross 1980, p. 116). Thus, physicians prescribed the lungs of the fox (known for its endurance) for asthmatics, and the yellow spice turmeric for jaundice. Again, disease and cure are linked because they resemble one another.

Or consider the popularity of homeopathy, which derives from the eighteenth-century work of the German physician Samuel Hahnemann (Barrett 1987). One of the bedrock principles of homeopathy is Hahnemann's "law of similars," according to which the key to discovering what substance will cure a particular disorder lies in noting the effect that various substances have on healthy people. If a substance causes a particular reaction in an unafflicted person, then it is seen as a likely cure for a disease characterized by those same symptoms. As before, the external symptoms of a disease are used to identify a cure for the disease—a cure that manifests the same external characteristics.

Of course, there are instances in which substances that cause particular symptoms *are* used effectively as part of a therapeutic regimen to cure, alleviate, or prevent those very symptoms. Vaccines deliver small quantities of disease-causing viruses to help individuals develop immunities. Likewise, allergy sufferers sometimes receive periodic doses of the exact substance to which they are allergic so that they will develop a tolerance over time. The problem with the dubious medical practices described above is the *general* assumption that the symptoms of a disease should resemble its cause, its cure, or both. Limiting the scope of possible cures to those that are representative of the disease can seriously impede scientific discovery. Such a narrow focus, for example, would have inhibited the discovery of the two most significant developments of modern medicine: sanitation and antibiotics.

Representativeness-thinking continues to abound in modern "alternative" medicine, a pursuit that appears to be gaining in perceived legitimacy (Cowley, King, Hager, and Rosenberg 1995). An investigation by Congress into health fraud and quackery noted several examples of what appear to be interventions inspired by the superficial appeal of representativeness (U.S. Congress, House

Subcommittee on Health and Long-Term Care 1984). In one set of suggested treatments, patients are encouraged to eat raw organ concentrates corresponding to the dysfunctional body part: e.g., brain concentrates for mental disorders, heart concentrates for cardiac conditions, and raw stomach lining for ulcers. Similarly, the fingerprints of representativeness are all over the practice of "rebirthing," a New Age therapeutic technique in which individuals attempt to reenact their own births in an effort to correct personality defects caused by having been born in an "unnatural" fashion (Ward 1994). One person who was born breech (i.e., feet first) underwent the rebirthing procedure to cure his sense that his life was always going in the wrong direction and that he could never seem to get things "the right way round." Another, born Caesarean, sought the treatment because of a lifelong difficulty with seeing things to completion, and always relying on others to finish tasks for her. As one author quipped, "God knows what damage forceps might inflict . . . a lifelong neurosis that you're being dragged where you don't want to go?" (Ward 1994, p. 90).

A more rigorous examination of the kind of erroneous beliefs about health and the human body that can arise from the appeal of representativeness has dealt with the adage, "You are what you eat." Just how far do people take this idea? In certain respects, the saying is undeniably true: Bodies are composed to a large extent of the molecules that were once ingested as food. Quite literally, we are what we have eaten. Indeed, there are times when we take on the character of what we ingest: People gain weight by eating fatty foods, and a person's skin can acquire an orange tint from the carotene found in carrots and tomatoes. But the notion that we develop the characteristics of the food we eat sometimes goes beyond such examples to almost magical extremes. The Hua of Papua New Guinea, for example, believe that individuals will grow quickly if they eat rapidly growing food (Meigs 1984, cited by Nemeroff and Rozin 1989).

But what about a more "scientifically minded" population? Psychologists Carol Nemeroff and Paul Rozin (1989) asked college students to consider a hypothetical culture known as the "Chandorans," who hunt wild boar and marine turtles. Some of the students learned that the Chandorans hunt turtles for their shells, and wild boar for their meat. The others heard the opposite: The tribe hunts turtles for their meat, and boar for their tusks.

After reading one of the two descriptions of the Chandorans, the students were asked to rate the tribe members on numerous characteristics. Their responses reflected a belief that the characteristics of the food that was eaten would "rub off" onto the tribe members. Boar-eaters were thought to be more aggressive and irritable than their counterparts—and more likely to have beards! The turtle-eaters were thought to live longer and be better swimmers.

However educated a person may be (the participants in Nemeroff and Rozin's experiment were University of Pennsylvania undergraduates), it can be difficult to get beyond the assumption that like goes with like. In this case, it leads to the belief that individuals tend to acquire the attributes of the food they ingest. Simple representativeness.

REPRESENTATIVENESS AND PSEUDOSCIENTIFIC BELIEFS

A core tenet of the field of astrology is that an individual's personality is influenced by the astrological sign under which he or she was born (Huntley 1990). A glance at the personality types associated with the various astrological signs reveals an uncanny concordance between the supposed personality of someone with a particular sign and the characteristics associated with the sign's namesake (Huntley 1990; Howe 1970; Zusne and Jones 1982). Those born under the sign of the goat (Capricorn) are said to be tenacious, hardworking, and stubborn; whereas those born under the lion (Leo) are proud, forceful leaders. Likewise, those born under the sign of Cancer (the crab) share with their namesake a tendency to appear hard on the outside; while inside their "shells" they are soft and vulnerable. One treatment of astrology goes so far as to suggest that, like the crab, those born under the sign of Cancer tend to be "deeply attached to their homes" (Read et al. 1978).

What is the origin of these associations? They are not empirically derived, as they have been shown time and time again to lack validity (e.g., Carlson 1985; Dean 1987; for reviews see Abell 1981: Schick and Vaughn 1995: Zusne and Jones 1982). Instead, they are conceptually driven by simple, representativeness-based assessments of the personalities that *should* be associated with various astrological signs. After all, who is more likely to be retiring and modest than a Virgo (the virgin)? Who better to be well balanced, harmonious, and fair than a Libra (the scales)? By taking advantage of people's reflexive associations, the system gains plausibility among those disinclined to dig deeper.

And it doesn't stop there. Consider another elaborate "scientific" system designed to assess the "secrets" of an individual's personality—graphology, or handwriting analysis. Corporations pay graphologists sizable fees to help screen job applicants by developing personality profiles of those who apply for jobs (Neter and Ben-Shakhar 1989). Graphologists are also called upon to provide "expert" testimony in trial proceedings, and to help the Secret Service determine if any real danger is posed by threatening letters to government officials (Scanlon and Mauro 1992). How much stock can we put in the work of handwriting analysts?

Unlike astrology, graphology is not worthless. It has been, and continues to be, the subject of careful empirical investigation (Nevo 1986), and it has been shown that people's handwriting can reveal certain things about them. Particularly shaky writing can be a clue that an individual suffers from some neurological disorder that causes hand tremors; whether a person is male or female is often apparent from his or her writing. In general, however, what handwriting analysis can determine most reliably tends to be things that can be more reliably ascertained through other means. As for the "secrets" of an individual's personality, graphology has yet to show that it is any better than astrology.

This has not done much to diminish the popularity of handwriting analysis, however. One reason for this is that graphologists, like astrologers, gain some surface plausibility or "face validity" for their claims by exploiting the tendency for people to employ the representativeness heuristic. Many of their claims have a superficial "sensible" quality, rarely violating the principle that like goes with like. Consider, for instance, the "zonal theory" of graphology, which divides a person's handwriting into the upper, middle, and lower regions. A person's "intellectual," "practical," and "instinctual" qualities supposedly correspond to the different regions (Basil 1989). Can you guess which is which? Could our "lower" instincts be reflected anywhere other than the lower region, or our "higher" intellect anywhere other than the top?

The list of such representativeness-based "connections" goes on and on. Handwriting slants to the left? The person must be holding something back, repressing his or her true emotions. Slants to the right? The person gets carried away by his or her feelings. A signature placed far below a paragraph suggests that the individual wishes to distance himself or herself from what was written (Scanlon and Mauro 1992). Handwriting that stays close to the left margin belongs to individuals attached to the past, whereas writing that hugs the right margin comes from those oriented toward the future.

What is ironic is that the very mechanism that many graphologists rely upon to argue for the persuasive value of their endeavor—that the character of the handwriting resembles the character of the person—is what ultimately betrays them: They call it "common sense"; we call it judgment by representativeness.

REPRESENTATIVENESS AND PSYCHOANALYSIS

Two prominent social psychologists, Richard Nisbett and Lee Ross, have argued that "the enormous popularity of Freudian theory probably lies in the fact that, unlike all its competitors among contemporary views, it encourages the layperson to do what comes naturally in causal explanation, that is, to use the representativeness heuristic" (Nisbett and Ross 1980, p. 244). Although this claim would be difficult to put to empirical test, there can be little doubt that much of the interpretation of symbols that lies at the core of psychoanalytic theory is driven by representativeness. Consider the interpretation of dreams, in which the images a client reports from his or her dreams are considered indicative of underlying motives. An infinite number of potential relationships exist between dream content and underlying psychodynamics, and it is interesting that virtually all of the "meaningful" ones identified by psychodynamically oriented clinicians are ones in which there is an obvious fit or resemblance between the reported image and inner dynamics. A man who dreams of a snake or a cigar is thought to be troubled by his penis or his sexuality. People who dream of policemen are thought to be concerned about their fathers or authority figures. Knowledge of the representativeness heuristic compels one to wonder whether such connections reflect something important about the psyche of the client, or whether they exist primarily in the mind of the therapist.

One area of psychodynamic theorizing in which the validity of such superficially plausible relationships has been tested and found wanting is the use of projective tests. The most widely known projective test is the Rorschach, in which clients report what they "see" in ambiguous blotches of ink on cards. As in all projective tests, the idea is that in responding to such an unstructured stimulus, a person must "project," and thus reveal, some of his or her inner dynamics. Countless studies, however, have failed to produce evidence that the test is valid—that is, that the assessments made about people on the basis of the test correspond to the psychopathological conditions from which they suffer (Burros 1978).[3]

The research findings notwithstanding, clinicians frequently report the Rorschach to be extremely helpful in clinical practice. Might representativeness contribute to this paradox of strongly held beliefs coexisting with the absence of any real relationship? You be the judge. A person who interprets the whole Rorschach card, and not its specific details, is considered by clinicians to suffer from a need to form a "big picture," and a tendency toward grandiosity, even paranoia. In contrast, a person who refers only to small details of the ink blots is considered to have an obsessive personality—someone who attends to detail at the expense of the more important holistic aspects (Dawes 1994). Once again, systematic research has failed to find evidence for these relationships, but the sense of representativeness gives them some superficial plausibility.

Conclusion

We have described numerous erroneous beliefs that appear to derive from the overuse of the representativeness heuristic. Many of them arise in domains in which the reach for solutions to important problems exceeds our grasp—such as the attempt to uncover (via astrology or handwriting analysis) simple cues to the complexities of human motivation and personality. In such domains in which no simple solutions exist, and yet the need or desire for such solutions remains strong, people often let down their guard. Dubious cause-effect links are then uncritically accepted because they satisfy the principle of like goes with like.

Representativeness can also have the opposite effect, inhibiting belief in valid claims that violate the expectation of resemblance. People initially scoffed at Walter Reed's suggestion that malaria was carried by the mosquito. From a representativeness standpoint, it is easy to see why: The cause (a tiny mosquito) is not at all representative of the result (a devastating disease). Reed's claim violated the notion that big effects should have big causes, and thus was difficult to accept (Nisbett and Ross 1980). Although skepticism is a vital component of critical thought, it should not be based on an excessive adherence to the principle that like goes with like.

Indeed, it is often those discoveries that violate the expected resemblance between cause and effect that are ultimately hailed a significant breakthroughs, as with the discovery of *Helicobacter pylori*, as the ulcer-causing bacterium is now named. As one author put it, "The discovery of *Helicobacter* is no crummy little shift. It's a mindblower—tangible, reproducible, unexpected, and, yes, revolutionary. Just the fact that a bug causes peptic ulcers, long considered the cardinal example of a psychosomatic illness, is a spear in the breast of New Age medicine" (Monmancy 1993, p. 68). Given these stakes, one might be advised to avoid an overreliance on the shortcut of representativeness, and instead to devote the extra effort needed to make accurate judgments and decisions. (But not too much effort—you wouldn't want to give yourself an ulcer.)

Notes

We thank Dennis Regan for his helpful comments on an earlier draft of this article.

1. The reason that the heuristic has been dubbed "representativeness" rather than, say, "resemblance" or "similarity" is that it also applies in circumstances in which the assessment of "fit" is not based on similarity. For example, when assessing whether a series of coin flips was produced by tossing a fair coin, people's judgments are influenced in part by whether the sequence is representative of one produced by a fair coin. A sequence of five heads and five tails is a representative outcome, but a sequence of nine heads and one tail is not. Note, however, that a fifty-fifty split does not make the sequence "similar" to a fair coin, but is does make it representative of one.

2. Some theories of the link between stress and ulcers are even more tinged with representativeness. Since the symptoms of an ulcer manifest themselves in the stomach, the cause "should" involve something that is highly characteristic of the stomach as well, such as hunger and nourishment. Thus, one theorist asserts, "The critical factor in the development of ulcers is the frustration associated with the wish to receive love—when this wish is rejected, it is converted into a wish to be fed," leading ultimately "to an ulcer." Echoing such ideas, James Masterson writes in his book *The Search for the Real Self* that ulcers affect those who are "hungering for emotional supplies that were lost in childhood or that were never sufficient to nourish the real self" (both quoted in Monmaney 1993).

3. Actually, a nonprojective use of the Rorschach, called the Exner System, has been shown to have some validity (Exner 1986). The system is based on the fact that some of the inkblots *do* look like various objects, and a person's responses are scored for the number and proportion that fail to reflect this correspondence. Unlike the usual Rorschach procedure, which is subjectively scored, the Exner system is a standardized test.

References

Abell, G. O. 1981. Astrology. In *Science and the Paranormal: Probing the Existence of the Supernatural*, ed. by G. O. Abell and B. Singer. New York: Charles Scribner's Sons.

Barrett, S. 1987. Homeopathy: Is it medicine? SKEPTICAL INQUIRER 12(1) (Fall): 56–62.

Basil, R. 1989. Graphology and personality: Let the buyer beware. SKEPTICAL INQUIRER 13 (3) (Spring): 241–243.

Burros, O. K. 1978. *Mental Measurement Yearbook*. 8th ed. Highland Park, N.J.: Gryphon Press.

Carlson, S. 1985. A double-blind test of astrology. *Nature* 318: 419–425.

Cowley, G., P. King, M. Hager, and D. Rosenberg. 1995. Going mainstream. *Newsweek* June 26: 56–57.

Dawes, R. M. 1994. *House of Cards: Psychology and Psychotherapy Built on Myth*. New York: Free Press.

Dawes, R. M., and M. Mulford. 1993. Diagnoses of alien kidnappings that result from conjunction effects in memory. SKEPTICAL INQUIRER 18(1) (Fall): 50–51.

Dean, G. 1987. Does astrology need to be true? Part 2: The answer is no. SKEPTICAL INQUIRER 11(3) (Spring): 257–273.

Deutsch, R. M. 1977. *The New Nuts among the Berriex: How Nutrition Nonsense Captured America.* Palo Alto, Calif.: Ball Publishing.

Evans-Pritchard, E. E. 1937. *Witsberuft, Oracles and Magic among the Axands.* Oxford: Clarendon.

Exnet, J. E. 1986. *The Rorschach: A comprehensive System.* 2d ed. New York: John Wiley.

Gilovich, T. 1991. *How We Know What Isn't So: The Fallibility of Human Reason in Everyday Life.* New York: The Free Press.

Glavin, G. B., and S. Szabo. 1992. Experimental gastric muscatel injury: Laboratory models reveal mechanisms of pathogenesis and new therapeutic strategies. *FASEB Journal* 6:825–831.

Hanslin, J. M. 1967. Craps and magic. *American Journal of Sociology* 73:316–330.

Hentschel, E., G. Brandstattet, B, Dragosics, A. M. Hirschel, H. Nemec, K. Schurze, M. Taufer, and H. Wurzet. 1993. Effect of ranitidine and amoxicillin plus metronidazole on the eradication of Helicobacter pylori and the recurrence of duodenal ulcer. *New England Journal of Medicine* 328: 308–312.

Howe, E. 1970. Astrology. In *Man, Myth, and Magic: An Illustrated Encyclopedia of the Supernatural,* ed. by R. Cavendish. New York: Marshall Cavendish.

Hunter, B. T. 1993. Good news for gastric sufferers. *Consumer's Research* 76 (October): 8–9.

Huntley, J. 1990. *The Elements of Astrology.* Shaftesbury, Dorset, Great Britain: Element Books.

Kahneman, D., and A. Tversky. 1972. Subjective probability: A judgment of representativeness. *Cognitive Psychology* 3: 430–454.

Kahneman, D., and A. Tversky. 1973. On the psychology of prediction. *Psychological Review* 80: 237–251.

Meigs, A. S. 1984. *Food, Sex, and Pollution: A New Guinea Religion.* New Brunswick, N.J.: Rutgers University Press.

Monmaney, T. 1993. Marshall's hunch. *The New Yorker* 69 (September 20): 64–72.

Nemeroff, C., and P. Rozin. 1989. 'You are what you eat': Applying the demand-free "impressions" technique to an unacknowledged belief. *Erhos* 17: 50–69.

Neter, E., and G. Ben-Shakhar. 1989. The predictive validity of graphological inferences: A meta-analytic approach. *Personality and Individual Differences* (10) 737–745.

Nevo, B. 1986. ed. *Scientific Aspects of Graphology: A Handbook.* Springfield, Ill.: Charles C. Thomas.

Nisbett, R., and L. Ross. 1980. *Human Inference: Strategies and Shortcomings of Social Judgment.* Englewood Cliffs, N.J.: Prentice-Hall.

Peterson, W. L. 1991. Helicobacter pylori and peptic ulcer disease. *New England Journal of Medicine* 324: 1043–1048.

Read, A. W. et al. eds. 1978. *Funk and Wagnall's New Comprehensive International Dictionary of the English Language.* New York: Publishers Guild Press.

Scanlon, M., and J. Mauro. 1992. The lowdown on handwriting analysis: Is it for real? *Psychology Today* (November/December): 46–53; 80.

Schick, T., and L. Vaughn. 1995. *How to Think about Weird Things: Critical Thinking for a New Age.* Mountain View, Calif.: Mayfield Publishing Company.

Soll, A. H. 1990. Pathogenesis of peptic ulcer and implications for therapy. *New England Journal of Medicine* 322: 909–916.

Tversky, A., and D. Kahneman. 1974. Judgment under uncertainty: Heuristics and biases. *Science* 185: 1124–1131.

Tversky, A., and D. Kahneman. 1982. Judgments of and by representativeness. In *Judgment under Uncertainty: Heuristics and Biases.* ed. by D. Kahneman, P. Slovic, and A. Tversky. Cambridge: Cambridge University Press.

Tversky, A., and D. Kahneman. 1983. Extensional versus intuitive reasoning: The conjunction fallacy in probability judgment. *Psychological Review* 90: 293–315.

U.S. Congress. 1984. *Quackery. A $10 Billion Scandal: A Report by the Chairman of the (House) Subcommittee on Health and Long-Term Care.* Washington, D.C.: United States Government Printing Office.

Wandyez, K. 1993. The H. Pylori factor. *Forbes* 152 (August 2): 128.

Ward, R. 1994. Maternity ward. *Mirabella* (February): 89–90.

Zusne, L. and W. H. Jones 1982. *Anomalistic Psychology.* Hillsdale, N.J.: Lawrence Erlbaum Associates.

Review and Contemplate

1. What is the representativeness heuristic?
2. Give two examples of how the representativeness heuristic can lead to mistaken medical beliefs.
3. Give two examples of how the representativeness heuristic can lead to pseudoscientific beliefs.
4. Explain how the representativeness heuristic plays a role in clinicians' beliefs about the validity of the Rorschach inkblot test.

7.3 *Some Systematic Biases of Everyday Judgment /*
THOMAS GILOVICH

While writing this introduction, I came across the Web site for a man named Brian who claims to have predictive dreams, 84% of which he says have come true. He claims to have predicted (a) Hurricane Katrina's landfall and the resulting flooding of New Orleans, (b) a school shooting in Tennessee, (c) a fireman waking up after 10 years in a coma, and many more events. Every day he updates his Web site with a number of scanned images of his "dream drawings" from the previous night. The drawings often consist of words and figures hastily scrawled on a piece of paper, and Brian typically interprets the drawing in a brief sentence placed below the image. Visitors to the Web site are invited to use a Web search engine to search for news stories or events that appear to match Brian's prediction. For example, on February 6, 2006, Brian posted a drawing that read "ship sinks." Later that same month, a visitor posted a story about 50 people who were missing after a ferry sank in a river in Bangladesh on February 27; thus, Brian's prediction was apparently confirmed.

Is Brian really psychic, or might believers in his psychic abilities be misled by normal cognitive tendencies that make Brian's predictive dreams seem more accurate than they actually are? In this article, Gilovich discusses several cognitive tendencies that may lead people to develop inaccurate, pseudoscientific, or paranormal beliefs. One of these tendencies—that Gilovich calls the "compared to what?" problem—is people's failure to consider a relevant baseline of comparison or control group. For example, with respect to Brian's "ship sinks" prediction, how frequent are events that involve a ship or boat sinking? Predicting a frequent event is not exactly an impressive feat. For example, I could predict that an automobile accident will occur in the near future on a major highway, but it's not a very impressive prediction because such accidents happen regularly. When I typed Brian's "ship sinks" prediction into a Web search engine, I found a number of stories consistent with Brian's prediction, including a freighter that sank in China, a cargo ship that sank off the coast of Egypt, and an Egyptian passenger ship that sank in the Red Sea. All of these events happened within a six-week period, so which one is the event he predicted?

Of course, there are additional reasons why people might overestimate the accuracy of Brian's dreams, one of which is his use of "ambiguous specificity," a topic discussed in the first article in this chapter. Other reasons are discussed in this article by Gilovich.

APA Reference

Gilovich, T. (1997, March/April). Some systematic biases of everyday judgment. *Skeptical Inquirer, 21,* 31–35.

Skeptics have long thought that everyday judgment and reasoning are biased in predictable ways. Psychological research on the subject conducted during the past quarter century largely confirms these suspicions.

Two types of explanations are typically offered for the dubious beliefs that are dissected in SKEPTICAL INQUIRER. On one hand, there are motivational causes: Some beliefs are comforting, and so people embrace that comfort and convince themselves that a questionable proposition is true. Many types of religious beliefs, for example, are often explained this way. On the other hand, there are cognitive causes: faulty processes of reasoning and judgment that lead people to misevaluate the evidence of their everyday experience. The skeptical community is convinced that everyday judgment and reasoning leave much to be desired.

Why are skeptics so unimpressed with the reasoning abilities and habits of the average person? Until recently, this pessimism was based on simple observation, often by those with a particularly keen eye for the foibles of human nature. Thus, skeptics often cite such thinkers as Francis Bacon, who stated:

> . . . all superstition is much the same whether it be that of astrology, dreams, omens, retributive judgment, or the like . . . [in that] the deluded believers observe events which are fulfilled, but neglect or pass over their failure, though it be much more common. (Bacon 1899/1620)

John Stuart Mill and Bertrand Russell are two other classic scholars who, along with Bacon, are often quoted for their trenchant observations on the shortcomings of human judgment. It is also common to see similar quotes of more recent vintage—in SKEPTICAL INQUIRER and elsewhere—from the likes of Richard Feynman, Stephen Jay Gould, and Carl Sagan.

During the past twenty-five years, a great deal of psychological research has dealt specifically with the quality of everyday reasoning, and so it is now possible to go beyond simple observation and arrive at a truly rigorous assessment of the shortcomings of everyday judgment. In so doing, we can determine whether or not these scholars we all admire are correct. Do people misevaluate evidence in the very ways and for the very reasons that Bacon, Russell, and others have claimed? Let us look at the research record and see.

Thomas Gilovich, professor of psychology at Cornell University and a fellow of CSICOP, is the author of How We Know What Isn't So: The Fallibility of Human Reason in Everyday Life. This article is based on his presentation at the twentieth-anniversary conference of CSICOP, June 20–23, 1996, Amherst, N.Y.

THE "COMPARED TO WHAT?" PROBLEM

Some of the common claims about the fallibility of human reasoning stand up well to empirical scrutiny. For example, it is commonly argued that people have difficulty with what might be called the "compared to what" problem. That is, people are often overly impressed with an absolute statistic without recognizing that its true import can only be assessed by comparison to some relevant baseline.

For instance, a 1986 article in *Discover* magazine (cited in Dawes 1988) urges readers who fly in airplanes to "know where the exits are and rehearse in your mind exactly how to get to them." Why? The article approvingly notes that someone who interviewed almost two hundred survivors of fatal airline accidents found that ". . . more than 90% had their escape routes mentally mapped out beforehand." Good for them, but note that whoever did the study cannot interview anyone who perished in an airplane crash. Air travel being as scary as it is to so many people, perhaps 90 percent or more of those who died in airline crashes rehearsed their escape routes as well. Ninety percent sounds impressive because it is so close to 100 percent. But without a more pertinent comparison, it really does not mean much.

Similarly, people are often impressed that, say, 30 percent of all infertile couples who adopt a child subsequently conceive. That is great news for that 30 percent to be sure, but what percentage of those who do not adopt likewise conceive? People likewise draw broad conclusions from a cancer patient who goes into remission after steadfastly practicing mental imagery. Again, excellent news for that individual, but might the cancer have gone into remission even if the person had not practiced mental imagery?

This problem of failing to invoke a relevant baseline of comparison is particularly common when the class of data that requires inspection is inherently difficult to collect. Consider, for example, the commonly expressed opinion, "I can always tell that someone is wearing a hairpiece." Are such claims to be believed, or is it just that one can tell that someone is wearing a hairpiece . . . when it is obvious that he is wearing a hairpiece? After all, how can one tell whether some have gone undetected? The goal of a good hairpiece is to fool the public, and so the example is one of those cases in which the confirmations speak loudly while the disconfirmations remain silent.

A similar asymmetry should give pause to those who have extreme confidence in their "gaydar," or their ability to detect whether someone is gay. Here, too, the confirmations announce themselves. When a person for whatever reason "seems gay" and it is later determined that he is, it is a salient triumph for one's skill at detection. But people who elude one's gaydar rarely go out of their way to announce, "By the way, I fooled you: I'm gay."

At any rate, the notion that people have difficulty invoking relevant comparisons has received support from psychological research. Studies of everyday reasoning have shown that the logic and necessity of control groups, for example, is often lost on a large segment of even the educated population (Boring 1954; Einhorn and Hogarth 1978; Nisbett and Ross 1980).

THE "SEEK AND YE SHALL FIND" PROBLEM

Another common claim that stands up well to empirical research is the idea that people do not assess hypotheses even-handedly. Rather, they tend to seek out confirmatory evidence for what they suspect to be true, a tendency that has the effect of "seek and ye shall find." A biased search for confirmatory information frequently turns up more apparent support for a hypothesis than is justified.

This phenomenon has been demonstrated in numerous experiments explicitly designed to assess people's hypothesis-testing strategies (Skov and Sherman 1986; Snyder and Swann 1978). But it is so pervasive that it can also be seen in studies designed with an entirely different agenda in mind. One of my personal favorites is a study in which participants were given the following information (Shafir 1993):

> Imagine that you serve on the jury of an only-child sole-custody case following a relatively messy divorce. The facts of the case are complicated by ambiguous, economic, social, and emotional considerations, and you decide to base your decision entirely on the following few observations. To which parent would you award sole custody of the child?

> Parent A: average income
>   average health
>   average working hours
>   reasonable rapport with the child
>   relatively stable social life
> Parent B: above-average income
>   minor health problems
>   lots of work-related travel
>   very close relationship with the child
>   extremely active social life

Faced with this version of the problem, the majority of respondents chose to award custody to Parent B, the "mixed bag" parent who offers several advantages (above-average income), but also some disadvantages (health problems), in comparison to Parent A. In another version of the problem, however, a different group is asked to which parent they would *deny* custody of the child. Here, too, a majority selects Parent B. Parent B, then, is paradoxically deemed both more and less worthy of caring for the child.

The result is paradoxical, that is, unless one takes into account people's tendencies to seek out confirming information. Asked which parent should be *awarded* the child, people look primarily for positive qualities that warrant being awarded the child—looking less vigilantly for negative characteristics that would lead one to favor the other parent. When asked which parent should be *denied* custody, on the other hand, people look primarily for negative qualities that would disqualify a parent. A decision to award or deny, of course, should be based on a comparison of the positive *and* negative characteristics of the two parents, but the way the question is framed channels respondents down a narrower path in which they focus on information that would confirm the type of verdict they are asked to render.

The same logic often rears its head when people test certain suppositions or hypotheses. Rumors of some dark conspiracy, for example, can lead people to search disproportionately for evidence that supports the plot and neglect evidence that contradicts it.

The Selective Memory Problem

A third commonly sounded complaint about everyday human thought is that people are more inclined to remember information that fits their expectations than information at variance with their expectations. Charles Darwin, for example, said that he took great care to record any observation that was inconsistent with his theories because "I had found by experience that such facts and thoughts were far more apt to escape from the memory than favourable ones" (cited in Clark 1984).

This particular criticism of the average person's cognitive faculties is in need of revision. Memory research has shown that often people have the easiest time recalling information that is *inconsistent* with their expectations or preferences (Bargh and Thein 1985; Srull and Wyer 1989). A little reflection indicates that this is particularly true of those "near misses" in life that become indelibly etched in the brain. The novelist Nicholson Baker (1991) provides a perfect illustration:

> [I] told her my terrible story of coming in second in the spelling bee in second grade by spelling *keep* "c-e-e-p" after successfully tossing off *microphone,* and how for two or three years afterward I was pained every time a yellow garbage truck drove by on Highland Avenue and I saw the capitals printed on it, "Help Keep Our City Clean," with that impossible irrational K that had made me lose so humiliatingly. . . .

Baker's account, of course, is only an anecdote, possibly an apocryphal one at that. But it is one that, as mentioned above, receives support from more systematic studies. In one study, for example, individuals who had bet on professional football games were later asked to recall as much as they could about the various bets they had made (Gilovich 1983). They recalled significantly more information about their losses—outcomes they most likely did not expect to have happen and certainly did not *prefer* to have happen (see Figure 7.2).

Thus, the simple idea that people remember best that which they expect or prefer needs modification. Still, there is something appealing and seemingly true about the idea, and it should not be discarded prematurely. When considering people's belief in the accuracy of psychic forecasts, for example, it certainly seems to be fed by selective memory for successful predictions.

How then can we reconcile this idea with the finding that often *inconsistent* information is better recalled? Perhaps the solution lies in considering when an event is *eventful.* With respect to their capacity to grab attention, some events are one-sided

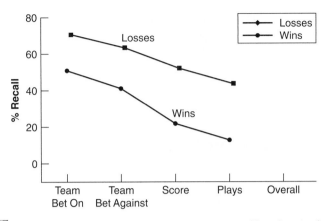

FIGURE 7.2 Gamblers' recall of information about bets won and lost. (From Gilovich 1983.)

and others two-sided. Two-sided events are those that stand out and psychologically register as events regardless of how they turn out. If you bet on a sporting event or an election result, for example, either outcome—a win or a loss—has emotional significance and is therefore likely to emerge from the stream of everyday experience and register as an event. For these events, it is doubtful that confirmatory information is typically better remembered than disconfirmatory information.

In contrast, suppose you believe that "the telephone always rings when I'm in the shower." The potentially relevant events here are one-sided. If the phone happens to ring while showering, it will certainly register as an event, as you experience great stress in deciding whether to answer it, and you run dripping wet to the phone only to discover that it is someone from AT&T asking if you are satisfied with your long-distance carrier. When the phone does *not* ring when you are in the shower, on the other hand, it is a non-event. Nothing happened. Thus, with respect to the belief that the phone always rings while you are in the shower, the events are inherently one-sided: Only the confirmations stand out.

Perhaps it is these one-sided events to which Bacon's and Darwin's comments best apply. For one-sided events, as I discuss below, it is often the outcomes consistent with expectations that stand out and are more likely to be remembered. For two-sided events, on the other hand, the two types of outcomes are likely to be equally memorable; or, on occasion, events inconsistent with expectations may be more memorable.

But what determines whether an event is one- or two-sided? There are doubtless several factors. Let's consider two of them in the context of psychic predictions. First, events relevant to psychic predictions are inherently one-sided in the sense that such predictions are disconfirmed not by any specific event, but by their accumulated failure to be confirmed. Thus, the relevant comparison here is between confirmations and non-confirmations, or between events and non-events. It is no surprise, surely, that events are typically more memorable than non-events.

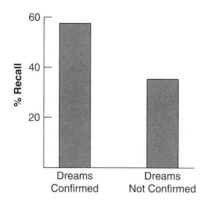

FIGURE 7.3  Participants' recall of dream prophecies that were either confirmed or unconfirmed. (Adapted from Madey 1993.)

In one test of this idea, a group of college students read a diary purportedly written by another student, who described herself as having an interest in the prophetic nature of dreams (Madey 1993). To test whether there was any validity to dream prophecy, she decided to record each night's dreams and keep a record of significant events in her life, and later determine if there was any connection between the two. Half of the dreams (e.g., "I saw lots of people being happy") were later followed by events that could be seen as fulfilling ("My professor cancelled our final, which produced cheers throughout the class"). The other half went unfulfilled.

After reading the entire diary and completing a brief "filler" task, the participants were asked to recall as many of the dreams as they could. As Figure 7.3 shows, they recalled many more of the prophecies that were fulfilled than those that were not. This result is hardly a surprise, of course, because the fulfillment of a prophecy reminds one of the original prediction, whereas a failure to fulfill it is often a non-event. The relevant outcomes are therefore inherently one-sided, and the confirmations are more easily recalled. The end result is that the broader belief in question—in this case, dream prophecy—receives spurious support.

The events relevant to psychic predictions are one-sided in another way as well. Psychic predictions are notoriously vague about when the prophesied events are supposed to occur. "A serious misfortune will befall a powerful leader" is a more common prophecy than "The President will be assassinated on March 15th." Such predictions are *temporally unfocused,* in that there is no specific moment to which interested parties are to direct their attention. For such predictions, confirmatory events are once again more likely to stand out because confirmations are more likely to prompt a recollection of the original prophecy. The events relevant to temporally unfocused expectations, then, tend to be one-sided, with the confirmations typically more salient and memorable than disconfirmations.

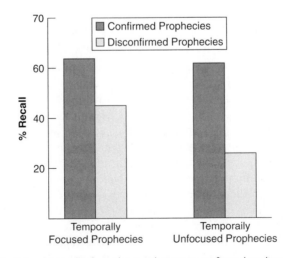

Temporally focused expectations, on the other hand, are those for which the timing of the decisive outcome is known in advance. If one expects a particular team to win the Super Bowl, for example, one knows precisely when that expectation will be confirmed or refuted—at the end of the game. As a result, the events relevant to temporally focused expectations tend to be two-sided because one's attention is focused on the decisive moment, and both outcomes are likely to be noticed and remembered.

In one study that examined the memory implications of temporally focused and unfocused expectations, participants were asked to read the diary of a student who, as part of an ESP experiment, was required to try to prophesy an otherwise unpredictable event every week for several weeks (Madey and Gilovich 1993). The diary included the student's weekly prophecy as well as various passages describing events from that week. There were two groups of participants in the experiment. In the *temporally unfocused* condition, the prophecies made no mention of when the prophesied event was likely to occur ("I have a feeling that I will get into an argument with my Psychology research group"). In the *temporally focused* condition, the prediction identified a precise day on which the event was to occur ("I have a feeling that I will get into an argument with my Psychology research group on Friday"). For each group, half of the prophecies were confirmed (e.g., "Our professor assigned us to research groups, and we immediately disagreed over our topic") and half were disconfirmed (e.g., "Our professor assigned us to research groups, and we immediately came to a unanimous decision on our topic"). Whether confirmed or disconfirmed, the relevant event was described in the diary entry for the day prophesied in the temporally focused condition. After reading the diary and

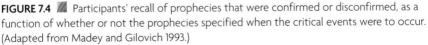

FIGURE 7.4 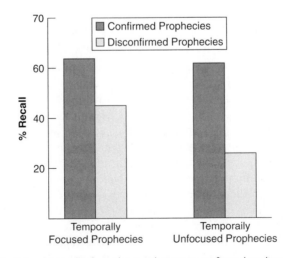 Participants' recall of prophecies that were confirmed or disconfirmed, as a function of whether or not the prophecies specified when the critical events were to occur. (Adapted from Madey and Gilovich 1993.)

completing a short distracter task, the participants were asked to recall as many prophecies and relevant events as they could.

Knowing when the prophesied events were likely to occur helped the respondents' memories, but only for those prophecies that were disconfirmed (see Figure 7.4). Confirmatory events were readily recalled whether temporally focused or not. Disconfirmations, on the other hand, were rarely recalled unless they disconfirmed a temporally focused prediction. When one considers that most psychic predictions are temporally unfocused, the result, once again, is that the evidence for psychic predictions can appear more substantial than it is.

CONCLUSION

There is, of course, much more psychological research on the quality of everyday judgment than that reviewed here (see, for example, Baron 1988; Dawes 1988; Gilovich 1991; Nisbett and Ross 1980; Kahneman, Slovic, and Tversky 1982). But even this brief review is sufficient to make it clear that some of the reputed biases of everyday judgment turn out to be real, verifiable shortcomings. Systematic research by and large supports the suspicions of much of the skeptical community that everyday judgment is not to be trusted completely. At one level, this should not come as a surprise: It is precisely because everyday judgment cannot be trusted that the inferential safeguards known as the scientific method were developed. It is unfortunate that those safeguards are not more widely taught or more generally appreciated.

References

Bacon, F. 1899. *Advancement of Learning and the Novum Organum* (rev. ed.). New York: Colonial Press. (Original work published 1620).

Baker, N. 1991. *Room Temperature*. New York: Vintage.

Bargh, J. A., and R. D. Thein. 1985. Individual construct accessibility, person memory, and the recall-judgment link: The case of information overload. *Journal of Personality and Social Psychology* 49: 1129–1146.

Baron, J. 1988. *Thinking and Deciding*. New York: Cambridge University Press.

Boting, E. G. 1954. The nature and history of experimental control. *American Journal of Psychology* 67: 573–589.

Clark, R. W. 1984. *The Survival of Charles Darwin: A Biography of a Man and an Idea*. New York: Random House.

Dawes, R. M. 1988. *Rational Choice in an Uncertain World*. San Diego, Calif.: Harcourt Brace Jovanovich.

Einhorn, H. J., and R. M. Hogarth. 1978. Confidence in judgment: Persistence in the illusion of validity. *Psychological Review* 85: 395–416.

Gilovich, T. 1983. Biased evaluation and persistence in gambling. *Journal of Personality and Social Psychology* 44: 1110–1126.

——. 1991. *How We Know What Isn't So: The Fallibility of Human Reason in Everyday Life*. New York: Free Press.

Kahneman, D., P. Slovic, and A. Tversky. 1982. *Judgment under Uncertainty: Heuristics and Biases.* Cambridge: Cambridge University Press.

Madey, S. E. 1993. Memory for expectancy-consistent and expectancy-inconsistent information: An investigation of one-sided and two-sided events. Unpublished doctoral dissertation, Cornell University.

Madey, S. F., and T. Gilovich. 1993. Effect of temporal focus on the recall of expectancy-consistent and expectancy-inconsistent information. *Journal of Personality and Social Psychology* 65: 458–468.

Nisbett, R. E., and L. Ross. 1980. *Human Inference: Strategies and Shortcomings of Social Judgment.* Englewood Cliffs, N.J.: Prentice-Hall.

Shafir, E. 1993. Choosing versus rejecting: Why some options are both better and worse than others. *Memory and Cognition* 21: 546–556.

Skov, R. B., and S. J. Sherman. 1986. Information-gathering processes: Diagnosticity, hypothesis-confirmatory strategies, and perceived hypothesis confirmation. *Journal of Experimental Social Psychology* 22: 93–121.

Snyder, M., and W. B. Swann. 1978. Hypothesis-testing processes in social interaction. *Journal of Personality and Social Psychology* 36: 1202–1212.

Stull, T. K., and R. S. Wyer. 1989. Person memory and judgment. *Psychological Review* 96: 58–83.

Review and Contemplate

1. Describe and give an example of the "compared to what?" problem.
2. Describe and give an example of the "seek and ye shall find" problem.
3. Describe and give an example of the "selective memory" problem.
4. Explain why we are more likely to remember information that *confirms* psychic predictions (give two reasons).
5. In the introduction to this article, I described how Brian's predictive dreams were related to the "compared to what?" problem. Explain how Brian's dreams are related to the "seek and ye shall find" problem and the "selective memory" problem.

CHAPTER 8
Personality and Psychological Testing

8.1   *What's Wrong with This Picture?/*
Scott Lilienfeld, James Wood, and Howard Garb

During the 1960s, psychologists Loren and Jean Chapman noticed a disturbing problem with clinicians' beliefs about a psychodiagnostic test called the Draw-a-Person Test (DAP). In the DAP a client draws pictures of people, and the clinician examines these drawings to infer information about the person's personality or psychological problems. There was fairly consistent agreement among the clinicians who used the DAP that people with certain psychological symptoms drew pictures with particular characteristics. For example, the clinicians believed that people who were paranoid or suspicious of other people drew pictures with atypical eyes and that men who were worried about their manliness drew broad-shouldered, muscular figures. The problem was that even though experienced clinicians believed in the existence of these correlations between drawing characteristics and the psychological symptoms of the test takers, research studies showed their beliefs were erroneous. In other words, paranoid or suspicious people did not draw atypical eyes more often than those who were not paranoid or suspicious. The clinicians had developed illusory correlations—that is, they perceived relationships that did not exist. Apparently, the clinicians saw these illusory correlations because they expected to see them, even though the data they observed showed no such correlations. This is a good example of a point raised in Chapter 1: difficulties we have with statistical reasoning can lead to pseudoscientific beliefs. In this case, difficulties with statistical reasoning led to the belief that the DAP accurately measured personality and psychological problems.

Projective tests, which include the DAP and other tests, are used by psychologists to assess personality, identify mental disorders, and estimate a person's violent or criminal tendencies. These tests involve ambiguous stimuli, such as inkblots or drawings, that test takers are asked to interpret. People's responses to these ambiguous stimuli supposedly reflect their hidden or unconscious motives, thoughts, and conflicts. Lilienfeld, Wood, and Garb discuss the scientific evidence concerning the reliability and validity of a variety of projective techniques, including the Rorschach inkblot test, Thematic Apperception Test, and Draw-a-Person Test.

APA Reference

Lilienfeld, S. O., Wood, J. M., & Garb, H. N. (2001). What's wrong with this picture? *Scientific American, 284*(5), 81–87.

What if you were asked to describe images you saw in an inkblot or to invent a story for an ambiguous illustration—say, of a middle-aged man looking away from a woman who was grabbing his arm? To comply, you would draw on your own emotions, experiences, memories and imagination. You would, in short, project yourself into the images. Once you did that, many practicing psychologists would assert, trained evaluators could mine your musings to reach conclusions about your personality traits, unconscious needs and overall mental health.

But how correct would they be? The answer is important because psychologists frequently apply such "projective" instruments (presenting people with ambiguous images, words or objects) as components of mental assessments, and because the outcomes can profoundly affect the lives of the respondents. The tools often serve, for instance, as aids in diagnosing mental illness, in predicting whether convicts are likely to become violent after being paroled, in evaluating the mental stability of parents engaged in custody battles, and in discerning whether children have been sexually molested.

We recently reviewed a large body of research into how well projective methods work, concentrating on three of the most extensively used and best-studied instruments. Overall our findings are unsettling.

BUTTERFLIES OR BISON?

The Famous Rorschach inkblot test—which asks people to describe what they see in a series of 10 inkblots—is by far the most popular of the projective methods, given to hundreds of thousands, or perhaps millions, of people every year. The research discussed below refers to the modern, rehabilitated version, not to the original construction, introduced in the 1920s by Swiss psychiatrist Hermann Rorschach.

The initial tool came under server attack in the 1950s and 1960s, in part because it lacked standardized procedures and a set of norms (averaged results from the general population). Standardization is important because seemingly trivial differences in the way an instrument is administered can affect a person's responses to it. Norms provide a reference point for determining when someone's responses fall outside an acceptable range.

In the 1970s John E. Exner, Jr., then at Long Island University, ostensibly corrected those problems in the early Rorschach test by introducing what he called the Comprehensive System. This set of instructions established detailed rules for delivering the inkblot exam and for interpreting the responses, and it provided norms for children and adults.

In spite of the Comprehensive System's current popularity, it generally falls short on two crucial criteria that were also problematic for the original Rorschach: scoring reliability and validity. A tool possessing scoring reliability yields similar results regardless of who grades and tabulates the responses. A valid technique measures what it aims to measure: its results are consistent with those produced by other trustworthy instruments or are able to predict behavior, or both.

To understand the Rorschach's scoring reliability defects, it helps to know something about how reactions to the inkblots are interpreted. First, a psychologist rates the collected reactions on more than 100 characteristics, or variables. The evaluator, for instance, records whether the person looked at whole blots or just parts, notes whether the detected images were unusual or typical of most test takers, and indicates which aspects of the inky swirls (such as form or color) most determined what the respondent reported seeing.

Then he or she compiles the findings into a psychological profile of the individual. As part of that interpretive process, psychologists might conclude that focusing on minor details (such as stray splotches) in the blots, instead of on whole images, signals obsessiveness in a patient and that seeing things in the white spaces within the larger blots, instead of in the inked areas, reveals a negative, contrary streak.

For the scoring of any variable to be considered highly reliable, two different assessors should be very likely to produce similar ratings when examining any given person's responses. Recent investigations demonstrate, however, that strong agreement is achieved for only about half the characteristics examined by those who score Rorschach responses; evaluators might well come up with quite different ratings for the remaining variables.

Equally troubling, analyses of the Rorschach's validity indicate that it is poorly equipped to identify most psychiatric conditions—with the notable exceptions of schizophrenia and other disturbances marked by disordered thoughts, such as bipolar disorder (manic-depression). Despite claims by some Rorschach proponents, the method does not consistently detect depression, anxiety disorders or psychopathic personality (a condition characterized by dishonesty, callousness and lack of guilt).

Moreover, although psychologists frequently administer the Rorschach to assess propensities toward violence, impulsiveness and criminal behavior, most research suggests it is not valid for these purposes either. Similarly, no compelling evidence supports its use for detecting sexual abuse in children.

Other problems have surfaced as well. Some evidence suggests that the Rorschach norms meant to distinguish mental health from mental illness are unrepresentative of the U.S. population and mistakenly make many adults and children seem maladjusted. For instance, in a 1999 study of 123 adult volunteers

RORSCHACH TEST

Wasted Ink?

"It looks like two dinosours with huge heads and tiny bodies. They're moving away from each other but looking back. The black blob in the middle reminds me of a spaceship."

Once deemed an "x-ray of the mind," the Rorschach inkblot test remains the most famous—and infamous—projective psychological technique. An examiner hands 10 symmetrical inkblots one at a time in a set order to a viewer, who says what each blot resembles. Five blots contain color; five are black and gray. Respondents can rotate the images. The one on the right is an inverted version of an Andy Warhol rendering; the actual Rorschach blots cannot be published.

Responses to the inkblots purportedly reveal aspects of a person's personality and mental health. Advocates believe, for instance, that references to moving animals—such as the dinosaurs mentioned above—often indicate impulsiveness, whereas allusions to a blot's "blackness"—as in the spaceship—often indicate depression.

Swiss psychiatrist Hermann Rorschach probably got the idea of showing inkblots from a European parlor game. The test debuted in 1921 and reached high status by 1945. But a critical backlash began taking shape in the 1950s, as researchers found that psychologists often interpreted the same responses differently and that particular responses did not correlate well with specific mental illnesses or personality traits.

Today the Comprehensive System, meant to remedy those weaknesses, is widely used to score and interpret Rorschach responses. But it has been criticized on similar grounds. Moreover, several recent findings indicate that the Comprehensive System incorrectly labels many normal respondents as pathological.

at a California blood bank, one in six had scores supposedly indicative of schizophrenia.

The inkblot results may be even more misleading for minorities. Several investigations have shown that scores for African-Americans, Native Americans, Native Alaskans, Hispanics, and Central and South Americans differ markedly from the norms. Together the collected research raises serious doubts about the use of the Rorschach inkblots in the psychotherapy office and in the courtroom.

DOUBTS ABOUT TAT

Another projective tool—the Thematic Apperception Test (TAT)—may be as problematic as the Rorschach. This method asks respondents to formulate a story based on ambiguous scenes in drawings on cards. Among the 31 cards available to psychologists are ones depicting a boy contemplating a violin, a distraught woman clutching an open door, and the man and woman who were mentioned at the start of this article. One card, the epitome of ambiguity, is totally blank.

The TAT has been called "a clinician's delight and a statistician's nightmare," in part because its administration is usually not standardized: different clinicians present different numbers and selections of cards to respondents. Also, most clinicians interpret people's stories intuitively instead of following a well-tested scoring procedure. Indeed, a recent survey of nearly 100 North American psychologists practicing in juvenile and family courts discovered that only 3 percent relied on a standardized TAT scoring system. Unfortunately, some evidence suggests that clinicians who interpret the TAT in an intuitive way are likely to over-diagnose psychological disturbance.

Many standardized scoring systems are available for the TAT, but some of the more popular ones display weak "test-retest" reliability: they tend to yield inconsistent scores from one picture-viewing session to the next. Their validity is frequently questionable as well; studies that find positive results are often contradicted by other investigations. For example, several scoring systems have proved unable to differentiate normal individuals from those who are psychotic or depressed.

A few standardized scoring systems for the TAT do appear to do a good job of discerning certain aspects of personality—notably the need to achieve and a person's perceptions of others (a property called "object relations"). But many times individuals who display a high need to achieve do not score well on measures of actual achievement, so the ability of that variable to predict a person's behavior may be limited. These scoring systems currently lack norms and so are not yet ready for application outside of research settings, but they merit further investigation.

FAULTS IN THE FIGURES

In contrast to the Rorschach and the TAT, which elicit reactions to existing images, a third projective approach asks the people being evaluated to draw the pictures. A number of these instruments, such as the frequently applied Draw-a-Person Test, have examinees depict a human being; others have them draw houses or trees as well. Clinicians commonly interpret the sketches by relating specific "signs"—such as features of the body or clothing—to facets of personality or to particular psychological disorders. They might associate large eyes with paranoia, long ties with sexual aggression, missing facial features with depression, and so on.

THEMATIC APPERCEPTION TEST

Picture Imperfect

The Thematic Apperception Test [TAT], created by Harvard University psychiatrist Henry A. Murray and his student Christiana Morgan in the 1930s, is among the most commonly used projective measures. Examiners present individuals with a subset [typically five to 12] of 31 cards displaying pictures of ambiguous situations, mostly featuring people. Respondents then construct a story about each picture, describing the events that are occurring, what led up to them, what the characters are thinking and feeling, and what will happen later. Many variations of the TAT are in use, such as the Children's Apperception Test, featuring animals in-

teracting in ambiguous situations, and the Blacky Test, featuring the adventures of a black dog and its family.

Psychologists have several ways of interpreting responses to the TAT. One promising approach—developed by Boston University psychologist Drew Westen—relies on a specific scoring system to assess people's perceptions of others ["object relations"]. According to that approach, if someone wove a story about an older woman plotting against a younger person in response to the image visible in the photograph above, the story would imply that the respondent tends to see malevolence in others—but only if similar themes turned up in stories told about other cards.

Surveys show, however, that most practitioners do not use systematic scoring systems to interpret TAT stories, relying instead on their intuitions. Unfortunately, research indicates that such "impressionistic" interpretations of the TAT are of doubtful validity and may make the TAT a projective exercise for both examiner and examinee.

As is true of the other methods, the research on drawing instruments gives reason for serious concern. In some studies, raters agree well on scoring, yet in others the agreement is poor. What is worse, no strong evidence supports the validity of the sign approach to interpretation; in other words, clinicians apparently have no grounds for linking specific signs to particular personality traits or psychiatric diagnoses. Nor is there consistent evidence that signs purportedly linked to child sexual abuse (such as tongues or genitalia) actually reveal a history of molestation. The only positive result found repeatedly is that, as a group, people who draw human figures poorly have somewhat elevated rates of psychological disorders. On the other hand, studies show that clinicians are likely to attribute mental illness to many normal individuals who lack artistic ability.

Certain proponents argue that sign approaches can be valid in the hands of seasoned experts. Yet one group of researchers reported that experts who administered the Draw-a-Person Test were less accurate than graduate students at distinguishing psychological normality from abnormality.

A few global scoring systems, which are not based on signs, might be useful. Instead of assuming a one-to-one correspondence between a feature of a drawing and a personality trait, psychologists who apply such methods combine many aspects of the pictures to come up with a general impression of a person's adjustment. In a study of 52 children, a global scoring approach helped to distinguish normal individuals from those with mood or anxiety disorders. In another report, global interpretation correctly differentiated 54 normal children and adolescents from those who were aggressive or extremely disobedient. The global approach may work better than the sign approach because the act of aggregating information can cancel out "noise" from variables that provide misleading or incomplete information.

Our literature review, then, indicates that, as usually administered, the Rorschach, TAT and human figure drawings are useful only in very limited circumstances. The same is true for many other projective techniques, some of which are described in the box on the following page.

We have also found that even when the methods assess what they claim to measure, they tend to lack what psychologists call "incremental validity": they rarely add much to information that can be obtained in other, more practical ways, such as by conducting interviews or administering objective personality tests. (Objective tests seek answers to relatively clear-cut questions, such as, "I frequently have thoughts of hurting myself—true or false?") This shortcoming of projective tools makes the costs in money and time hard to justify.

WHAT TO DO?

Some mental health professionals disagree with our conclusions. They argue that projective tools have a long history of constructive use and, when administered and interpreted properly, can cut through the veneer of respondents'

OTHER PROJECTIVE TOOLS

What's the Score?

Psychologists have dozens of projective methods to choose from beyond the Rorschach Test, the TAT and figure drawings. As the sampling below indicates, some stand up well to the scrutiny of research, but many do not.

Hand Test

Subjects say what hands pictured in various positions might be doing. This method is used to assess aggression, anxiety and other personality traits, but it has not been well studied.

Handwriting Analysis (Graphology]

Interpreters rely on specific "signs" in a person's handwriting to assess personality characteristics. Though useless, the method is still used to screen prospective employees.

Lüscher Color Test

People rank colored cards in order of preference to reveal personality traits. Most studies find the technique to lack merit.

Play with Anatomically Correct Dolls

Research finds that sexually abused children often play with the dolls' genitalia, however, that behavior is not diagnostic, because many nonabused children do the same thing.

Rosenzweig Picture Frustration Study

After one cartoon character makes a provocative remark to another, a viewer decides how the second character should respond. This instrument, featured in the movie *A Clockwork Orange*, successfully predicts aggression in children.

Sentence Completion Test

Test takers finish a sentence, such as, "If only I could..." Most versions are poorly studied, but one developed by Jane Loevinger of Washington University is valid for measuring aspects of ego development, such as morality and empathy.

Szondi Test

From photographs of patients with various psychiatric disorders, viewers select the ones they like most and least, this technique assumes that the selections reveal something about the choosers' needs, but research has discredited it.

HUMAN FIGURE DRAWINGS

Misleading Signs

Psychologists have many projective drawing instruments at their disposal, but the Draw-a-Person Test is among the most popular—especially for assessing children and—adolescents. A clinician asks the child to draw someone of the same sex and then someone of the opposite sex in any way that he or she wishes. [A variation involves asking the child to draw a person, house and tree.] Those who employ the test believe that the drawings reveal meaningful information about the child's personality or mental health.

In a sketch of a man, for example, small feet would supposedly indicate insecurity or instability—a small head, inadequacy. Large hands or teeth would be considered signs of aggression; short arms, a sign of shyness. And feminine features—such as long eyelashes or darkly colored lips—would allegedly suggest sex-role confusion.

Yet research consistently shows that such "signs" bear virtually no relation to personality or mental illness. Scientists have denounced these sign interpretations as "phrenology for the 20th century," recalling the 19th-century pseudoscience of inferring people's personalities from the pattern of bumps on their skulls.

Still, the sign approach remains widely used. Some psychologists even claim they can identify sexual abuse from certain key signs. For instance, in the child's drawing at the right, alleged signs of abuse include a person older than the child, a partially unclothed body, a hand near the genitals, a hand hidden in a pocket, a large nose and a mustache. In reality, the connection between these signs and sexual abuse remains dubious, at best.

self-reports to provide a picture of the deepest recesses of the mind. Critics have also asserted that we have emphasized negative findings to the exclusion of positive ones.

Yet we remain confident in our conclusions. In fact, as negative as our overall findings are, they may paint an overly rosy picture of projective techniques because of the so-called file drawer effect. As is well known, scientific journals are more likely to publish reports demonstrating that some procedure works than reports finding failure. Consequently, researchers often quietly file away their negative data, which may never again see the light of day.

We find it troubling that psychologists commonly administer projective instruments in situations for which their value has not been well established by multiple studies; too many people can suffer if erroneous diagnostic judgments influence therapy plans, custody rulings or criminal court decisions. Based on our findings, we strongly urge psychologists to curtail their use of most projective

HOW OFTEN THE TOOLS ARE USED

Popularity Poll

In 1995 a survey asked 412 randomly selected clinical psychologists in the American Psychological Association how often they used various projective and non-projective assessment tools, including those listed below. Projective instruments present people with ambiguous pictures, words or things; the other measures are less open-ended. The number of clinicians who use projective methods might have declined slightly since 1995, but these techniques remain widely used.

Projective Techniques	Use Always Or Frequently	Use At Least Occasionally
Rorschach	43%	82%
Human Figure Drawings	39%	80%
Thematic Apperception Test [TAT]	34%	82%
Sentence Completion Tests	34%	84%
CAT [Children's versions of the TAT]	6%	42%

Nonprojective Techniques*	Use Always Or Frequently	Use At Least Occasionally
Weshler Adult Intelligence Scale [WAIS]	59%	93%
Minnesota Multiphasic Personality Inventory-2 [MMPI-2]	58%	85%
Weschler Intelligence Scale for Children [WISC]	42%	69%
Beck Depression Inventory	21%	71%

*These listed are the most community used nonprojective tests for assessing adult IQ (WAIS) personality (MMPI-2), childhood IQ (WISC) and depression [Beck Depression inventory).
Source: "Contemporary Practice of Psychological Assessment by Clinical Psychologists" by C.E. Watkins et al. In *Professional Psychology Research and Practice*, Vol. 26: No. 1, pages 54–60, 1995.

techniques and, when they do select such instruments, to limit themselves to scoring and interpreting the small number of variables that have been proved trustworthy.

Our results also offer a broader lesson for practicing clinicians, psychology students and the public at large: even seasoned professionals can be fooled by their intuitions and their faith in tools that lack strong evidence of effectiveness. When a substantial body of research demonstrates that old intuitions are wrong, it is time to adopt new ways of thinking.

More to Explore

The Rorschach: A Comprehensive System. Vol. 1: Basic Foundations. Third edition. John E. Exner. John Wiley & Sons, 1993.

The Comprehensive System for the Rorschach: A Critical Examination. James M. Wood, M. Teresa Nezworski and William J. Stejskal in *Psychological Science*, Vol. 7, No 1, pages 3–10; January 1995.

Studying the Clinician: Judgment Research and Psychological Assessment. Howard N. Garb. American Psychological Association, 1998.

Evocative Images: The Thematic Apperception Test and the Art of Projection. Edited by Lon Gieser and Morris I. Stein. American Psychological Association, 1999.

Projective Measures of Personality and Psychopathology: How Well Do They Work? Scott D. Lilienfeld in *Skeptical Inquirer,* Vol. 23, No. 5, pages 32–39; September/October 1999.

The Scientific Status of Projective Techniques. Scott D. Lilienfeld, James M. Wood and Howard N. Garb in *Psychological Science in the Public Interest,* Vol. 1, No. 2, pages 27–55 November 2000. Available at www.psychologicalscience.org/newsresearch/publications/journals/pips1_2.html

Review and Contemplate

1. Define *scoring reliability* and *validity.*
2. Briefly describe the Rorschach inkblot test. What does research indicate about the validity of this test?
3. Briefly describe the Thematic Apperception Test (TAT). What does research indicate about the validity of this test with respect to diagnosing mental disorders and personality?
4. What does it mean to say that projective tests such as the Rorschach and TAT lack incremental validity?
5. Explain why professional clinicians might believe in the validity of projective tests despite research evidence suggesting that these tests are not valid (HINT: The reason is related to statistical reasoning).

About the Author

SCOTT O. LILIENFELD, JAMES M. WOOD and HOWARD N. GARB all conduct research on psychological assessment tools and recently collaborated on an extensive review of research into projective instruments that was published by the American Psychological Society [see "More to Explore."]. Lilienfeld and Wood are associate professors in the departments of psychology at Emory University and the University of Texas at El Paso, respectively. Garb is a clinical psychologist at the Pittsburgh Veterans Administration Health Care System and the University of Pittsburgh and author of the book *Studying the Clinician: Judgment Research and Psychological Assessment.*

8.2

Polygraph Testing and Sexual Abuse: The lure of the magic lasso/
THEODORE CROSS AND LEONARD SAXE

In February 2003, U.S. Secretary of State Colin Powell addressed the United Nations Security Council about whether Iraq had complied with a U.N. resolution that required Iraq to destroy its alleged weapons of mass destruction. Mr. Powell presented evidence suggesting that Iraq still possessed weapons of mass destruction and had failed to comply with the resolution, setting the stage for the United States to invade Iraq in March 2003. Part of the evidence presented by Mr. Powell was information from an Iraqi defector who told U.S. intelligence officials that Iraq had mobile biological weapons factories. Because the informant had passed a polygraph test, his information appeared reliable. But should a polygraph test be trusted as an accurate lie detector in matters of such importance? Unfortunately, intelligence officials later acknowledged that the informant may have fabricated or exaggerated the information about the mobile weapons factories. No such mobile factories were ever found in Iraq.

Polygraph testing involves measuring people's physiological responses to questions designed to determine if they are guilty of deceit or some misdeed. You've probably heard of many examples of the use of polygraph testing in professional settings, such as by police to determine if a suspect is guilty of a crime or by the CIA to determine if their employees are involved in espionage. Polygraph use is also prevalent in the popular media. On several talk shows, it's been used to determine whether men have had sexual affairs. On one reality television show, it was used when a man's children wanted to determine which of several women would be a suitable marriage partner for him. On another reality show, it was used when the parents of an attractive young woman wanted to learn which of several young men would be a suitable dating partner for their daughter.

A crucial question underlying all uses of the polygraph is whether it can accurately detect when people are lying. In this article, Cross and Saxe present scientific evidence on the validity of the polygraph test and discuss whether it is a useful tool in sexual abuse cases.

APA Reference

Cross, T. P., & Saxe, L. (2001). Polygraph testing and sexual abuse: The lure of the magic lasso. *Child Maltreatment, 6,* 195–206.
CHILD MALTREATMENT, Vol. 6, No. 3, August 2001 195–206 ©2001 Sage Publications

Polygraph tests to assess veracity are widely promoted for application in sexual abuse matters. The use of polygraph tests is advocated despite substantial differences in professional and scientific opinion about the validity of such techniques. Polygraph diagnoses of an individual's deception are inferences made by an examiner who compares physiological reactions to a set of questions. The test situation, however, is also used to induce examinees to admit crimes. In addition to their use in investigations, polygraph tests are used by defendants seeking exculpatory evidence and by treatment and probation programs to assess and monitor sexual offenders. Although there are dissenters, most knowledgeable scientists consider polygraph testing as unvalidated. Professionals need to access the literature on polygraph testing, evaluate the efficacy and ethics of polygraph tests in their community, and further develop standards for their use.

P olygraph tests to determine an individual's truthfulness are being widely promoted to assess sexual abuse. They are used in investigations and as a component of treatment and probation programs for sex offenders. The application of polygraph testing in sexual abuse matters has grown despite skeptical analysis of lie detection and despite legal and public policy curbs on its use (cf. Cross & Saxe, 1992; Saxe & Ben-Shakhar, 1999). Highly divergent opinions have appeared in the professional literature on sexual abuse. Some professionals who work with children have been critical of the use of polygraph testing with alleged perpetrators (Corwin, 1988; Faller, 1997), and their use with alleged victims of abuse has also been criticized (Sloan, 1995). Some professionals, however, who work with or study sexual offenders advocate use of polygraph tests in treatment and probation programs (see, e.g., English, 1998; English, Jones, Patrick, Pasini-Hill, & Gonzalez, 2000; English, Pullen, & Jones, 1996, 1997; Leberg, 1997).

What underlies the contradictory response to the use of polygraph tests? Although many scientists believe polygraph testing fails to meet the standards for a valid test (see, e.g., Cross & Saxe, 1992; Iacono & Lykken, 1997a; Saxe, 1991; Saxe & Ben-Shakhar, 1999), it may succeed as psychological manipulation (see Goldzband, 1999). An apt metaphor for this manipulation came from Marston (1917), a Harvard-trained psychologist who nearly 80 years ago developed the systolic blood pressure test, the progenitor of modern polygraphy for the detection of deception. Marston also created the comic book character Wonder Woman, who possesses a "magic lasso" that forces all who she corrals with it to tell the truth (see Wonder Woman pages, available at http://www.hastur.com/Wonder-Woman/marston.html; see also Lykken, 1998). Rather than working through magic, however, polygraph examinations create a situation in which examinees are psychologically pressured to confess or provide self-incriminating information. A former police polygrapher called this power a "psychological billy club" (Williams quoted in Parson, 2000), whereas a psychologist-polygrapher has likened it to a Rorschach test (Lawrence, 1998). Although Marston represented polygraphy as a scientific test, belief in it may make it a sort of psychological magic lasso or placebo, regardless of its actual validity (see Saxe, 1991).

HOW POLYGRAPH TESTS WORK

Although present-day polygraph tests have the appearance of sophisticated technology, the technique was developed more than 50 years ago and has not fundamentally changed (see, e.g., Matte, 1996; Saxe, Dougherty, & Cross, 1983, 1985). A typical polygraph instrument consists of a set of devices to measure and record breathing, cardiovascular activity, and palmar sweating. The instrument includes a set of stationary pens that record these measures on a moving roll of paper. The latest technology digitizes polygraph data and stores the results on a personal computer. Computerized polygraphs permit more efficient collection and analysis of subjects' responses but do not change the phenomena being measured.

Test Questions

The diagnosis of deception is an inference about the meaning of physiological responses to a series of questions (see Katkin, 1987). The central problem with the use of a polygraph to detect deception is that there is no known physiological response that is unique to lying (see, e.g., Saxe et al., 1983). The most common polygraph procedure is the Control Question Test (CQT). A CQT includes three basic types of questions. Irrelevant questions such as "Is your name Joe?" are included as a baseline but not scored. The key questions on which examiners base their diagnosis are relevant and control questions. Relevant questions concern the crime or misdeed at issue, for example, "Did you insert your finger in Betty's vagina?" Control questions (also called comparison questions) are designed to be emotionally arousing for all subjects, regardless of whether they are being deceptive or nondeceptive. They are typically posed as questions about a subject's general honesty and usually concern possible misdeeds in a subject's history prior to the period under investigation. Polygraph examiners assume that they can detect deception by comparing reactions between control and relevant questions. This assumption is, however, disputed between polygraph proponents (e.g., Raskin, Honts, & Kircher, 1997) and opponents (e.g., Iacono & Lykken, 1997a).

Consider a typical control question used to test for sexual abuse: "Between the ages of 18 and 24, do you remember ever engaging in an unnatural sex act?" (Matte, 1996, p. 252). Polygraph examiners expect a nondeceptive suspect to react more strongly to this question than to a relevant question. The assumption is that the nondeceptive suspect will be less concerned about questions regarding the criminal charge, which they know they are telling the truth about, and more concerned with questions about their previous life. It is assumed that innocent subjects will lie in response to control questions or will be very concerned about whether they will be seen as truthful. Their primary fear, it is thought, will be failing the test because of their responses to the control questions. Examinees who react substantially more to relevant questions than to control questions are judged deceptive, whereas examinees who react substantially more to control questions are judged to be truthful. Lack of a substantial difference leads to an inconclusive result.

Innocent persons, however, might actually react more strongly to the relevant questions. Relevant questions, for example, may strike subjects as more threatening than control questions, regardless of subjects' guilt or innocence. Innocent subjects may be more alarmed about questions on a crime they are suspected of and could get punished for than about vague questions about past behavior that is not under investigation and not even necessarily criminal.

There are, likewise, a host of reasons why a deceptive person would react more strongly to control questions. The reaction could, for example, occur because control questions are novel or because examinees know or believe that they have other criminal behavior to hide. Guilty examinees may also have habituated (i.e., no longer be reactive) to a relevant question because they have been asked about it repeatedly. For both deceptive and nondeceptive subjects, it is not possible to rule out alternative explanations and to objectively determine whether differences in reaction are due to deception. As several psychological experts have noted, the theory underlying the CQT is implausible (Ben-Shakhar & Furedy, 1990; Iacono & Lykken, 1997a; Lykken, 1998; see also Saxe, 1991).

The traditional control question is referred to as a probable lie (examiner believes that the subject is lying about this issue). But some polygraphers (e.g., Honts, Raskin, Amato, Gordon, & Devitt, 2000) promote use of the directed lie. A directed lie comparison asks the subject to knowingly lie (e.g., "Have you ever told a lie?"). Intense debate on this matter among polygraphers in ongoing (e.g., Abrams, 1999; Honts et al., 2000; Matte, 2000). The debate illustrates how little agreement there is, even among polygraphers, about control questions—the central feature of most polygraph tests about specific allegations.

The Guilty Knowledge Test is a polygraph test based on an entirely different theory (see, e.g., Lykken, 1998). Instead of assessing deception the Guilty Knowledge Test tests whether examinees' have a different physiological response to information that only a guilty party would have (e.g., the victim's clothing when the crime was committed). Because of the difficulty of obtaining sufficient guilty knowledge in most situations and because of concerns about the validity of these tests (Raskin et al., 1997), they are used infrequently. Thus, the remainder of this discussion concerns the CQT.

Polygraph tests are sometimes conducted with adolescent perpetrators and victims (see Chambers, 1994), but developmental factors have not been adequately studied, and it is difficult to say whether the test is different with minors. Abrams (1975) suggested that children younger than the age of 11 are poor polygraph subjects, and Matte (1996) argued that testing child victims is inadvisable because it makes them relive traumatic events.

Tests as Manipulation

The test involves more than the operation of the polygraph instrument. The examiner interacts with the participant before, during, and after the examination (see, e.g., P. W. Davis & McKenzie-Rundle, 1984; Matte, 1996; Reid & Inbau, 1977).

A pretest interview helps the examiner to learn about subjects' background and to influence them to believe in the test. The examiner often will quote high accuracy rates and conduct so-called stimulation tests to demonstrate the power of the instrument. For example, subjects may pick a number, and examiners will determine which number they chose by looking at the polygraph tracings made when a series of numbers were presented to them. The stim test, however, is based on different psychophysiological principles than the standard polygraph test and is sometimes rigged (Lykken, 1998).

If an examiner believes that a subject is deceptive, the subject will typically be interrogated at the conclusion of the test. In this posttest phase, the examiner confronts a subject with the results and tries to elicit a confession. Subjects may confess or reveal self-incriminating information during the pretest or posttest questioning. False confessions have occurred following polygraph-aided interrogation (Lykken, 1998) and examinees may provide false information to "satisfy" an examiner. No systematic data are available on the frequency of such outcomes.

The key issue, however, is that belief that a polygraph test can determine honesty serves as a powerful tool. If subjects are convinced that the test can detect lying, they may conclude that they have nothing to lose by revealing the truth and may even perceive an advantage (more leniency) if they acknowledge a misdeed. Or they may offer rationalizations, distortions, or other responses that inadvertently incriminate them or provide clues for investigation or assessment. The typical polygraph examiner has been trained in skills to elicit confessions (see, e.g., Holmes, 1995). To the extent that the polygrapher relies on the polygraph test outcome, guilty subjects who "beat" the test will not be interrogated. Thus, they are less likely to confess and their crimes may remain undetected.

Proponents suggest that the power of the polygraph in probation or treatment programs generalizes to the period before the examination (e.g., Abrams, 1991b; L. Jones et al., 1996). They argue that offenders may be more honest in nonpolygraph interviews if they know they will later be subjected to a polygraph test. The ability to induce confessions and self-incriminating reports is, perhaps, the major reason that polygraphy has been accepted for at least some uses in sexual abuse matters. In the absence of physical evidence or other corroboration, investigators, probation officers, and treatment staff members need additional information.

Social psychological laboratory research sheds light on the manipulative power of lie detectors (Saxe, 1991; Saxe et al., 1985). To mitigate social desirability effects and to increase the likelihood of honest responses from research participants in matters such as racial attitudes, E. E. Jones and Sigall (1971) devised the "bogus pipeline" procedure. Research participants were "hooked up" to an impressive-looking electronic device that was actually a "pile of electronic junk." Participants were told that the device was a lie detector that would accurately assess deviations from their true opinions. Indeed, those surveyed under bogus pipeline conditions provided responses that were more politically incorrect. Because subjects believe their honesty can be accurately measured, they perceive that it is in their interest to tell the truth (even if it reflects badly on them) rather than be caught telling a lie (see, e.g., Aguinis, Pierce, & Quigley, 1995). A meta-analysis of 20 years of research suggests that subjects offer socially undesirable information because of their fear of the bogus pipeline and not just because of the expectations of the experimenters (Roese & Jamieson, 1993). Although bogus pipeline research does not directly concern the efficacy of polygraph tests, it supports the present analysis of the placebo function of polygraph testing.

SEXUAL ABUSE CASES

Polygraph testing is used in a variety of ways to assess sexual abuse (Williams, 1999), ranging from investigative applications, to use by suspects or defendants seeking exculpatory evidence, to use to monitor sex offenders and aid in their assessment.

Investigative

The polygraph is used in different investigative settings as a test of specific allegations of abuse. Some police agencies or prosecutors conduct polygraph tests with alleged perpetrators and, sometimes, alleged victims of abuse (see Pence & Wilson, 1994; Sloan, 1995). Federal law enforcement agencies, including the Federal Bureau of Investigation (FBI) and the armed services, also use polygraph tests to assess sexual abuse allegations. However, the former chief of the FBI's polygraph unit has argued that polygraph results do not meet standards to be admitted as evidence in a criminal proceeding (Murphy & Murphy, 1997). The results of a polygraph examination are often used to help investigators decide whether to pursue a criminal charge. Employers sometimes contract with private polygraphers to assess sexual abuse or sexual harassment allegations against employees (Matte, 1996). Polygraph examiners have promoted investigative use of polygraph examinations in sexual abuse cases (e.g., Abrams & Abrams, 1993; Holden, 2000; Raskin & Steller, 1989) but much less so than for assessing known offenders.

It is difficult to know how widespread investigative use is because there is no requirement to report use of polygraph tests. Smith and Goretsky-Elstein (1993) found that a polygraph test was conducted in 15% of a sample of child abuse cases ($N = 297$) screened by prosecutors in 10 jurisdictions. However, criminal justice systems varied in their adoption of polygraph testing, and the 15% appeared to be from a small number of jurisdictions that used polygraph tests frequently. Police officers initiated testing for 77% of polygraphs, defendants for 15%, and others for 8%. Faller and Henry (2000) profiled another such jurisdiction, in which 37.5% of criminal court cases of child sexual abuse featured polygraph tests.

Exculpatory

There have long been efforts to introduce the results of polygraph tests as evidence in criminal and civil proceedings on behalf of defendants who claim innocence. Lykken (1998) reported that at least 17 states admitted the results of stipulated polygraph tests, that is, tests that are administered based on prior agreement by defense and prosecution. Marston himself first tried to introduce a blood pressure test as evidence of a defendant's innocence in the early 1920s (see Lykken, 1998). The case *United States v. Frye* (1923) led to the precedent that governed the introduction of scientific evidence in U.S. courts for nearly 70 years. The court rejected Marston's testimony because the test had not gained acceptance by the relevant scientific community. The *United States v. Frye* precedent has been superceded by a 1993 Supreme Court decision, *Daubert v. Merrell Dow Pharmaceuticals, Inc.* (1993). *Daubert v. Merrell Dow Pharmaceuticals, Inc.* gives courts the discretion to weight the validity of evidence, including whether it has gained acceptance by the scientific community (see Murphy & Murphy, 1997; Saxe & Ben-Shakhar, 1999).

Daubert v. Merrell Dow Pharmaceuticals, Inc. (1993) has led courts to reconsider the potential value of polygraph evidence. For example, lawyers for au pair Louise Woodward, who was accused of first-degree murder in a case involving a shaken baby, unsuccessfully attempted to introduce polygraph evidence (*Commonwealth of Massachusetts v. Woodward*, 1998; see also, e.g., Saxe & Ben-Shakhar, 1999; *United States v. Frank Javier Cordoba*, 1998). *Daubert v. Merrell Dow Pharmaceuticals, Inc.* is interpreted by some courts as compelling a hearing on admissibility of polygraph results, if requested by a defendant. There are, however, only a few examples in which such requests have been successful (cf. Honts et al., 2000). The U.S. Supreme Court ruled that a defendant's constitutional rights were not violated when a military court refused to admit polygraph results (*United States v. Scheffer*, 1998; see also Goldzband, 1999). This has discouraged attempts to admit polygraph evidence, although, because the matter involved a military court martial, the ruling may not be broad enough to limit all efforts to introduce polygraph test results.

Assessing and Monitoring Sexual Offenders

Polygraph testing is being used systematically in a number of probation and treatment programs to uncover current and past sexual abuse (see, e.g., Abrams, 1989, 1991a, 1991b; Abrams & Abrams, 1993; Baranowski, 1998; Blasingame, 1998; English, Colling-Chadwick, Pullen, & Jones, 1996; Hager, 1989; Hagler, 1995; Matte, 1996; Pullen, Olsen, Brown, & Amich, 1996; Schlank & Shaw, 1996). An initial examination is often used to uncover information about the offender's past behavior, as an aid to assessment and treatment contracting. Periodic exams are also used to monitor offenders' behavior while in a treatment program or on probation (see, e.g., Abrams, 1989, 1991a, 1991b; Blasingame, 1998). Examinations often test for risky behavior, such as sexual fantasies about children as well as sexual offenses, and can be conducted as frequently as every 3 to 6 months (Matte, 1996). Polygraph testing is used as only one of several bases for decision making, although some experts suggest establishing standardized sanctions and privileges based on whether offenders are judged deceptive or nondeceptive on the polygraph (Ahlmeyer, Heil, McKee, & English, 2000; Cooley-Towell, Pasini-Hill, & Patrick, 2000). L. Davis, McShane, and Williams (1995) advocated using polygraph testing to monitor access to the Internet for sex offenders on probation.

In a 1994 national sample ($N = 732$), 10% of probation supervisors and 9% of parole supervisors reported that offenders in their programs were often or always required to take polygraph tests for treatment or supervision (English, Colling-Chadwick, et al., 1996). About the same time, a national survey of treatment programs found that 24% used the polygraph with sexual offenders (Knopp, Freeman-Longo, & Stevenson, 1994).

Use has probably increased substantially since these surveys. English, Pullen, et al. (1996, 1997; see also English, 1998) have recommended polygraph testing as one leg, along with treatment and correctional supervision, in a triangle of containment for community management of sex offenders. The federally funded Center for Sex Offender Management (2000) described polygraph testing as "an important asset in treatment and supervision" (p. 11). Sex offender treatment professionals have offered training programs and presentations together with polygraph examiners (Gatlin, Criss, & Porter, 1999; Sinclair Seminars, 1998). Statewide programs or initiatives using polygraph assessment of offenders are active in Colorado (Heil, Ahlmeyer, McCullar, & McKee, 2000), Hawaii (Branson, 1999), Massachusetts (Center for Sex Offender Management, 1999), Oregon (Oregon Department of Corrections, 1995), and Vermont (Center for Sex Offender Management, 1999). In a recent survey of 122 supervision and corrections departments in Texas, more than three quarters of agencies used polygraph testing to supervise and treat sex offenders (McKay, 2000).

RESEARCH ON ACCURACY

Over the past 30 years, those who have reviewed the evidence for the validity of the CQT have come to radically different conclusions (see, e.g., Abrams, 1973; Ansley, 1990; Ben-Shakhar & Furedy, 1990; Forensic Research, 1997; Iacono & Lykken, 1997a; Raskin et al., 1997; Saxe, 1991; Saxe & Ben-Shakhar, 1999; Saxe, 1983, 1985; Williams, 1995, 1999). Differences in assessments of polygraphy represent significant theoretical disagreements as well as conflicting analysis of the adequacy of research.

The core of the debate concerns field studies. In field studies, a sample of polygraph tests conducted in actual investigations are compared against a measure of "ground truth"—some other method for determining whether examinees are lying or telling the truth. Developing an adequate field study is challenging because of the difficulty of establishing ground truth. Indicators of the truth such as physical evidence, eyewitness testimony, or DNA evidence are often unavailable in polygraph cases. Note that sexual abuse cases especially lack such evidence of ground truth (see, e.g., Myers, 1998). Most studies use confession as a criterion of ground truth, whereas a few use the decision of a panel of experts reviewing case evidence (see Iacono & Lykken, 1997a; Raskin et al., 1997).

Compared with critics, supporters of polygraph testing, such as Ansley, Williams, and Raskin, consider as valid a larger number of field studies, many from polygraph and criminal justice professional journals (e.g., *Polygraph, Journal of Police Science and Administration*). Supporters often report accuracy rates exceeding 90%. But critics have rejected many of the studies included by proponents. Iacono and Lykken (1997a) argued that these studies lack adequate peer review and had fatal methodological flaws.

The most damning criticism is that the use of confession to measure ground truth introduces a selection bias (Iacono, 1991; Iacono & Lykken, 1997a; Patrick & Iacono, 1991). The sample of guilty subjects in most studies consists primarily of those subjects who were found deceptive by the polygraph. Confessions were typically elicited by polygraph examiners themselves when they confronted examinees in the posttest interview. But not all examinees are confronted, only those who "fail." Cases in which a guilty subject beats the polygraph are unlikely ever to be included in research studies. Reliance on confession as a criterion of accuracy is likely, thus, to artificially inflate polygraph accuracy rates. Iacono (1991; see also Iacono & Lykken, 1997a; Patrick & Iacono, 1991) demonstrated how an examiner making judgments with chance accuracy could accumulate a sample of cases in this way that suggested accuracy close to 100%.

Given these problems, Iacono and Lykken (1997a) identified only a handful of adequate field studies, which have much lower accuracy rates. They found no evidence for the validity of polygraph testing in field studies and raised concerns about the percentages of false positives and negatives in these studies. Similar controversy envelops other polygraph studies. For example, Raskin et al. (1997) argued for polygraph validity based on laboratory analogue studies with an aggregate accuracy rate of approximately 90%. But Iacono and Lykken (1997a) argued that laboratory studies are too dissimilar from field polygraph tests to speak to real polygraph accuracy. Iacono and Lykken argued further that countermeasures are a real threat, whereas Raskin et al. claimed that successful use of countermeasures is unlikely. Results of surveys of scientists have been put forward on both sides (Iacono & Lykken, 1997a; Raskin et al., 1997). Sixty-two percent of scientists in a Gallup Organization (1984) survey and 60% in Amato and Honts (1994) study agreed that the polygraph test was a "useful diagnostic tool when considered with other reliable information." But in Iacono and Lykken's (1997b) surveys of scientists, only 36% in one and 30% in the other agreed that "the CQT is based on scientifically sound psychological principles or theory" (p. 430), and smaller percentages felt that courts should admit CQT polygraphs as evidence.

Regardless of one's position about the evidence, the clear conclusion is that there is no agreement among scientists. Notably, most scientific supporters of polygraph testing were originally affiliated with one research program at the University of Utah. Most other scientists who have written about polygraph test validity have been critics (Bashore & Rapp, 1993; Ben-Shakhar & Furedy, 1990; Furedy, 1996; Iacono & Lykken, 1997a; Kleinmuntz & Szucko, 1984; Saxe, 1991; Saxe & Ben-Shakhar, 1999; Saxe et al., 1983, 1985). At a minimum, it is fair to say that no overall accuracy rates for polygraph testing are accepted.

Research on Sexual Abuse Applications

The validity of a psychological test must be considered separately for different applications of the test and populations (American Psychological Association, 1999). Arguably, sexual abuse represents a very different offense from other felonies, and sexual offenders and victims are very different populations. Cross and Saxe (1992) critiqued the validity of polygraph tests in child sexual abuse cases because the validity of polygraph tests generally had not been demonstrated, field research on the validity of polygraph tests in sexual abuse cases had not been conducted, and the nature of sexual abuse made polygraph assessment particularly problematic. It was argued that the denial and the tendency to rationalize and minimize that is characteristic of sexual offenders might make lying about sexual offenses especially difficult to detect. Williams (1995, 1999), in response, claimed that other criminals cognitively distort their crime and thus that polygraphing sexual offenders is not a special case. But concerns with the potential effects of cognitive distortion by any offender raises concerns, given the lack of demonstrated validity for polygraph testing in general. An additional problem is the difficulty of designing suitable control questions related to sexual abuse.

Faller (1997) studied the relationship of polygraph findings to other assessments of child sexual abuse. A sample of 42 child sexual abuse cases involving polygraph testing was assembled from a university clinic and from solicitations to child abuse professionals. Data abstractors using case files completed questionnaires for the clinic cases, and the referring professionals completed them for the submitted cases. Faller created measures of evidence of child sexual abuse based on corroborating information external to the child interview (e.g., medical evidence, confession, other victim or witness information), on corroborating information from the child (e.g., sexual knowledge, sexual behavior, psychological testing), and on a number of contextual details. Polygraph findings were not statistically related to any of these measures, although the sample size was probably insufficient to assess this question. Passing police polygraph tests significantly predicted cases not being prosecuted, but failing the tests did not predict prosecution. In a borderline finding, polygraph results predicted substantiation by child protective services. But polygraph results were not related to substantiation by health and mental health professionals.

Faller (1997) is not a validity study, however, because it lacks an objective measure of ground truth. Indeed, we know of no field research that specifically tests the validity of polygraph examinations in sexual abuse cases (cf. Cross & Saxe, 1992). Not surprisingly, however, its manipulative effect has begun to be studied.

RESEARCH ON MANIPULATIVE EFFECTS

Some research has looked specifically at the effect of polygraph tests on the information that sexual offenders in treatment, on parole, or in prison report about their crimes. These studies have found that offenders reveal more self-incriminating information when the polygraph was added to criminal history and self-report. In one or more of these studies, the polygraph condition produced more self-incriminating information on the following variables:

- number of offenses, victims, or rate of offending (Abrams, Hoyt, & Jewell, 1991; Colorado Department of Corrections, 1998; Emerick & Dutton, 1993; O'Connell, 1998; Office of Research and Statistics, 2000; "Research Disputes Assumptions," 1988; see also Harrison & Kirkpatrick, 2000);
- number of types of offenses (e.g., rape, exhibitionism, etc.) (Emerick & Dutton, 1993; O'Connell, 1998; Office of Research and Statistics, 2000);
- reports of "hands-off" deviant behaviors and high-risk behaviors (e.g., exhibitionism, voyeurism, bestiality, masturbation to a deviant fantasy) (Emerick & Dutton, 1993; Office of Research and Statistics, 2000);
- degree of force (Emerick & Dutton, 1993);
- degree of intrusion (Emerick & Dutton, 1993);
- number of age groups abused (Office of Research and Statistics, 2000);
- number of types of relationships with victims (Emerick & Dutton, 1993; Office of Research and Statistics, 2000);
- number of genders abused (Emerick & Dutton, 1993; Office of Research and Statistics, 2000); and
- use and severity of pornography (Emerick & Dutton, 1993; Office of Research and Statistics, 2000).

Abrams et al. (1991) found that participants ($N = 71$) in a sexual abuse treatment clinic made an average of 2.34 admissions of sexually deviant behavior prior to being polygraphed. They interpreted this as evidence that anticipation of being subjected to a polygraph also has effects.

These studies suffer from methodological limitations such as the difficulty of disentangling the effects of polygraph testing and treatment (Office of Research and Statistics, 2000) and flaws in statistical analysis (Emerick & Dutton, 1993). In addition, the effects have not been found in all studies with all groups (see Ahlmeyer et al., 2000), and the accuracy of these admissions has not been validated. It would not be surprising to learn that offenders provide such information because they believe it is expected of them. Nevertheless, the consistency of the results of these studies and the breadth of the self-incriminating information revealed suggest the power of the test. The empirical literature on the bogus pipeline provides added support (see Saxe, 1991; Saxe et al., 1983).

Abrams and Ogard (1986; see also Abrams, 1989) examined recidivism for offenders on polygraph and probation supervision versus those on probation supervision alone. Overall, offenders who were polygraphed had lower rates of recidivism, although the number of sexual offenders in the study was too small for significance testing as a separate group. Small sample size ($N = 28$) is also a problem for Harrison and Kirkpatrick's (2000) study, in which some sex offenders reported that the polygraph led to avoidance of risky behaviors that may have resulted in treatment or parole violations.

IMPLICATIONS

How should sexual abuse professionals respond to use of the polygraph? They may be reluctant to discourage use of a tool that may help probation and treatment professionals confront intractable denial. Yet, they may not want to lend support to a procedure that has not been validated and is used to exculpate offenders, sometimes in the face of strong evidence of guilt. There is risk. If the polygraph as test is confused with its function as psychological manipulation, it is likely to be misused. At the very least, polygraph testing may lose some of its manipulative effect the more it is used. A placebo can function, but over time, the manipulated subjects may realize it has little power. Sexual abuse professionals can take several useful steps to limit the misuse of the polygraph test.

Knowledge is Power

Regardless of a professional's stance toward polygraph testing, understanding the technique is essential. Gaining knowledge about polygraph testing is important to be able to treat claims about polygraph testing with appropriate skepticism. It is possible to develop serviceable knowledge quickly in response to a sudden initiative to use a polygraph test in an individual case or program. This knowledge can then be passed on to a judge, administrator, or other decision maker. Even a quick scan of the literature can tell the reader the following:

- The polygraph is not a simple, objective test;
- accuracy rates vary depending on which studies you consider;
- scientists disagree about which studies adequately test polygraph validity;
- some scientists consider the test valid, and many scientists do not;
- circumstances of testing may affect the outcome;
- countermeasures may be effective with the right training and practice;
- the magic lasso or bogus pipeline effect needs to be taken into account; and
- many programs find them helpful to assess and manage sex offenders.

For those interested in accessing the literature, Lykken's (1998) *A Tremor in the Blood* provides a wide-ranging and entertaining overview. Matte (1996) appears to be the most comprehensive publication in print in support of polygraph testing. Raskin et al. (1997) and Iacono and Lykken (1997a) are thorough, scholarly works, one mostly pro- and one mostly anti-polygraph, designed specifically to address *Daubert v. Merrell Dow Pharmaceuticals, Inc.*, (1993) criteria and presented in the same volume in point-counterpoint fashion. Saxe and Ben-Shakhar (1999) have also reviewed the issue of legal admissibility, summarizing much of the extant literature. Other good sources for professionals include Ben-Shakhar and Furedy (1990), Iacono and Patrick (1987, 1988), Saxe (1991), and Saxe et al. (1983, 1985). . . .

CONCLUSION

Sexual abuse professionals need to understand polygraph testing, whether they support it or not. The issues raised by lie detectors are too important to be left in the hands of true believers. Far less attention has been paid to understanding and critically evaluating polygraph testing than to the various methods of assessing children for the validity of allegations (see, e.g., Fisher & Whiting, 1998). Research that specifically assesses the validity of polygraph tests in sexual abuse matters is urgently needed.

Basic research is needed on the underlying psychophysiological reactions of sexual abusers to a wide variety of stimuli, including polygraph procedures. A particular focus should be the interaction of sexual fantasy with memory and verbal statements. Research should also examine repeated testing. Although common in monitoring sexual offenders, it has little precedent elsewhere. Repeated administrations may lead to habituation or to the subject's learning countermeasures and may increase chances of a wrongful decision because of the increased probability of at least one error over the multiple tests.

Field studies of the validity of polygraph testing are complex because of the difficulties of ascertaining ground truth, yet if polygraph testing continues to be employed, such studies are essential. Iacono and Lykken (1997a) suggested a research design in which polygraph tests are conducted in actual cases but examiners avoid making the results known during the investigation. The polygraph charts would be independently scored, and cases would be followed up later to see if corroborating evidence supported polygraph results. This would avoid the selection bias associated with using polygraph-induced confessions as ground truth.

Polygraph tests may have utility to elicit important information about offenders, but the potential cost is substantial. Errors with deceptive individuals can lead to new offenses against children, whereas errors with truthful individuals can devastate people's lives. Association with the technique may affect the integrity and credibility of sexual abuse professionals. We would certainly want to employ a device that could objectively evaluate vexing questions about the honesty of sexual abusers. But it may be wishful thinking to believe that such an instrument exists.

References

Abrams, S. (1973). Polygraph validity and reliability: A review. *Journal of Forensic Sciences, 17*, 313–327.

Abrams, S. (1975). The validity of the polygraph technique with children. *Journal of Police Science and Administration, 3*, 310–311.

Abrams, S. (1989). Probation polygraph surveillance of child abusers. *The Prosecutor, 22*, 29–38.

Abrams, S. (1991a). Lies: The polygraph as a tool in the treatment of sex abusers. *Preventing Sexual Abuse, 2*, 10–15.

Abrams, S. (1991b). The use of polygraphy with sex offenders. *Annals of Sex Research, 4*, 239–263.

Abrams, S. (1999). A response to Honts on the issue of the discussion of questions between charts. *Polygraph, 28*, 223–228.

Abrams, S., & Abrams, J. (1993). *Polygraph testing of the pedophile*, Portland, OR: Ryan Guinner.

Abrams, S., Hoyt, D., & Jewell, C. (1991). The effectiveness of the disclosure test with sex abusers of children. *Polygraph, 20*, 197–203.

Abrams, S., & Ogard, E. (1986). Polygraph surveillance of probationers. *Polygraph, 15*, 174–182.

Aguinis, H., Pierce, C. A., & Quigley, B. M. (1995). Enhancing the validity of self-reported alcohol and marijuana consumption using a bogus pipeline procedure: A meta-analytic review. *Basic and Applied Social Psychology, 16*, 515–527.

Ahlmeyer, S., Heil, P., McKee, B., & English, K. (2000). Impact of polygraph on admissions of victims and offenses in adult sexual offenders. *Sexual Abuse: A Journal of Research and Treatment*, 12, 123–138.

Amato, S. L., & Honts, C. R. (1994). What do psychophysiologists think about polygraph tests: A survey of the membership of SPR. *Psychophysiology, 31*, S22.

American Academy of Child and Adolescent Psychiatry. (1997). *Forensic evaluation of children and adolescents who may have been sexually abused.* Washington, DC: Author.

American Psychological Association. (1999). *Standards for educational and psychological testing.* Washington, DC: Author.

Ansley, N. (1990). The validity and reliability of polygraph decisions in real cases. *Polygraph*, 19, 169–181.

Association for the Treatment of Sexual Abusers. (1997). *Ethical standards and principles for the management of sexual abusers.* Beaverton, OR: Author.

Baranowski, G. H. (1998). Managing sex offenders in the community with the assistance of polygraph testing. *Polygraph*, 27, 75–88.

Bashore, T. R., & Rapp. P. E. (1993). Are there alternatives to traditional polygraph procedures? *Psychological Bulletin*, 113, 3–22.

Ben-Shakhar, G., & Furedy, J. (1990). *Theories and applications in the detection of deception.* New York/Berlin: Springer-Verlag.

Blasingame, G. D. (1998). Suggested clinical uses of polygraphy in community-based sexual offender-treatment programs. *Sexual Abuse: A Journal of Research and Treatment, 10*, 37–45.

Branson, H. K. (1999). How Hawaii's treatment for sex offenders works: Intense follow-up is the key. *Corrections Technology and Management, 3*, 54–56.

Center for Sex Offender Management. (1999). *Case studies on the Center for Sex Offender Management's national research sites.* Silver Spring, MD: Author.

Center for Sex Offender Management. (2000). *Community supervision of the sex offender: An overview of current and promising practices.* Silver Spring, MD: Author.

Chambers, H. (1994). *Snohomish County Juvenile Court Sex Offender Treatment Program: Policy statement on the use of polygraph in treatment of juvenile sex offenders.* Everten, WA: Snohomish County Juvenile Court Services.

Colorado Department of Corrections. (1998). *Evaluation report: Integration of polygraph testing with adult sex offenders.* Denver: Colorado Division of Criminal Justice.

Commonwealth of Massachusetts v. Woodward, SJC-07635 (D. Boston, 1998).

Cooley-Towell, S., Pasini-Hill, D., & Patrick, D. (2000). Value of the post-conviction polygraph: The importance of sanctions. *Polygraph, 29*, 6–19.

Corwin, D. L. (1988). Early diagnosis of sexual abuse: Diminishing the lasting effects. In G. E. Wyatt & G. J. Powell (Eds.). *Lasting effects of child sexual abuse* (pp. 251–269). Newbury Park, CA: Sage.

Cross, T. P., & Saxe, L. (1992). A critique of the validity of polygraph testing in child sexual abuse cases. *Journal of Child Sexual Abuse, 1*, 19–33.

Daubert v. Merrell Dow Pharmaceuticals, Inc., 113 C. Ct. Supp. 2786 (1993).

Davis, L., McShane, M. D., & Williams, F. P. (1995). Controlling computer access to pornography: Special conditions for sex offenders. *Federal Probation, 59*, 43–48.

Davis, P. W., & McKenzie-Rundle, P. (1984). The social organization of lie-detector tests. *Urban Life, 13*, 177–205.

Emerick, R. L., & Dutton, W. A. (1993). The effect of polygraphy on the self report of adolescent sex offenders: Implications for risk assessment. *Annals of Sex Research, 6*, 83–103.

English, K. (1998). The containment approach: An aggressive strategy for the community management of adult sex offenders. *Psychology, Public Policy, & Law Special Issue: Sex Offenders: Scientific, Legal, and Policy Perspectives, 4*, 218–235.

English, K., Colling-Chadwick, S., Pullen, S., & Jones, L. (1996). *How are adult felony sex offenders managed on production and panule?* Denver: Colorado Division of Criminal Justice.

English, K., Jones, L., Patrick, D., Pasini-Hill, D., & Gonzalez, S. (2000). We need you to become experts in the post-conviction polygraph. *Polygraph, 29*, 44–62.

English, K., Pullen, S., & Jones, L. (1996). *Managing adult sex offenders: A containment approach*. Lexington, KY: American Probation and Parole Association.

English, K., Pullen, S., & Jones, L. (Eds.). (1997). *Managing adult sex offenders: A containment approach* (National Institute of Justice Research Brief NCJ163387). Washington, DC: National Institute of Justice.

Faller, K. (1997). The polygraph, its use in cases of alleged sexual abuse: An exploratory study. *Child Abuse & Neglect, 21*, 995–1008.

Faller, K. C., & Henry, J. (2000). Child sexual abuse; A case study in community collaboration. *Child Abuse & Neglect, 24*, 1215–1225.

Fisher, C. B., & Whiting, K. A. (1998). How valid are child sexual abuse validations? In S. Ceci & H. Hembrooke (Eds.), *Expert witnesses in child abuse cases: What can and should be said in court* (pp. 159–184). Washington, DC: American Psychological Association.

Forensic Research. (1997). Validity and reliability of polygraph testing. *Polygraph, 26*, 215–239.

Furedy, J. J. (1996). The North American polygraph and psychophysiology: Disinterested, uninterested, and interested perspectives. *International Journal of Psychophysiology, 21*, 97–105.

Gallup Organization. (1984). Survey of members of the society for psychophysiological research concerning their opinions of polygraph test interpretation. *Polygraph, 13*, 153.

Gatlin, C. H., Criss, S. E., & Porter, W. D. (1999, September). *The development of a collaborative program for sex offender treatment using the treatment triangle approach*. Paper presented at the meeting of the Association for Treatment of Sexual Abusers, Lake Buena Vista, FL.

Goldzband, M. G. (1999). Polygraphy revisited: U.S. v. Scheffer. *Journal of the American Academy of Psychiatry & the Law, 27*, 133–142.

Hager, D. M. (1989). A guide to conducting polygraph examinations in sexual matters. *Polygraph, 18*, 78–89.

Hagler, H. L. (1995). Polygraph as a measure of progress in the assessment, treatment, and surveillance of sex offenders. *Sexual Addiction and Compulsivity, 2*, 98–111.

Harrison, J. S., & Kirkpatrick, B. (2000). Polygraph testing and behavioral change with sex offenders in an outpatient setting: An exploratory study. *Polygraph, 29*, 20–25.

Heil, P., Ahlmeyer, S., McCullar, B., & McKee, B. (2000). Integration of polygraph testing with sexual offenders in the Colorado Department of Corrections. *Polygraph, 29*, 26–35.

Holden, E. J. (2000). Pre-and post-conviction polygraph: Building blocks for the future— Procedures, principles, and practices. *Polygraph, 29*, 69–98.

Holmes, W. D. (1995). Interrogation. *Polygraph, 24*, 237–258.

Honts, C. R., Raskin, D. C., Amato, S. L., Gordon, A., & Devin, M. (2000). The hybrid directed-lie test, the overemphasized comparison question, chimeras and other inventions: A rejoinder to Abrams (1999). *Polygraph, 29*, 156–168.

Iacono, W. (1991). Can we determine the accuracy of polygraph tests? In J. R. Jennings & P. K. Ackles (Eds.), *Advances in psychophysiology: A research annual* (Vol. 4. pp. 201–207). London: Jessica Kingsley.

Iacono, W., & Lykken, D. T. (1997a). The scientific status of research on polygraph techniques: The case against polygraph tests. In D. L. Faigman, D. H. Kaye, M. J. Saks, & J. Sanders (Eds.), *Modern scientific evidence: The law and science of expert testimony* (pp. 582–618). St. Paul, MN: West.

Iacono, W. G., & Lykken, D. T. (1997b). The validity of the lie detector: Two surveys of scientific opinion. *Journal of Applied Psychology, 82*, 426–433.

Iacono, W. G., & Patrick, C. J. (1987). What psychologists should know about lie detection. In I. B. Weiner & A. K. Hess (Eds.), *Handbook of forensic psychology* (pp. 460–489). New York: John Wiley.

Iacono, W. G., & Patrick, C. J. (1988). Assessing deception: Polygraph techniques. In R. Rogers (Ed.), *Clinical assessment of malingering and deception* (pp. 203–233). New York: Guilford.

Jones, E. E., & Sigall H. (1971). The bogus pipeline: A new paradigm for measuring affect and attitude. *Psychological Bulletin, 76*, 349–364.

Jones, L., Pullen, S., English, K., Crouch, J., Colling-Chadwick, S., & Patzman, J. (1996). Summary of the national telephone survey of probation and parole supervisors. In K. English, S. Pullen, & L. Jones (Eds.), *Managing adult sex offenders: A containment approach* (pp. 3.1–3.14). Lexington, KY: American Probation and Parole Association.

Katkin, E. S. (1987). Psychophysiological assessment for decision-making: Conceptions and misconceptions. In D. R. Peterson & D. B. Fishman (Eds.), *Assessment for decision. Rutgers symposia on applied psychology* (Vol. 1, pp. 107–133). New Brunswick, NJ: Rutgers University Press.

Kleinmuntz, B., & Szucko, J. J. (1984). Lie detection in ancient and modern times: A call for contemporary scientific study. *American Psychologist, 39*, 766–776.

Knopp, F. H., Freeman-Longo, R., & Stevenson, W. (1994). *Nation-wide survey of juvenile and adult sex offender treatment program and models*. Orwell, VT: Safer Society.

Lawrence, S. (1998, August). Shedding light on the polygraph [Letter to the editor]. *APA Monitor, 29*, 3.

Leberg, E. (1997). *Understanding child molesters: Taking chargr.* Thousand Oaks, CA: Sage.

Lykken, D. (1998). *A tremor in the blood: Uses and abuses of the lie detector* (2nd ed.). Reading, MA: Perseus.

Marston, W. M. (1917). Systolic blood pressure symptoms of deception. *Journal of Experimental Psychology, 2*, 117–163.

Matte, J. A. (1996). *Forensic psychophysiology using the polygraph: Scientific truth verification—Lie detection.* Williamsville, NY: J.A.M. (Available on the World Wide Web: http://www.mattepolygraph.com)

Matte, J. A. (2000). A critical analysis of Honts' study: The discussion (stimulation) of comparison questions. *Polygraph, 29*, 146–150.

McKay, B. (2000). State of polygraph testing on sex offenders under community supervision in Texas. *Polygraph, 29*, 36–39.

Murphy, C. A., & Murphy, J. K. (1997). Polygraph admissibility: A critical analysis under standards set by Daubert v. Merrell Dow Pharmaceutical. *Update, 10*, 1–2.

Myers, J. B. (1998). *Legal issues in child abuse and neglect practice* (2nd ed.). Thousand Oaks, CA: Sage.

O'Connell, M. A. (1998). Using polygraph testing to assess deviant sexual history of sex offenders (Doctoral dissertation, University of Washington, 1998). *Dissertation Abstracts International, 58*, 3023.

Office of Research and Statistics. (2000). Combo of polygraph & treatment reveals many sex offenders offend across multiple relationship, age, gender, & crime type categories. *Elements of Change: Highlighting Trends and Issues in the Criminal Justice System, 5*, 1–7.

Oregon Department of Corrections. (1995). *Sex offender community notification in Oregon* (Report for the Oregon legislature, NCJ No. 155233). Washington, DC: National Institute of Justice.

Parson, A. (2000, August 15). The quest for truth. *The Boston Globe*, pp. F1, F3.

Patrick, C. J., & Iacono, W. G. (1991). Validity of the control question polygraph test: The problem of sampling bias. *Journal of Applied Psychology, 76*, 229–238.

Pence, D., & Wilson, C. (1994). *Team investigation of child sexual abuse: The uneasy alliance*. Thousand Oaks, CA: Sage.

Pullen, S., Olsen, S., Brown, G., & Amich, D. (1996). Using the polygraph. In K. English, S. Pullen, & L. Jones (Eds.), *Managing adult sex offenders: A containment approach* (pp. 15.1–15.18). Lexington, KY: American Probation and Parole Association.

Raskin, D. C., Honts, C. R., & Kircher, J. C. (1997). The scientific status of research on polygraph tests: The case for polygraph tests. In D. L. Faigman, D. Kaye, M. J. Saks, & J. Sanders (Eds.), *The West companion to scientific evidence* (pp. 565–582). St. Paul, MN: West.

Raskin, D. C., & Steller, M. (1989). Assessing credibility of allegations of child sexual abuse: Polygraph examinations and statement analysis. In H. Wegener, F. Lösel, & J. Haisch (Eds.), *Criminal behavior and the justice system: Psychological perspectives* (pp. 290–302). New York/Berlin: Springer-Verlag.

Reid, J. E., & Inbaut, F. E. (1977). *Truth and deception—The polygraph technique* (3rd ed.). Baltimore: Williams & Wilkins.

Research disputes assumptions. (1988). *National District Attorneys Association Bulletin, 7*, 1–3.

Roese, N.J., & Jamieson, D.W. (1993). Twenty years of bogus pipeline research: A critical review and meta-analysis. *Psychological Bulletin, 114*, 363–375.

Saxe, L. (1991). Science and the CQT polygraph: A theoretical critique. *Integrative Physiological and Behavioral Science, 26*, 223–231.

Saxe, L., & Ben-Shakhar, G. (1999). Admissibility of polygraph tests: The applications of scientific standards post-Daubert. *Psychology, Public Policy, & Law, 5*, 203–223.

Saxe, L., Dougherty, D., & Cross, T. P. (1983). *Scientific validity of polygraph testing* (OTA-TM-H-15) (Report for the U.S. Congress, Office of Technology Assessment). Washington, DC: Government Printing Office.

Saxe, L., Dougherty, D., & Cross, T. P. (1985). The validity of polygraph testing: Scientific analysis and public controversy. *American Psychologist, 40*, 355–366.

Schlank, A. M., & Shaw, T. (1996). Treating sexual offenders who deny their guilt: A pilot study. *Sexual Abuse: A Journal of Research and Treatment, 8*, 17–23.

Sinclair Seminars. (1998). *Sex offender evaluation and treatment training program* [Brochure]. Madison, W1: Author.

Sloan, L. M. (1995). Revictimization by polygraph: The practice of polygraphing survivors of sexual assault. *Medicine & Law, 14*, 255–267.

Smith, B. E., & Goretsky-Elstein, S. (1993). *The prosecution of child sexual and physical abuse cases* (Final report of a grant from the National Center on Child Abuse and Neglect). Washington, DC: American Bar Association.

Task Force on the Psychosocial Evaluation of Suspected Sexual Abuse in Children. (1997). *Psychosocial evaluation of suspected sexual abuse in children* (2nd ed.). Chicago: American Professional Society on the Abuse of Children.

Task Force on the Use of Anatomical Dolls in Child Sexual Abuse Assessments. (1995). *Use of anatomical dolls in child sexual abuse assessments.* Chicago: American Professional Society on the Abuse of Children.

United States v. Frank Javier Cordoba, 158 (D. California, 1998), *aff'd*, SA CR 95–39-GLT[SF].

United States v. Frye, 293 F. 1013, 1013 (D.C. Cir. 1923).

United States v. Scheffer, 118 S. CL. Supp. 1261 (D. Washington, 1998), *aff'd*, USCA DKL No. 95–0521/AF. (U.S. Court of Appeals for the Armed Forces).

Williams, V. L. (1995). Response to Cross and Saxe's "A critique of the validity of polygraph testing in child sexual abuse cases." *Journal of Child Sexual Abuse, 4*, 55–71.

Williams, V. L. (1999). Response to Cross and Saxe's "A critique of the validity of polygraph testing in child sexual abuse cases." *Polygraph, 28*, 105–116.

Theodore P. Cross, Ph.D., is a research associate at the Crimes Against Children Research Center, at the University of New Hampshire, and in the Department of Psychology at Brandies University. He has conducted research for the past decade on the criminal justice response to child maltreatment and the evaluation of a varisty of interventions for troubled children. He is the principal investigator for the National Evaluation of Children's Advocacy Centers. With Saxe, he coauthored the 1983 Congressional Office of Technology Assessment report on the validity of polygraph testing and has served as an expert witness and court expert on polygraph testing in several cases. He teaches graduate-level statistics and maintains a practice in child clinical psychology.

Leonard Saxe, Ph.D., is a social psychologist on the faculty of the Heller School of Social Welfare at Brandies University. His work concerns the evaluation of social interventions, and he has long-standing involvement in assessing the validity of polygraph tests. He was a Congressional Science Fellow at the Congressional Office of Technology Assessment and was principal author of its study of the scientific issues of polygraph testing. He has coauthored a number of monographs, book chapters, and journal articles on the conduct of applied research. He has also served as an expert witness and court expert in numerous cases involving the use of psychological tests. Saxe received the American Psychological Association's award for Research in the Public Interest (Early Career) and has been a Fulbright scholar.

Review and Contemplate

1. What is the "central problem" with the use of the polygraph to detect deception?
2. What is the most common polygraph procedure? Explain how it is conducted and what pattern of responses supposedly indicates deception.
3. Briefly explain how polygraph tests are used in sexual abuse cases for (a) investigative, (b) exculpatory, and (c) monitoring purposes.
4. What overall accuracy rate for polygraphs is accepted by scientists? What accuracy rates are reported by supporters of polygraphs? Is there any evidence that polygraph tests in child sexual abuse cases are accurate?
5. Explain why the use of the polygraph test for detecting deception might be considered a pseudoscientific practice.

Authors' Note: The Family Violence Research Seminar at the University of New Hampshire was instrumental to the preparation of this article. We also wish to thank Elise Cantor, Monique Simone, Elizabeth McDonald, and Erica Kibbe for their assistance. Correspondence concerning this article should be directed to the first author at the Crimes Against Children Research Center, 126 Horton Social Science Center, University of New Hampshire, Durham, New Hampshire 03824 or by e-mail at ted.cross@unh.edu.

8.3

A position statement by the International Graphonomics Society on the use of graphology in personnel selection testing,

MARVIN SIMNER AND RICHARD GOFFIN

Graphology involves analyzing people's handwriting to determine their personality traits or other attributes. Graphologists examine characteristics such as the spacing between words, the slant of the writing, and the pressure used against the paper; the characteristics of a person's writing are thought to provide information about the person's attributes. For example, wide spacing between words supposedly suggests a person is isolated or lonely; those who crowd their words together are desperate for companionship; people who write large letters supposedly think big or are confident; and a woman whose signature reveals larger capitals in her given name than her husband's surname is said to have an unhappy marriage (if you read Article 7.2, you might recognize that graphologists appear to rely on the representativeness heuristic because they assume that there is a similarity between the characteristics of our handwriting and the characteristics of our personality).

Despite the scientific evidence that casts doubt on the validity of graphology, people who have used it may come away with a sense that it works. One reason is that a graphologist's analysis of a person's personality may contain a number of vague statements that apply to many people. For example, a handwriting analysis I requested of my daughter's handwriting showed that she "has a healthy imagination and displays a fair amount of trust," she is a "practical person whose goals are planned," she "likes to have all the facts before making a decision," and "her emotions are stirred by sympathy and heart-rending stories." Yes, that sounds like a fairly accurate description of my daughter. But it also sounds like a fairly accurate description of me, my colleagues, and most of the other people I know. People's tendency to accept vague, general statements as accurate descriptions of their own personalities is what psychologists call the Barnum Effect. This tendency may help explain why people believe that graphology is a valid technique for assessing personality. The Barnum Effect is another good example of one of the themes of this book discussed in Chapter 1: normal cognitive and social processes contribute to pseudoscientific and paranormal beliefs.

One popular use of graphology is in selecting employees for positions in various businesses. Simner and Goffin discuss the scientific evidence on whether graphology is useful for testing potential employees. They conclude with a position statement by the International Graphonomics Society—an organization that studies handwriting issues such as the development of graphic skills and computer recognition of handwriting—on the use of graphology in personnel selection testing.

APA Reference

Simner, M. L., & Goffin, R. D. (2003). A position statement by the International Graphonomics Society on the use of graphology in personnel selection testing. *International Journal of Testing, 3,* 353–364.

Among the various tests employed in personnel selection, handwriting analysis, or graphology, has enjoyed long-standing international popularity despite being highly contentious. This report contains not only an evaluation of the current published scientific reviews on the use of graphology in personnel selection, but also an evaluation of several additional studies graphologists provided that seemed to have been overlooked. The latter were obtained by contacting nine of the foremost institutes offering graphological training, consulting services, or both to ensure that the graphologists themselves would be fairly represented. Even with this additional information we found no reason to counter conclusions the scientific community has reached, namely that (a) the continued use of graphology in personnel selection could prove harmful to many individuals and firms, and (b) it fails to approach the level of criterion validity of other widely available and less expensive screening devices used for personnel selection. This article ends with a position statement about this matter, which the International Graphonomics Society[1] endorsed.

Graphology is the study of character or personality through handwriting. Although the term originated in 1868, the practice of using handwriting as a means of determining certain personality characteristics dates back to the 17th century (Le Guen, 1976). Whereas several systems of graphology exist today, the most popular ones focus on what are often referred to as general signs and special signs in individual letter strokes. Examples of general signs include small, angular, rounded, or uneven strokes, and special signs refer to words in which the letters are of unequal height, cramped, unconnected, or written in small groups of three or four. These signs, in turn, are then said to be associated with different

---

Requests for reprints should be sent to Marvin L. Simner, Department of Psychology, Social Science Centre, University of Western Ontario, London, Ontario, Canada N6A 5C2. E-mail: msimner@uwo.ca

---

[1]The International Graphonomics Society was established in 1987 to advance basic and applied research on a broad range of topics dealing with handwriting. Although membership is open to professionals in many disciplines, most members are involved in handwriting investigations in areas such as computer science; motor control; experimental, developmental, and educational psychology; and forensic document examination.

personality types such as sociability, responsibility, self-discipline, integrity, and intellectual efficiency (see International Graphoanalysis Society, 1975).

Among the many advantages said to be associated with the use of graphology is the ability of graphologists to make personnel selection decisions in business (Currer-Briggs, Kennett, & Paterson, 1973). Over the years, however, a substantial amount of evidence has accumulated on the validity of these decisions. Despite the fact that this evidence shows only a marginal relation between these decisions and supervisor ratings of actual on-the-job performance (for reviews of the evidence see Dean, 1992; Klimoski & Rafaeli, 1983; Neter & Ben-Shakhar, 1989), the practice of using handwriting analysis in making employment recommendations seems to be continuing unabated throughout much of the world (Beyerstein & Beyerstein, 1992; Edwards & Armitage, 1992; Tett & Palmer, 1997). According to Edwards and Armitage, for example, "In Israel and France … an estimated 80% of firms now use graphologists when appointing staff, and the practice is spreading rapidly in Germany, Switzerland, the U.S.A., and Britain." N. Bradley (personal communication, January 17, 2002) compiled a list of more than 150 multinational corporations using this approach, and Ann Mahony, a practicing graphologist, on her current Web site (http://iac.classroomdoor.com/bios/ag_Mahony.asp) claims to have worked for firms such as Coldwell Banker, Bank of America, Barclay's Bank, Pacific Bell, Federal Express, United Parcel Service, and Dow Chemical.

During a recent meeting of the International Graphonomics Society, the Board of Directors approved a motion to determine if the evidence linking graphology to personnel selection is indeed sufficiently meager to warrant a position statement dealing with this matter. The statement would alert the public to the harm that might result if this practice continues. Hence, this article evaluates the evidence to determine whether such a statement is warranted.

METHOD

To gather the necessary information we used two procedures. First we conducted a computer search of the PsycINFO database, which is a comprehensive listing of journal articles, technical reports, and dissertations published since 1967 that deal with the international literature in psychology and related disciplines. From this database we located several correlational studies linking graphology to job performance, all of which (and then some) Dean (1992) had previously reviewed. In his review, Dean not only reported the outcome of the individual studies, but also the outcome of a meta-analysis he performed on the findings to provide a statistical summary of the results.

Next we contacted the graphologists themselves to ensure that they would receive a fair hearing, which we considered important because graphologists often reject the conclusions derived from reviews, such as the one Dean conducted, on grounds that the studies contained in these reviews were not properly performed and so the evidence was biased against the profession (Edwards & Armitage, 1992; Sackheim, 1990). To this end, the following letter was sent via e-mail in January 2002 to 9 graphological training institutes and consulting firms[2] that listed personnel selection on their Web sites as an aspect of graphology.

> (We) are currently working on an article reviewing the use of handwriting analysis as a way of evaluating job applicants. Prior to writing this article, we would, of course, like to familiarize ourselves with all of the relevant scientific literature that assesses the use of handwriting analysis for personnel selection purposes. (We) are contacting you to ask for your help in locating relevant scientific literature on this topic. Would you be so kind as to send (us) a list of any articles that you are aware of that deal with this topic?
>
> We have already consulted the relevant psychology journals dealing with this topic but in the interests of conducting a thorough search we also thought it would be advisable to contact your organization.

Several of the organizations subsequently forwarded the letter to practitioners throughout the world. Over the next few months we received numerous replies, many of which contained references. Although many of these only provided descriptive information or anecdotal accounts that favored graphology, six of the references did report empirical findings that were directly relevant to personnel selection, and four used procedures that yielded correlational results (Ben-Shakhar, Bar-Hillel, Bilu, Ben-Abba, & Flug, 1986; Bornstein, 1985; Hofsommer & Holdsworth, 1963; Keinan, Barak, & Ramati, 1984). The other two (Edwards & Armitage, 1992; Satow & Rector, 1995) employed a matching or sorting procedure that did not readily lend itself to this form of analysis.

Because graphologists provided all six investigations, we reasonably assumed that they would offer an appraisal of graphology acceptable to practitioners in the field. Of added importance, the four investigations that yielded correlational findings were already included in Dean's (1992) meta-analysis.

RESULTS

Table 8.1 reports the findings from each of the 16 correlational investigations Dean (1992, see Appendix B, p. 335) reviewed; they are arranged according to whether the script that was evaluated was autobiographical or nonautobiographical. The reason for this division is that although graphologists normally prefer to use autobiographical scripts (Ben-Shakhar et al., 1986, p. 646), nonautobiographical or neutral material should be employed in empirical investigations to eliminate the possibility of bias due to the content of the material (see Sackheim, 1990, p. 165–166).

As mentioned, the studies by Edwards and Armitage (1992) and Satow and Rector (1995) did not report the outcome of their work in terms of correlations

---

[2]A to Z Handwriting Specialists Inc., American Graphological Centers, Graph-O-Logica.com, Handwriting Analysis Inc., Handwriting Research Corporation, Handwriting University.com, International Graphoanalysis Society, Anna Koren Graphology Center Ltd., and Ocampa Handwriting Analysis.

TABLE 8.1 ▰▰▰▰▰▰▰▰▰▰▰▰▰▰▰▰▰▰▰▰▰▰▰▰▰▰▰▰▰▰

Correlations Reported in Dean (1992) Between Handwriting Analyses Performed on Autobiographical Versus Nonautobiographical Material by Graphologists, and Subsequent Supervisory Ratings of Job Performance

Investigation[a]	Sample Size/ Nature	Number of Graphologists	Correlation Type	Mean Correlation
Autobiographical material				
Ben-Shakhar et al. (1986)	58/Bank	3	r	.21
Bornstein (1985)[a]	214/Military	3	r	.14
Drory (1986)	60/Drink plant	1	r	.36
Esroni, Rolnik, & Livnat (1985)[a]	23/Military	1	ph	.19
Esroni et al.(1985)[a]	125/Military	1	ph	.01
Esroni et al.(1985)[a]	49/Military	1	r	.03
Esroni et al.(1985)[a]	45/Military	1	r	.06
Hofsummer, Holdsworth, & Seifert (1962)[a]	54/Foresters	2	rs	.55
Hofsommer & Holdsworth (1963)[a]	141/Pilots	1	rp	.20
Jansen (1973); (Study 3)	20/Commercial	10	ph	.23[b]
Jansen (1973); (Study 4)	9/Administration	6	rs	.09
Keinan, Barak, & Ramati (1984)	65/Military	6	r	.23
Rafaeli & Klimoski (1983)	55/Real estate sales	20	r	.03
Shilo (1979)[a]	15/Moshav	?	?	.18
Sonnemann & Kernan (1962)	37/Executives	1	r	.43
Strolovitch (1980)[a]	25/Technical	2	r	−.19
Wallner (1963)[a]	89/Executives	2	r	.05
Nonautobiographical material				
Ben-Shakhar et al. (1986)	36/Professionals	5	k	.08
Bornstein (1985)[a]	214/Military	3	r	.12
Cox & Tapsell (1991)	50/Executives	2	r	.00
Rafaeli & Klimoski (1983)	55/Real estate sales	20	r	.09
Super (1941)	24/Students–SVIB	1	ph	−.02
Zdep & Weaver (1967)	63/Insurance sales	2	r	.08

Note. k = Cohen's kappa; ph = phi coefficient; r = Pearson correlation; rp = point biserial r; rs = Spearman rank order correlation; SVIB = strong vocational interest blank.
[a]Data obtained from secondary sources (see Dean, 1992, for explanation).
[b]Corrected for range expansion.

due to the experimental methods that they employed and, hence, were not part of Dean's (1992) review. In Edwards and Armitage's study, samples of handwriting were obtained from people who were said to be either successful or unsuccessful in their given occupations (i.e., secretaries, executives) according to information their employers provided. The four graphologists were to identify the successful people versus the unsuccessful people by virtue of their handwriting alone. Table 8.2 reports the results from this study.

In the Satow and Rector (1995) study, samples of handwriting were obtained from two groups of 40 people each. The first group consisted of entrepreneurs

TABLE 8.2

Percentage of Successful Matches Across the Two Employment Situations for Each of Four Graphologists

Employment Category	Number of Writers	Graphologist			
		A	**B**	**C**	**D**
Secretaries	50	60%	66%	68%	72%
Executives					
Men	42	66%	57%	60%	57%
Women	18	67%	69%	61%	67%

with proven success in business. These were all chief executive officers in top-ranked "privately owned companies which showed the largest sales growth in the past five years." The second group, which served as a control, were people "randomly selected from a national database of American households with telephones." The samples of writing from the two groups were then sorted into pairs with each pair consisting of one sample from the control group and one from the entrepreneur group. Three graphologists were then employed, each of whom received the 40 pairs of handwriting samples. Here the task required the graphologists to determine, for each pair, which person belonged to the entrepreneur group and which to the control group. Table 8.3 shows the results Satow and Rector obtained. For ease of interpretation we converted the raw data Satow and Rector reported into percentage of correct choices.

DISCUSSION

What are we to make of these results? First, and most striking, is the variability in the magnitude of the findings. The correlations reported in Table 8.1 ranged from −.19 to +.55 across investigations. Similarly, whereas the graphologists in the Edwards and Armitage (1992; Table 8.2) study were correct, on average, 64% of the time (which is only 14% above a 50% chance level), the graphologists in the Satow and Rector (1995; Table 8.3) study were correct, on average, 83% of the time. Admittedly, some variation is always to be expected across studies in part because of sample differences and study design. But beyond these differences, this variation could have resulted from the level of expertise of the particular graphologists who were employed in the investigations.

TABLE 8.3

Percentage of Correct Choices for Each of Three Graphologists Graphologist

Employment Category	Number of Writers	Graphologist		
		A	**B**	**C**
Enterpreneurs	40	78%	85%	85%

This latter possibility should not be dismissed lightly. Graphologists themselves have often commented on the fact that different results are likely to emerge from different studies depending on the qualifications of the graphologist. If this is indeed the case, how then is a firm to know whether the advice of a particular graphologist is valid? Clearly, the only appropriate way to answer this question is to have the graphologist perform an empirical investigation according to professional standards (e.g., Society for Industrial and Organizational Psychology, 1987), similar to the follow-up investigations described earlier, to validate his or her own practice. The replies we received in response to our e-mail inquiry suggested that this type of evidence is decidedly lacking.

Moreover, we would assume that collectively the graphologists who took part in the existing peer-reviewed published literature are reasonably representative of graphologists in general. This point raises a second concern that has to do with the meaning of the validity of the graphological judgements as reported in this literature.In concert with the view that differences in study design and other factors may account for variability in study findings, consider the overall findings that emerged from the meta-analysis Dean (1992) performed on the data in Table 8.1. Dean's results are much more persuasive than are the results of Edwards and Armitage (1992) or Satow and Rector (1995) discussed earlier because Dean's combined sample size is much larger. The overall mean correlation between the graphological judgements and job performance that resulted from the studies using writing samples containing autobiographical material was .16, whereas the overall mean validity that resulted from the nonautobio-graphical material was only .09 (Dean, 1992).

As mentioned earlier, we have good reason to believe that studies using nonautobiographical material should be considered the most rigorous because they remove, or at least reduce, the potentially serious confound the content of the writing sample introduced. That is, graphologists claim that their judgements are derived from the characteristics of the handwriting, not from the personality-related or autobiographical content of the handwriting sample.[3] The aforementioned difference in size between validities derived from content-laden (r = .16) versus content-free (r = .09) writing samples does, in fact, suggest that the content of the material might well influence the graphologists' judgement. Moreover, this content by itself has been suggested to be a predictor of later job performance, albeit a weak one. As part of the evidence available to Dean (1992), psychologists with no prior knowledge of graphology rendered judgements in five of the

---

[3]We recognize that graphologists claim not to use the autobiographical content of writing samples. Nonetheless, if the graphologist is using the autobiographical or personality-related content of the writing sample, this type of content is not being exploited as effectively as possible. Specifically, qualified personnel selection professionals can readily obtain standardized questionnaires that measure autobiographical information (i.e., biodata tests) and personality tests. Biodata tests and personality tests have been meta-analytically shown to predict job performance at .35 and .31 – .41 respectively (Schmidt & Hunter, 1998), which, even allowing for differences in statistical corrections between the Schmidt and Hunter and the Dean meta-analyses, is far better than the .16 relationship obtained from graphologists who used autobiographical writing samples (i.e., Dean, 1992).

investigations. The psychologists' task was to read the autobiographical material in the writing samples and make their judgements solely on the basis of the global character descriptions derived from the content of this material. The mean correlation that resulted from the meta-analysis of this work was .18, which is nearly identical to the mean correlation of .16 the graphologists achieved when they also used the autobiographical writing samples (see the Dean, 1992, results described earlier). Thus, the content of the writing sample may very well influence the graphologists' judgments.

Regardless of whether one chooses to use the nonautobiographical or the autobiographical evidence, however, these two values of .09 and .16 not only place graphology at the lower end of the validity continuum with respect to other more commonly used personnel selection methods (for a recent review of these methods see Schmidt and Hunter, 1998), but they also suggest that the continued use of graphology in personnel selection could result in large financial losses to organizations. In short, if the graphologist makes use of information derived solely from the physical characteristics of the script (or for that matter, even from the autobiographical content of the written material), the graphologist is relying on information that has little bearing on later actual job performance. In this regard it is worth pointing out that in North America at least, neither the applicant nor the firm has much in the way of legal recourse if the graphologist arrives at a conclusion that later proves to be invalid (see Carswell, 1992; Reagh, 1992).

Finally, also worth mentioning is that graphologists often attempt to justify their support of handwriting analysis in making hiring decisions by stating that the results they obtain are no different than the results obtained through other more objective employment screening measures because all such measures are imperfect. The fact that other established selection methods measuring different domains have been shown to generate higher criterion-related validity correlations than those graphologists produced clearly illustrates the fallacy of this reasoning. For example Schmidt and Hunter's (1998) meta-analysis found the criterion-related validity of both general mental ability (GMA) testing and structured employment interviews to be .51. Moreover, if used in combination, the structured employment interview and GMA testing result in a multiple correlation of .63. Hence, contrary to the views graphologists often express, other procedures are more likely than graphology to yield relatively accurate information when firms are called on to make personnel selection decisions.

CONCLUSION

Given the findings summarized herein we believe we have good reason to question the merit of using graphology as a means of judging a person's potential. Many others who have also evaluated this evidence have reached the same conclusion:

> "The present state of knowledge on this topic can best be described by saying its use in applied settings is premature. Although the literature on this topic suffers

from significant methodological negligence, the general trend of findings is to suggest that graphology is not a viable assessment method" (Klimoski & Rafaeli, 1983).

"Although the person reading a graphological character analysis has a distinct sense that an integrated, whole personality has been put together, and that he or she now actually knows the person described, the sense of being now able to predict that person's behavior is not supported by the facts" (Ben-Shakhar et al., 1986).

"From a practical point of view, it is doubtful whether graphology is to be recommended as a device for selection of personnel" (Nevo, 1988, p. 94).

"In summary, this experiment, while rejecting the null hypothesis that graphology cannot discriminate at all between individuals with different types of personality, offers scant support to the claims made by professional practitioners of graphology that their 'science' is sufficiently developed to have practical reliability" *(Edwards & Armitage, 1992, p. 73).*

In essence we feel sufficient grounds indeed exist to justify the following position statement, which the International Graphonomics Society endorsed in November 2002:

Although the use of handwriting analysis in making personnel selection decisions has a very long history, the evidence available to date fails to support this practice. Whereas the International Graphonomic Society does not wish to recommend any particular personnel selection device, the Society does recommend that firms that wish to continue to employ the services of graphologists should exercise extreme caution when accepting their judgements and carefully consider the scientific evidence, which, on balance, suggests that the use of graphological judgements for personnel selection is much less effective than several other readily available personnel selection methods.

References

Ben-Shakhar, G., Bar-Hillel, M., Bilu, Y., Ben-Abba, E., & Flug, A. (1986). Can graphology predict occupational success? Two empirical studies and some methodological ruminations. *Journal of Applied Psychology, 71,* 645–653.

Beyerstein, B. L., & Beyerstein, D. F. (Eds.). (1992). *The write stuff: Evaluations of graphology—The study of handwriting analysis.* Buffalo, NY: Prometheus.

Bornstein, Y. (1985). *Examination of the efficiency of graphology as a selection tool in the Israel Defense Forces.* Master's thesis, University of Haifa, Israel.

Brogden, H. E. (1949). When testing pays off. *Personnel Psychology, 2,* 171–183.

Carswell, R. S. (1992). Graphology: Canadian legal implications. In B. L. Beyerstein & D. F. Beyerstein (Eds.), *The write stuff: Evaluations of graphology—The study of handwriting analysis.* Buffalo, NY: Prometheus.

Cascio, W. F. (1991). *Costing human resources: The financial impact of behavior in organizations.* Boston: PWS-Kent.

Cox, J., & Tapsell, J. (1991). *Graphology and its validity in personnel assessment.* Paper presented at the BPS Occupational Psychology Conference, Cardiff, Wales.

Cronbach, L. J., & Gleser, G. C. (1965). *Psychological tests and personnel decisions.* Urbana, IL: University of Illinois Press.

Currer-Briggs, N., Kennett, B., & Paterson, J. (1973). *Handwriting analysis in business: The use of graphology in personnel selection.* New York: Wiley.

Dean, G. A. (1992). The bottom line: Effect size. In B. L. Beyerstein & D. F. Beyerstein (Eds.), *The write stuff: Evaluations of graphology—The study of handwriting analysis.* Buffalo, NY: Prometheus.

Drory, A. (1986). Graphology and job performance—A validation study. In B. Nevo (Ed.), *Scientific aspects of graphology.* Springfield, IL: Thomas.

Edwards, A. G. P., & Armitage, P. (1992). An experiment to test the discriminating ability of graphologists. *Personality and Individual Differences, 13,* 69–74.

Esroni, G., Rolnik, A., & Livnat, E. (1985). *Studies evaluating the validity of graphology in a voluntary military unit.* Paper presented at the 20th Israeli Psychological Association Conference.

Hofsommer, W., & Holdsworth, R. (1963). Die Validitatder Handschriften analyse beider Auswahlvon Piloten. *Psychol. prax, 7,* 175–178.

Hofsommer, W., Holdsworth, R., & Seifert, T. (1962). Zur Bewahrungskontrolle Graphologischer Diagnosen. *Psychol. Beit., 7,* 397–401.

International Graphoanalysis Society. (1975). *Evaluated traits of graphoanalysis.* Chicago, IL: Author.

Jansen, A. (1973). *Validation of graphological judgments: An experimental study.* Paris: Mouton.

Keinan, G., Barak, A., & Ramati, T. (1984). Reliability and validity of graphological assessment in the selection process of military officers. *Perceptual and Motor Skills, 58,* 811–821.

Klimoski, R., & Rafaeli, A. (1983). Inferring personal qualities through handwriting analysis. *Journal of Occupational Psychology, 56,* 191–202.

Le Guen, M. (1976). *Graphology.* Barcelona, Spain: Media Books.

Murphy, K. R., & Davidshofer, C. O. (1998). *Psychological testing: Principles and applications.* Upper Saddle River, NJ: Prentice Hall.

Neter, E., & Ben-Shakhar, G. (1989). The predictive validity of graphological inferences: A meta-analytic approach. *Personnel and Individual Differences, 10,* 737–745.

Nevo, B. (1988). Yes, graphology can predict occupational success: Rejoinder to Ben-Shakhar et al. *Perceptual and Motor Skills, 66,* 92–94.

Rafaeli, A., & Klimoski, R. J. (1983). Predicting sales success through handwriting analysis: An evaluation of the effects of training and handwriting sample content. *Journal of Applied Psychology, 68,* 212–217.

Reagh, J. D. (1992). Legal implications of graphology in the United States. In B. L. Beyerstein & D. F. Beyerstein (Eds.), *The write stuff: Evaluations of graphology—The study of handwriting analysis.* Buffalo, NY: Prometheus.

Sackheim, K. K. (1990). *Handwriting analysis and the employee selection process: A guide for human resource professionals.* New York: Quorum.

Satow, R., & Rector, J. (1995). Using gestalt graphology to identify entrepreneurial leadership. *Perceptual and Motor Skills, 81,* 263–270.

Schmidt, F. L., & Hunter, J. E. (1998). The validity and utility of selection methods in personnel psychology: Practical and theoretical implications of 85 years of research findings. *Psychological Bulletin, 124,* 262–274.

Schmidt, F. L., Hunter, J. E., McKenzie, R. C., & Muldrow, T. W. (1979). Impact of valid selection procedures on work-force productivity. *Journal of Applied Psychology, 64,* 609–626.

Shilo, S. (1979). *Prediction of success on a moshav according to graphological scores as compared to prediction of the same criterion by psychological scores.* Internal Research Report, Hadassa Institute for Career Guidance Counselling, Jerusalem, Israel.

Society for Industrial and Organizational Psychology (1987). *Principles for the validation and use of personnel selection procedures* (3rd ed.). College Park, MD: Author.

Sonneman, U., & Kernan, J. P. (1962). Handwriting analysis—A valid selection tool. *Personnel, 39*(6), 8–14.

Super, D. E. (1941). A comparison of the diagnoses of a graphologist with the results of psychological tests. *Journal of Consulting Psychology, 5,* 127–133.

Strolovitch, I. (1980). *Impact of personal variables and job variables on the predictive validity of some personnel selection practices for scientific–technical positions.* Master's thesis, Technion, Haifa, Israel.

Tett, R. P., & Palmer, C. A. (1997). The validity of handwriting elements in relation to self-report personality trait measures. *Personality and Individual Differences, 22,* 11–18.

U.S. Department of Labor. (2000). *Employment cost indexes, 1975–99.* Washington, DC: Author.

Viswesvaran, C., Ones, D. S., & Schmidt, F. L. Comparative analysis of the reliability of job performance ratings. *Journal of Applied Psychology, 81,* 557–574.

Wallner, T. (1963). Uber die Validitat Graphologischer Aussagen. *Diagnostica, 9,* 26–35.

Zdep, S. M., & Weaver, H. B. (1967). The graphoanalytic approach to selecting life insurance salesmen. *Journal of Applied Psychology, 51,* 295–299.

Review and Contemplate

1. What is graphology? What "signs" do graphologists look for, and what do they claim they can determine from such signs?

2. Simner and Goffin (2003) reviewed scientific studies that examined whether graphology is a valid technique for personnel selection. Briefly describe their overall conclusions.

3. What evidence suggests that graphologists' judgments are influenced by the *content* of one's writing rather than the *characteristics* of the handwriting? How does the accuracy of graphologists compare with that of psychologists who have no special training in graphology (i.e., when both groups' judgments are based on autobiographical writing)?

4. How does the validity of graphology compare with established personnel selection methods such as general mental ability testing and structured employment interviews?

5. What is the Barnum Effect? How might it explain why people believe in the validity of graphology despite scientific evidence to the contrary?

CHAPTER 9
Psychological Disorders and Therapies

9.1 *Multiple Personality Disorder:* Witchcraft Survives in the Twentieth Century/
AUGUST PIPER JR.

The 1976 movie Sybil was based on the true story of a woman who was diagnosed with multiple personality disorder (currently known as dissociative identity disorder). Her psychiatrist, Dr. Cornelia Wilbur, believed that Sybil developed the disorder as a way to cope with the severe abuse she received as a child by her cruel mother. Sybil's 16 personalities included a self-assured blonde woman, a male carpenter, a baby, and a carefree, fun-loving teenage girl. It's a fascinating story, but psychologists now question whether Sybil ever had multiple personalities. In the late 1990s, after reviewing tape recordings of conversations between Dr. Wilbur and the author of a book about Sybil, psychologist Robert Rieber concluded that Sybil's personalities may have been created during therapy as a result of suggestions given by Dr. Wilbur. Similarly, Dr. Herbert Spiegel, who served as Sybil's psychiatrist when Dr. Wilbur was out of town, suspected that Sybil's multiple personalities came about as a result of Dr. Wilbur's therapeutic technique of assigning people's names to various emotional states Sybil exhibited and encouraging her to be those people while describing her past experiences.

In the 1970s there were fewer than two hundred cases of people diagnosed with multiple personality disorder. By the 1990s clinicians specializing in the treatment of the disorder estimated there were tens of thousands of cases, most of which were in North America. Psychologists now question whether dissociative identity disorder more likely reflects a pseudoscientific social phenomenon than a psychological disorder brought about by childhood trauma. Piper discusses the controversy surrounding this disorder and the problems with the theory that trauma causes multiple personality disorder.

APA Reference

Piper, A. (1998, May/June). Multiple personality disorder: Witchcraft survives in the twentieth century. *Skeptical Inquirer, 22,* 44–50.

Any people, given over to the power of contagious passion, may be swept by desolation, and plunged into ruin. —Charles W. Upham, 1867

Since 1980, some psychotherapists have claimed that thousands of Americans are afflicted with multiple personality disorder. Believing such claims requires ignoring their many serious deficiencies.

An epidemic of psychiatric illness is sweeping through North America. Before 1980, a total of no more than about two hundred cases had ever been found in the entire world, throughout the entire recorded history of psychiatry. Yet today, some proponents of the condition claim that it afflicts at least a tenth of all Americans, and perhaps 30 percent of poor people—more than twenty-six million individuals. An industry involving significant sums of money, many specialty hospitals, and numerous self-described experts, has rapidly grown up around the disorder.

The illness is multiple personality disorder (MPD), a condition that has always attracted a few wisps of controversy. Lately, these wisps have coalesced into clouds that, in drenching rainbursts, pour criticism on the disorder. An examination of the flawed reasoning, unsound claims, and logical inconsistencies of the MPD literature shows that well-founded concerns drive this storm of criticism.

WHAT IS MPD?

MPD is classified as a dissociative disorder. The term *dissociation* refers to disruption in one or more mental operations that constitute the central idea of "consciousness": forming and holding memories, assimilating sensory impressions and making sense of them, and maintaining a sense of one's own identity (American Psychiatric Association 1994, 477). The essence of dissociation is that material not in awareness influences behavior, mood, and thought (Spiegel and Schleflin 1994). Thus, the behavioral disturbances prominently manifested in dissociative disorders are considered to be unconscious: that is, resulting from forces beyond the patient's awareness, beyond voluntary control.

August Piper Jr., M. D. is a psychiatrist in private practice in Seattle. His book, *Hoax and Reality: The Bizarre World of Multiple Personality Disorder*, was published in January 1997 by Jason Aronson, Inc.

The king of dissociative disorders is MPD,[1] also called dissociative identity disorder. Afflicted people episodically fail to recall vital data about themselves, but what distinguishes MPD from all other psychiatric conditions is the putative cause for these memory failures. The condition's proponents claim the memory failures occur because patients are periodically taken over by one or more "alter personalities" (variously referred to as "identities," "ego states," "alters," or "personality states"). These guest personalities, submerged since being formed during childhood—more on this later—rise to the surface and impose their own memories, thoughts, and behaviors on patients.

The essential feature of MPD, it is said, is that an individual's behavior is controlled by two or more alters (Putnam et al. 1990); the separate identities are assumed involuntarily (Sarbin 1995; Watkins and Watkins 1984). One personality may feel "carried along in a panicked helpless state" as another endangers it or engages in behavior repugnant to it (Kluft 1983, 75). Patients are said to experience a sense of being *made to* misbehave or hurt themselves (Putnam 1991). Some theorists even claim the existence of "omnipotent alters," which can simply compel patients to do their bidding (Lewis and Bard 1991). As an example, C. A. Ross writes of alters that "force [the patient] to jump in front of a truck. [The alters] then go back inside just before impact, leaving the [patient] to experience the pain" (Ross 1989, 115).

The image of all this is of an invading army usurping a government, an operator taking control of a machine, or a parasite attacking another organism. For example, contributors to the MPD literature frequently make statements such as, "If [the patient] drops her guard, the alters take over" (Bliss 1980, 1393). Proponents describe the original personality as the "host" —again recalling notions of a parasite—and describe the change from host to alter, or from one alter to another, as "switching." Thus, a librarian may one minute be her forty-two-year-old true shy self, but behave in the next like a nine-year-old child, a deep-voiced, foul-mouthed logger, or a promiscuous woman who picks up men in bars (Putnam 1989, 111, 119–120).

These guest personalities, or "alters," are believed to have many truly remarkable capabilities and qualities. Some have the task of reproducing—of creating new alters. Others, it is claimed, determine which alter will take control of the body at any particular time (Kluft 1995, 364). There are alters of people of the opposite sex, of the treating therapist, of infants, television characters, and demons. Alters of Satan and God, of dogs, cats, lobsters, and stuffed animals—even of people thousands of years old or from another dimension—have been reported by MPD proponents (*Fifth Estate* 1993; Ganaway 1989; Hendrickson et al. 1990; Kluft 1991b, 166; Kluft 1995, 366; Ross 1989, 112; Ross et al. 1989).

MPD proponents assert that all manner of activities—creating a work of art, driving a car, fighting, doing schoolwork, engaging in prostitution, cleaning a bathtub, or even baking chocolate-chip cookies—are performed by alters (Braun 1988; Putnam 1989, 104; Ross 1989, 112).

Alters are often wily, secretive, and elusive. For instance, R. P. Kluft (1991a) says he has identified guest personalities whose role is to deny that the patient has MPD, thus obscuring the diagnosis. Personalities are also said to try to trick therapists by hiding and impersonating each other (Putnam 1989, 113). They are said to be plastic: "Alter A may be somewhat different when it has been preceded by alter B than when it follows alter C" (Kluft 1988, 49). They are said to multiply: each alter can undergo a cascade of splits, resulting in what is called "polyfragmented" MPD (*Frontline* 1995; Ross 1994, 60). Or the opposite may occur: during therapy, several alters may coalesce into a kind of "superalter" (Kluft 1988). It is even claimed that they can permanently stop growing at some time, or temporarily stop aging by going into "inner hibernation" and then emerging to resume growing older (Ross 1989, 112). Cases reported in the last few years have shown a median number of two alters at the time of diagnosis; however, during treatment, a further six or twelve usually appear (Putnam et al. 1986; Ross et al. 1989). Sometimes many more are found: as many as one quarter of cases have twenty-six or more alters (Kluft 1988). And the longer patients remain in treatment, the more guest personalities are discovered (Kluft 1988; Kluft 1989): "It is the rule rather than the exception for previously unknown personalities to enter the treatment" (Kluft 1988, 54). Patients with 300 and 4,500 personalities have now been reported (Kluft 1988; Ross 1989, 121; Ross et al. 1989). Kluft has been consulted "several times" on cases where therapists claim—wrongly, Kluft says—to have counted "upward of 10,000 alters" (Kluft 1995, 363).

Why this nearly endless flowering of personalities? According to MPD proponents, it occurs because each trauma or major life change experienced by an MPD patient causes some or all of the alters to be created anew (Kluft 1988).

WHAT CAUSES MPD?

According to proponents, extraordinary childhood traumas—usually sexual or other abuse by adults—lead to MPD.

The theory is as follows. Because the child cannot physically escape the pain, its only option is to escape mentally: by dissociating. Dissociation is said to defend against pain by allowing the maltreatment to be experienced as if it were happening to someone else (Archison and McFarlane 1994; Braun 1989; Kluft 1985a; Kluft 1987; Ross 1995). The distress of this childhood maltreatment is also endured by employing *repression*, a mental mechanism that supposedly allows the child to forget that the abuse happened at all (Lynn and Nash 1994): "Now, not only is the abuse not happening to me, [but] I don't even remember it" (Ross 1995, 67).

Eventually, MPD proponents claim, these defenses begin to be overused—that is, enlisted more and more to cope with commonplace, everyday stressors (Braun 1986, 66; Putnam 1991). The abuse victim's "dissociated internal structures are slowly crystallized" until they become personalities (Archison and McFarlane 1994; Putnam 1989, 53–54; Ross 1995a, 67). As mentioned earlier, this alter-building process is supposed to occur almost exclusively in early child-hood (Greaves 1980; Vincent and Pickering 1988).

WHAT'S WRONG HERE?

So stands the tottering house of MPD theory. Its foundation crumbles and ter-mites gnaw; the storm beats upon it.

The house suffers from at least four serious ailments.

The first: What, exactly, is an "alter personality"?

One might believe that the disorder's proponents would long ago have taken the elementary step of answering this fundamental question. Such a belief would be mistaken. The MPD literature contains not one single plain, under-standable definition that would allow an alter to be recognized if it were en-countered on the street, in a person one has known intimately for years, or even in oneself.

The vagueness and imprecision of the alter concept are shown by the fre-quency with which even MPD experts contradict each other on the fundamen-tal attributes of these entities. As an example, Ross (1990) says patients' minds are no more host to many distinct personalities than their bodies are to different people; another theorist believes that alter personalities are imaginary constructs (Bliss 1984). But in contradiction, *DSM-IV* and the writings of several MPD the-orists repeatedly stress that alters are well-developed, district from one another, complex, and well-integrated (Kluft 1984b, Kluft 1987; Taylor and Martin 1944). Also, MPD-focused practitioners routinely report patients who have dozens or hundreds of personalities—yet Spiegel (1995) has recently claimed that because MPD patients cannot integrate various emotions and memories, such patients actually have less than one personality, not more than one.

Contradictions abound elsewhere, too. On the one hand, Bliss (1984) be-lieves personalities have specific and limited functions, and possess only a nar-row range of moods. But on the other, Braun (1984) and other proponents (Putnam 1989, 104; Ross 1989, 81) say that *fragments* do not have a wide range of mood or affect. One proponent states that *fragments* "carry out a limited task in the person's life" (Ross 1989, 81), but then later in the same publication (111–118) argues that *personalities* may perform only one specific function, rep-resent only a single mood or memory, or exhibit only a narrow range of skills.

This failure to rigorously define the concept of a guest personality leads to all manner of excesses. For example, MPD proponents discover MPD in people whose close relatives, and others who have known those people for years, have never once seen any evidence of alters (Ganaway 1995). Kluft (1985b), for in-stance, diagnosed the disorder in a series of people—even though he himself acknowledged that almost half of them showed "no overt signs" of MPD. These proponents also find MPD even in people who lack any knowledge whatever of having the condition (Bliss 1980; Bliss 1984; Kluft 1985b), and at least one enthusiast recommends that people be treated for MPD even if they claim not to have the disorder (Putnam 1989, 139, 215).

The imprecision of the alter concept allows MPD adherents to claim that scores of patient behaviors should signal the possible presence of guest personalities. Thus, adherents claim that the following behaviors—and many others—are important diagnostic clues for MPD: glancing around the therapist's office; frequently blinking one's eyes; changing posture, or the voice's pitch or volume; rolling the eyes upward; laughing or showing anger suddenly; covering the mouth; allowing the hair to fall over one's face; developing a headache; scratching an itch; touching the face, or the chair in which one sits; changing hairstyles between sessions or wearing a particular color of clothing or item of jewelry (Franklin 1990; Loewenstein 1991; Putnam 1989, 118–123; Ross 1989, 232). In one case known to the author, a leading MPD proponent claimed that the diagnosis was supported by behavior no more remarkable than the fact that the patient changed clothes several times daily and liked to wear sunglasses.

These beliefs about personalities raise some difficult questions that MPD enthusiasts fail to answer. First, how does alter-induced behavior differ from behavior people show every day—say, when they are angry or happy (Piper 1994a)? Do indwelling alters or fragments cause all feelings? If not, how does one determine which emotions result from the activities of alters, which from those of fragments, and which from neither? One proponent acknowledges the difficulty posed by these questions: he says alters may be indistinguishable from the original personality (Kluft 1991b).

Second, how do persons claiming they are overpowered by "irresistible alters" differ from those who attempt to avoid legal sanctions by claiming that, when they committed crimes, they couldn't control their behavior (Piper 1994c)?

Finally, one wonders how seriously to take MPD enthusiasts' claims that they can accurately keep track of fifteen or thirty invisible alters—or 4,500— when those alters are deceiving the therapist, growing, splitting, ceasing to age, reproducing, coalescing, going into "inner hibernation," and changing their characteristics depending on which personality preceded or followed their appearance.

In summary, knowing how to test or prove an assertion that an individual has more than one personality, or how to clinically distinguish between personalities, ego states, identities, fragments, personality states, or the like, is impossible in the absence of agreement about what any of these terms mean (Dinwiddie et al. 1993; Aldridge-Morris 1993, ch. 1). It follows, then, that few limits exist to the number of "personalities" one may unearth. The number is restrained only by the interviewer's energy and zeal in searching, and by his or her subjective—and perhaps idiosyncratic—sense of what constitutes an alter (Dinwiddie et al. 1993).

Enthusiasts thus expand the concept of personality beyond all bounds. If such a grandly expansive definition is employed, finding thousands of MPD "patients" becomes simple. Without clear behavioral criteria allowing the observer to know when a personality has been encountered, the term *personality* comes to mean anything and everything patient and clinician want it to. It thus comes to mean nothing.

The second affliction of the house of MPD is laid bare by one startling fact: the disorder's most dramatic signs appear after, not before, patients begin therapy with MPD proponents.

Those eventually given this diagnosis seek professional help because of many different kinds of psychiatric difficulties. When first presenting for treatment, these patients can exhibit signs or symptoms of each and every psychiatric condition (Coons et al. 1988; Putnam et al. 1986; Bliss 1984). One complaint, however, is conspicuously absent: evidence of separate alter personalities (Brick and Chu 1991; Franklin 1990; Kluft 1984a; Kluft 1985a; Ross 1989, 93).

But when the patients enter MPD-focused therapy, signs of alters' behaviors skyrocket. For instance, one patient's guest personalities created apparent grand mal seizures (Kluft 1995); another sold drugs when the host was supposed to be at work (the host would supposedly "come to" miles away) (Putnam 1989, 198). According to proponents, much of the behavior of MPD patients results from alters' "personified intrapsychic conflicts" (Putnam et al. 1986, 291); the personalities create crises in the patient's life by attempting to dominate, sabotage, and destroy one another (Kluft 1983; Kluft 1984c). As one example, an alter may lead the patient into compromising circumstances—say, a sexual encounter, an episode of firesetting, or an illegal drug purchase. This personality then vanishes, leaving the patient, who "wakes up" not knowing how he or she got into the situation, to handle the problem (Confer and Ables 1983; Kluft 1991b).

MPD patients often significantly deteriorate during treatment (Kluft 1984c; Ofshe and Watters 1994, ch. 10; Pendergrast 1995, ch. 6). One of the disorder's leading adherents acknowledges that MPD psychotherapy "causes significant disruption in a patient's life outside the treatment setting" and that suicide attempts may occur in the weeks following the diagnosis (Putnam 1989, 98, 299). As MPD psychotherapy progresses, patients may become more dissociative, more anxious, or more depressed (Braun 1989); the longer they remain in treatment, the more florid, elaborate, and unlikely their stories about their alleged childhood maltreatment tend to become (Ganaway 1995; Spanos 1996, ch. 20). This worsening contributes to the lengthy hospitalizations—some costing millions of dollars (*Frontline* 1995; Piper 1994b)—that often occur when MPD patients who are well-insured are treated by the disorder's enthusiasts. Hospitalizations occur more frequently after the MPD diagnosis is made (Piper 1994b; Ross and Dua 1993).

MPD focused therapists have struggled mightily to explain these rather embarrassing results of their interventions. Examining these explanations is beyond the scope of this article: see Piper 1995; Piper 1997; Simpson 1995. However, several recent malpractice juries have found the explanations unimpressive. The juries have preferred a simple and logical explanation for the worsening status of these patients: patients worsen after beginning MPD-focused therapy because therapists cause them to do so—by, among other things, encouraging ever-more-dramatic displays of "alters."

One important way in which therapists encourage such displays is to behave as if alter personalities were real. For example, leading authorities in this field routinely call alters out, hypnotize them, engage in "lengthy monologues" with them, name them, establish treatment alliances with them, talk to their stuffed animals, take them for walks to McDonald's ("The outside world often seems very big and frightening to child personalities"), engage in playful parody and sarcasm with them, allow them to work on age-appropriate childrens' projects in occupational therapy ("to show respect for the alter"), and recruit one alter to keep another from hurting still a third (Ross 1989, 227, 252–254; Ross and Gahan 1988). Other MPD adherents encourage alters to solve problems among themselves, to learn the Golden Rule, to participate in "internal group therapy," and even to decide whether or not the host should enter treatment (Caul 1984; Kluft 1993; Ross 1989, 209).

In 1988, Vincent and Pickering noted that in the published reviews of the literature, exactly *one* case presenting in childhood was reported in the 135 years prior to 1979. After reviewing the literature published since 1979, they were able to gather a mere twelve cases. (It seems, however, that Vincent and Pickering had to stretch a bit to find even those—four of the twelve were examples not of MPD, but rather of something the authors called "incipient MPD.") Nine additional cases were found by Peterson (1990).

These minuscule numbers, standing in stark contrast to the thousands of adult cases discovered in recent years, reveal the third weakness: if MPD results from child abuse, then why have so few cases been discovered in children?

The fourth and final weakness of the house is that it is built in a bog, namely, the belief that childhood maltreatment causes MPD. The literature strongly implies that childhood trauma has been unequivocally established as the primary cause of the disorder, and that severe sexual abuse more or less directly leads to MPD (Braun 1989, 311; Ellason and Ross 1997; Putnam 1989, 47; Ross 1989, 101; Ross 1995, 505; Schafer 1986).

Several commentators have recently noted this formulation's deficiencies. Esman (1994) warns of the dangers of attempting to discover unitary causes of psychiatric disorders; he urges "measured skepticism" about assigning a role for sexual abuse, independently of other aspects of disturbed family function, in the genesis of later adult psychopathology. Numerous investigators, raising similar cautions, state that general family pathology in childhood better predicts adult dysfunction than does childhood sexual abuse alone (Bifulco et al. 1991; Fromuth 1986; Harter et al. 1988; Levitt and Pinnell 1995; Nash et al. 1993). Further, studies repeatedly note the difficulty of separating effects of abuse from the "matrix of disadvantage" giving rise to that abuse (Nash et al. 1993; Bushnell et al. 1992; Hussey and Singer 1993; Mullen et al. 1993). And finally, recent studies warn of the "very real uncertainties that surround evidence" concerning the relationship between childhood sexual abuse and psychiatric disorders (Fergusson et al. 1997), and conclude that available evidence to date does not support sweeping generalizations about childhood sexual abuse as an isolated cause of adult psychopathology (Beichtman et al. 1992; Finkelhor 1990; Levitt and Pinnell 1995).

The evidence for and against a relationship between trauma and dissociative pathology has also been examined. The data should "inspire skepticism, or at least serve to mute the grand conclusions about univariate cause and effect between trauma and dissociation that abound in the professional and lay literatures" (Tillman et al. 1994, 409).

Yet another weakness of this literature is inadequate verification of its child-abuse claims (Frankel 1993; Piper 1994a; Piper 1997). MPD patients very often report bizarre and extremely improbable experiences. For example, in a recent case familiar to the author, one patient claimed to have witnessed a baby being barbecued alive at a family picnic in a city park; another patient alleged repeated sexual assaults by a lion, a baboon, and other zoo animals in her parents' back yard—in broad daylight. (It should be mentioned that both therapists in these cases are prominent MPD adherents, and neither appeared to have any difficulty believing these allegations). Despite the frequency of claims of this type, "repressed memory patients are seldom referred to medical doctors for examination and possible corroboration of past abuse [though one would assume that] the horrific physical abuse allegedly experienced . . . would require medical care at some point" (Parr 1996). (Space limitations limit discussion of this weakness; see Jones and McGraw 1987; Lindsay and Read 1994; Ofshe and Watters 1994; Pendergrast 1994, chs. 3–5; Spanos 1996, ch. 20; Wakefield and Underwager 1995, ch. 10).

The logic of the claim that childhood trauma causes MPD demonstrates a final serious flaw. If the claim were true, the abuse of millions of children over the years should have caused many cases of MPD. A case in point: children who endured unspeakable maltreatment in the ghettoes, boxcars, and concentration camps of Nazi Germany. However, no evidence exists that any developed MPD (Bower 1994; Des Pres 1976; Eitinger 1980; Krystal 1991; Sofsky 1997) or that any dissociated or repressed their traumatic memories (Eisen 1988; Wagenaar and Groeneweg 1990). Similarly, the same results hold in studies of children who saw a parent murdered (Eth and Pynoos 1994; Malmquist 1986); studies of kidnapped children (Terr 1979; Terr 1983); studies of children known to have been abused (Gold et al. 1994); and in several other investigations (Chodoff 1963; Pynoos and Nader 1989; Strom et al. 1962). Victims neither repressed the traumatic events, forgot about them, nor developed MPD.

CONCLUDING COMMENTS

In the epigraph that begins this article, Upham speaks of the excesses of the seventeenth-century New England witchcraft craze. The story of Sarah Good exemplifies those excesses (Rosenthal 1993). In March of 1692, when thirty-eight years old and pregnant, she heard her husband denounce her to the witchcraft tribunal. He said that either she already was a witch, "or would be one very quickly" (Rosenthal 1993, 89). No one had produced evidence that she had engaged in witchcraft, no one had seen her do anything unusual, no one had come forward to say they had participated in satanic activities with her. But no matter.

On July 19, 1692, Sarah Good died on the gallows.

Three hundred years later, a woman in Chicago consulted a psychiatrist for depression (*Frontline* 1995). He concluded that she suffered from MPD, that she had abused her own children, and that she had gleefully participated in Satan-worshiping cult orgies where pregnant women were eviscerated and their babies eaten. Her failure to recall these events was attributed to alters that blocked her awareness. No one had produced any evidence for the truth of any of this, no one had seen her do anything unusual, no one had come forward to say they had participated in satanic activities with her. But no matter.

The doctor notified the state that the woman was a child molester. Then, after convincing her that she had killed several adults because she had been told to do so by satanists, he threatened to notify the police about these "criminal activities."

The woman's husband believed the doctor's claims. He divorced her. And, of course, because she was a "child molester," she lost custody of her children.

Charles Upham recognized the importance of erecting barricades against addlepated ideas blown by gales of illogic. The twentieth-century fad of multiple personality disorder indicates that even after a third of a millennium, such bulwarks have yet to be built.

References

Aldridge-Morris, R. 1993. *Multiple Personality: An Exercise in Deception.* Hove, U.K.: Erlbaum.

American Psychiatric Association. 1994. *Diagnostic and Statistical Manual of Mental Disorders.* 4th ed. Washington, D.C.: American Psychiatric Association.

Atchison, M., and A. C. McFarlane. 1994. A review of dissociation and dissociative disorders. *Australian and New Zealand Journal of Psychiatry* 28: 591–599.

Beitchman, J. H., K. J. Zucker, J. E. Hood, G. A. DaCosta, D. Akman, and E. Cassavia. 1992. A review of the long-term effects of child sexual abuse. *Child Abuse and Neglect* 16: 101–118.

Bifulco, A., G. W. Brown, and Z. Alder. 1991. Early sexual abuse and clinical depression in late life. *British Journal of Psychiatry* 159: 115–122.

Bliss, E. L. 1980. Multiple personalities: A report of 14 cases with implications for schizophrenia and hysteria. *Archives of General Psychiatry* 37: 1388–1397.

———. 1984. Spontaneous self-hypnosis in multiple personality disorder. *Psychiatric Clinics of North America* 7: 135–148.

Bower, H. 1994. The concentration camp syndrome. *Australian and New Zealand Journal of Psychiatry* 28: 391–397.

Braun, B. G. 1984. Hypnosis creates multiple personality: Myth or reality? *International Journal of Clinical and Experimental Hypnosis* 32: 191–197.

————. 1986. *Treatment of Multiple Personality Disorder.* Washington, D. C.: American Psychiatric Press.

————. 1988. The BASK model of dissociation. *Dissociation* 1: 4–23.

————. 1989. Psychotherapy of the survivor of incest with a dissociative disorder. *Psychiatric Clinics of North America* 12: 307–324.

Brick, S. S., and J. A. Chu. 1991. The simulation of multiple personalities: A case report. *Psychotherapy* 28: 267–272.

Bushnell, J. A., J. E. Wells, and M. A. Oakley-Brown. 1992. Long-term effects of intrafamilial sexual abuse in childhood. *Acta Psychiatrica Scandinavica* 85: 136–142.

Caul, D. 1984. Group and videotape techniques for multiple personality disorder. *Psychiatric Annals* 14: 43–54.

Chodoff, P. 1963. Late effects of the concentration camp syndrome. *Archives of General Psychiatry* 8: 323–333.

Confer, W. N., and B. S. Ables. 1983. *Multiple Personality: Etiology, Diagnosis, and Treatment.* New York: Human Series Press.

Coons, P. M., E. S. Bowman, and V. Milstein. 1988. Multiple personality disorder: A clinical investigation of 50 cases. *Journal of Nervous and Mental Disease* 176: 519–527.

Des Pres, T. 1976. *The Survivor: An Anatomy of Life in the Death Camps.* New York: Washington Square Press.

Dinwiddie, S. H., C. S. North, and S. H. Yutzy. 1993. Multiple personality disorder: Scientific and medicolegal issues. *Bulletin of the American Academy of Psychiatry and Law* 21: 69–79.

Eisen, G. 1988. *Children and Play in the Holocaust: Games Among the Shadows.* Amherst, Mass.: University of Massachusetts Press.

Eitinger, L. 1980. The concentration camp syndrome and its late sequelae. In *Survivors, Victims, and Perpetrators. Essays on the Nazi Holocaust,* edited by J. E. Dimsdale, Washington, D.C.: Hemisphere Press.

Ellason, J. W., and Ross, C. A. 1997. Two-year follow-up of inpatients with dissociative identity disorder. *American Journal of Psychiatry* 154: 832–839.

Esman, A. H. 1994. "Sexual abuse," pathogenesis, and enlightened skepticism. *American Journal of Psychiatry* 151: 1,101–1,103.

Eth, S., and R. S. Pynoos. 1994. Children who witness the homicide of a parent. *Psychiatry* 57: 287–306.

Fergusson, D. M., M. T. Lynskey, and L. J. Horwood. 1997. Childhood sexual abuse and psychiatric disorder in young adulthood: II. Psychiatric outcomes of childhood sexual abuse. *Journal of the American Academy of Child and Adolescent Psychiatry* 34: 1,365–1,374.

Fifth Estate. 1993. *Multiple Personality Disorder,* videotape shown on November 9. CTV Canadian Television Network.

Finkelhor, D. 1990. Early and long-term effects of child sexual abuse: An update. *Professional Psychology: Research and Practice* 21: 325–330.

Frankel, F. H. 1993. Adult reconstruction of childhood events in the multiple personality literature. *American Journal of Psychiatry* 150: 954–958.

Franklin, J. 1990. The diagnosis of multiple personality disorder based on subtle dissociative signs. *Journal of Nervous and Mental Disease* 178: 4–14.

Fromuth, M. E. 1986. The relationship of childhood sexual abuse with later psychological and sexual adjustment in a sample of college women. *Child Abuse and Neglect* 10: 5–15.

Frontline. 1995. *Searching for Satan:* videotape shown on October 24. PBS.

Ganaway, G. K. 1989. Historical versus narrative truth: Clarifying the role of exogenous trauma in the etiology of MPD and its variants. *Dissociation* 2: 205–220.

———. 1995. Hypnosis, childhood trauma, and dissociative identity disorder: Toward an integrative theory. *International Journal of Clinical and Experimental Hypnosis* 43: 127–144.

Gold, S. N., D. Hughes, and L. Hohnecker. 1994. Degrees of repression of sexual abuse memories. *American Psychologist* 49: 441–442.

Greaves, G. B. 1980. Multiple personality 165 years after Mary Reynolds *Journal of Nervous and Mental Disease* 168: 577–595.

Harter, S., P. Alexander, and R. A. Neimeyer. 1988. Long-term effects of incestuous child abuse in college women: Social adjustment, social cognition, and family characteristics. *Journal of Consulting and Clinical Psychology* 56: 5–8.

Hendrickson, K. M., T. McCarty, and J. M. Goodwin. 1990. Animal alters: Case reports. *Dissociation 3:* 218–221.

Hussey, D. L., and M. Singer, 1993. Psychological distress, problem behaviors, and family functioning of sexually-abused adolescent inpatients. *Journal of the American Academy of Child and Adolescent Psychiatry* 32: 954–961.

Jones, D. P. H., and J. M. McGraw. 1987. Reliable and fictitious accounts of sexual abuse to children. *Journal of Interpersonal Violence* 2: 27–45.

Kluft, R. P. 1983. Hypnotherapeutic crisis intervention in multiple personality. *American Journal of Clinical Hypnosis* 26: 73–83.

———. 1984a. Treatment of multiple personality disorder: A study of 33 cases. *Psychiatric Clinics of North America* 7: 9–29.

——— 1984b. An introduction to multiple personality disorder. *Psychiatric Annals* 14: 19–24.

———. 1984c. Aspects of the treatment of multiple personality disorder. *Psychiatric Annals* 14: 51–55.

———. 1985a. *Childhood Antecedents of Multiple Personality.* Washington, D.C.: American Psychiatric Press.

———. 1985b. Making the diagnosis of multiple personality disorder. *Directions in Psychiatry* 5: 1–11.

———. 1987. An update on multiple personality disorder. *Hospital and Community Psychiatry* 38: 363–373.

———. 1988. The phenomenology and treatment of extremely complex multiple personality disorder. *Dissociation* 1: 47–58.

———. 1989. Iatrogenic creation of new alter personalities. *Dissociation,* 2: 83–91.

———. 1991a. *Multiple personality disorder.* In *American Psychiatric Press Review of Psychiatry.* Washington, D.C.: American Psychiatric Press, 161–188, v. 10.

———. 1991b. Clinical presentations of multiple personality disorder. *Psychiatric Clinics of North America* 14: 741–756.

———. 1993. The initial stages of psychotherapy in the treatment of multiple personality disorder patients. *Dissociation* 6: 145–161.

———. 1995. Current controversies surrounding dissociative identity disorder. In *Dissociative Identity Disorder. Theoretical and Treatment Controversies,* edited by L. Cohen, J. Berzoff, and M. Elin Northvale, N.J.: Jason Aronson, pp. 347–377.

Krystal, H. 1991. Integration and self-healing in poss-traumatic states: A ten year retrospective. *American Image* 48: 93–118.

Levitt, E. E., and C. M. Pinnell. 1995. Some additional light on the childhood sexual abuse-psychopathology axis. *International Journal of Clinical and Experimental Hypnosis* 43: 145–162.

Lewis, D. O., and J. S. Bard. 1991. Multiple personality and forensic issues. *Psychiatric Clinics of North America* 14: 741–756.

Lindsay, D. S., and J. D. Read. 1994. Psychotherapy and memories of childhood sexual abuse: A cognitive perspective. *Applied Cognitive Psychology* 8: 281–338.

Lowenstein, R. J. 1991. An office mental status examination for complex chronic dissociative symptoms and multiple personality disorder. *Psychiatric Clinics of North America* 14: 567–604.

Lynn, S. J., and M. R. Nash. 1994. Truth in memory: Ramifications for psychotherapy and hypnotherapy. *American Journal of Clinical Hypnoses* 36: 194–208.

Malmquist, C. P. 1986. Children who witness parental murder: Post-traumatic aspects. *Journal of the American Academy of Child and Adolescent Psychiatry* 25: 320–325.

Mullen, P. E., J. L. Martin, J. C., Anderson, S. E. Romans, and G. P. Herbison. 1993. Childhood sexual abuse and mental health in adult life. *British Journal of Psychiatry* 163: 721–732.

Nash, M. R., T. L. Hulsey, M. C. Sexton, T. L. Harralson, and W. Lambert. 1993. Long-term sequelae of childhood sexual abuse: Perceived family environment, Psychopathology, and dissociation. *Journal of Consulting and Clinical Psychology* 61: 276–283.

Ofshe, R., and E. Watters. 1994. *Making Monsterss: Fahe Memories, Psychotherapy, and Sexual Hytteria,* New York: Scribners.

Parr, L. E. 1996. *Repressed Memory Claims in the Crime Victims Compensation Program.* Olympia, Wash.: Department of Labor and Industries Public Affairs.

Pendergrast, M. 1995. *Victims of Memory: Incent Accusations and Shattered Lives.* Hinesburg, Vt.: Upper Access.

Peterson, G. 1990. Diagnosis of childhood multiple personality disorder. *Dissociation* 3: 3–9.

Piper, A. 1994a. Multiple personality disorder. *British Journal of Psychiatry* 164: 600–612.

———. 1994b. Treatment for multiple personality disorder: At what cost? *American Journal of Psychotherapy* 48: 392–400.

———. 1994c. Multiple personality disorder and criminal responsibility: Critique of a paper by Elyn Saks. *Journal of Psychiatry and Law* 22: 7–49.

———. 1995. A skeptical look at multiple personality disorder. In *Dissociative Identity Disorder: Theoretical and Treatment Controversies,* edited by L. Cohen, J. Berzoff, and M. Elin. Northvale, NJ.: Jason Aronson, pp. 135–173.

———. 1997. *Hoax and Reality: The Entire World of Multiple Personality Disorder.* Northvale, N.J.: Jason Aronson.

Putnam, F. W. 1989. *Diagnosis and Treatment of Multiple Personality Disorder.* New York: Guilford.

———. 1991. Dissociative Phenomena. In *American Psychiatric Press Review of Psychiatry,* v. 10, edited by A. Tasman and S. M. Goldfinger, Washington, D.C.: American Psychiatric Press: 145–160.

Putnam, F. W., J. J. Guroff, E. K. Silberman, L. Barban, and R. M. Post. 1986. The clinical phenomenology of multiple personality disorder: Review of 100 recent cases. *Journal of Clinical Psychiatry* 47: 285–293.

Putnam, F. W., T. P. Zahn, and R. M. Post. 1990. Differential autonomic nervous system activity in multiple personality disorders. *Psychiatric Research* 31: 251–260.

Pynoos, R. S., and K. Nader. 1989. Children's memory and proximity to violence. *Journal of the American Academy of Child Psychiatry* 28: 236–241.

Rosenthal, B. 1993. *Salem Story: Reading the Witch Trials of 1692.* Cambridge, U.K.: Cambridge University Press.

Ross, C. A. 1989. *Multiple Personality Disorder: Diagnosis, Clinical Features, and Treatment,* New York: Wiley.

————. 1990. Twelve cognitive errors about multiple personality disorder. *American Journal of Psychotherapy* 44: 348–356.

————. 1994. *The Osiris Complex: Case Studies in Multiple Personality Disorder.* Toronto: University of Toronto Press.

————. 1995a. The validity and reliability of dissociative identity disorders. In *Dissociative Identity Disorder: Theoretical and Treatment Controversies*, edited by L. Cohen, J. Berzoff, and M. Elin. Northvale, N. J.: Jason Aronson, pp. 65–84.

————. 1995b. Current treatment of dissociative identity disorder. In *Dissociative Identity Disorder: Theoretical and Treatment Controversies*, edited, by L. Cohen, J. Berzoff, and M. Elin, Northvale, N.J.: Jason Aronson, pp. 413–434.

Ross, C. A., and P. Gahan. 1988. Techniques in the treatment of multiple personality disorder. *American Journal of Psychithrapy* 42: 40–52.

Ross, C. A., G. R. Norton, and G. A. Fraser 1989. Evidence against the latiogenesis of multiple personality disorder. *Dissociation* 2: 61–65.

Ross, C. A. and V. Dua. 1993. Psychiatric health case costs of multiple personality disorder. *American Journal of Psychotherapy* 47: 103–112.

Satbin, T. R. 1995. On the belief that one body may be host to two or more personalities: *International Journal of Clinical and Experimental Hypnosis* 33: 163–183.

Schafer, D. W. 1986. Recognizing multiple personality patients. *American Journal of Psychotherapy* 15: 500–510.

Simpson, M. 1995. Gullible's travels, or the importance of being multiple. In *Dissociative Identity Disorder. Theoretical and Treatment Controversies*, edited by L. Colsen, J. Berzoff, and M. Elin. Northvale, N.J.: Jason Aronson pp. 87–134.

Sofsky, W. 1997. *The Order of Terror: The Concentration Camp.* Princeton: Princeton University Press.

Spanos, N. P. 1996. *Multiple Identities and False Memories: A Socicognitive Perspective.* Washington, D.C.: American Psychological Association.

Spiegel, D. 1995. Psychiatry disabused (l + r). *Nature Medicine* 1: 490–491.

Spiegel, D., and A. W. Schleflin, 1994. Dissociated or fabricated? Psychiatric aspects of repressed memory in criminal and civil cases. *International Journal of Clinical and Experimental Hypnosis* 42: 413–432.

Storm, A., S. B. Refsum, L. Eitinger. 1962. Examination of Norwegian ex-concentration camp prisoners. *Journal of Neurospychiatry* 4: 43–62.

Taylor, W. S., and M. E. Martin. 1944. Multiple personality. *Journal of Abnormal and Social Psychology* 39: 281–300.

Terr, I. C., 1979. Children of Chowchilla. *Psychoanalytic Study of the Child* 34: 547–623.

————. 1983. Chowchilla revisited: The effects of psychic trauma four years after a school-bus kidnapping. *American Journal of Psychiatry* 140: 1,543–1,550.

Tillman, J. G., M. R. Nash, and P. M. Lerner. 1994. Does trauma cause dissociative pathology? In *Dissociation: Clinical and Theoretical Perspectives*, edited by S. J. Lynn and J. W. Rhue, New York: Guilford, pp. 394–414.

Vincent, M., and M. R. Pickering. 1988. Multiple personality disorder in childhood. *Canadian Journal of Psychology* 53: 527–529.

Wagenaar W. A., and J. Groeneweg. 1990. The memory of concentration camp survivors. *Applied Cognitive Psychology* 4: 77–87.

Wakefield, H., and R. Underwager. 1994. *Return of the Furies. An Investigation into Recovered-Memory Therapy.* Chicago: Open Court.

Watkins, J. G., and H. H. Watkins. 1984. Hazards to the therapist in the treatment of multiple personalities. *Psychiatric Clinics of North America* 7: 111–119.

Note

1. In the fourth and latest edition of the American Psychiatric Association's *Diagnostic and Statistical Manual*, the disorder has been renamed. Although the third edition called the condition MPD, the fourth calls it *disractative identity disorder*. The differences between the two disorders' diagnostic criteria are slight and mainly cosmetic: in the newer criteria, terms such as *identities* or *personality* states are employed, rather than the older *personalities*. Also, the newer definition emphasizes the patient's inability to recall important personal information.

   Whether the newer term will become popular has yet to be seen; because *MPD* has the distinct advantage of familiarity, it will be used in this paper.

Review and Contemplate

1. Describe the essential features of MPD (or dissociative identity disorder). According to proponents of MPD, what causes the disorder?
2. How has the prevalence of MPD changed since 1980?
3. Briefly describe the "four serious ailments" or problems with MPD theory.
4. Which of the "four serious ailments" seems to explain how Sybil developed MPD? Explain your answer.

9.2   *Can we Really Tap Our Problems Away?* A Critical Analysis of Thought Field Therapy/
BRANDON GAUDIANO AND JAMES HERBERT

In August of 1998, Dr. Jenny Edwards, a practitioner of thought field therapy, was in Nairobi, Kenya, conducting a training program for human service workers when the U.S. Embassy was bombed. She went to a nearby hospital to help the bombing victims, and she encountered a woman whose shoes had been blown off in the bombing. The woman was just staring into space. After talking with the woman, Dr. Edwards discovered that she was very traumatized, had an extreme level of pain, and could not stop thinking that a bomb might go off any minute in the hospital. Dr. Edwards quickly performed thought field therapy—which involves tapping various parts of the body in specific sequences—on the woman and found that her pain, trauma, and intrusive thoughts disappeared. Dr. Edwards then moved on to another woman who "was just staring into space; her arm was bandaged, and her hand was limp. . . . she was a '10' on both trauma and pain." After performing thought field therapy, the woman's trauma and pain disappeared, and "she was moving her hand all around, color was restored to her face, and she was smiling and laughing."

Today the Web site for Dr. Roger Callahan's thought field therapy explains that it is "a powerful therapy exerted through nature's healing system to balance the body's energy system." It is used primarily for weight loss, stress relief, and treating anxiety and trauma. In this article, Gaudiano and Herbert discuss why thought field therapy should be considered a pseudoscientific practice.

APA Reference

Gaudiano, B. A., & Herbert, J. D. (2000, July/August). Can we really tap our problems away? A critical analysis of thought field therapy. *Skeptical Inquirer, 24,* 29–33, 36.

Thought Field Therapy is marketed as an extraordinarily fast and effective body-tapping treatment for a number of psychological problems. However, it lacks even basic empirical support and exhibits many of the trappings of a pseudoscience.—Brandon A. Gaudiano and James D. Herbert

Brandon A. Gaudiano is a doctoral candidate in clinical psychology at MCP Hahnemann University (Department of Clinical and Health Psychology, Mail Stop 988, 245 N. 15th St., Philadelphia, PA 19102–1192). **James D. Herbert, Ph.D.,** is associate professor of psychology at MCP Hahnemann University and is the director of the Social Anxiety Treatment Program.

It is nothing new to find enterprising entrepreneurs seeking to profit from their novel inventions, which are often claimed to produce miraculous results for their users. The field of mental health is no exception. In fact, there has recently been a surge of putatively revolutionary treatments for various psychological problems that claim to be far superior to standard treatments in both effectiveness and efficiency. Known as "power" or "energy" therapies (Gist, Woodall, and Magenheimer 1999; Herbert et al. in press; Swenson 1999), these treatments are gaining widespread acceptance among mental health practitioners, despite their frankly bizarre theories and techniques, extraordinary claims, and absence of scientific support. One of the most popular of these power therapies, known as Eye Movement Desensitization and Reprocessing (EMDR), involves a therapist waving his or her fingers in front of the patient's eyes while the client imagines various disturbing scenes that are thought to be related to the patient's problems. In fact, EMDR, a "power therapy" that alludes to neural networks instead of energy fields for its theoretical basis, has been described as a prototypical case of pseudoscience within mental health (Herbert et al. in press; Lohr, Montgomery, Lilienfeld, and Tolin 1999; Lilienfeld 1996).

There is another treatment approach on the rise that threatens to overtake EMDR as the premiere power therapy for the twenty-first century: Thought Field Therapy (TFT; Callahan 1985). Roger Callahan, TFT's inventor, claims that he can train therapists to be over 97% effective using his "revolutionary" procedures in treating a variety of common psychological problems including anxiety and depression. Since the history of psychotherapy is replete with treatments that failed to live up to their initial hype, it seems prudent to take a closer look at TFT.

ORIGINS AND METHODS

Callahan (1997) states that he accidentally discovered TFT while treating a client named Mary, who had a severe fear of water. Inspired by an acupuncture class he was taking at the time, Callahan instructed Mary to firmly tap the area under her eye with her fingers, leading to a miraculous and immediate resolution of Mary's phobia. Callahan subsequently developed the comprehensive set of techniques and theory that is now known as TFT. The therapy is based on the idea that invisible energy fields called "thought fields" exist within the body (Callahan and Callahan 1997). Environmental traumas and inherited predispositions are theorized to cause blockages, or what Callahan terms "perturbations," in the flow of energy in these thought fields. Callahan theorizes that the commonly observed neurochemical, behavioral, and cognitive indicators of disorders such as depression are the result of these perturbations. In other words, the root cause of all psychological problems are blockages in energy fields.

In order to correct these perturbations, clients are directed by the TFT therapist to tap on the body's "energy meridians" in specific sequences, called "algorithms," which vary based on the particular problem being treated (Callahan and Callahan 1997). For example, the client may be instructed to tap at the corner of the eyebrow five times and then continue tapping on other parts of the body in a specific sequence as instructed by the therapist. In addition, the clients are told to roll their eyes, count, and hum a few bars of a song at various points during the treatment. Callahan states that when the thought field is "attuned," that is, when the person is thinking about the distressing event or image, perturbations are able to be located and corrected. The tapping is theorized to add energy to the system, which then re-balances the overall energy flow, thereby eliminating the distress at the source.

THEORETICAL UNDERPINNINGS

The theory behind TFT is a hodgepodge of concepts derived from a variety of sources. Foremost among these is the ancient Chinese philosophy of *chi,* which is thought to be the "life force" that flows throughout the body. Beyerstein and Sampson (1996) argue that *chi* is more accurately conceptualized as a philosophy, not a science, and its existence is not empirically supported. In addition, they note that while acupuncture, a procedure used to correct the flow of *chi,* has been shown to provide some minor analgesic effects, its utility has not been demonstrated for treating illnesses or diseases. TFT also borrows techniques from a procedure known as Applied Kinesiology that is used to test muscles for "weaknesses" caused by certain food or chemical pathogens (Sampson and Beyerstein 1996). Applied Kinesiology is a scientifically discredited procedure. For example, Kenny, Clemens, and Forsythe (1988) found that those using the techniques did no better than chance in determining nutritional status using muscle testing. Finally, TFT even borrows some of its concepts from quantum physics. For instance, the idea of active information, in which small amounts of energy can affect large systems, is used to support the existence of perturbations (Bohm and Hiley 1993). There are obvious problems with the theoretical basis for TFT, not the least of which is the complete lack of scientific evidence for the existence of "thought fields."

TFT, as with other new "energy" therapies, is based on misconceptions or outright distortions of the concept of energy as it is used by scientists (Saravi 1999). In physics, energy is defined simply as the capacity to do work, and energy exchanges are observable and measurable. Energy therapists, in contrast, use the term to describe a kind of universal life force that influences health, but they provide no direct data to document the presence of such a force. Saravi concludes that "New Agers' and psychobabblers' 'energy' has only a remote relationship with its physical, scientific counterpart. For them, it is just a word conveniently invoked to explain phenomena whose very existence is far from certain" (47).

EXTRAORDINARY CLAIMS OF SUCCESS

TFT is marketed primarily through the Internet. To attract potential therapists to take TFT courses and to persuade prospective clients to pay for this therapeutic approach, amazing claims are presented on several TFT-related Web sites. For example, Callahan's primary Web site[1] claims that TFT allows individuals "to eliminate most negative emotions within minutes." In addition, Callahan asserts that TFT's effectiveness increases with higher levels of training. For example, another Web site[2] publicizes that therapists can achieve an 80 percent effectiveness rate from learning to use specific algorithms, a 90–95 percent effectiveness rate from using "Causal Diagnostic" techniques, and an over 97 percent effectiveness rate using a technique mysteriously termed "Voice Technology." Yet another Web site,[3] this one based in the United Kingdom, states that TFT is the only psychotherapy that can "genuinely claim to offer a cure." TFT claims to be able to "cure" people of a variety of psychological problems, including phobias, panic, post-traumatic stress disorder, addictions, sexual problems, pain, depression, anger, general distress, and even other less serious problems such as fingernail biting (Hooke 1998a). One noted TFT therapist even claims to have cured her dog of a fear of heights using the trauma algorithm (Danzig 1998).

Despite these miraculous assertions, no controlled studies have been published in peer-reviewed scientific journals to provide evidence for TFT's claims. Instead, testimonials and uncontrolled case studies are offered to support these astonishing declarations of success (Callahan 1995). The vast majority of these claims are made via Internet postings (Lohr, Montgomery, et al. 1999). Such anecdotes, however, do not constitute probative data on the question of TFT's efficacy. Callahan often claims that his public demonstrations of TFT on television shows such as *The Leeza Gibbons Show* (aired October 12, 1996) provide dramatic proof of success, thereby circumventing the need for empirical research. However, such vivid but uncontrolled presentations are not evidential, given the extraordinary demand characteristics (i.e., the implicit pressure engendered by the situation for clients to behave in accordance with their beliefs about what is expected of them) inherent in such settings, not to mention the lack of objective, standardized assessments of improvement in symptoms (Hooke 1998b). Given that Callahan claims to have been using his techniques for over twenty years, it is curious why no controlled studies have been conducted. It should be quite easy to demonstrate the effects of a treatment with a 97 percent effectiveness rate using accepted methods of clinical science.

THE LIMITED RESEARCH FINDINGS

TFT has recently attracted the attention of two Florida State University researchers. In considering their work, it is important to note that none of their findings have been published in peer-reviewed journals; instead they report their results in one of the researcher's self-published Internet "journal." Carbonell and Figley (1999) tested four controversial treatments for trauma, including TFT. Thirty-nine individuals who reported distress from having experienced a traumatic event were given one of the four treatments for up to one week. Overall, Carbonell and Figley reported that participants demonstrated some improvement in self-rated distress and on questionnaire measures from pre-treatment to six-month follow-up. This study is so seriously flawed, however, that the results are completely uninterpretable. The most critical flaw is the absence of any control for the passage of time. In the absence of a no-treatment or a placebo control group, there is no way to know if any observed improvement was a function of factors such as the natural remission of symptoms over time, statistical regression to the mean (i.e., the tendency for extreme scores on a measure to be less extreme upon retest), or placebo effects. This concern is heightened by the absence of measures taken immediately following treatment, as the only outcome measures were reported six months following treatment. Also, subjects were not diagnosed with post-traumatic stress disorder using standard diagnostic criteria, and it is not clear how much subjects were impaired by their traumatic experiences. Moreover, daily diaries and recordings of distress revealed that subjects appeared to have difficulty distinguishing distress associated with the normal ups and downs of life from distress associated with their trauma. For example, a participant who had suffered childhood abuse reported high distress, but upon query disclosed that this distress was due to her car getting a flat tire rather than her trauma, raising questions about the reliability of these subjective distress ratings (Huber 1997).

Furthermore, the authors did not report subjecting their data to statistical analysis, instead relying on their visual inspection of the data for interpretation. Interestingly, even these data do not support the large effect sizes claimed by TFT supporters. On the contrary, mean scores on the self-report questionnaires showed only relatively paltry changes in symptoms, far below the claims of miraculous improvement that Callahan and others have consistently claimed. Thus, Carbonell and Figley's (1999) study, which is the most serious research attempt to date, does not support the effectiveness of TFT. Nevertheless, the results of this study, originally presented at a 1995 symposium, are frequently cited by Callahan and others as providing evidence of TFT's efficacy (Callahan and Callahan 1997). The only other "research" on TFT is either presented in internally circulated publications such as Callahan's newsletter *The Thought Field*, nonscientific magazine reports (e.g., Shamis 1996), or on Web sites (e.g., Carbonell 1996; see Swenson 1999 for a review).

ALTERNATE EXPLANATIONS

Occam's Razor is a principle often applied in science indicating that, all things being equal, the most parsimonious explanation for a phenomenon is the preferred one. Applying this principle to TFT, there is little need for concepts such as energy fields and perturbations to explain any effects that TFT might show. TFT highlights specific tapping sequences as its proposed mechanism of action; however, other components of the treatment protocol may be responsible for any observed benefits. In addition to the absence of controls for spontaneous remission, no research has ruled out factors that are common—to greater or lesser degrees—in all psychotherapies. These include placebo effects resulting from the mere expectation for improvement, demand characteristics, therapist enthusiasm and support, therapist-client alliance, and effort justification (i.e., the tendency to report positive changes in order to justify the effort exerted; Lohr, Lilienfeld, Tolin, and Herbert 1999). Thus, despite the absence of empirical evidence to support TFT's claims of tremendous effectiveness, it would not be surprising to find that the procedure sometimes produces benefits for some individuals owing to these common mechanisms shared by all forms of psychotherapy. Serious psychotherapy innovators go to great lengths to conduct studies to demonstrate that the hypothesized active ingredients of their procedures outperform these so-called "nonspecific" effects. No such effort has been made by the promoters of TFT.

Callahan, however, dismisses the possibility that TFT could be explained by such mechanisms. He asserts that "clinical evidence" has ruled out the possibility of nonspecific or placebo effects accounting for TFT's results, but fails to support this claim (Callahan and Callahan 1997). He frequently states that placebo effects cannot be operative in TFT because some clients express skepticism that the tapping will work (Hooke 1998a). This argument demonstrates a misunderstanding of the placebo concept, which does not necessarily require the individual to fully believe in the practitioner's explanation for why a procedure works (Bootzin 1985; Dodes 1997). Callahan (1999) also reports case studies in which he claims to have observed a "re-balancing" of the autonomic nervous system after treatment with TFT, and that this somehow refutes the placebo explanation. In fact, it is well accepted that the autonomic nervous system, including phenomena such as pulse, blood pressure, and electrocardiogram changes, can be influenced by various psychological events, including placebos (Ross and Buckalew 1985).

In addition to nonspecific and placebo effects, TFT appears to incorporate procedures from existing, well-established therapies. TFT therapists instruct clients to focus repeatedly on distressing thoughts and images during the tapping sequences. Such repeated exposure to distressing cognitions is a well-known behavior therapy technique called imagery exposure (Foa and Meadows 1997). Furthermore, TFT therapists utilize cognitive coping statements throughout treatment (e.g., "I accept and forgive them for what they did"), which represent another established cognitive therapy technique. In short, any effects that TFT might show can be readily explained by known mechanisms, without invoking unfounded concepts such as "perturbations" and "thought fields" (Hooke 1998a).

TFT AND EFT

Since the emergence of TFT, several therapists have recently developed offshoot therapies based on treating the body's energy fields. The most successful of these TFT derivatives was developed by Gary Craig. Craig (1997), who has a degree in engineering and formerly studied under Callahan, created what he calls Emotional Freedom Techniques (EFT). EFT is very similar to TFT, except that it employs one simplified and ubiquitous tapping procedure instead of applying different algorithms to treat different problems. On his Web site[4], Craig asserts that Callahan's reliance on differing algorithms is unnecessary because he has witnessed TFT therapists tap in the wrong order or apply the wrong algorithm to the particular problem and still obtain improvements. Craig's anecdotal evidence appears to contradict Callahan's anecdotal evidence. Furthermore, Craig extends his tapping therapy far beyond the realm of mental health, reporting testimonials from individuals who claim to have successfully used EFT to treat everything from autism to warts and various other medical problems with positive results. In the latest developments, Craig has reported on the positive effects of "surrogate tapping," in which therapists tap on themselves to treat the problems of others.

A scientifically minded investigator would have then taken Craig's observations a step further and tested a completely "placebo" algorithm which did not tap on any supposed energy meridians to see if it produced similar results. However, Craig reports that he has never carried out his simple experiment nor does he know of anyone who has (Craig, personal communication, January 14, 2000). Furthermore, Craig speculates that a placebo algorithm may be impossible because tapping anywhere on the body will affect the body's energy meridians. This position conveniently renders Craig's theory unfalsifiable and therefore outside the realm of science.

PSEUDOSCIENCE IN PSYCHOTHERAPY

Lilienfeld (1998) argues that the proliferation of pseudoscience in psychotherapy is threatening the public welfare and damaging the reputation of psychology. Lohr, Montgomery et al. (1999) assert that the contemporary commercial promotion of treatments for the sequelae of trauma, such as EMDR and TFT, are commonly characterized by a host of pseudoscientific practices. In general, pseudoscience can be identified as consisting of "claims presented so that they appear scientific even though they lack supporting evidence and plausibility" (Shermer 1997, 33). For example, TFT incorporates scientific-sounding terminology by speaking of "bioenergies" and taking concepts from quantum physics out of context in an attempt to gain credibility. No empirical evidence is provided for the existence of central concepts such thought fields or perturbations, which are instead inferred through ad hoc, circular reasoning. For example, Callahan and Callahan (1997) state that perturbations are ultimately demonstrated through their effects, meaning that a perturbation in the thought field must have existed because after treatment the person no longer experiences distress.

The hallmark of a science is falsifiability (Popper 1965). A scientific proposition must specify, a priori, predictions that can be refuted, at least in principle. Callahan has not provided a framework by which his theory could be brought under scientific investigation. As is characteristic of pseudoscience, only confirming evidence of TFT is sought out and presented by advocates (Lohr, Montgomery, et al. 1999). Neither Callahan nor other proponents, including Carbonell and Figley (1999), have subjected TFT to controlled evaluation using accepted scientific methods and published results in peer-reviewed journals.

The objective of a pseudoscience is often persuasion and promotion, in lieu of responsible investigation of claims (Bunge 1967). Web sites advertise courses and multilevel training in TFT techniques for thousands of dollars. The highest level of training in TFT is called Voice Technology (VT), which supposedly allows the therapist to diagnosis perturbations and treat clients entirely over the telephone by analyzing their voices. The effectiveness of VT is said to approach 100 percent (Callahan 1998). Callahan sells this technique for $100,000, and trainees must sign nondisclosure contracts that forbid them from discussing or revealing any aspects of the technique. Recently, the Arizona Board of Psychologist Examiners put a psychologist on probation for refusing to provide specific information about VT to back up his assertion of its high degree of effectiveness (Foxhall 1999; Lilienfeld and Lohr 2000). Interestingly, on his Web site[5] Gary Craig, who was trained in the method, stresses that the putative "secret" behind VT is readily available "in the public domain and can be learned at a weekend workshop for a few hundred dollars." The mystery surrounding VT only has the effect of obfuscating independent examination and investigation.

Finally, pseudosciences explain away or reinterpret failures as actually providing confirmatory evidence (Lakatos 1978). Callahan proposes the existence of a phenomenon termed "psychological reversal" to explain instances in which TFT fails to work. Psychological reversal is claimed to result in self-sabotaging attitudes and behaviors and is manifested in the reversed flow of energy that blocks the effects of the treatment (Callahan 1998). The prescribed treatment for such a condition involves reciting more cognitive coping statements (e.g., "I accept myself, even though I have this problem") that may alleviate distress independent of tapping. In addition, "energy toxins" are claimed to be substances that negatively affect the thought field, even if the person is not physically allergic to these supposed pathogens. These substances are proposed to cause a previously eliminated symptom to return (Joslin 1999). Using "muscle testing" procedures and VT, the offending pathogen can allegedly be identified, then removed until the treatment works again. Both psychological reversal and energy toxins are prime examples of post hoc reasoning and attempts to ignore disconfirming evidence by creating uncorroborated explanations of TFT failures.

CONCLUSION AND IMPLICATIONS

Despite extraordinary claims to the contrary, TFT is not supported by scientific evidence. The theoretical basis of TFT is grounded in unsupported and discredited concepts including the Chinese philosophy of *chi* and Applied Kinesiology. Many of the practices of TFT proponents are much more consistent with pseudoscience than science. Controlled studies evaluating the efficacy of TFT will be required for the treatment to be taken seriously by the scientific community.

TFT is only now beginning to garner negative press, and critiques are starting to appear in the popular literature. For example, Swenson (1999) recently reviewed the extraordinary claims for TFT made by Callahan and others, and noted the absence of controlled research to support these claims. Recently in the SKEPTICAL INQUIRER, Lilienfeld and Lohr (2000) reported on the American Psychological Association's decision in late 1999 to prohibit its sponsors of continuing education programs for psychologists from offering credits for training in TFT, as well as the sanctioning of an Arizona psychologist for using TFT and Voice Technology within the practice of psychology.

Nevertheless, thousands of therapists from various professional disciplines continue to pay for TFT training courses. Much of TFT's marketing success can be attributed to the prevalence of pro-TFT Web sites that promote strong claims of its effectiveness. TFT therapists, some of whom have no traditional training in psychology or psychotherapy, appear to be satisfied with TFT's vivid anecdotal stories of success, and are not aware of or not bothered by the overwhelming lack of empirical support for the procedure. Englebretsen (1995), among others, points to the alarming rise of postmodernist attitudes currently permeating the mental health field, exemplified by the willingness of some clinicians to value compelling anecdotal stories over controlled empirical data. This postmodernist mindset promotes the notion that all truth is relative and contextual; science is only one of many modes of thinking, each of which is equally valid. Such attitudes render the mental health field fertile breeding ground for pseudoscientific therapies such as TFT and its derivatives. Healthy skepticism competes head-to-head with extraordinary claims and, as is often the case, many mental health clinicians choose to ignore the facts in favor of miraculous possibilities.

Notes

1. http://www.tftrx.com
2. http://www.thoughtfield.com
3. http://homepages.enterprise.net/ig/
4. http://www.emofree.com/scien-i.htm
5. http://www.emofree.com/about.htm

References

Beyerstein, B. L., and W. Sampson. 1996. Traditional medicine and pseudoscience in China: A report of the second CSICOP delegation (part I) SKEPTICAL INQUIRER 20(4): 18–27.

Bohm, D. and B. Hiley. 1993. *The Undivided Universe: An Ontological Interpretation of Quantum Theory*. New York: Routledge.

Bootzin, R.R. 1985. The role of expectancy in behavior change. In *Placebo: Theory, Research, and Mechanisms*, edited by L. White, B. Tursky, and G. Schwartz. New York: Guilford, pp. 196–210.

Bunge, M. 1967. *Scientific Research*. New York, Springer.

Callahan, R. 1985. *Five Minute Phobia Cure*. Wilmington, DE: Enterprise.

———. 1995. Thought Field Therapy (TFT) algorithm for trauma: A reproducible experiment in psychotherapy. Paper delivered at the Annual Meeting of the American Psychological Association.

————. 1997. Thought Field Therapy: The case of Mary. Electronic Journal of Traumatology 3(1). Available: http://www.fsu.edu/-trauma/T039.html.

————. 1998. Response to Hooke's review of TFT. Electronic Journal of Traumatology 3(2). Available: http://www.fsu.edu/-trauma/v3i2art4.html.

————. 1999. TFT and Heart Rate Variability. *The Thought Field Newsletter* 5(2).

Callahan, R.J., and J. Callahan. 1997. Thought Field Therapy: Aiding the bereavement process. In *Death and Trauma: The Traumatology of Grieving*, edited by C. Figley, B. Bride, and N. Mazza. Washington, D.C.: Taylor & Francis, pp. 249–267.

Carbonell, J.L. 1996. An experimental study of TFT and acrophobia. Available: http://www.tftrx.com/ref_articles/6heights.html.

Carbonell, J.L., and C. Figley. 1999. A systematic clinical demonstration of promising PTSD treatment approaches. Electronic Journal of Traumatology 5(1). Available: http://www.fsu.edu/trauma/promising.html.

Craig, G. 1997. Six days at the VA: Using Emotional Freedom Therapy-Produced by Gary Craig. Videocassette.

Danzig, V. 1998. CT-TFT changes Karma. *The Thought Field Newsletter* 4(2).

Dodes, J.E. 1997. The mysterious placebo. Skeptical Inquirer 21(1): 44–46

Englebrersen, G. 1995. The filling of scholarly vacuums. Skeptical Inquirer 21(4): 57–59.

Foa, E.B., and E.A. Meadows. 1997. Psychosocial treatments for posttraumatic stress disorder: A critical review. *Annual Review of Psychology* 48: 449–480.

Fohall, K. 1999. Arizona board sanctions psychologist for use of Thought Field Therapy. *American Psychological Association Monitor* 30(8): 8.

Gist, R., S.J. Woodall, and L.K. Magenheimer. 1999. "And then you do the Hokey-Pokey and you turn yourself around . . ." In *Response to Disaster: Psychosocial, Community, and Ecological Approaches*, edited by R. Gist and B. Lubin. Philadelphia: Brunner/Mazel, 269–290.

Herbert, J.D., S.O. Lilienfeld, J.M. Lohr, R.W. Montgomery, W.T. O'Donohue, G.M. Rosen, and D.F. Tolin. in press. Science and pseudoscience in the development of Eye Movement Desensitization and Reprocessing: Implications for clinical psychology. *Clinical Psychology Review.*

Hooke, W. 1998a. A review of Thought Field Therapy. Electronic Journal of Traumatology 3(2). Available: http://www.fsu.edu/-trauma/v3i2art3.html.

Hooke, W. 1998b. Wayne Hooke's reply to Roger Callahan. Electronic Journal of Traumatology 3(2). Available:http://www.fsu.edu/-trauma/v3i2art5.html.

Huber, C.H. 1997. PTSD: A search for "active ingredients." *Family Journal* 5(2): 144–148.

Joslin, G. 1999. A follow-up toxin treatment for a previously treated multiple personality patient. *The Thought Field Newsletter* 5(2).

Kenny J.J., R. Clemens, K.D. Forsythe. 1988. Applied Kinesiology unreliable for assessing nurrient status. *Journal of the American Dietetic Association* 88(6): 698–704.

Lakatos, I. 1978. Introduction: Science and pseudoscience. In *The Methodology of Scientific Research Programs: Philosophical Papers*, edited by J. Worrall and G. Currie. Cambridge, England: cambridge University Press.

Leonoff, G. 1995. The successful treatment of phobias and anxiety by telephone and radio: A replication of Callahan's 1987 study. *The Thought Field Newsletter* 1(2).

Lilienfeld, S.O. 1996. EMDR treatment: Less than meets the eys? Skeptical Inquirer 20(1): 25–31.

————. 1998. Pseudoscience in contemporary clinical psychology: What it is and what we can do about it. *The Clinical Psychologist* 51(4): 3–9.

Lilienfeld, S.O. Lilienfeld, D.F. Tolin, and J.D. Herbert. 1999. Eye Movement Desensitization and Reprocessing: An analysis of specific versus nonspecific treatment factors. *Journal of Anxiety Disorders* 13(1–2): 185–207.

Lohr, J.M., R.W. Montgomery, S.O. Lilienfeld, and D.F. Tolin. 1999. Pseudoscience and the commercial promotion of trauma treatments. In *Response to Disaster: Psychosocial, Community, and Ecological Approaches* edited by R. Gist and R. Lubin. Philadelphia: Brunner/Mazel, pp. 291–326.

Popper, K. 1965. *The Logic of Scientific Disovery.* New York: Harper.

Ross, S., and L.W. Buckalew. 1985. Placebo agentry: Assesment of drug and placebo effects. In *Placebo: Theory, Research, and Mechanism,* ed. L. White, B. Tursky, and G. Schwartz. New York: Guilford, 67–82.

Sampson, W., and B.L. Beyerstein. 1996. Traditional medicine and pseudoscience in China: A report of the second CSICOP delegation (part 2). Skeptical Inquirer 20(5): 27–36.

Saravi, F.D. 1999. Energy and the brain: Facts and fantasies. In *Mind Myths: Exploring Popular Assumptions about the Mind and Brain,* edited by S. Della Sala. New York: Wiley & Sons, 43–58.

Shamis, B. 1996. Thought Field Therapy. *Visions Magazine* 8 (Nov): 8–9, 32–33.

Shermer, M. 1997. *Why People Believe Weird Things: Pseudoscience, Superstition, and other Confusions of Our Time.* New York: W.H. Freeman.

Swenson, D.X. 1999. Thought Field Therapy: Still searching for the quick fix. *Skeptic* 7(4): 60–65.

Review and Contemplate

1. What is thought field therapy (TFT)? Briefly explain how TFT is claimed to work and what disorders it is used to treat.

2. How is the concept of "energy" in energy therapies different from the concept of energy in physics?

3. Briefly describe the evidence for the effectiveness of TFT, including the study by Carbonell and Figley (1999). What are some limitations of this evidence?

4. TFT proponents claim that specific tapping sequences that affect thought fields produce any positive improvements TFT patients might exhibit. What are some alternative explanations for such improvements?

5. Which of the six characteristics of pseudoscience, discussed in Chapter 1, seem most closely related to TFT?

9.3   *Perception of Conventional Sensory Cues as an Alternative to the Postulated "Human Energy Field" of Therapeutic Touch/*

REBECCA LONG, PAUL BERNHARDT, AND WILLIAM EVANS

In an article published in *Orthopaedic Nursing,* Dr. Sherron Herdtner (2000) told the story of a man named Paul who fell 20 feet from a ladder and shattered his elbow. Paul had surgery to repair his elbow, but he was in pain and was not able to work or help his wife with their newborn baby. Although Paul wasn't sure whether Therapeutic Touch (TT) would help him, he gave it a try. Dr. Herdtner explained that after his first TT session Paul "experienced greater movement in his wrist and arm and did not feel pain on movement . . . . That night he did yard work, helped his wife with the dishes, and took his children out for ice cream." She concluded, "Paul's experience with therapeutic touch helped him physically, emotionally, and spiritually."

Imagine that a nurse could promote the healing of wounds, relieve pain, reduce stress and anxiety, alleviate symptoms of Alzheimer's disease or AIDS, and treat cancer by simply sweeping her hands slightly above a patient's body. These are some of the miraculous claims made about TT, a practice that has become popular among nurses. TT practitioners believe that they can use their hands to detect problems with a person's "human energy field" (HEF), which they claim to realign or balance to promote healing.

In 1996, a 9-year-old girl named Emily Rosa designed an experiment to test TT practitioners for her fourth-grade science fair project. The practice of TT rests on practitioners' claims that they can detect the HEF and manipulate it, so Emily decided to find out if they could actually detect such "energy" by simply asking them to detect whether her hand was above their right or left hand (which they could not see). She discovered that the TT practitioners who participated in her study failed the test. Emily's research was published in the prestigious *Journal of the American Medical Association* in 1998. Other signs also point to the improbability of TT practitioners' claimed ability to detect the HEF. More than $1 million has been offered by the James Randi Educational Foundation to anyone who can demonstrate an ability to detect a human energy field under controlled conditions, but so far not one person has demonstrated such an ability. In fact, only one of the tens of thousands of American TT practitioners has agreed to be tested (in 1996 when the prize was $742,000), and she failed.

Despite the failure of TT practitioners to demonstrate an ability to detect the HEF, the practice of TT continues and practitioners still claim they can detect and manipulate the HEF with their hands. TT practitioners often report feeling warm or tingling sensations through their hands, which they believe is evidence that they are detecting the HEF. Are TT practitioners merely imagining these sensations, can they actually detect the HEF, or might there be another explanation? Long, Bernhardt, and Evans explore these questions in the following article. While reading this article, consider how it illustrates the difference between pseudoscientific and scientific approaches (see Chapter 1) to gaining knowledge about whether people can actually detect a "human energy field."

APA Reference

Long, R., Bernhardt, P., & Evans, W. (1999). Perception of conventional sensory cues as an alternative to the postulated "human energy field" of therapeutic touch. *Scientific Review of Alternative Medicine, 3,* 53–61.

ABSTRACT   Background—Therapeutic Touch (TT) proponents claim that humans emit a metaphysical "Human Energy Field" (HEF) that TT practitioners can sense and manipulate via their hands even without direct physical contact between practitioner and patient. As evidence, proponents note that TT practitioners commonly report various tactile sensations as they sweep their hands just above their patients' bodies. An experiment was conducted to determine if, and under what conditions, human subjects could detect via their hands the presence of a nearby human body that they could not see or touch. **Methods**—Twenty-six subjects were tested to determine whether or not they could detect the presence of an investigator's unseen hand that was steadied just above one of the subject's hands. Subjects were tested at various distances between hands of subject and investigator and in trials in which various sensory cues were systematically added and removed. **Results**—Subjects performed well at 3 inches between hands, offering correct guesses regarding the location of the investigator's unseen hand more than 70 percent of the time. Subjects' abilities remained strong at 4 inches between hands but diminished at 6 inches between hands. Subjects performed no better than chance would predict when body heat was shielded. Subjects who were purposefully miscued by investigators performed significantly worse than subjects who were not miscued. **Conclusions**—Participants in Therapeutic Touch sessions may be mistaking conventional sensory cues such as radiated body heat for evidence of a metaphysical phenomenon.

Rebecca Long, a nuclear engineer, is President of the Georgia Skeptics and the Georgia Council Against Health Fraud, Inc. Paul Bernhardt is a Ph.D. candidate in the Department of Educational Psychology at the University of Utah and a member of the Rocky Mountain Skeptics. William Evans, Ph.D., is Associate Professor in the Department of Communication at Georgia State University and a member of Georgia Skeptics and the Georgia Council Against Health Fraud, Inc.

P ractitioners of the alternative nursing practice known as Therapeutic Touch (TT) claim that they use their hands to sense and manipulate a metaphysical "Human Energy Field" (HEF) that emanates from their patients. TT practitioners claim that manipulation of the HEF can facilitate physical and psychological healing. Moreover, TT practitioners contend that they can sense and manipulate the HEF without touching their patients. Indeed, TT is typically conducted with the practitioner's hand a few inches from the patient's body.

Despite this lack of direct physical contact between TT practitioners and patients, both practitioners and patients often report feeling sensations of warmth and tingling during TT sessions. TT proponents claim that these sensations stem from perception of a special type of energy that cannot be accounted for by conventional science. These sensations are often adduced by TT proponents as evidence of the efficacy of TT and the validity of its metaphysical constructs. For their part, some skeptics suggest that TT practitioners and patients may be merely imagining the sensations of warmth and tingling that are so often reported in TT testimonials. In this view, TT participants are victims of the power of suggestion and their desire to find corroborating evidence for their metaphysical worldview.

This article reports the results of an experiment designed to address these issues. More specifically, our experiment assessed (1) whether or not human subjects can detect, without using sight or touch, the presence of a human hand when the hand is placed just above the subjects' hands, and (2) the role that conventional sensory cues such as radiated body heat may play in subjects' abilities to detect the presence of a human hand that they cannot see or touch. If subjects are unable to detect the presence of a nearby human hand when all significant sources of conventional sensory cuing have been eliminated, this would constitute evidence against the claim that humans can sense (or manipulate) a metaphysical HEF.

BACKGROUND

TT is today among the most commonly utilized alternative health therapies. TT has enjoyed particular success in the nursing community, where it has been embraced by several mainstream nursing organizations and utilized by nurses in many hospitals in North America and around the world.[1,2] TT enjoys frequent and largely favorable coverage in nursing journals and periodicals.[3]

The success of TT in terms of the number and prestige of its practitioners has drawn the attention of researchers who have attempted to empirically assess the effectiveness of TT, especially in treating stress, pain, and a variety of mood disturbances. Rosa et al. report that 83 research studies that focus at least in part on TT had been published through 1997.[4] As Meehan notes, this research has been inconclusive.[5] The relatively few studies to report positive results for TT have been beset with methodological problems. These problems include the lack of control groups, failure to use blind protocols, the use of only a small number of subjects, and an over-reliance on subjects' self-reports regarding the effectiveness of TT interventions. Meehan suggests that much of the TT research conducted to date has done too little to control for possible placebo effects.[6] In a recent meta-analysis, Peters reports that the many methodological limitations of the existing TT research make it difficult or even impossible to say anything conclusively about the effectiveness of TT.[7] Earlier literature reviews, such as a report commissioned by the University of Colorado Health Sciences Center,[8] have also noted similar methodological problems and limitations.

Perhaps in frustration with the great methodological difficulties (and high financial costs) associated with TT research that examines health outcomes, some researchers have moved from attempts to assess TT's therapeutic effectiveness to investigations of the TT practitioner; avowed ability to sense and manipulate the HEF.

Within the theoretical constructs of TT the HEF is a metaphysical manifestation of the flow of vitalistic life energy through the body. Persons who are ill are said to have deficits, blockages, or imbalances in their vital energy flow. TT practitioners claim they can use their hands to detect disturbances in the HEF, correct blockages by "unruffling" the field, and correct imbalances by channeling healing energy.[9] Again, the HEF is said to be sensed and manipulated without physical contact between practitioner and patient. Practitioners typically move their hands over the patient's body at a distance of 2 to 4 inches,[10] although slightly greater distances are cited by some proponents.

Dolores Krieger, one of the cofounders of TT, notes that TT practitioners almost always describe their perceptions of disturbances in the HEF in one of the following six ways: "heat," "cold," "tingling," "pressure," "electric shocks," or "pulsations." The phrase most often used is "temperature differential."[11] TT proponents do not believe that these sensations are responses to ordinary sensory stimuli. Instead, they maintain that TT participants perceive an energy force that scientific instruments cannot detect and that conventional scientific theories cannot explain. For example, Krieger writes that the terms used by TT practitioners to describe the sensations—indicate a common experience for which we do not as yet have an adequately expressive language."[12] According to Krieger, the sensation of heat "is not the sense of heat one feels when a hot stove is touched or a finger is passed through a flame." Rather, Krieger explains, "Therapeutic Touch deals with a very different aspect or conception of temperature differential than the one we currently understand in biophysics."[13]

To determine whether or not TT practitioners can sense an HEF, Rosa et al.[14] designed an experiment in which TT practitioners were asked to detect the presence of an unseen human hand that hovered above one of the practitioner's hands. Subjects and investigators were seated at a table divided by an opaque partition. Subjects placed their hands through holes in the partition. Twenty-one TT practitioners were tested. In 280 trials, these TT practitioners could correctly identify the hand over which an investigators unseen hand hovered only 44 percent of the time, a rate that is no better than that which would be expected by chance. Ball and Alexander[15] conducted an experiment in which a single blindfolded TT practitioner was asked to detect the presence or absence of a human body that, when present, was positioned (on a massage table) 4 inches from the practitioner's hands. This practitioner was successful in 7 out of 10 trials, a success rate that Ball and Alexander deemed insufficient to warrant concluding that the TT practitioner was able to detect HEFs.

The results reported by Rosa et al.[16] and Ball and Alexander[17] make sense in terms of science. Given what we know about electromagnetic fields and human physiology, it does indeed seem unlikely that HEFs exist and function in the manner that TT proponents believe them to. But science would also suggest that several sensory cues might be readily available to help humans determine when an unseen human body is in very close proximity. For example, radiant body heat might provide a salient sensory cue. Similarly, rustling of clothing or movements of air caused by even the slightest body movements might provide cues that a body is nearby. In this context, it might seem strange to expect that subjects would fail to perform at better-than-chance rates when asked to discern the presence or absence of an unseen but very close human body.

In order to adequately blind a test of whether or not human hands can detect the HEF of a nearby human body, it is necessary to eliminate any conventional sensory stimuli that could either (1) cue the subjects as to the presence of the body, or (2) miscue the subjects. The experimental apparatuses and procedures themselves may introduce confounding sensory cues. Investigator speech and behavior during experimental protocols may introduce them. Cuing often creeps into experimental protocols in the most surprising and sometimes seemingly inexplicable ways.[18] The seeming inevitability of subtle but nonetheless confounding cues such as rustling shirt sleeves and investigator tone of voice have led experimenters in sciences such as medicine, psychology, and sociology to adopt double-blind conditions whenever possible.

We discovered during pilot testing that subjects could seemingly be cued (and miscued) by investigators' body movements. For example, subtle sounds associated with the rustling of clothing or paperwork by the investigator were sufficient to cue some test subjects. In addition, some subjects could detect a very slight flow of air onto the hand if the investigator's hand was placed over it too rapidly or with a downward movement. Curiously, this slight breeze cued some subjects and miscued others who interpreted the sensation as coolness and therefore selected the wrong (i.e., warmer) hand. Similar subtle but significant cuing and miscuing effects were observed with some test subjects when an air conditioning system was running and the placement of the investigator's hand over the subject's hand blocked the flow of air.

Subjects were seemingly cued (and miscued) when the investigator rested an elbow on the experimental table, which turned out to be a common investigator tendency, especially when testing time was lengthy. Subjects displayed an ability to sense the vibrations or slight change in table alignment caused by this practice, and tended to preferentially guess the hand in front of the investigator's elbow. This resulted in both cuing and miscuing because the investigator's elbow was not always in front of the subject's hand over which the investigator's hand was placed.

Subjects were also seemingly cued and miscued when investigators gave a verbal signal (e.g., "okay," "ready") to indicate that their hand was in position. Investigators tended to look at the hand they were holding in place and subjects could seemingly detect the direction from which the audible signal was issued. We found evidence to suggest that investigators could miscue subjects by issuing an audible signal while looking at the wrong hand, as investigators did on occasion.

Rosa et al.[19] asked subjects to place their palms in an upward position, a procedure we adopted (even if the palms-upward position is not typically used in TT practice). However, we discovered that subject who were asked to keep their palms turned upward often complained of discomfort and reported "tingling," "pulsating," and "electrical" sensations in their hands. Subjects understandably expressed concerns that these sensations might interfere with their ability to detect sensations relevant to the experiment.

In short, there is a danger that experimental designs of this type may introduce sensory cues that threaten the validity of the study. Investigators may intentionally or (more likely) unintentionally introduce confounding sensory cues, and subjects may consciously or unconsciously make use of these cues. Because it is impractical to double-blind such an experiment, it is especially important to rigorously blind the subjects with respect to the investigator. In designing our experiment, we tried to minimize these threats to validity. We also designed our experiment in part of assess the potential role of investigator cuing and miscuing in experimental assessments of TT practitioners.

METHODS

Twenty-six subjects were tested under blinded conditions to determine if they could detect the presence of an investigator's hand that they could neither see nor touch. Subjects were recruited from among acquaintances of Rebecca Long (the first author of this report). There were 13 male and 13 female subjects, ranging in age from 10 to 81 years. (A twenty-seventh subject was tested but his data was excluded from our analysis because he did not follow the protocol as instructed.) None of the subjects were TT practitioners, and none had ever been treated by a TT practitioner. None had more than a superficial familiarity with TT practices and claims.

The experiment utilized an apparatus very similar to that used by Rosa et al.[20] Subjects were seated at a table and placed their hands through holes in a large opaque screen. Subjects rested their hands on the table, palms upward. The position of the screen and the placement of holes in the screen were informed by the pilot testing discussed above and designed to minimize physical sensations caused by the awkward hand position. To further minimize potentially confounding hand sensations, care was taken to minimize testing time. Subject comfort was verified before and after each set of experimental trials.

A towel was placed over subjects' forearms to prevent them from seeing through the holes in the screen. All reflective surfaces visible to subjects while in place for testing were covered to preclude the possibility that subjects would receive visual cues via reflected light. No air conditioning or heating system was run while testing was in progress. Room temperature was 64°F during all trials on one of the two days on which subjects were tested; it was 74°F during the second day of trials.

Two investigators participated in the experiment. Investigator 1 was Rebecca Steinbach, an 11-year-old female. Investigator 2 was Rebecca Long, a female adult. Another person stood nearby to monitor subject and investigator adherence to experimental protocols and to verify the accuracy of the recorded data. Data were recorded by another participant, who was shielded from view of the subjects and who operated the LED device utilized in the experiment (described below).

Investigators 1 and 2 each tested a different group of 13 subjects, one week apart. Each subject underwent 10 trials in each of the experimental conditions under which he or she was tested. In each trial, an investigator steadied her hand in place over one of the subject's hands. Whether the investigator placed her hand over the subject's left or right hand was determined in advance using a random number table (odd-numbered integers were associated with the subject's right hand and even-numbered integers with the subject's left hand). To avoid creating air movement, the investigator's hand was moved into position over the subject's hand slowly and with a horizontal movement, parallel to the table. Investigators wore clothing that did not rustle. Investigators were not permitted to lean on the table.

To eliminate the possibility of verbal cuing, a red "ready" light was used to signal the subject that the investigator's hand was in place. An LED device was also used to signal the investigator regarding whether to place her hand over the subject's left or right hand. The lights used to signal investigators were enclosed in a box that prevented light leakage that might have cued subjects. Pilot testing confirmed that the LEDs generated no light or heat that was detectable by subjects.

Trials were conducted at each of three different distances between the hands of subjects and investigators: 3, 4, and 6 inches. Hand distances were measured from the center of the subject's palm to the palm of the investigator's hand. A series of colored lines were placed on the investigator's side of the partition to help investigators judge where to place their hands.

In addition to varying the distance between hands, we used two additional experimental manipulations to assess the possible role of conventional sensory cues in subjects' guesses. In one set of trials, the possible role of body heat as a sensory cue was evaluated by interposing a thin piece of glass (from a picture frame) between the hands of subject and investigator. The glass was placed 3 inches above the palm of the subject. The investigator's hand was placed on the surface of the glass.

In a separate set of trials, conducted at a distance of 6 inches between hands, deliberate investigator miscuing was introduced. Instead of using the "ready" light to signal subjects, the investigator spoke the word "okay" while looking in the direction of the incorrect hand. At the same time, the investigator gently rested her elbow on the table in front of the incorrect hand.

Although subjects were given no time limits, all made their guesses rather rapidly, and in all cases the sets of 10 trials were completed in less than one minute per set. After testing, each subject was invited to comment about the trials. These comments were recorded, as were all unsolicited comments made by the subjects during the trials.

RESULTS

Subjects were assessed in six different experimental conditions. Subjects could be expected to make correct guesses 50 percent of the time based on chance alone. Results are reported in Table 9.1, where reported significance levels are based on two-tailed t-tests against the null hypothesis of chance accuracy (5 out of 10 correct guesses).

Subjects performed significantly better than chance would predict at distances of 3 and 4 inches between hands. At 3 inches, subjects tested by Investigator 1 made correct guesses an average of 7.62 times out of 10, with a standard deviation of 1.76 (t = 5.36; df = 12; p = 12; p = .0002). Subjects tested by Investigator 2 offered correct guesses an average of 7.69 times out of 10, with a standard deviation of 1.32 (t = 7.38; df = 12; p = .0001). Fifteen of the 26 subjects offered at least 8 out of 10 correct guesses. Three subjects scored a perfect 10 out of 10. No subject guessed incorrectly more than 5 times out of 10. One subject who scored 10 out of 10 was retested and proved able to offer correct guesses 30 out of 30 times (these retesting data are not included in our statistical analyses).

TABLE 9.1

Mean Correct Subject Guesses, by Experimental Condition

Experimental Condition[a]	Mean Correct Guesses Out of 10	Standard Deviation	t(df)	Significance[b]
3 inches[c]	7.62	1.76	5.36(12)	*p* = .0002
3 inches[d]	7.69	1.32	7.38(12)	*p* = .0001
4 inches[c]	6.54	1.90	2.92(12)	*p* = .0128
6 inches[c]	5.77	1.42	1.95(12)	*p* = .0751
3 inches, with glass barrier[e]	5.20	1.21	0.64(14)	*p* = .5314
6 inches, with negative cuing[f]	3.90	1.66	−2.09(9)	*p* = .0660

[a]Inches refers to distance between hands of subjects and investigator
[b]Based on two-tailed t-test against the null hypothesis of chance accuracy
[c]Investigator 1; 13 subjects
[d]Investigator 2; 13 subjects
[e]Investigators 1 and 2; 15 subjects
[f]Investigator 1; 10 subjects

At 4 inches between hands, subjects made correct guesses an average of 6.54 times out of 10, with a standard deviation of 1.90 (t = 6.54; df = 12; p = .0128). At this distance, 5 of 13 subjects achieved scores of at least 8 out of 10, and one subject scored 10 out of 10.

At 6 inches between hands, subjects did not perform better than chance would predict, although the results could be interpreted as marginally significant. At this distance, subjects made correct guesses an average of 5.77 times out of 10, with a standard deviation of 1.42 (t = 5.77; df = 12; p = .0751). One subject who scored 8 out of 10 correct guesses at this distance was retested and achieved a total score of 27 out of 30 correct guesses (this was the same subject who scored 30 out of 30 at 3 inches between hands).

When a glass barrier was interposed between the hands of subjects and investigator, subjects performed neither better nor worse than chance would predict, making correct guesses an average of 5.20 times out of 10, with a standard deviation of 1.21 (t = 0.64; df = 14; p = .5314). Fifteen subjects were tested at 3 inches between hands both with and without the glass barrier. A repeated measures analysis of variance reveals that these subjects were significantly more likely to offer correct guesses when the glass barrier was not in place (F = 26.62; df = 1,14; p <.0001).

When deliberate miscuing was introduced subjects performed neither better or worse than chance would predict, although the results could be interpreted as marginally significant. Subjects made correct guesses only 3.90 times out of ten, with a standard deviation of 1.66 (t = −2.09; df = 9; p = .0660). Again, this condition involved a distance of 6 inches between hands. A repeated analysis of variance measure indicates that there was a significant difference in subjects' abilities to offer correct guesses at 6 inches between the uncued and miscued conditions (F = 9.875; df = 1.9; p = .012). That is, subjects made significantly more successful guesses when deliberate miscuing was absent. . . .

In describing the sensations they felt during the trials, most subjects referred to sensations of heat. In fact, "body heat" was the phrase most commonly used by subjects—both during and after the trials—to refer to their perceptions. Many subjects reported that they made their guesses on the basis of a heat differential they perceived between their hands when the "ready" light signaled them. Two subjects reported "tingling" feelings in their palms, but most subjects identified the sensations as heat.

DISCUSSION

The simplest explanation for our findings is that subjects were using radiant body heat to discern the presence of the investigator's unseen hand. The experimental protocol was designed to eliminate all salient sources of sensory cuing other than body heat. Subjects' abilities to discern the investigators' hand were high when the distance between the hands of subject and investigator was small. Subjects' abilities diminished as the distance was increased. Regression analysis confirmed that subjects' abilities were indeed a function of distance between hands, as would be expected if real energy such as radiant body heat was involved. Subjects performed no better than chance would predict when a piece of glass was interposed between the hands of subject and investigator, a finding that also suggests that body heat was the most salient cue. Finally, in their self-reported accounts of their sensations subjects routinely used the term "body heat" and spoke of discerning heat differentials between their hands when an investigator's hand was in place over one of the subject's hands. Both the trial data and subjects' self-reports are consistent with the explanation that body heat provided a highly salient and effective cue.

Our subjects manifested substantial variation in individual ability to detect the investigator's unseen and untouched hand. Moreover, subjects' scores in the test trials were consistent with their self-reported ability to detect body heat. A number of subjects volunteered that they felt body heat at 3 inches but not at 4 inches. Others stated that they felt body heat at 3 and 4 inches but did not feel body heat at 6 inches. Some reported that they could distinctly feel body heat at 6 inches. No subjects reported that they could feel body heat at 6 inches but not at 4 inches. And in all cases, subjects guessed more accurately in trials in which they professed to feel body heat than in trials in which they offered no such professions.

Our findings regarding investigator cuing suggest that such cuing can influence and even potentially contaminate experimental results. We tested the effects of only two sources of cuing: voice signaling and leaning on the table. Future research would be needed to evaluate the effects of other potential sources of investigator cuing or miscuing.

The results reported here would seem consistent with Ball and Alexander's[21] report in which a single blindfolded subject made correct guesses regarding the presence or absence of a human body in 7 out of 10 attempts. In attempts where a body was present, Ball and Alexander maintained a distance of 4 inches between the body and the subject's hands. The subjects in our experiment made successful guesses an average of 6.54 times out of 10 at a distance of 4 inches between the hands of subject and investigator.

The results reported here are inconsistent with results reported by Rosa et al.,[22] who report that the TT practitioners they tested could not perform at better-than-chance rates when asked to discern the presence of an investigator's hand placed 8 to 10 centimeters (approximately 3 to 4 inches) above one of the subject's hands. Additional research would seem to be required to address these discrepancies and to provide conclusive evidence regarding the abilities of humans to detect nearby but unseen and untouched human bodies.

CONCLUSION

The results of our experiment provide evidence against the claim that humans can perceive (or manipulate) a metaphysical HEF which emanates from the human body. When salient sources of conventional sensory cuing were eliminated, our experimental subjects could not discern the presence of an unseen human hand.

Our experiment has demonstrated that individuals who are untrained in TT can readily discern the presence of an unseen human hand at the distance at which TT is typically practiced (i.e., 3 to 4 inches) when body heat is not shielded. Although TT practitioners may detect an "energy field" of sorts, the most parsimonious explanation is that the "heatlike" sensations perceived by TT practitioners are due to radiant body heat. In addition, our pilot testing suggested conventional explanations for the "tingling," "pulsating," and "electrical" sensations sometimes reported in the TT literature. We found that such sensations may be caused by the hand position used in TT (palms and fingers flattened and stretched), and by the continual back-and-forth movements of the hands. Certainly, our findings suggest that one can readily explain the sensations reported by TT practitioners without recourse to metaphysical theories that invoke unconventional energy fields.

TT proponents may dispute our conclusions because our experimental subjects were not trained TT practitioners. TT proponents may also object that we have not conclusively ruled out the possibility that our subjects were sensing the HEF rather than body heat. Indeed, we do not claim to have definitively falsified the claim that TT practitioners can sense an HEF. However, within the theoretical system of TT, the universal vital energy force of which the HEF is a manifestation is said to transcend matter and to be everywhere. Although glass effectively shields the transmission of radiant body heat, a universal vital energy such as is postulated in TT would presumably penetrate glass just as it penetrates other matter. If the HEF exists and functions as TT proponents claim then trained TT practitioners should be able to sense the HEF when conventional sensory cues such as body heat have been eliminated. The burden of proof now rests with the practitioners of TT, who must demonstrate an ability to detect the HEF that is distinct from an ability to detect radiant body heat.

Our findings suggest that skeptics should no longer discount the sensory experiences reported in TT testimonials as being merely the products of wishful thinking or autosuggestion. Rather, the implications of these perceived sensations should be accounted for in future TT research. During TT sessions, participants who have embraced TT may fully expect to sense the HEF and its manipulation. The conventional sensory cues that our research suggests are readily available might then provide TT participants which sensations they interpret as "proof" of the efficacy of TT. This process could likely facilitate a placebo effect among TT patients.

The authors thank Jon Cadle, Dale Heatherington, Beth Holley, Sandefur, Rebecca Steinbach, and Harry Taylor for their assistance in conducting the experiment. Additional information about the experiment reported here can be found online at http://www.hcrc.org/t-touch/.

References

1. Meehan, T.C. Therapeutic Touch as a nursing intervention. *J. Adv. Nurs.* 1998; 28: 117–125.
2. Rosa, L., Rosa, E., Sarner, L., Barrett, S. A close look at Therapeutic Touch. *JAMA.* 1998; 279:1005–1010.

3. Meehan., Therapeutic Touch as a nursing intervention.
4. Rosa, Rosa, Sarner, and Barrett. A Close Look at Therapeutic Touch.
5. Meehan, Therapeutic Touch as a nursing intervention.
6. *Ibid.*
7. Peters, R.M., The effectiveness of Therapeutic Touch: a meta-analytic review. *Nurs. Sci. Q.* 1999; 2:52–61.
8. Claman, H.N., Freeman, R., Quissel, D., et al. *Report of the Chancellor's Committee on Therapeutic Touch.* Denver, CO: University of Colorado Health Sciences Center; 1994.
9. Krieger, D. *The Therapeutic Touch: How to Use Your Hands to Help or Heal.* New York, NY: Prentice Hall; 1992.
10. Rosa, Rosa, Sarner, and Barrett. A Close Look at Therapeutic Touch.
11. Krieger, *The Therapeutic Touch.*
12. *Ibid.*
13. Krieger, D. *Accepting Your Power to Heal: The Personal Practice of Therapeutic Touch.* Santa Fe, NM: Bear; 1993.
14. Rosa, Rosa, Sarner, and Barrett. A Close Look at Therapeutic Touch.
15. Ball, T.S., Alexander, D.K., Catching up with eighteenth century science in the evaluation of Therapeutic Touch. *Skeptical Inquirer.* 1998; 22.(4):31–34.
16. Rosa, Rosa, Sarner, and Barrett. A Close Look at Therapeutic Touch.
17. Ball and Alexander. Catching up with eighteenth century science in the evaluation of Therapeutic Touch.
18. Rosenthal, R. *Experimenter Effects in Behavioral Research.* New York, NY: Irvington; 1976.
19. Rosa, Rosa, Sarner, and Barrett. A Close Look at Therapeutic Touch.
20. *Ibid.*
21. Ball and Alexander, Catching up with eighteenth century science in the evaluation of Therapeutic Touch.
22. Rosa, Rosa, Sarner, and Barrett. A Close Look at Therapeutic Touch.

Review and Contemplate

1. What is Therapeutic Touch (TT)? How is it performed, and for what types of ailments is it used?
2. Long et al. briefly discussed the results of previous studies designed to empirically assess the effectiveness of TT (i.e., in treating stress, pain, mood disturbances, etc.). What overall conclusion do they reach about whether TT is an effective therapy?
3. Briefly describe the procedure used by Long et al. to test their 26 participants and state the results.
4. Explain why Long et al. concluded that their results "provide evidence against the claim that humans can perceive (or manipulate) a metaphysical HEF." Which aspect of their results provides evidence for this conclusion?
5. Which of the six characteristics of pseudoscience, discussed in Chapter 1, seem most closely related to TT?

10.1 — *Mass Delusions and Hysterias:* Highlights from the Past Millennium/ ROBERT BARTHOLOMEW AND ERICH GOODE

On the evening of September 1, 1944, Mrs. Kearney went to bed with her 3-year-old daughter in Mattoon, Illinois. That evening she detected a sweet smell in her bedroom. As the smell grew stronger, she began to feel paralysis in her legs and lower body. She suspected someone had gassed her, but a neighbor and the police could find no evidence of the mysterious gasser. Later, her husband reported seeing a prowler—dressed in dark clothes and a tight-fitting cap—near the bedroom window. Mr. Kearney chased the prowler, but the person escaped. The police were called a second time, but a thorough search of the neighborhood turned up nothing. On September 2, the local newspaper reported the story with the headline, "'Anesthetic Prowler' on Loose." It wasn't long before Mattoon police received dozens of calls about similar gas attacks involving nearly 30 victims.

Today scientists believe that the "Mad Gasser of Mattoon" never existed. Social psychologists who study social influence have known for a long time that people sometimes rely on others to help them interpret events and determine what actions to take, especially when they are unsure of themselves or when the situation is ambiguous. Thus, Mattoon residents who smelled an unusual odor or experienced ambiguous physical symptoms (e.g., nausea or a burning feeling in the throat) might have followed the lead of earlier "victims" by interpreting the event as gasser-related and calling the police, even though no gasser existed.

In this article, Bartholomew and Goode (2000) discuss this event and other historical examples of mass delusions and hysterias, which illustrate the power of social forces to create widespread beliefs in paranormal or nonexistent phenomena. Thus, this article is a good illustration of how normal social processes can lead to paranormal beliefs, a point raised in Chapter 1.

APA Reference

Bartholomew, R. E., & Goode, E. (2000, May/June). Mass delusions and hysterias: High-lights from the past millennium. *Skeptical Inquirer, 24,* 20–28.

Over the past millennium, mass delusions and hysterical outbreaks have taken many forms. Sociologists Robert Bartholomew and Erich Goode survey some of the more colorful cases.

The turn of the second millennium has brought about, in the Western world at least, an outpouring of concern about cosmic matters. A major portion of this concern has taken a delusional, even hysterical turn, specifically in imagining an end-of-the-world scenario. "The end of the world is near," predicts Karl de Nostredame, supposedly the "last living descendent" of Nostradamus; "White House knows doomsday date!" he claims (Wolfe 1999, 8). Against this backdrop, it seems an appropriate time to survey a sample of social delusions and group hysterias from the past millennium. Given the enormous volume of literature, we will limit our list to the more colorful episodes.

The study of collective delusions most commonly falls within the domain of sociologists working in the sub-field of collective behavior, and psychologists specializing in social psychology. Collective delusions are typified as the spontaneous, rapid spread of false or exaggerated beliefs within a population at large, temporarily affecting a particular region, culture, or country. Mass hysteria is most commonly studied by psychiatrists and physicians. Episodes typically affect small, tightly knit groups in enclosed settings such as schools, factories, convents and orphanages (Calmeil 1845; Hirsch 1883; Sirois 1974).

Mass hysteria is characterized by the rapid spread of conversion disorder, a condition involving the appearance of bodily complaints for which there is no organic basis. In such episodes, psychological distress is converted or channeled into physical symptoms. There are two common types: anxiety hysteria and motor hysteria. The former is of shorter duration, usually lasting a day, and is triggered by the sudden perception of a threatening agent, most commonly a strange odor. Symptoms typically include headache, dizziness, nausea, breathlessness, and general weakness. Motor hysteria is prevalent in intolerable social situations such as strict school and religious settings where discipline is excessive. Symptoms include trance-like states, melodramatic acts of rebellion known as histrionics, and what physicians term "psychomotor agitation" (whereby pent-up anxiety built up over a long period results in disruptions to the nerves or neurons that send messages to the muscles, triggering temporary bouts of twitching, spasms, and shaking). Motor hysteria appears gradually over time and usually takes weeks or months to subside (Wessely 1987; Bartholomew and Sirois 1996). The term mass hysteria is often used inappropriately to describe collective delusions, as the overwhelming majority of participants are not exhibiting hysteria, except in extremely rare cases. In short, all mass hysterias are collective delusions as they involve false or exaggerated beliefs, but only rarely do collective delusions involve mass hysteria as to do so, they must report illness symptoms.

Many factors contribute to the formation and spread of collective delusions and hysterical illness: the mass media; rumors; extraordinary anxiety or excitement; cultural beliefs and stereotypes; the social and political context; and reinforcing actions by authorities such as politicians, or institutions of social control such as the police or military. Episodes are also distinguishable by the redefinition of mundane objects, events, and circumstances and reflect a rapidly spreading folk belief which contributes to an emerging definition of the situation. . . .

MILAN, ITALY, 1630

British journalist Charles Mackay (1852, 261–265) described a poisoning scare that terrorized Milan, Italy, in 1630, coinciding with pestilence, plague, and a prediction that the Devil would poison the city's water supply. On one April morning people awoke, and became fearful upon finding "that all the doors in the principal streets of the city were marked with a curious daub, or spot." Soon there was alarm that the sign of the awaited poisoning was at hand, and the belief spread that corn and fruit had also been poisoned. Many people were executed. One elderly man was spotted wiping a stool before sitting on it, when he was accused of smearing poison on the seat. He was seized by an angry mob of women and pulled by the hair to a judge, but died on the way. In another incident, a pharmacist and barber named Mora was found with several preparations containing unknown potions and accused of being in cahoots with the Devil to poison the city. Protesting his innocence, he eventually confessed after prolonged torture on the rack, admitting to cooperating with the Devil and foreigners to poisoning the city and anointing the doors. Under duress he named several accomplices who were eventually arrested and tortured. They were all pronounced guilty and executed. Mackay states that "The number of persons who confessed that they were employed by the Devil to distribute poison is almost incredible," noting that "day after day persons came voluntarily forward to accuse themselves" (264).

LILLE, FRANCE, 1639

Mackay (1852, 539–540) reports that in 1639 at an all-girls' school in Lille, France, fifty pupils were convinced by their overzealous teacher that they were under Satanic influence. Antoinette Bourgignon had the children believing that "little black angels" were flying about their heads, and that the Devil's imps were everywhere. Soon, each of the students confessed to witchcraft, flying on broomsticks and even eating baby flesh. The students came close to being burned at the stake but were spared when blame shifted to the headmistress, who escaped at the last minute. The episode occurred near the end of the Continental European witch mania of 1400 to 1650, when at least 200,000 people were executed following allegations of witchcraft.

SALEM, MASSACHUSETTS, 1691–1693

In 1692, Salem Village (now Danvers, Massachusetts) was the scene of a moral panic that spread throughout the region and involved witchcraft accusations which led to trials, torture, imprisonment, and executions. Others died in jail or during torture. At least twenty residents lost their lives. Social paranoia was such that two dogs were even accused and executed! All convictions were based on ambiguous evidence. The witch mania began in December 1691, when eight girls living in the vicinity of Salem exhibited strange behaviors including disordered speech, convulsive movements, and bizarre conduct. Explanations for the "fits" range from outright fakery to hysteria to ergot poisoning of the food supply. By February 1692, the affected girls had accused two elderly women and a servant from Barbados named Tibula of being witches, and they were arrested. Soon hundreds of residents were accused of witchcraft, and trials were held. In May 1693, the episode ended when Governor Phips ordered that all suspects be released (Nevins 1916; Caporael 1976; Karlsen 1989).

LONDON, ENGLAND, 1761

On February 8, 1761, a minor earthquake struck London, damaging several chimneys. When another tremor occurred on the following month on the exact day as the first (March 8), the coincidence became the subject of widespread discussion. According to Mackay (1852), a lifeguard named Bell then predicted that London would be destroyed in a third quake on April 5, "As the awful day approached, the excitement became intense, and great numbers of credulous people resorted to all the villages within a circuit of twenty miles, awaiting the doom of London" (259). People paid exorbitant fees to temporarily board with households in such places as Highgate, Hampstead, Islington, Blackheath, and Harrow. The poor stayed in London until two or three days before the predicted event before leaving to camp in fields in the countryside. When the designated time arrived, nothing happened.

LEEDS, ENGLAND, 1806

In 1806, a panic spread through Leeds and the surrounding communities that the end of the world was at hand. The "panic terror" began when a hen from a nearby village was said to begin laying eggs inscribed with the message, "Christ is coming." Large numbers flocked to the site to examine the eggs and see the "miracle" firsthand. Many were convinced that the end was near and suddenly became devoutly religious. Mackay (1852, 261) states that excitement then quickly turned to disappointment when a man "caught the poor hen in the act of laying one of her miraculous eggs" and soon determined "that the egg had been inscribed with some corrosive ink, and cruelly forced up again into the bird's body. . . ."

BRITISH SOUTH AFRICA, 1914

In the war scare setting of British South Africa in 1914, local newspapers erroneously reported that hostile monoplanes from adjacent German South West Africa were making reconnaissance flights as a prelude to an imminent attack. The episode coincided with the start of World War I. Despite the technological impossibility of such missions (the maneuvers reported by witnesses were beyond those of airplanes of the period and their capability of staying aloft for long periods), thousands of residents misperceived ambiguous, nocturnal aerial stimuli (stars and planets) as representing enemy monoplanes (Bartholomew 1989).

ISLAND OF BANDA, INDONESIA, 1937

During March 1937, the first Indonesian Prime Minister, Soetan Sjahrir, was living on the Moluccan island of Banda, where he described a head-hunting rumor-panic which swept through his village. The episode coincided with rumors that a tjoelik (someone who engages in head-hunting for the government) was operating in the area and searching for a head to be placed near a local jetty that was being rebuilt. According to tradition, government construction projects will soon crumble without such an offering. Sjahrir (1949) said that "people have been living in fear" and were "talking and whispering about it everywhere" (162), and after 7 p.m. the streets were nearly deserted. There were many reports of strange noises and sightings. Sjahrir stated: "Every morning there are new stories, generally about footsteps or voices, or a house that was bombarded with stones, or an attack on somebody by a tjoelik with a noose, or a cowboy lasso. Naturally, the person who was attacked got away from the tjoelik in a nick of time!" (164). Sjahrir described the scare as an example of "mass psychosis."

USA, 1938

On Halloween Eve 1938, a live fictional radio drama produced by Orson Welles was broadcast across much of the United States by the CBS Mercury Theatre. It depicted an invasion by Martians who had landed in Grovers Mill, New Jersey, and soon began attacking with heat rays and poison gas. Princeton University psychologist Hadley Cantril (1940) concluded that an estimated 1.2 million listeners became excited, frightened, or disturbed. However, subsequent reviews of Cantril's findings by sociologists David Miller (1985), William Sims Bainbridge

(1987), and others, concluded that there was scant evidence of substantial or widespread panic. For instance, Miller found little evidence of mobilization, an essential ingredient in a panic. Hence, it was a collective delusion and not a true panic. Cantril also exaggerated the extent of the mobilization, attributing much of the typical activity at the time to the "panic." In short, many listeners may have expressed concern but did not do anything in response, like try to flee, grab a gun for protection, or barricade themselves inside a house. Either way one looks at this episode, it qualifies as a collective delusion. If, as Cantril originally asserted, many listeners were frightened and panicked, it is a mass delusion. Conversely, if we are to accept the more recent and likely assessments that the "panic" was primarily a media creation inadvertently fueled by Cantril's flawed study, then erroneous depictions of a mass panic that have been recounted in numerous books and articles for over six decades constitute an equally remarkable social delusion.

MAD GASSER OF MATTOON, 1944

During the first two weeks of September 1944, residents of Mattoon, Illinois, were thrust into the world media spotlight after a series of imaginary gas attacks by a "phantom anesthetist." On Friday night, September 1, Mattoon police received a phone call that a woman and her daughter had been left nauseated and dizzy after being sprayed with a sweet-smelling gas by a mysterious figure lurking near their bedroom window. The woman also said she experienced slight, temporary difficulty in walking. Despite the ambiguous circumstances and lack of evidence, the following evening the incident was afforded sensational coverage in the Mattoon Daily Journal-Gazette ("Anesthetic Prowler on Loose"). After seeing the story, two other Mattoon families recounted for police similar "gas attacks" in their homes just prior to the incident.

Before the reports ceased (after September 12), police logged over two dozen separate calls involving at least twenty-nine victims, most of whom were females. University of Illinois researcher Donald Johnson (1945) investigated the episode, concluding that it was a case of mass hysteria. Their transient symptoms included nausea, vomiting, dry mouth, palpitations, difficulty walking, and in one instance, a burning sensation in the mouth. Given the influential role of the Mattoon news media, it may be that victims were redefining mundane symptoms such as a panic attack, chemical smell, one's leg "falling asleep," and the consequences of anxiety such as nausea, insomnia, shortness of breath, shakiness, dry mouth, dizziness, etc. as gasser-related.

"MIRACLE" IN PUERTO RICO, 1953

At 11 a.m. on May 25, 1953, an estimated 150,000 people converged on a well at Rincorn, Puerto Rico, to await the appearance of the Virgin Mary as predicted by seven local children. Over the next six hours, a team of sociologists led by Melvin Tumin and Arnold Feldman (1955) mingled in the crowd conducting interviews. During this period, some people reported seeing colored rings encircling the sun, and a silhouette of the Virgin in the clouds, while others experienced healings, and a general sense of well-being. Others neither saw nor experienced anything extraordinary. A media frenzy preceded the event, and a local mayor enthusiastically organized the visionaries to lead throngs of pilgrims in mass prayers and processions. Tumin and Feldman found that the majority of pilgrims believed in the authenticity of the children's claim, and were seeking cures for conditions that physicians had deemed incurable. Various ambiguous objects in the immediate surroundings (clouds, trees, etc.) mirrored the hopeful and expectant religious state of mind of many participants.

SEATTLE WINDSHIELD PITTING EPIDEMIC, 1954

On March 23, 1954, reports appeared in Seattle newspapers of damaged automobile windshields in a city eighty miles to the north. While initially suspecting vandals, the number of cases spread, causing growing concern. In time, reports of damaged windshields moved closer to Seattle. According to a study by Nahum Medalia of the Georgia Institute of Technology and Otto Larsen of the University of Washington (1958), by nightfall on April 14, the mysterious pits first reached the city, and by the end of the next day, weary police had answered 242 phone calls from concerned residents, reporting tiny pit marks on over 3,000 vehicles. In some cases, whole parking lots were reportedly affected. The reports quickly declined and ceased. On April 16 police logged forty-six pitting claims, and ten the next day, after which no more reports were received.

The most common damage report involved claims that tiny pit marks grew into dime-sized bubbles embedded within the glass, leading to a folk theory that sandflea eggs had somehow been deposited in the glass and later hatched. The sudden presence of the "pits" created widespread anxiety as they were typically attributed to atomic fallout from hydrogen bomb tests that had been recently conducted in the Pacific and received saturation media publicity. At the height of the incident on the night of April 15, the Seattle mayor even sought emergency assistance from President Dwight Eisenhower.

In the wake of rumors of radioactive fallout and a few initial cases amplified in the media, residents began looking at, instead of through, their windshields. An analysis of the mysterious black, sooty grains that dotted many windshields was carried out at the Environmental Research Laboratory at the University of Washington. The material was identified as cenospheres—tiny particles produced by the incomplete combustion of bituminous coal. The particles had been a common feature of everyday life in Seattle, and could not pit or penetrate windshields.

Medalia and Larsen noted that because the pitting reports coincided with the H-Bomb tests, media publicity seems to have reduced tension about the possible consequences of the bomb tests—"something was bound to happen to us as a result of the H-bomb tests—windshields became pitted—it's happened—now that threat is over" (186). Secondly, the very act of phoning police and appeals by the mayor to the governor and even President of the United States "served to give people the sense that they were 'doing something' about the danger that threatened" (186).

PHANTOM SLASHER OF TAIWAN, 1956

For a two-week period in 1956, residents in the vicinity of Taipei, Taiwan, lived in fear that they would be the next victim of a crazed villain who was prowling the city and slashing people at random with a razor or similar type weapon. At least twenty-one slashing victims were reported during this period, mostly women and children of low income and education. Norman Jacobs was teaching in Taipei at the time, and conducted a survey of local press coverage of the slasher. Jacobs concluded that those affected had erroneously attributed mundane slash marks to a dastardly slasher (Jacobs 1965).

Rumors amplified by sensational press coverage treating the slasher's existence as real served to foment the scare by altering the public's outlook to include the reality of a daring slasher. Police eventually concluded that the various "slashings" had resulted from inadvertent, everyday contact in public places, that ordinarily would have gone relatively unnoticed. For instance, one man told police in detail how he had been slashed by a man carrying mysterious black bag. When a doctor determined that the wound was made by a blunt object and not a razor, the "victim" admitted that he could not recall exactly what had happened, but assumed that he had been slashed "because of all the talk going around." In another case, it was not the supposed victim but physicians who were responsible for creating an incident. An elderly man with a wrist laceration sought medical treatment but the attending doctor grew suspicious and contacted police when the man casually noted that a stranger had coincidentally touched him at about the same time when he first noticed the bleeding. A more thorough examination led to the conclusion that the "slash" was an old injury that had been re-opened after inadvertent scratching.

On May 12 police announced the results of their investigation: they concluded that the episode was entirely psychological in origin. Of the twenty-one slashing claims examined by their office, they determined that "five were innocent false reports, seven were self-inflicted cuts, eight were due to cuts other than razors, and one was a complete fantasy" (Jacobs, 1965, 324).

FIRST FLYING SAUCER WAVE, 1947

On June 24, 1947, Kenneth Arnold was piloting his private plane near the Cascade mountains in Washington state when he saw what appeared to be nine glittering objects flying in echelon-like formation near Mount Rainier. He kept the objects in sight for about three minutes before they traveled south over Mount Adams and were lost to view (Arnold 1950; Arnold and Palmer 1952; Gardner 1988; Clark 1998, 139–143).

Worried that he may have observed guided missiles from a foreign power, Arnold eventually flew to Pendleton, Oregon, where he tried reporting what he saw to the FBI office there. But the office was closed, so he went to the offices of The East Oregonian newspaper. After listening to Arnold's story, journalist Bill Bequette produced a report for the Associated Press. It is notable that at this point, Arnold had described the objects as crescent-shaped, referring only to their movement as "like a saucer would if you skipped it across the water" (Gardner 1957, 56; Story 1980, 25; Sachs 1980, 207–208). However, the Associated Press account describing Arnold's "saucers" appeared in over 150 newspapers.

The AP report filed by Bequette was the proto-article from which the term "flying saucer" was created by headline writers on June 25 and 26, 1947 (Strentz 1970). Of key import was Bequette's use of the term "saucer-like" in describing Arnold's sighting. Bequette's use of the word "saucer" provided a motif for the worldwide wave of flying saucer sightings during the summer of 1947, and other waves since. There are a few scattered historical references to disc-shaped objects, but no consistent pattern emerges until 1947, with Arnold's sighting. There have only been a handful of occasions prior to 1947 that a witness has actually used the word "saucer" to describe mysterious aerial objects. Hence, the global 1947 flying saucer wave can be regarded as a media-generated collective delusion unique to the twentieth century. . . .

THE HISPANIC GOATSUCKER, 1975 TO PRESENT

Between February and March 1975, reports circulated in Puerto Rico of a mysterious creature attacking domestic and farm animals, draining their blood and scooping out chunks of their flesh. Residents claimed that they heard loud screeches and/or flapping wings coinciding with the attacks. Academics and police examined the carcasses, blaming everything from humans to snakes to vampire bats. Locals referred to the attacker as "The Vampire of Moca." This incident may have been spurred by the better known "cattle mutilation mystery" (Ellis 1996, 3). In November 1995, similar attacks were reported on the island. Called chupacabras or goatsucker, (named after a crepuscular bird that steals goat's milk), the bizarre being was described as a "bristly, bulge-eyed rat with the hind legs of a kangaroo, capable of escaping after its crimes in high speed sprints" (Preston 1996). It also exuded a sulfur-like stench. Stories described the bodies of animals disemboweled and drained of blood. One member of a Civil Defense team in a small city in the affected area says he spends half his time responding to chupacabras calls. Some people, he reported, have been so distraught "that they have had to be taken to the hospital" (Navarro 1996). Interest in the creature ran so high on May 1996 that a chupacabras Web site received enough hits to be ranked in the top 5 percent of all Web sites (Ellis 1996, 2). By March 1996, goatsucker stories had spread to Hispanic communities in Florida; by May, accounts of chupacabras attacks began to circulate in Mexico and soon after, to the Mexican-American community in Arizona. The chupacabras flap ended abruptly in mid-1996, and almost nothing has been reported on its since. . . .

WEST BANK, JORDAN, 1983

Between March and April 1983, 947 mostly female residents of the Israeli-occupied Jordan West Bank reported various psychogenic symptoms: fainting, headache, abdominal pain, and dizziness (Modan et al., 1983). The episode was precipitated by poison gas rumors and a long-standing Palestinian mistrust of Jews. The medical complaints appeared during a fifteen-day period, amid rumors and intense media publicity that poison gas was being sporadically targeted at Palestinians. The episode began in, and was predominantly confined to, schools in several adjacent villages. In one incident on March 27, sixty-four residents in Jenin were rushed for local medical care after believing that they had been poisoned when thick smoke belched from an apparently faulty exhaust system on a passing car. In all, 879 females were affected. Following negative medical tests, it became evident that no gassings had occurred, the hypothesis was discredited, and the transient symptoms rapidly ceased.

MASS DELUSION BY PROXY IN GEORGIA, 1988

A rarely reported form of what could be described as mass delusion by proxy occurred at a Georgia elementary school near Atlanta in 1988. It involved the re-labelling of mundane symptoms that were instigated and maintained by erroneous beliefs among hypervigilant parents. The episode began during a routine social gathering of parents and students at the school cafeteria in early September. A student's mother commented that, ever since the term began, her child had experienced numerous minor health problems and looked pale. Other mothers at the meeting noted similar signs and symptoms in their children since the beginning of the school term: pallor, dark circles under the eyes, headaches, fatigue, nausea and occasional vomiting. They soon suspected that something in the school building was to blame, a view confirmed on October 11 when the school was evacuated after a minor natural gas leak occurred during routine maintenance. When intermittent minor gas leaks continued over the next month, concerned parents picketed the school and appealed to the local media, which highlighted their fears. After negative environmental and epidemiological studies, Philen et al. (1989) concluded that mothers had almost exclusively redefined common and everpresent childhood illnesses, while the children in question neither sought attention nor were overly concerned with their symptoms, maintaining high attendance levels throughout the term.

KOSOVO, 1990

On March 14, 1990, at least four thousand residents in the Serbian province of Kosovo, in the former Yugoslavia, were struck down by a mystery illness that persisted for some three weeks. According to Dr. Zoran Radovanovic (1995), the head of the community medicine faculty at Kuwait University, the symptoms were psychogenic in nature and prompted by ethnic Albanian mistrust of Serbs. The transient complaints were almost exclusively confined to young adolescent ethnic Albanians, and included headache, dizziness, hyperventilation, weakness, burning sensations, cramps, chest pain, nausea, and dry mouth. The episode began at a high school in Podujevo, and rapidly spread to dozens of schools within the province. An outbreak of respiratory infection within a single class appears to have triggered fears that Serbs may have dispensed poison. Influential factors included rumors, the scrutinization of mundane odors and substances, visits by health authorities that served to legitimate fears, ethnic tension between Serbs and Albanians, and mass communication. The dramatic proliferation of cases across the province on March 22 coincided with the implementation of an emergency disaster plan whereby ethnic Albanians seized control of public health services.

NIGERIAN GENITALIA VANISHING EPIDEMIC OF 1990

During 1990, an episode of "vanishing" genitalia caused widespread fear across Nigeria. Native psychiatrist Sunny Ilechukwu (1992) said that most reports of attacks involved male victims. Accusations were usually triggered by incidental body contact with a stranger in a public place, after which the "victim" would feel strange scrotum sensations and grab their genitals to confirm that they were still there. Then they would confront the person as a crowd would gather, accusing them of being a genital thief, before stripping naked to convince bystanders that their penis was really missing. Many "victims" claimed that the penis had been returned once the alarm had been raised or that, although the penis was now back, "it was shrunken and so probably a 'wrong' one or just the ghost of a penis" (95). The accused was often threatened or beaten until the penis had been "fully restored," and in some instances, the accused was beaten to death. Ilechukwu (1992, 96) described the scene in one city: Men could be seen in the streets of Lagos holding on to their genitalia either openly or discreetly with their hands in their pockets. Women were also seen holding on to their breasts directly or discreetly by crossing the hands across the chest. It was thought that inattention and a weak will facilitated the "taking" of the penis or breasts. Vigilance and anticipatory aggression were thought to be good prophylaxis.

Social and cultural traditions contributed to the outbreak as many Nigerian ethnic groups "ascribe high potency to the external genitalia as ritual and magical objects to promote fecundity or material prosperity to the unscrupulous" (Ilechukwu 1988, 313). The belief in vanishing genitalia was not only plausible but institutionalized; many influential Nigerians expressed outrage when police released suspected genital thieves. A Christian priest even claimed that a Bible passage where Jesus asked "Who touched me?" because the "power had gone out of him," referred to genital stealing (101–102).

CONCLUDING REMARKS

The next one thousands years will yield a new batch of social delusions and hysterical outbreaks that will reflect the hopes and fears of future generations. While it is not possible to know the exact nature of these episodes, we can confidently predict one of the first delusions of this period. For at the start of the second Christian millennium, we should be mindful that the millennial notion is itself a social delusion. The concept does not exist in nature but is a human creation—a product of history and circumstance. It has no significance beyond the meaning that humans attach to it. Yet, students of history know well that the consequences of beliefs can enormously influence the course of history.

References

Arnold, K. 1950. *The Flying Saucer As I Saw It.* Boise, Idaho: Self-published.

Arnold, K., and R. A. Palmer. 1952. *The Coming of the Saucers: A Documentary Report on Sky Objects that Have Mystified the World.* Amherst, Wisconsin: Self-published.

Bainbridge, W. S. 1987. Collective behavior and social movements. Pp. 544–576. In R. Stark (ed.), *Sociology.* Belmont, California: Wadsworth.

Bartholomew, R. E. 1989. The South African monoplane hysteria: An evaluation of the usefulness of Smelser's Theory of Hysterical Beliefs. *Sociological Inquiry 59*(3): 287–300.

Bartholomew, R. E., and F. Sirois. 1996. Epidemic hysteria in schools: An international and historical overview. *Educational Studies 22*(3): 285–311.

Barnes, R. H. 1993. Construction sacrifice, kidnapping and headhunting rumours on flores and elsewhere in Indonesia. *Oceania 64:* 146–158.

Bulgatz, J. 1992. *Ponzi Schemes, Invaders from Mars & More Extraordinary Popular Delusions and the Madness of Crowds.* New York: Harmony Books.

Calmell, L. F. 1845. *De la Folie, Consideree Sous le Point de vue Pathologigue, Philosophique, Historique et Judiciaire* [On the Crowd, Considerations on the Point of Pathology, Philosophy, History and Justice]. Parls: Ballere.

Cantril, H. 1940 [1947]. *The Invasion From Mars: A Study in the Psychology of Panic.* Princeton, New Jersey: Princeton University Press.

Caporael, L. 1976. Ergotism: The Satan loosed in Salem? *Science 192:*21–26.

Clark, J. 1998. *The UFO Encyclopedia: The Phenomenon from the Beginning.* Volume One: A-K (second edition). Omnigraphics, Incorporated: Detroit, Michigan.

Darnton, R. 1984. *The Great Cat Massacre and Other Episodes in French Cultural History.* New York: Basic Books.

Drake, R. A. 1989. Construction sacrifice and kidnapping: Rumor panics in Borneo. *Oceania 59:*269–278.

Ellis, B. 1996. Chupacabras mania spreads. *Foaftale News 39:*2–3.

Forth, G. 1991. Construction sacrifice and head-hunting rumours in central Flores (Eastern Indonesia): A Comparative Note. *Oceania 61:*257–266.

Gardner, M. 1988. *The New Age: Notes of a Fringe Watcher.* Buffalo, New York: Prometheus Books.

Gardner, M. 1957. *Fads and Fallacies in the Name of Science.* New York: Dover.

Griggs, W. N. 1852. *The Celebrated 'Moon Story.'* New York: Bunnell and Price.

Hecker, J. F. C. 1844. *Epidemics of the Middle Ages* (translated from German by B. Babington) London: The Sydenham Society.

Hirsch, A. 1883. Handbook of Geographical and Historical Pathology. New Sydenham Society: London.

Ilechukwu, S. T. C. 1992. Magical penis loss in Nigeria: Report of a recent epidemic of a koro-like syndrome. Transcultural Psychiatric Research Review 29:91–108.

———. Letter from S. T. C. Ilechukwu, M. D. (Lagos, Nigeria) which describes interesting koro-like syndromes in Nigeria. Transcultural Psychiatric Research Review 25:310–314.

Jacobs, N. 1965. The phantom slasher of Taipei: Mass hysteria in a non-western society. Social Problems 12:318–328.

Johnson, D. M. 1945. The "Phantom Anesthetist" of Mattoon: A field study of mass hysteria. Journal of Abnormal and Social Psychology 40:175–186.

Johnston, F. 1980. When Millions Saw Mary. Chulmleigh, England: Augustine Publishing.

Karlsen, C. F. 1989. The Devil in the Shape of a Woman: Witchcraft in Colonial New England. New York: Vintage.

Mackay, C. 1852. Memoirs of Extraordinary Popular Delusions and the Madness of Crowds Volume 2. London: Office of the National Illustrated Library.

Madden, R. R. 1857. Phantasmata or Illusions and Fanaticisms of Protean of Protean Forms Productive of Great Evils. T. C. Newby: London.

Medalia, N. Z., and O. Larsen. 1958. Diffusion and belief in a collective delusion. Sociological Review 23:180–186.

Miller, D. 1985. Introduction to Collective Behavior. Belmont, Calif.: Wadsworth.

Modan, B., M. Tirosh, E. Weissenberg, C. Acker, T., Swartz, C. Coston, A., Donagi, M. Revach, and G. Vettorazzi. 1983. The Arjenyattah epidemic. Lancet ii:1472–1476.

Navarro, M. 1996. A monster on loose? Or is it fantasy? The New York Times, January 26, p. A10.

Nevins, W. S. 1916. Witchcraft in Salem Village. Franklin: New York.

Persinger, M., and J. Derr. 1989. Geophysical variables and behavior: LIV. Zeitoun (Egypt) Apparitions of the Virgin Mary as tectonic strain-induced luminosities. Perceptual and Motor Skills 68:123–128.

Philen, R. M., E. M. Kilbourn, and T. W. McKinley. 1989. Mass sociogenic illness by proxy: Parentally reported in an elementary school. Lancet ii: 1372–1376.

Preston, J. 1996. In the tradition of Bigfoot and Elvis, the Goatsucker. The New York Times, June, 2, p. 2E.

Radovanovic, Z. 1995. On the origin of mass casualty incidents in Kosovo, Yugoslavia, in 1990. European Journal of Epidemiology 11:1–13.

Rockney, R. M., and T. Lemke. 1992. Casualties from a junior high school during the Persian Gulf War: Toxic poisoning or mass hysteria? Journal of Developmental and Behavioral Pediatrics 13:339–342.

Sachs, M. 1980. The UFO Encyclopedia. New York: Perigee.

Sirois, F. 1974. Epidemic hysteria. Acta Psychiatrica Scandinavica Supplementum 252:7–46.

Sjahrir, S. 1949. Out of Exile (translated from Dutch by Charles Wolf). New York: Greenwood Press.

Story, R. 1980. The Encyclopedia of UFOs. New York: Doubleday.

Strentz, H. J. 1970. A Survey of Press Coverage of Unidentified Flying Objects, 1947–1966. Doctoral Dissertation, Northwestern University, Department of Journalism.

Tumin, M. M., and A. S. Feldman. 1955. The miracle at Sabana Grande. Public Opinion Quarterly 19:124–139.

Wessely, S. 1987. Mass hysteria: Two syndromes? Psychological Medicine 17:109–120.

Wolfe, R. 1999. Weekly World News, September 28:8–9.

About the Authors

Robert E. Bartholomew is a sociologist at James Cook University in Townsville 4811, Queensland, Australia (e–mail: art-reb2@jcu.edu.au).

Erich Goode is professor of sociology at The State University of New York at Stony Brook, Stony Brook, NY 11794 (e-mail: Egoode2001@aol.com).

Review and Contemplate

1. What are collective delusions and mass hysteria? Which term best characterizes the poisoning scare of Milan, Italy, in 1630?
2. Describe the "miracle" in Puerto Rico in 1953 and explain how it is related to the concept of perceptual set (consult an introductory psychology textbook for information about perceptual set).
3. What evidence suggests that flying saucer sightings in 1947 were a collective delusion prompted by the media?
4. Describe two historical examples of mass hysteria.
5. Which of the two major themes of this book, discussed in Chapter 1, seem most closely related to this article? Explain your answer.

10.2   *How to Sell a Pseudoscience/*
ANTHONY PRATKANIS

Pseudoscientists are famous for promising amazing benefits or results that may seem real but cannot actually be obtained using the techniques they advocate. In previous chapters, we've seen the claims that (a) the Q-Ray bracelet can relieve pain by regulating the imbalance of positive and negative ions in your body, (b) people can unlock their hidden potential for psychic powers by learning to utilize more than the usual 10% of their brains, (c) children's intelligence can be improved by listening to Mozart, (d) subliminal tapes can boost your self-esteem, and (e) therapeutic touch can relieve symptoms of Alzheimer's disease. As Pratkanis explains in the following article, creating a phantom—a desirable goal that cannot be reached—is one of many tactics used by pseudoscientists to persuade people to buy into their practice.

Pratkanis also discusses how a number of other persuasion tactics studied by social psychologists are used by pseudoscientists to "sell" their ideas and products to others. For example, social psychologists know that we are likely to obey and be persuaded by people whom we consider to be credible and trustworthy authorities. For example, it makes perfect sense for you to follow the advice of a trusted medical doctor if he or she says you have a sinus infection and should take antibiotics to treat it. After all, your medical doctor probably knows much more than you do about infections and how to treat them, so it is reasonable to follow his or her advice. However, problems can arise when we blindly obey authority figures who seem credible and trustworthy due to their "official" titles, credentials, or clothes because these signs of authority can be forged or meaningless. A pseudoscientific health practitioner might wear a white lab coat and be a "certified" therapist, but this might not tell you anything about whether this person uses effective treatments. For example, someone can become a "certified aromatherapist," but that just means this person was trained in a practice that is widely considered a pseudoscience.

APA Reference

Pratkanis, A. (1995, July/August). How to sell a pseudoscience. *Skeptical Inquirer, 19,* 19–25.

Want your own pseudoscience? Here are nine effective persuasion tactics for selling all sorts of flimflam.

Every time I read the reports of new pseudosciences in the SKEPTICAL INQUIRER or watch the latest "In Search Of"-style television show I have one cognitive response, "Holy cow, how can anyone believe that?" Some recent examples include: "Holy cow, why do people spend $3.95 a minute to talk on the telephone with a 'psychic' who has never foretold the future?" "Holy cow, why do people believe that an all uncooked vegan diet is natural and therefore nutritious?" "Holy cow, why would two state troopers chase the planet Venus across state lines thinking it was an alien spacecraft?" "Holy cow, why do people spend millions of dollars each year on subliminal tapes that just don't work?"

There are, of course, many different answers to these "holy cow" questions. Conjurers can duplicate pseudoscientific feats and thus show us how sleights of hand and misdirections can mislead (e.g., Randi 1982a, 1982b, 1989). Sociologists can point to social conditions that increase the prevalence of pseudoscientific beliefs (e.g., Lett 1992; Padgett and Jorgenson 1982; Victor 1993). Natural scientists can describe the physical properties of objects to show that what may appear to be supernatural is natural (e.g., Culver and Ianna 1988; Nickell 1983, 1993). Cognitive psychologists have identified common mental biases that often lead us to misinterpret social reality and to conclude in favor of supernatural phenomena (e.g., Blackmore 1992; Gilovich 1991; Hines 1988). These perspectives are useful in addressing the "holy cow" question; all give us a piece of the puzzle in unraveling this mystery.

I will describe how a social psychologist answers the holy cow question. Social psychology is the study of social influence—how human beings and their institutions influence and affect each other (see Aronson 1992; Aronson and Prarkanis 1993). For the past seven decades, social psychologists have been developing theories of social influence and have been testing the effectiveness of various persuasion tactics in their labs (see Cialdini 1984; Pratkanis and Aronson, 1992). It is my thesis that many persuasion tactics discovered by social psychologists are used every day, perhaps not totally consciously, by the promoters of pseudoscience (see Feynman 1985 or Hines 1988 for a definition of pseudoscience).

To see how these tactics can be used to sell flimflam, let's pretend for a moment that we wish to have our very own pseudoscience. Here are nine common propaganda tactics that should result in success.

1. CREATE A PHANTOM

The first thing we need to do is to create a phantom—an unavailable goal that looks real and possible; it looks as if it might be obtained with just the right effort, just the right belief, or just the right amount of money, but in reality it can't be obtained. Most pseudosciences are based on belief in a distant or phantom goal. Some examples of pseudoscience phantoms: meeting a space alien, contacting a dead relative at a séance, receiving the wisdom of the universe from

Anthony R. Pratkanis is associate professor of psychology, University of California, Santa Cruz, CA 95064. This article is based on a paper presented at the conference of the Committee for the Scientific Investigation of Claims of the Paranormal, June 23–26, 1994, in Seattle, Washington.

a channeled dolphin, and improving one's bowling game or overcoming the trauma of rape with a subliminal tape.

Phantoms can serve as effective propaganda devices (Pratkanis and Farquhar 1992). If I don't have a desired phantom, I feel deprived and somehow less of a person. A pseudoscientist can take advantage of these feelings of inferiority by appearing to offer a means to obtain that goal. In a rush to enhance self-esteem, we suspend better judgment and readily accept the offering of the pseudoscience.

The trick, of course, is to get the new seeker to believe that the phantom is possible. Often the mere mention of the delights of a phantom will be enough to dazzle the new pseudoscience recruit (see Lund's 1925 discussion of wishful thinking). After all, who wouldn't want a better sex life, better health, and peace of mind, all from a $14.95 subliminal tape? The fear of loss of a phantom also can motivate us to accept it as real. The thought that I will never speak again to a cherished but dead loved one or that next month I may die of cancer can be so painful as to cause me to suspend my better judgment and hold out hope against hope that the medium can contact the dead or that Laetrile works. But at times the sell is harder, and that calls for our next set of persuasion tactics.

2. SET A RATIONALIZATION TRAP

The rationalization trap is based on the premise: Get the person committed to the cause as soon as possible. Once a commitment is made, the nature of thought changes. The committed heart is not so much interested in a careful evaluation of the merits of a course of action but in proving that he or she is right.

To see how commitment to a pseudoscience can be established, let's look at a bizarre case—mass suicides at the direction of cult leader Jim Jones. This is the ultimate "holy cow" question: "Why kill yourself and your children on another's command?" From outside the cult, it appears strange, but from the inside it seems natural. Jones began by having his followers make easy commitments (a gift to the church, attending Wednesday night service) and then increased the level of commitment—more tithes, more time in service, loyalty oaths, public admission of sins and punishment, selling of homes, forced sex, moving to Guyana, and then the suicide. Each step was really a small one. Outsiders saw the strange end-product; insiders experienced an ever increasing spiral of escalating commitment. (See Pratkanis and Aronson 1992 for other tactics used by Jones.)

This is a dramatic example, but not all belief in pseudoscience is so extreme. For example, there are those who occasionally consult a psychic or listen to a subliminal tape. In such cases, commitment can be secured by what social psychologists call the foot-in-the-door technique (Freedman and Fraser 1966). It works this way: You start with a small request, such as accepting a free chiropractic spine exam (Barrett 1993a), taking a sample of vitamins, or completing a free personality inventory. Then a larger request follows—a $1,000 chiropractic realignment, a vitamin regime, or an expensive seminar series. The first small request sets the commitment: Why did you get that bone exam, take those vitamins, or complete that test if you weren't interested and didn't think there might be something to it? An all too common response, "Well gosh, I guess I am interested." The rationalization trap is sprung.

Now that we have secured the target's commitment to a phantom goal, we need some social support for the newfound pseudoscientific beliefs. The next tactics are designed to bolster those beliefs.

3. MANUFACTURE SOURCE CREDIBILITY AND SINCERITY

Our third tactic is to manufacture source credibility and sincerity. In other words, create a guru, leader, mystic, lord, or other generally likable and powerful authority, one who people would be just plain nuts if they didn't believe. For example, practitioners of alternative medicine often have "degrees" as chiropractors or in homeopathy. Subliminal tape sellers claim specialized knowledge and training in such arts as hypnosis. Advocates of UFO sightings often become directors of "research centers." "Psychic detectives" come with long résumés of police service. Prophets claim past successes. For example, most of us "know" that Jeane Dixon predicted the assassination of President Kennedy but probably don't know that she also predicted a Nixon win in 1960. As modern public relations has shown us, credibility is easier to manufacture than we might normally think (see Ailes 1988; Dilenschneider 1990).

Source credibility is an effective propaganda device for at least two reasons. First, we often process persuasive messages in a half-mindless state—either because we are not motivated to think, don't have the time to consider, or lack the abilities to understand the issues (Perry and Cacioppo 1986). In such cases, the presence of a credible source can lead one to quickly infer that the message has merit and should be accepted.

Second, source credibility can stop questioning (Kramer and Alstad 1993). After all, what gives you the right to question a guru, a prophet, the image of the Mother Mary, or a sincere seeker of life's hidden potentials? I'll clarify this point with an example. Suppose I told you that the following statement is a prediction of the development of the atomic bomb and the fighter aircraft (see Hines 1988):

> They will think they have seen the Sun at night
> When they will see the pig half-man:
> Noise, song, battle fighting in the sky perceived,
> And one will hear brute beasts talking.

You probably would respond: "Huh? I don't see how you get the atomic bomb from that. This could just as well be a prediction of an in-flight showing of the Dr. Doolittle movie or the advent of night baseball at Wrigley field." However, attribute the statement to Nostradamus and the dynamics change. Nostradamus was a man who supposedly cured plague victims, predicted who would be pope, foretold the future of kings and queens, and even found a poor dog lost by the king's page (Randi 1993). Such a great seer and prophet can't be wrong. The implied message: The problem is with you: instead of questioning, why don't you suspend your faulty, linear mind until you gain the needed insight?

4. ESTABLISH A GRANFALLOON

Where would a leader be without something to lead? Our next tactic supplies the answer: Establish what Kurt Vonnegut (1976) terms a "granfalloon," a proud and meaningless association of human beings. One of social psychology's most remarkable findings is the ease with which granfalloons can be created. For example, the social psychologist Henri Tajfel merely brought subjects into his lab, flipped a coin, and randomly assigned them to be labeled either Xs or Ws (Tajfel 1981; Turner 1987). At the end of the study, total strangers were acting as if those in their granfalloon were their close kin and those in the other group were their worst enemies.

Granfalloons are powerful propaganda devices because they are easy to create and, once established, the granfalloon defines social reality and maintains social identities. Information is dependent on the granfalloon. Since most granfalloons quickly develop out-groups, criticisms can be attributed to those "evil ones" outside the group, who are thus stifled. To maintain a desired social identity, such as that of a seeker or a New Age rebel, one must obey the dictates of the granfalloon and its leaders.

The classic séance can be viewed as an ad-hoc granfalloon. Note what happens as you sit in the dark and hear a thud. You are dependent on the group led by a medium for the interpretation of this sound. "What is it? A knee against the table or my long lost Uncle Ned? The group believes it is Uncle Ned. Rocking the boat would be impolite. Besides, I came here to be a seeker."

Essential to the success of the granfalloon tactic is the creation of a shared social identity. In creating this identity, here are some things you might want to include:

a. *rituals and symbols* (e.g., a dowset's rod, secret symbols, and special ways of preparing food): these not only create an identity, but provide items for sale at a profit.

b. *jargon and beliefs* that only the in-group understands and accepts (e.g., thetans are impeded by engrams, you are on a cusp with Jupiter rising): jargon is an effective means of social control since it can be used to frame the interpretation of events.

c. *shared goals* (e.g., to end all war, to sell the faith and related products, or to realize one's human potential): such goals not only define the group, but motivate action as believers attempt to reach them.

d. *shared feelings* (e.g., the excitement of a prophecy that might appear to be true or the collective rationalization of strange beliefs to others): shared feelings aid in the *we* feeling.

e. *specialized information* (e.g., the U.S. government is in a conspiracy to cover up UFOs): this helps the target feel special because he or she is "in the know."

f. *enemies* (e.g., alternative medicine opposing the AMA and the FDA, subliminal-tape companies spurning academic psychologists, and spiritualists condemning Randi and other investigators): enemies are very important because you as a pseudoscientist will need scapegoats to blame for your problems and failures.

5. Use Self-Generated Persuasion

Another tactic for promoting pseudoscience and one of the most powerful tactics identified by social psychologists is self-generated persuasion—the subtle design of the situation so that the targets persuade themselves. During World War II, Kurt Lewin (1947) was able to get Americans to eat more sweetbreads (veal and beef organ meats) by having them form groups to discuss how they could persuade others to eat sweetbreads.

Retailers selling so-called nutritional products have discovered this technique by turning customers into salespersons (Jarvis and Barrett 1993). To create a multilevel sales organization, the "nutrition" retailer recruits customers (who recruit still more customers) to serve as sales agents for the product. Customers are recruited as a test of their belief in the product or with the hope of making lots of money (often to buy more products). By trying to sell the product, the customer-turned-salesperson becomes more convinced of its worth. One multilevel leader tells his new sales agents to "answer all objections with testimonials. That's the secret to motivating people" (Jarvis and Barrett 1993), and it is also the secret to convincing yourself.

6. Construct Vivid Appeals

Joseph Stalin once remarked: "The death of a single Russian soldier is a tragedy. A million deaths is a statistic." (See Nisbett and Ross 1980.) In other words, a vividly presented case study or example can make a lasting impression. For example, the pseudosciences are replete with graphic stories of ships and planes caught in the Bermuda Triangle, space aliens examining the sexual parts of humans, weird goings-on in Borley Rectory or Amityville, New York, and psychic surgeons removing cancerous tumors.

A vivid presentation is likely to be very memorable and hard to refute. No matter how many logical arguments can be mustered to counter the pseudoscience claim, there remains that one graphic incident that comes quickly to mind to prompt the response: "Yeah, but what about that haunted house in New York? Hard to explain that." By the way, one of the best ways to counter a vivid appeal is with an equally vivid counter appeal. For example, to counter stories about psychic surgeons in the Philippines, Randi (1982a) tells an equally vivid story of a psychic surgeon palming chicken guts and then pretending to remove them from a sick and now less wealthy patient.

7. USE PRE-PERSUASION

Pre-persuasion is defining the situation or setting the stage so you win, and sometimes without raising so much as a valid argument. How does one do this? At least three steps are important.

First, establish the nature of the issue. For example, to avoid the wrath of the FDA, advocates of alternative medicine define the issue as health freedom (you should have the right to the health alternative of your choice) as opposed to consumer protection or quality care. If the issue is defined as freedom, the alternative medicine advocate will win because "Who is opposed to freedom?" Another example of this technique is to create a problem or disease, such as reactive hypoglycemia or yeast allergy, that then just happens to be "curable" with whatever quackery you have to sell (Jarvis and Barrett 1993).

Another way to define an issue is through differentiation. Subliminal-tape companies use product differentiation to respond to negative subliminal-tape studies. The claim: "Our tapes have a special technique that makes them superior to other tapes that have been used in studies that failed to show the therapeutic value of subliminal tapes." Thus, null results are used to make a given subliminal tape look superior. The psychic network has taken a similar approach—"Tired of those phoney psychics? Ours are certified," says the advertisement.

Second, set expectations. Expectations can lead us to interpret ambiguous information in a way that supports an original hypothesis (Greenwald, Pratkanis, Leippe, and Baumgardner 1986). For example, a belief in the Bermuda Triangle may lead us to interpret a plane crash off the coast of New York City as evidence for the Triangle's sinister effects (Kusche 1986; Randi 1982a). We recently conducted a study that showed how an expectation can lead people to think that subliminal tapes work when in fact they do not (Greenwald, Spangenberg, Pratkanis, and Eskenazi 1991; Pratkanis, Eskenanzi, and Greenwald 1994; for a summary see Pratkanis 1992). In our study, expectations were established by mislabeling half the tapes (e.g., some subjects thought they had a subliminal tape to improve memory but really had one designed to increase self-esteem). The results showed that about half the subjects thought they improved (though they did not) based on how the tape was labeled (and not the actual content). The label led them to interpret their behavior in support of expectations, or what we termed an "illusory placebo" effect.

A third way to pre-persuade is to specify the decision criteria. For example, psychic supporters have developed guidelines on what should be viewed as acceptable evidence for paranormal abilities—such as using personal experiences as data, placing the burden of proof on the critic and not the claimant (see Beloff 1985), and above all else keeping James Randi and other psi-inhibitors out of the testing room. Accept these criteria and one must conclude that psi is a reality. The collaboration of Hyman and Honorton is one positive attempt to establish a fair playing field (Hyman and Honorton 1986).

"Source credibility can stop questioning. After all, what gives you the right to question a guru, a prophet, the image of the Mother Mary, or a sincere seeker of life's hidden potentials?"

8. Frequently Use Heuristics and Commonplaces

My next recommendation to the would-be pseudoscientist is to use heuristics and commonplaces. Heuristics are simple if-then rules or norms that are widely accepted; for example, if it costs more it must be more valuable. Commonplaces are widely accepted beliefs that can serve as the basis of an appeal; for example, government health-reform should be rejected because politicians are corrupt (assuming political corruption is a widely accepted belief). Heuristics and commonplaces gain their power because they are widely accepted and thus induce little thought about whether the rule or arguments is appropriate.

To sell a pseudoscience, liberally sprinkle your appeal with heuristics and commonplaces. Here are some common examples.

a.   The *scarcity heuristic,* or if it is rare it is valuable. The Psychic Friends Network costs a pricey $3.95 a minute and therefore must be valuable. On the other hand, an average University of California professor goes for about 27 cents per minute and is thus of little value.[1]

b.   The *consensus or bandwagon* heuristic, or if everyone agrees it must be true. Subliminal tapes, psychic phone ads, and quack medicine (Jarvis and Barrett 1993) feature testimonials of people who have found what they are looking for (see Hyman 1993 for a critique of this practice).

c.   The *message length* heuristic, or if the message is long it is strong. Subliminal-tape brochures often list hundreds of subliminal studies in support of their claims. Yet most of these studies do not deal with subliminal influence and thus are irrelevant. An uninformed observer would be impressed by the weight of the evidence.

d.   The *representative* heuristic or if an object resembles another (on some salient dimension) then they act similarly. For example, in folk medicines the cure often resembles the apparent cause of the disease. Homeopathy is based on the notion that small amounts of substances that can cause a disease's symptoms will cure the disease (Barrett 1993b). The Chinese Doctrine of Signatures claims that similarity of shape and form determine therapeutic value; thus rhinoceros horns, deer antlers, and ginseng root look phallic and supposedly improve vitality (Tyler 1993).

e.   The *natural* commonplace, or what is natural is good and what is made by humans is bad. Alternative medicines are promoted with the word "natural." Psychic abilities are portrayed as natural, but lost, abilities. Organic food is natural. Of course mistletoe berries are natural too, and I don't recommend a steady diet of these morsels.

f.   The *goddess-within* commonplace, or humans have a spiritual side that is neglected by modern materialistic science. This commonplace stems from the medieval notion of the soul, which was modernized by Mesmer as animal magnetism and then converted by psychoanalysis into the powerful, hidden unconscious (see Fuller 1982, 1986). Pseudoscience plays to this commonplace by offering ways to tap the unconscious, such as subliminal tapes, to prove this hidden power exists through extrasensory perception (ESP) and psi, or to talk with the remnants of this hidden spirituality through channeling and the séance.

g. The *science* commonplaces. Pseudosciences use the word "science" in a contradictory manner. On the one hand, the word "science" is sprinkled liberally throughout most pseudosciences: subliminal tapes make use of the "latest scientific technology"; psychics are "scientifically tested"; health fads are "on the cutting edge of science." On the other hand, science is often portrayed as limited. For example, one article in *Self* magazine (Sharp 1993) reported our subliminal-tapes studies (Greenwald et al. 1992; Pratkanis et al. 1994) showing no evidence that the tapes worked and then stated: "Tape makers dispute the objectivity of the studies. They also point out that science can't always explain the results of mainstream medicine either" (p. 194). In each case a commonplace about science is used: (1) "Science is powerful" and (2) "Science is limited and can't replace the personal." The selective use of these commonplaces allows a pseudoscience to claim the power of science but have a convenient out should science fail to promote the pseudoscience.

9. ATTACK OPPONENTS THROUGH INNUENDO AND CHARACTER ASSASSINATION

Finally, you would like your pseudoscience to be safe from harm and external attack. Given that the best defense is a good offense, I offer the advice of Cicero: "If you don't have a good argument, attack the plaintiff."

Let me give a personal example of this tactic in action. After our research showing that subliminal tapes have no therapeutic value was reported, my coauthors, Tony Greenwald, Eric Spangenberg, and Jay Eskenazi, and I were the target of many innuendoes. One subliminal newsletter edited by Eldon Taylor, Michael Urban, and others (see the *International Society of Peripheral Learning Specialists Newsletter,* August 1991) claimed that our research was a marketing study designed not to test the tapes but to "demonstrate the influence of marketing practices on consumer perceptions." The article points out that the entire body of data presented by Greenwald represents a marketing dissertation by Spangenberg and questions why Greenwald is even an author. The newsletter makes other attacks as well, claiming that our research design lacked a control group, that we really found significant effects of the tapes, that we violated American Psychological Association ethics with a hint that an investigation would follow, that we prematurely reported our findings in a manner similar to those who prematurely announced cold fusion, and that we were conducting a "Willie Horton"-style smear campaign against those who seek to help Americans achieve their personal goals.

Many skeptics can point to similar types of attacks. In the fourteenth century, Bishop Pierre d'Arcis, one of the first to contest the authenticity of the Shroud of Turin, was accused by shroud promoters as being motivated by jealousy and a desire to possess the shroud (Nickell 1983: 15). Today, James Randi is described by supporters of Uri Geller as "a powerful psychic trying to convince the world that such powers don't exist so he can take the lead role in the psychic world" (Hines 1988: 91).

Why is innuendo such a powerful propaganda device? Social psychologists point to three classes of answers. First, innuendoes change the agenda of discussion. Note the "new" discussion on subliminal tapes isn't about whether these tapes are worth your money or not. Instead, we are discussing whether I am ethical or not, whether I am a competent researcher, and whether I even did the research.

Second, innuendoes raise a glimmer of doubt about the character of the person under attack. That doubt can be especially powerful when there is little other information on which to base a judgment. For example, the average reader of the subliminal newsletter I quoted probably knows little about me— knows little about the research and little about the peer review process that evaluated it, and doesn't know that I make my living from teaching college and not from the sale of subliminal tapes. This average reader is left with the impression of an unethical and incompetent scientist who is out of control. Who in their right mind would accept what that person has to say?

Finally, innuendoes can have a chilling effect (Kurtz 1992). The recipient begins to wonder about his or her reputation and whether the fight is worth it. The frivolous lawsuit is an effective way to magnify this chilling effect.

CAN SCIENCE BE SOLD WITH PROPAGANDA?

I would be remiss if I didn't address one more issue: Can we sell science with the persuasion tactics of pseudoscience? Let's be honest; science sometimes uses these tactics. For example, I carry in my wallet a membership card to the Monterey Bay Aquarium with a picture of the cutest little otter you'll ever see. I am in the otter granfalloon. On some occasions skeptics have played a little loose with their arguments and their name-calling. As just one example, see George Price's (1955) *Science* article attacking Rhine's and Soal's work on ESP— an attack that went well beyond the then available data. (See Hyman's [1985] discussion.)

I can somewhat understand the use of such tactics. If a cute otter can inspire a young child to seek to understand nature, then so be it. But we should remember that such tactics can be ineffective in promoting science if they are not followed up by involvement in the process of science—the process of questioning and discovering. And we should be mindful that the use of propaganda techniques has its costs. If we base our claims on cheap propaganda tactics, then it is an easy task for the pseudoscientist to develop even more effective propaganda tactics and carry the day.

More fundamentally, propaganda works best when we are half mindless, simplistic thinkers trying to rationalize our behavior and beliefs to ourselves and others. Science works best when we are thoughtful and critical and scrutinize claims carefully. Our job should be to promote such thought and scrutiny. We should be careful to select our persuasion strategies to be consistent with that goal.

Notes

I thank Craig Abbott, Elizabeth A. Turner, and Marlene E. Turner for helpful comments on an earlier draft of this article.

1. Based on 50 weeks a year at an average salary of $49,000 and a work week of 61 hours (as reported in recent surveys of the average UC faculty work load). Assuming a work week of 40 hours, the average faculty makes 41 cents a minute.

References

Ailes, R. 1988. *You Are the Message.* New York: Doubleday.

Aronson, E. 1992. *The Social Animal.* 6th ed. New York: W. H. Freeman.

Aronson, E., and A. R. Pratkanis. 1993. "What Is Social Psychology?" In *Social Psychology,* vol. 1, ed. by E. Aronson and A. R. Pratkanis, xiii–xx. Cheltenham, Gloucestershire: Edward Elgar Publishing.

Barrett, S. 1993a. "The Spine Salesmen." In *The Health Robbers,* ed. by S. Barrett and W. T. Jarvis, 161–190. Buffalo, N.Y.: Prometheus Books.

——. 1993b. "Homeopathy: Is it Medicine?" In *The Health Robbers,* ed. by S. Barrett and W. T. Jarvis, 191–202. Buffalo, N.Y.: Prometheus Books.

Beloff, J. 1985. "What Is Your Counter-explanation? A Plea to Skeptics to Think Again." In *A Skeptic's Handbook of Parapsychology,* ed. by P. Kurtz, 359–377. Buffalo, N.Y.: Prometheus Books.

Blackmore, S. 1992. Psychic experiences; Psychic illusions. SKEPTICAL INQUIRER, 16: 367–376.

Cialdini, R. B. 1984. *Influence.* New York: William Morrow.

Culver, R. B., and P. A. Ianna. 1988. *Astrology: True or False?* Buffalo, N.Y.: Prometheus Books.

Dilenschneider, R. L. 1990. *Power and Influence.* New York: Prentice-Hall.

Feynman, R. P. 1985. *Surely You're Joking Mr. Feynman.* New York: Bantam Books.

Freedman, J., and S. Fraser. 1966. Compliance without pressure. The foot-in-the-door technique. *Journal of Personality and Social Psychology,* 4:195–202.

Fuller, R. C. 1982. *Mesmerism and the American Cure of Souls.* Philadelphia: University of Pennsylvania Press.

——. 1986. *Americans and the Unconscious.* New York: Oxford University Press.

Gilovich, T. 1991. *How We Know What Isn't So.* New York: Free Press.

Greenwald, A. G., E. R. Spangenberg, A. R. Pratkanis, and J. Eskenazi. 1991. Double-blind tests of subliminal self-help audiotapes. *Psychological Science,* 2:119–122.

Greenwald, A. G., A. R. Pratkanis, M. R. Leippe, and M. H. Baumgardner. 1986. Under what conditions does theory obstruct research progress? *Psychological Review,* 93: 216–229.

Hines, T. 1988. *Pseudoscience and the Paranormal.* Buffalo, N.Y.: Prometheus Books.

Hyman, R. 1985. "A Critical Historical Overview of Parapsychology." In *A Skeptic's Handbook of Parapsychology,* ed. by P. Kurtz, 3–96. Buffalo, N.Y.: Prometheus Books.

———. 1993. Occult health practices, In *The Health Robbers,* ed. by S. Barrett and W. T. Jarvis, 55–66. Buffalo, N.Y.: Prometheus Books.

Hyman, R., and C. Honorton. 1986. A joint communique: The Psi Ganzfeld controversy. *Journal of Parapsychology,* 56: 351–364.

Jarvis, W. T., and S. Barrett. 1993. "How Quackery Sells." In *The Health Robbers,* ed. by S. Barrett and W. T. Jarvis, 1–22. Buffalo, N.Y.: Prometheus Books.

Kramer, J., and D. Alstad. 1993. *The Guru Papers: Masks of Authoritarian Power,* Berkeley, Calif.: North Atlantic Books/Frog Ltd.

Kurtz, P. 1992. On being sued: The chilling of freedom of expression. SKEPTICAL INQUIRER, 16:114–117.

Kusche, L. 1986. *The Bermuda Triangle Mystery Solved.* Buffalo, N.Y.: Prometheus Books.

Lett, J. 1992. The persistent popularity of the paranormal. SKEPTICAL INQUIRER, 16, 381–388.

Lewin, K. 1947. "Group Decision and Social Change." In *Readings in Social Psychology,* ed. by T. M. Newcomb and E. L. Hartley, 330–344. New York: Holt.

Lund, F. H. 1925. The psychology of belief. *Journal of Abnormal and Social Psychology,* 20: 63–81, 174–196.

Nickell, J. 1983. *Inquest on the Shroud of Turin.* Buffalo, N.Y.: Prometheus Books.

———. 1993. *Looking for a Miracle.* Buffalo, N.Y.: Prometheus Books.

Nisbett, R., and L. Ross. 1980. *Human Inference: Strategies and Shortcomings of Social Judgment.* Englewood Cliffs, N.J.: Prentice-Hall.

Padgett, V. R., and D. O. Jorgenson. 1982. Superstition and economic threat: Germany 1918–1940. *Personality and Social Psychology Bulletin,* 8:736–741.

Perry, R. E., and J. T. Cacioppo. 1986. *Communication and Persuasion: Central and Peripheral Routes to Attitude Change.* New York: Springer-Verlag.

Pratkanis, A. R. 1992. The cargo-cult science of subliminal persuasion. SKEPTICAL INQUIRER, 16: 260–272.

Pratkanis, A. R., and E. Aronson. 1992. *Age of Propaganda: Everyday Use and Abuse of Persuasion.* New York: W. H. Freeman.

Pratkanis, A. R., J. Eskenazi, and A. G. Greenwald. 1994. What you expect is what you believe (but not necessarily what you get): A test of the effectiveness of subliminal self-help audiotapes. *Basic and Applied Social Psychology,* 15:251–276.

Pratkanis, A. R., and P. H. Farquhar. 1992. A brief history of research on phantom alternatives: Evidence for seven empirical generalizations about phantoms. *Basic and Applied Social Psychology,* 13:103–122.

Price, G. R. 1955. Science and the supernatural. *Science,* 122:359–367.

Randi, J. 1982a. *Flim-Flam!* Buffalo, N.Y.: Prometheus Books.

———. 1982b. *The Truth About Uri Geller,* Buffalo, N.Y.: Prometheus Books.

———. 1989. *The Faith Healers.* Buffalo, N.Y.: Prometheus Books.

———. 1993. *The Mask of Nostradamus.* Buffalo, N.Y.: Prometheus Books.

Sharp, K. 1993. The new hidden persuaders. *Self,* March, pp. 174–175, 194.

Tajfel, H. 1981. *Human Groups and Social Categories.* Cambridge, U.K.: Cambridge University Press.

Turner, J. C. 1987. *Rediscovering the Social Group.* New York: Blackwell.

Tyler, V. E. 1993. "The Overselling of Herbs." In *The Health Robbers,* ed. by S. Barrett and W. T. Jarvis, 213–224. Buffalo, N.Y.: Prometheus Books.

Victor, J. S. 1993. *Satanic Panic: The Creation of a Contemporary Legend.* Chicago, Ill.: Open Court.

Vonnegut, K. 1976. *Wampeters, Foma, and Granfalloons.* New York: Dell.

Review and Contemplate

1. What is social influence, and how it is related to pseudoscience?
2. Name and describe five common propaganda tactics used by pseudoscientists.
3. Describe how two of the nine propaganda tactics discussed by Pratkanis may be related to the example of the Q-Ray bracelet (discussed in Chapter 1).
4. Chapter 1 discussed the point that normal cognitive and social processes can lead to pseudoscientific and paranormal beliefs. Choose two of the propaganda tactics discussed by Pratkanis, and explain how they illustrate this point.

10.3   *The Social Psychology of False Confessions:* Compliance, Internalization, and Confabulation/ SAUL KASSIN AND KATHERINE KIECHEL

During the evening of April 19, 1989, a 28-year-old woman was attacked and raped in New York City's Central Park. Her skull had been fractured, her body temperature had dropped to 84 degrees, and she had lost 75% of her blood. Although the woman recovered, she had no memory of the assault. Police suspected several African American and Latino teenagers who were in custody for other attacks in the park that night. Antron McCray was one of five teenagers who, after lengthy police interrogation, confessed to attacking the woman. He was convicted of rape and assault and was sentenced to 5–10 years in prison for his role in the crime. After serving 6 years in prison, Antron was released in 2002 after Matias Reyes, a convicted murderer and rapist who was not one of the five teenagers, confessed that he alone committed the crime. DNA evidence corroborated his confession.

Why would a teenager confess to a crime he did not commit? Doesn't his confession suggest that he must have played some role in the attack? Psychologists have found that although people believe that (a) confessions provide strong evidence of a person's guilt and (b) people do not confess unless they are guilty, under certain circumstances people may confess to crimes they did not commit. Kassin and Kiechel discuss the role of social influence and other factors in producing false confessions, and they present the results of their experiment that elicited false confessions from their participants.

APA Reference

Kassin, S. M., & Kiechel, K. L. (1996). The social psychology of false confessions: Compliance, internalization, and confabulation. *Psychological Science, 7,* 125–128.

ABSTRACT   An experiment demonstrated that false incriminating evidence can lead people to accept guilt for a crime they did not commit. Subjects in a fast- or slow-paced reaction time task were accused of damaging a computer by pressing the wrong key. All were truly innocent and initially denied the charge. A confederate then said she saw the subject hit the key or did not see the subject hit the key. Compared with subjects in the slow-pace/no-witness group, those in the fast-pace/witness group were more likely to sign a confession, internalize guilt for the event, and confabulate details in memory consistent with that belief. Both legal and conceptual implications are discussed.

In criminal law, confession evidence is a potent weapon for the prosecution and a recurring source of controversy. Whether a suspect's self-incriminating statement was voluntary or coerced and whether a suspect was of sound mind are just two of the issues that trial judges and juries consider on a routine basis. To guard citizens against violations of due process and to minimize the risk that the innocent would confess to crimes they did not commit, the courts have erected guidelines for the admissibility of confession evidence. Although there is no simple litmus test, confessions are typically excluded from trial if elicited by physical violence, a threat of harm or punishment, or a promise of immunity or leniency, or without the suspect being notified of his or her Miranda rights.

To understand the psychology of criminal confessions, three questions need to be addressed First, how do police interrogators elicit self-incriminating statements (i e, what means of social influence do they use)? Second, what effects do these methods have (i e, do innocent suspects ever confess to crimes they did not commit)? Third, when a coerced confession is retracted and later presented at trial, do juries sufficiently discount the evidence in accordance with the law? General reviews of relevant case law and research are available elsewhere (Gudjonsson, 1992, Wrightsman & Kassin, 1933). The present research adresses the first two questions.

Informed by developments in case law, the police use various methods of interrogation—including the presentation of false evidence (e.g. fake polygraph, fingerprints, or other forensic test results, staged eyewitness identifications), appeals to God and religion, feigned friendship, and the use of prison inform-ants. A number of manuals are available to advise detectives on how to extract confessions from reluctant crime suspects (Aubry & Caputo, 1965, O'Hara & O'Hara, 1981). The most popular manual is Inbau, Reid, and Buckley's (1986) *Criminal Interrogation and Confessions,* originally published in 1962, and now in its third edition.

After advising interrogators to set aside a bare, soundproof room absent of social support and distraction, Inbau et al (1986) describe in detail a nine-step procedure consisting of various specific ploys. In general, two types of ap-proaches can be distinguished. One is *minimization,* a technique in which the detective lulls the suspect into a false sense of security by providing face-saving excuses, citing mitigating circumstances, blaming the victim, and underplaying the charges. The second approach is one of *maximization,* in which the inter-rogator uses scare tactics by exaggerating or falsifying the characterization of ev-idence, the seriousness of the offense, and the magnitude of the charges. In a recent study (Kassin & McNall, 1991), subjects read interrogation transcripts in which these ploys were used and estimated the severity of the sentence likely to be received. The results indicated that minimization communicated an implicit offer of leniency, comparable to that estimated in an explicit-promise condition,

Address correspondence to **Saul Kassin,** Department of Psychology, Williams College, Williamstown, MA 01267.

whereas maximization implied a threat of harsh punishment, comparable to that found in an explicit-threat condition. Yet although American courts routinely exclude confessions elicited by explicit threats and promises, they admit those produced by contingencies that are pragmatically implied.

Although police often use coercive methods of interrogation, research suggests that juries are prone to convict defendants who confess in these situations. In the case of *Arizona v. Fulminante* (1991), the U. S. Supreme Court ruled that under certain conditions, an improperly admitted coerced confession may be considered upon appeal to have been nonprejudical, or "harmless error". Yet mock-jury research shows that people find it hard to believe that anyone would confess to a crime that he or she did not commit (Kassin & Wrightsman, 1980, 1981, Sukel & Kassin, 1994). Still, it happens. One cannot estimate the prevalence of the problem, which has never been systematically examined, but there are numerous documented instances on record (Bedau & Radelet, 1987, Borchard, 1932, Rattner, 1988). Indeed, one can distinguish three types of false confession (Kassin & Wrightsman, 1985) *voluntary* (in which a subject confesses in the absence of external pressure), *coerced-compliant* (in which a suspect confesses only to escape an aversive interrogation, secure a promised benefit, or avoid a threatened harm), and *coerced-internalized* (in which a suspect actually comes to believe that he or she is guilty of the crime).

This last type of false confession seems most unlikely, but a number of recent cases have come to light in which the police had seized a suspect who was vulnerable (by virtue of his or her youth, intelligence, personality, stress, or mental state) and used false evidence to convince the beleaguered suspect that he or she was guilty. In one case that received a great deal of attention, for example, Paul Ingram was charged with rape and a host of satanic cult crimes that included the slaughter of newborn babies. During 6 months of interrogation, he was hypnotized, exposed to graphic crime details, informed by a police psychologist that sex offenders often repress their offenses, and urged by the minister of his church to confess. Eventually, Ingram "recalled" crime scenes to specification, pleaded guilty, and was sentenced to prison. There was no physical evidence of these crimes, however, and an expert who reviewed the case for the state concluded that Ingram had been brainwashed. To demonstrate, this expert accused Ingram of a bogus crime and found that although he initially denied the charge, he later confessed—and embellished the story (Ofshe, 1992, Wright, 1994).

Other similar cases have been reported (e. g. Pratkanis & Aronson, 1991), but, to date, there is no empirical proof of this phenomenon. Memory researchers have found that misleading postevent information can alter actual or reported memories of observed events (Loftus, Donders, Hoffman, & Schooler, 1989, Loftus, Miller, & Burns, 1978, McCloskey & Zaragoza, 1985)—an effect that is particularly potent in young children (Ceci & Bruck, 1993, Ceci, Ross, & Toglia, 1987) and adults under hypnosis (Dinges et. al., 1992, Dywan & Bowers, 1983, Sheehan, Statham, & Jamieson, 1991). Indeed, recent studies suggest it is even possible to implant false recollections of traumas supposedly buried in the unconscious (Loftus, 1993). As related to confessions, the question is, can memory of one's own actions similarly be altered? Can people be induced to accept guilt for crimes they did not commit? Is it, contrary to popular belief, possible?

Because of obvious ethical constraints, this important issue has not been addressed previously. This article thus reports on a new laboratory paradigm used to test the following specific hypothesis. The presentation of false evidence can lead individuals who are vulnerable (i.e., in a heightened state of uncertainty) to confess to an act they did not commit and more important, to internalize the confession and perhaps confabulate details in memory consistent with that new belief.

METHOD

Participating for extra credit in what was supposed to be a reaction time experiment, 79 undergraduates (40 male, 39 female) were randomly assigned to one of four groups produced by a 2 (high vs. low vulnerability) × 2 (presence vs. absence of a false incriminating witness) factorial design.

Two subjects per session (actually, 1 subject and a female confederate) engaged in a reaction time task on an IBM PS2/Model 50 computer. To bolster the credibility of the experimental cover story, they were asked to fill out a brief questionnaire concerning their typing experience and ability, spatial awareness, and speed of reflexes. The subject and confederate were then taken to another room, seated across a table from the experimenter, and instructed on the task. The confederate was to read aloud a list of letters, and the subject was to type these letters on the keyboard. After 3 min, the subject and confederate were to reverse roles. Before the session began, subjects were instructed on proper use of the computer—and were specifically warned not to press the "ALT" key positioned near the space bar because doing so would cause the program to crash and data to be lost. Lo and behold, after 60 s, the computer supposedly ceased to function, and a highly distressed experimenter accused the subject of having pressed the forbidden key. All subjects initially denied the charge, at which point the experimenter tinkered with the keyboard, confirmed that data had been lost, and asked, "Did you hit the 'ALT' key?"

Two forensically relevant factors were independently varied. First, we manipulated subjects' level of *vulnerability* (i.e., their subjective certainty concerning their own innocence by varying the pace of the task. Using a mechanical metronome, the confederate read either at a slow and relaxed pace of 43 letters per minute or at a frenzied pace of 67 letters per minute (these settings were established through pretesting). Two-way analyses of variance revealed significant main effects on the number of letters typed correctly (Ms = 3301 and 6112, respectively, $F[1, 71] = 27893$, $p < 001$) and the number of typing errors made ($Ms = 112$ and 1090, respectively, $F[1, 71] = 3881$, $p < 001$) thus confirming the effectiveness of this manipulation.

Second, we varied the use of *false incriminating evidence,* a common interrogation technique. After the subject initially denied the charge, the experimenter turned to the confederate and asked, "Did you see anything?" In the false-witness condition, the confederate 'admitted' that she had seen the subject hit the 'ALT' key that terminated the program. In the no-witness condition, the same confederate said she had not seen what happened.

As dependent measures three forms of social influence were assessed compliance, internalization, and confabulation. To elicit *compliance,* the experimenter handwrote a standardized confession ("I hit the 'ALT' key and caused the program to crash. Data were lost") and asked the subject to sign it—the consequence of which would be a phone call from the principal investigator. If the subject refused, the request was repeated a second time.

To assess *internalization,* we unobtrusively recorded the way subjects privately described what happened soon afterward. As the experimenter and subject left the laboratory, they were met in the reception area by a waiting subject (actually, a second confederate who was blind to the subject's condition and previous behavior) who had overheard the commotion. The experimenter explained that the session would have to be rescheduled, and then left the room to retrieve his appointment calendar. At that point, the second confederate turned privately to the subject and asked, "What happened?" The subject's reply was recorded verbatim and later coded for whether or not he or she had unambiguously internalized guilt for what happened (e.g., "I hit the wrong button and ruined the program". "I hit a button I wasn't supposed to"). A conservative criterion was employed. Any reply that was prefaced by "he said" or "I may have" or "I think" was not taken as evidence of internalization. Two raters who were blind to the subject's condition independently coded these responses, and their agreement rate was 96%.

Finally, after the sessions seemed to be over, the experimenter reappeared, brought the subjects back into the lab, reread the list of letters they had typed, and asked if they could reconstruct how or when they hit the "ALT" key. This procedure was designed to probe for evidence of *confabulation,* to determine whether subjects would "recall" specific details to fit the allegation (e.g., "Yes, here, I hit it with the side of my hand right after you called out the 'A'"). The interrater agreement rate on the coding of these data was 100%.

At the end of each session, subjects were fully and carefully debriefed about the study—its purpose, the hypothesis, and the reason for the use of deception— by the experimenter and first confederate. Most subjects reacted with a combination of relief (that they had not ruined the experiment), amazement (that their perceptions of their own behavior had been so completely manipulated), and a sense of satisfaction (at having played a meaningful role in an important study). Subjects were also asked not to discuss the experience with other students until all the data were collected. Four subjects reported during debriefing that they were suspicious of the experimental manipulation. Their data were excluded from all analyses.

RESULTS AND DISCUSSION

Overall, 69% of the 75 subjects signed the confession 28% exhibited internalization, and 9% confabulated details to support their false beliefs. More important, between-group comparisons provided strong support for the main hypothesis.

As seen in Table 10.1, subjects in the slow-pace/no-witness control group were the least likely to exhibit an effect, whereas those in the fast-pace/witness group were the most likely to exhibit the effect on the measures of compliance ($\chi^2\{3\} = 23.84$, $p < .001$), internalization ($\chi^2\{3\} = 37.61$, $p < .001$). and confabulation ($\chi^2\{3\} = 18.0$, $p < .005$).

Specifically, although 34.78% of the subjects in the slow pace/no-witness group signed the confession, indicating compliance, not a single subject in this group exhibited internalization or confabulation. In contrast, the two independent variables had a powerful combined effect. Out of 17 subjects in the fast-pace/witness cell, 100% signed a confession, 65% came to believe they were guilty (in reality, they were not), and 35% confabulated details to support their false belief (via chi-square tests, the differences in these rates between the slow-pace/no-witness control group and fast-pace/witness group were significant at $ps < .001$, .001, and .005, respectively).

Additional pair-wise comparisons revealed that the presence of a witness alone was sufficient to significantly increase the rates of compliant and internalized confessions, even in the slow-pace condition ($\chi^2\{1\} = 12.18$, $p < .005$, and $\chi^2\{1\} = 16.39$, $p < .001$). There were no sex differences on any measures (i.e., make and female subjects exhibited comparable confession rates overall, and were similarly influenced by the independent variables).

The present study provides strong initial support for the provocative notion that the presentation of false incriminating evidence—an interrogation ploy that is common among the police and sanctioned by many courts—can induce people to internalize blame for outcomes they did not produce. These results provide an initial basis for challenging the evidentiary validity of confessions produced by this technique. These findings also demonstrate, possibly for the first time, that memory can be altered not only for observed events and remote past experiences, but also for one's own recent actions.

An obvious and important empirical question remains concerning the external validity of the present results. To what extent do they generalize to the interrogation behavior of actual crime suspects? For ethical reasons, we developed a laboratory paradigm in which subjects were accused merely of an unconscious act of negligence, not of an act involving explicit criminal intent (e.g., stealing

TABLE 10.1 ▬▬▬▬▬▬▬▬▬▬▬▬▬▬▬▬▬▬▬▬▬▬▬▬▬▬▬▬▬▬

Percentage of Subjects in Each Cell Who Exhibited the Three Forms of Influence

	No witness		Witness	
Form of influence	Slow pace	Fast pace	Slow pace	Fast pace
Compliance	35_a	65_b	89_{bc}	100_c
Internalization	0_a	12_{ab}	44_{bc}	65_c
Confabulation	0_a	0_a	6_a	35_b

Note. Percentages not sharing a common subscript differ at $p < 05$ via a chi-square test of significance equipment from the lab or cheating on an important test). In this paradigm, there was only a minor consequence for liability. At this point, it is unclear whether people could similarly be induced to internalize false guilt for acts of omission (i.e., neglecting to do something they were told to do) or for acts that emanate from conscious intent.

It is important, however, not to overstate this limitation. The fact that our procedure focused on an act of negligence and low consequence may well explain why the compliance rate was high, with roughly two thirds of all subjects agreeing to sign a confession statement. Effects of this sort on overt judgments and behavior have been observed in studies of conformity to group norms, compliance with direct requests, and obedience to the commands of authority. But the more important and startling result—that many subjects privately internalized guilt for an outcome they did not produce, and that some even constructed memories to fit that false belief—is not seriously compromised by the laboratory paradigm that was used. Conceptually, these findings extend known effects of misinformation on memory for observed events (Loftus et al., 1978, McCloskey & Zaragoza, 1985) and for traumas assumed to be buried in the unconscious (Loftus, 1993). Indeed, our effects were exhibited by college students who are intelligent (drawn from a population in which the mean score on the Scholastic Aptitude Test is over 1300), self-assured, and under minimal stress compared with crime suspects held in custody, often in isolation.

At this point, additional research is needed to examine other common interrogation techniques (e.g., minimization), individual differences in suspect vulnerability (e.g., manifest anxiety, need for approval, hypnotic susceptibility), and other risk factors for false confessions (e.g., blood alcohol level, sleep deprivation). In light of recent judicial acceptance of a broad range of self-incriminatory statements, increasing use of videotaped confessions at the trial level (Geller, 1993), and the U.S. Supreme Court's ruling that an improperly admitted coerced confession may qualify as a mere "harmless error" (*Arizona v. Fulminante,* 1991), further research is also needed to assess the lay jury's reaction to this type of evidence when presented in court.

ACKNOWLEDGMENTS

—This research was submitted as part of a senior honor's thesis by the second author and was funded by the Bronfman Science Center of Williams College.

References

Arizona v., Fulminante, 59 U. S. L. W. 4235 (1991).
Aubsy, A. & Caputo, R. (1965). *Criminal interrogation.* Springfield, IL. Charles C Thomas.
Bedau, H., & Radelet, M. (1987). Miscarriages of justice in potentially capital cases *Stanford Law Review 40* 21–179.
Borchard, E. M. (1932). *Convicting the innocent Errors of criminal justice.* New Haven, CT. Yale University Press.

Ceci, S. J., & Bruck, M. (1993) Suggestibility of the child witness. A historical review and synthesis. *Psychological Bulletin, 113,* 403–439.

Ceci S. J., Ross, D. F., & Toglia M. P. (1987). Suggestibility of children's memory. Psychological implications *Journal of Experimental Psychology General, 116,* 38–49.

Dinges, D. F. Whitehouse, W. G., Orne, E. C. Powell, J. W., Orne, M. T., & Erdelyi, M. H. (1992) Evaluating hypnotic memory enhancement (hypermnesia and reminiscence) using multitrial forced recall *Journal of Experimental Psychology Learning Memory and Cognition, 18,* 1139–1147.

Dywan, J. & Bowers, K. (1983) The use of hypnosis to enhance recall. *Science 222* 184–185.

Geller W. A. (1993). Videotaping interrogations and confessions (National Institute of Justice Research in Brief). Washington DC U. S. Department of Justice.

Gudjonsson G. (1992) The psychology of interrogations confessions and testimony London Wiley.

Inbau, F. E., Reid, J. E., & Buckley, J. P. (1986). Criminal interrogation and confessions (3rd ed) Baltimore MD Williams. & Wilkins.

Kaasin, S. M. & McNall, K. (1991). Police interrogations and confessions Commenting promises and threats by pragmatic implication *Law and Human Behavior 15* 233–251.

Kassin, S. M., & Wrightsman, L. S. (1980). Prior confessions and mock juror verdicts *Journal of Applied Social Psychology, 10,* 133–146.

Kassin, S. M., & Wrightsman, L. S. (1981). Coerced confessions judicial instruction and mock prior verdicts. *Journal of Applied Social Psychology, 11,* 489–506.

Kassin, S. M., & Wrightsman, L. S. (1985). Confession evidence. Is S. M. Kassin & L. S. Wrightsman (Eds). *The psychology of evidence and trail procedure* (pp. 67–94). Beverly Hills CA:Sage.

Loftus, E. F. (1993). The reality of represented memories, *American Psychologist 48,* 518–537.

Loftus, E. F., Donders K., Hoffman, H. G., & Schoolaer, J. W. (1999). Creating new memories that are quickly accessed and confidently held. *Memory and Cognition, 17,* 607–616.

Loftus, E. F., Miller, D. G., & Burns, H. J. (1978). Semantic integration of verbal information into visual memory. *Journal of Experimental Psychology Human Learning and Memory, 4,* 19–31.

McCloskey, M., & Zaragoza M. (1985). Misleading postevent information and memory for events. Arguments and evidence against memory impairment hypotheses. *Journal of Experimental Psychology, 114,* 3–18.

Ofshe, R. (1992). Inadvertent hypnosis during interrogation. False confession due to dissociative state misidentified multiple personality and the satanic cult hypothesis. *International Journal of Clinical and Experimental Hypnosis 40* 125–156.

O'Hara, C. E., & O'Hara, G. L. (1981). *Fundamentals of criminal investigation:* Springfield IL. Charles C. Thomas.

Pratkanis, A. & Aronson, E. (1991). *Age of propaganda. The everyday use and abuse of persuasion.* New York: W. H. Freeman.

Rattner, A. (1988) Convicted but innocent: Wrongful conviction and the criminal justice system. *Law and Human Behavior 12,* 283–293.

Sheehan, P. W. Statham, D. & Jamieson, G. A. (1991). Pseudomemory effects and their relationship to level of susceptibility to hypnosis and state instruction *Journal of Personality and Social Psychology 60,* 130–137.

Sukel, H. L. & Kassin, S. M. (1994 March). *Coerced confessions and the jury. An experimental test of the harmless error rule.* Paper presented at the biennial meeting of the American Psychology-Law Society, Sante Fe, NM.

Wright, L. (1994) *Remembering Satan*. New York: Alfred A. Knopf.

Wrightsman, L. S. & Kassin, S. M. (1993). *Confessions in the courtroom*. Hewbury Park, CA: Sage.

Review and Contemplate

1. Do American courts allow, as evidence in criminal cases, confessions elicited by explicit threats from police? Do they allow confessions elicited after police present the suspect with false evidence of his or her guilt?

2. Name and describe three types of false confessions. Which of these types were elicited from the participants in the experiment conducted by Kassin and Kiechel (1996)?

3. What do the results of Kassin and Kiechel's experiment suggest about the validity of confessions elicited from suspects who are given false incriminating evidence (e.g., false information that an eyewitness saw them commit the crime)?